Miracle at Joaseiro

Institute of Latin American Studies
Columbia University

Miracle at Joaseiro

by
RALPH DELLA CAVA

COLUMBIA UNIVERSITY PRESS   NEW YORK AND LONDON   1970

Ralph della Cava is Assistant Professor of History
at Queens College, City University of New York,
Flushing, New York

Dedicated to the memory of

Alba Frota,
Joaquim Alves,
Octávio Aires de Menezes,
Odílio Figueiredo,
and Rui Facó,

friends and scholars

The Institute of Latin American Studies of Columbia University was established in 1961 in response to a national, public, and educational need for a better understanding of the nations of Latin America and a more knowledgeable basis for inter-American relations. The major objectives of the Institute are to prepare a limited number of North Americans for scholarly and professional careers in the field of Latin American studies, to advance our knowledge of Latin America through an active program of research by faculty, graduate students, and visiting scholars, and to improve public knowledge through publication of a series of books on Latin America.

Miracle at Joaseiro by Ralph della Cava is a welcome and distinguished addition to this Institute series on Latin America. Dr. della Cava was associated with the Institute of Latin American Studies for several years. He was a graduate student of history at Columbia University and was enrolled also in several Institute courses. He was an Instructor of History and a member of the Institute staff when he began this book. His study of the remarkable events at Joaseiro and their aftermath reflect his ability to apply the concepts of other social sciences to history. The story of Padre Cicero of Joaseiro is an important part of Brazilian social history which has not been told in English in any detail until now. It is an exciting story of the spirit and the soul of the poverty-stricken, arid northeast of Brazil; for Padre Cicero is still very much alive in the minds and memories of the peasantry of the northeastern backlands. Dr. della Cava's study of this religious movement, and of its sociological setting, is, in a sense, a dramatic epilogue to that great Brazilian classic *Rebellion in the Backlands* by Euclides da Cunha. For the religious fanaticism of Canudos described by da Cunha was not an isolated phenomenon. In many respects it reappeared in Joaseiro just a generation later, and the germ still lives in the Brazilian backlands.

We are proud to include this book in our series on Latin America. The publication program of the Institute of Latin American studies is made possible in part by the financial assistance of the Ford Foundation.

Preface

In the fall of 1962, as my graduate studies in Latin American history were drawing to a close, I found it necessary to choose a subject worthy of research. I was certain of one thing: Brazil, the Latin American nation I knew least, attracted me most. A brief visit there had whetted my desire to become better acquainted with her gentle and optimistic people. Their expressive, New World Portuguese, which I was arduously struggling to master, tempted me still further.

Of special significance to me at the time was my conviction that Brazil—the proverbial "country of the future"—had for a decade been set on a course of profound social reforms. In the cities and in the countryside, hitherto dormant and oppressed peoples were awakening to their birthright as forgers of their own destiny. Joining with them were idealistic men and women, especially university students and young workers, who rallied behind a new and promising political leadership that had committed itself to the self-determination and welfare of *all* Brazil's people.

Professor Charles Wagley of Columbia University sympathetically encouraged me to combine these personal interests with my scholarly vocation. Moreover, it was at his suggestion that I took an interest in, and later decided to study, a popular religious protest movement that had arisen in the backland city of Joaseiro in the 1880s and that struck me at first as a precursor of the awakening then occurring throughout Brazil. Once in the field, however, I came to realize that the populist tendencies of the Joaseiro movement—like those at play in Brazil prior to 1964—were aborted. I then faced the necessity of abandoning my original perspective and of finding new ones from which to analyze the movement more accurately. In that task, Professor Lewis Hanke, my advisor at Columbia, was particularly helpful, while several Brazilian scholars and friends intimately familiar with Joaseiro reassured me that there was much to learn about Brazilian history from the movement's past.

To reconstruct that past, I resided in Brazil for fourteen months, about five of them in the city of Joaseiro. The next three years were spent intermittently in re-evaluating most of my original assumptions in the light of archival materials and recent scholarship. The results of that effort, completed in late 1967, are delineated in the pages that follow. Therein, I have attempted to reinvest persons, actions, and relationships with the rationality I am convinced they possessed but which other writers and the distance of history have hitherto denied them. It is also my hope that the reasons for and significance of Joaseiro's past are now clear, evident, intelligible, and stripped at last of myth, fantasy, and error.

This study is in no way offered as a definitive history of Joaseiro and the Joaseirenses. Yet, in retrospect, it is clear to me that this work might never have been written had it not been for the inhabitants of Joaseiro. They allowed me to share their lives, their hopes, their history, giving me a sense of the past that I otherwise could not have had.

My debt of gratitude extends even further. In addition to those mentioned, I should like also to record the names of James Berry, Octávio Ianni, Luis Martín, Leo McLaughlin, and Immanuel Wallerstein, whose assistance transcended the conventional boundaries of intellectual exchange. Dom Vicente de Araújo Matos, Bishop of Crato, generously and unconditionally granted me access to the ecclesiastical archives of his diocese, as did Father Gino Moratelli to those of the Colégio Salesiano "Dom João Bosco" in Joaseiro, which he directed in 1964. Mr. Milton do Nascimento of Fortaleza and the staff of the Biblioteca Nacional in Rio de Janeiro kindly helped me to microfilm portions of those archives. Other Brazilians aided me in countless ways: several put family papers, unpublished manuscripts, and bibliographical sources at my disposal; not a few gave me many hours of their time in detailed interviews and fruitful conversation. I have tried to acknowledge the help of each of them elsewhere in this book.

Several friends and their families also helped to make our stay in Brazil a memorable one: José Oswaldo de Araújo, Raimundo Carvalho, Eduardo Diatay Bezerra de Menezes, Giusseppe Sebasti, Madre Neli Sobreira, and Lívio Xavier.

A grant from the Foreign Area Fellowship Program made it possible for me and my family to reside in Brazil, while assistance from the Institute of Latin American Studies of Columbia University and the Department of History at Queens College, City University of New York, facilitated the completion of this study.

Throughout the course of this study, I enjoyed the enduring comradeship and affection of Olha Tatiana, Marco Rafael, and Miriam Firenza, for whom I can find no words that will convey the measure of my gratitude and my debt.

New York City, 13 June 1970

Contents

xiii

Miracle at Joaseiro

Introduction

This monograph is intended as a historical contribution to the recent literature on popular religious movements of the nineteenth and twentieth centuries. As such, the primary objective of this study is to provide a detailed political history of a single movement which flourished between 1889 and 1934 in the rural hamlet of Joaseiro, situated in the interior of the Brazilian Northeast.

A reputed miracle sparked that movement. On the morning of 1 March 1889, the devout chaplain of Joaseiro, Padre Cícero Romão Batista, administered communion to one of the hamlet's pious women. Within moments, the white host was believed to have miraculously transformed itself into blood, unquestioningly held to be the blood of Jesus Christ. This collective belief thereafter became the foundation stone of a popular religious movement while Padre Cícero, subsequently suspended from the priesthood by the Roman Catholic hierarchy, became the movement's celebrated leader. Among Brazilians, both the movement and its leader have long stimulated national interest, not a little controversy, and an extensive bibliography. Unfortunately, that bibliography has been intensely partisan: It essentially reflects the acrimonious religious and political controversies—among the most heated in the annals of Brazilian history—which the movement and Padre Cícero have inspired since 1889. Furthermore, a vast "mythic" literature has arisen: Northeastern bards of the backlands and troubadours (*cantadores*) have since about 1900 appropriated the messiah-like figure of Padre Cícero into their popular repertoire, and in doing so have transfigured the suspended priest into a powerful "miracle worker" and one of the region's legendary folk-heroes.

Only of late have Brazilian social scientists and political thinkers attempted to study Joaseiro and its leader from fresh, dispassionate, and more relevant perspectives. Despite this felicitous and welcomed change of attitude, some recent studies have failed to reap as fruitful a harvest as might have been hoped for. This failure lies less in the intent of the authors than in their dependence on abundant but nonetheless partisan and legendary sources. To remedy the latter shortcoming and provide a firmer base for future studies, this monograph attempts to reconstruct the first thorough and accurate historical account of the movement at Joaseiro and of its leader, Padre Cícero.

To that end, the present study is the first to rely extensively on two important archival sources, which, for the most part, have been hitherto inaccessible to interested students. The one comprises a goodly portion of Padre Cícero's extant personal, lifetime correspondence, preserved at present in the Colégio Salesiano "Dom João Bosco" in Joaseiro, Ceará. With the assistance of the Colégio's librarian, Fr. Manuel Isaú, this archive was collated, organized, and catalogued for the first time since Padre Cícero's death in 1934 by the author of this study in the latter half of 1964. The other archive, also incomplete but nonetheless substantial, is ecclesiastical in nature and constitutes the chief record of the movement—as perceived by the church hierarchy—from 1889 until about 1900. This archive originally pertained to the Diocese of Ceará in Fortaleza, but after 1914 or 1915, was transferred to the jurisdiction of the then newly established Diocese of Crato, in Crato, Ceará. In addition to these two fundamental sources, this study has benefited from considerable unpublished primary materials found in the personal family archives of several prominent residents of Joaseiro. Finally, many hitherto neglected books, published documents, and newspapers of the period, as well as extensive personal interviews conducted by the author in Joaseiro and elsewhere in Ceará during 1963 and 1964 round out the basic sources in which the present historical study is anchored.

As indicated earlier, the primary objective of this study is to record the *political* history of Joaseiro; its messianic and millenarian aspects have been purposely put into the background. This strategy was not arbitrary, despite the fact that Padre Cícero often appeared to some of his followers as a "messiah" and that at specific historical moments millenarian beliefs were articulated by certain social groups within the movement. However, neither a messianic nor a millenarian framework or theory seemed to the author to be capable of satisfactorily "explaining" a movement which endured for almost half a century and, at that, in a constant process of conflict, bargaining, and accommodation with both a hostile church and state. Nor did such theories seem to account adequately for changes within the movement itself, as evidenced by the malleability of Padre Cícero's followers, who began in 1889 as orthodox Catholics, were declared dissident believers in 1894 and finally constituted after 1900 the popular political base which then enabled the suspended priest to enter into the established and conservative political structures of the region, state, and nation. There are additional reasons to relegate the theories and incidents of messianism and millenarianism into the background, and they should become apparent in the course of this study. This is not to say that recent monographs based on these theories have not cast fresh light on how social cohesion is achieved within such movements or how a supposedly popular religious ideology can be in reality a vehicle for social protest. However, in our opinion, a too rigid *a priori* perception of every popular religious movement as *necessarily* and *exclusively* messianic and millenarian risks being as restricted today as were the earlier nineteenth century interpretations which branded almost all such movements as "fanatical," "deviant," "retrogressive," and the product of a culturally "backward" society. Too strict a millenarian perspective also risks neglecting the relationships of popular religious movements to the political realities within which they developed and were developed.

Partially, for these reasons, this monograph primarily seeks to recreate the *political* history of Joaseiro. Furthermore, this strategy to focus on the *totality* of relationships of the popular religious movement to the polity and not merely on its limited messianic and millenarian aspects was demanded by the concrete historical circumstances which enveloped the movement at Joaseiro. Some brief examples will suffice to illustrate this contention. From the outset, Joaseiro was enmeshed in what may be described as "ecclesiastical politics." The attempt of dissident believers to obtain Rome's approval of the alleged miracles of Joaseiro required them to act politically, *latu sensu,* within the framework of an international bureaucratic institution that is the Roman Catholic Church. Later, Padre Cícero—the long-time religious leader of Joaseiro—legally assumed the political office of prefect of Joaseiro; in 1912, he became a Vice-Governor of Ceará State; in 1913–1914, he lent his prestige to an armed movement which deposed the Governor of Ceará; and, in 1926, was elected as deputy to the Brazilian federal congress. During the last two decades of his life, he was reputedly the most powerful political figure in the Brazilian Northeast. These facts alone made it indispensable to inquire about the political base of the movement of Joaseiro and to explain how that popular religious movement became fully integrated into the prevailing political system of Brazil.

It should not be surprising that other data strongly suggested a parallel inquiry into the economic history of the movement. For example, there exists strong, albeit purely descriptive, evidence that the influx of religious pilgrims to Joaseiro had an immediate economic impact. As thousands of pilgrims became permanent settlers, they visibly transformed the rural hamlet-shrine of Joaseiro into a burgeoning agricultural, commercial, and artisan emporium of the Northeastern backlands—within less than twenty years. Furthermore, the surrounding region, known as the Cariry Valley, was also affected by Joaseiro's transformation and shortly thereafter assumed the title of "breadbasket of the Northeastern *sertão*." Moreover, if it is borne in mind that Joaseiro today is a city of about 80,000 inhabitants—one of the largest in the backlands—and that it is at present in the throes of an industrialization program, then it is impossible not to be interested in the historical origins of this remarkable change and in the original economic base of the popular religious movement. Unfortunately the lack of reliable statistical data and the overwhelming difficulties involved in reconstructing them from diverse and usually descriptive sources militated against any systematic economic inquiry. At best, the present study can be only broadly suggestive of the economic dimensions within which the popular religious movement at Joaseiro emerged and developed.

While the primary objective of this monograph is therefore to recreate the political history of the movement at Joaseiro (and to a lesser extent, illuminate some aspects of its economic history), a secondary but equally important objective is to illustrate a basic hypothesis: It is our contention that popular religious movements originate and develop within a total social context defined by the dominant structures of a national and world order. To be more specific, the popular religious movement at Joaseiro affected and was affected by: (1) an international ecclesiastical institution, the Church of Rome; (2) the national political system of Imperial and Republican Brazil; and (3) a changing national and international economy.

By implication, this perspective puts into question the validity of some earlier hypotheses which hold that popular religious movements are geographically and culturally isolated from the dominant structures of a national and world order. Furthermore, it recasts another long-held Brazilian perspective, popularized by the famous Brazilian writer, Euclydes da Cunha. In his renowned work, *Rebellion in the Backlands*, the emergence of a popular religious movement at Canudos was portrayed as symptomatic of the inherent conflict between the modern, sophisticated culture of Brazil's urban coastal centers, on the one hand, and the archaic, backward culture of Brazil's abandoned rural interior, on the other. This dualistic view of Brazilian society widely persists today. However, the present monograph suggests that that view has been greatly overstated. In fact, in Joaseiro, it is quite clear that even at the end of the nineteenth century backland society was integrated at many important levels into a single, national social order. Furthermore, the case of Joaseiro reveals that the conflict between a backland movement and the urbane civilization of the cities did not unfold—as da Cunha implied—because of the former's incapacity and unwillingness to accept the material and other gains achieved by the coast, but rather precisely because of the backland's quest to obtain a greater share of those advances.

This study's emphasis on the backland elites (priests and professional men, merchants and landowners) and on the means and degree of their incorporation "into a single, national social order" is not so self-evident as might be supposed. In fact, it departs considerably from the traditional historiographical view of the "Old Republic" as a federalist system in which national, state, and local forces operated with relative autonomy and independence of each other until 1930.

Insofar as the historiography of Joaseiro is concerned, the attempt to demonstrate the linkages of local elites into the total social system is an even more radical departure. Earlier studies of the movement of Joaseiro have attributed its origins and development almost entirely to the personality of Padre Cícero or, in another vein, to the "religious fanaticism" and folk culture of the rural masses. In an effort to counterbalance those distorted emphases—although neither is neglected nor denied in entirety—the thesis of this study is that the actors and events in which the movement of Joaseiro originated and developed were part and parcel of a national social order.

It is impossible to anticipate every objection which the above hypothesis may raise. One, however, is inescapable: Is the hypothesis validated by evidence derived from popular religious movements other than that at Joaseiro? Only a comparative analysis now and in the future would provide the answer. For that reason, it was necessary for us to test the hypothesis by reanalyzing at least one other movement, in this case, the celebrated Canudos movement referred to earlier. The results of that preliminary research, undertaken in 1966, and recently published under the title "Brazilian Messianism and National Institutions: A Reappraisal of Canudos and Joaseiro," fully validated, for our purposes, the fruitfulness of the approach employed in this study. Understandably, the scope of this work does not permit here either a lengthy comparative analysis of the two movements or the inclusion of the preliminary monograph. For the purpose of comparison with recent European movements of radical persuasion, E. J. Hobsbawm's *Primitive Rebels* was consulted and is here recommended. In contrast to Hobsbawm's concerns, this monograph deals with a Brazilian movement which, despite its clear potential for opposing the status quo, chose and was obliged to reintegrate itself into the traditional and conservative political structures of the Brazilian nation. These differences aside, both the Hobsbawm study and the present work stem from the assumption that popular religious movements evolve within a total social context.

There are objections of another order that will certainly arise. Students of Brazilian history will find that this study was obliged both to chart new courses in and revise old interpretations about Brazilian history since the 1880s. An example of a new course is our contention that Brazilian nationalism had taken root among a segment of the native-born clergy prior to 1900. Examples of revisionist interpretations are our implicit demonstration: (1) that backland political violence in the early twentieth century arose because of the growth of the national economy and political system and not because of either the persistence of traditional family feuds or the inherent moral decadence of backland civilization; (2) that by 1910 the national political structure was moving towards the creation of a highly centralized system of authority that was consolidated by the Vargas revolution of 1930 and not wrought by it.

These viewpoints were arrived at by perceiving Brazilian society through the historical prism of the movement at Joaseiro. From that standpoint, the viewpoints in question seemed evident and certain, even though it was not always possible to substantiate them as fully as it might have been desired. However, the merit of stating these new viewpoints, tenuous though they may be, seemed upon reflection to outweigh the merit of awaiting the results of additional research.

Also in order is a word about the form of this monograph. It was inevitable that the reconstruction of the fascinating and human story of Joaseiro and Padre Cícero would be marred if analysis were allowed to prevail over description. For that reason, a chronological narrative relying on richly descriptive archival sources—often quoted extensively in the text— was chosen as the most suitable vehicle by which the leading figures of the day could recount their own history. It was also inevitable that the intriguing personality of Padre Cícero and the heated and interminable controversy he still inspires would envelop the author in their grips until many of the prevailing errors and questions were resolved. To undo errors and resolve questions in the text, however, would have occasionally burdened the layman unnecessarily. For this reason, the footnotes have been reserved for an extensive dialogue between the author and a handful of scholars, epecially those in Ceará, who have also become impassioned biographers of the suspended priest and his movement.

Finally, it is necessary to clarify some of the orthographic forms of Brazilian Portuguese employed in this work. The word *padre* (priest) when used as a formal clerical title of address means "Father"; its Portuguese form is retained throughout the text when referring to Padre Cícero. There is no standard orthography for the place-name, Joaseiro; it may also appear in titles of published works as Joazeiro, Juaseiro, or Juàseiro; today it is officially designated by the Brazilian Institute of Geography and Statistics as Juàzeiro do Norte. Our preference has been to retain throughout the text the late nineteenth-century spelling, namely, Joaseiro; when citing published works and manuscripts containing this place-name, the original orthography is retained. So too is the original orthography retained in respect to the proper names of authors and several personalities referred to in the narrative. The text also follows the accepted Brazilian practice of sometimes referring to prominent persons, officials, etc., by their Christian names (e.g., Dr. Floro Bartholomeu da Côsta: Dr. Floro). Finally, the translation of uncommon Brazilian words is provided in parenthesis after the initial use of the word in the text.

1

The Social Origins
of the Miracle

The Arrival of a Visionary

On 11 April 1872, the recently ordained priest, Padre Cícero Romão Batista, arrived in the sparsely populated hamlet of Joaseiro.[1] That day he celebrated mass at the rustic Chapel of Our Lady of Sorrows, a simple plantation shrine and the only notable landmark of this outlying rural *distrito* at the northeastern edge of the prosperous *município* of Crato. Later that same day, the young priest—short in stature with dark hair and a fair complexion—continued to confess the local residents and administer to them the sacraments. Nothing in his demeanor or in the performance of his priestly duties indicated that in the Chapel of Our Lady of Sorrows, less than two decades later, he would become the protagonist of a miracle.[2]

In fact, in April 1872, there was every reason to believe that the clergyman's first visit to Joaseiro was to be his last. Only with reluctance had he made the three-hour journey from the nearby county seat of Crato—and on horseback, an art at which he was never proficient. He had come only to placate two of Joaseiro's most prominent citizens whom he had earlier

9

promised to spend a few days in the hamlet which was long without a resident curate.[3] Nor did the twenty-eight-year-old priest have any intention of accepting the vacated chaplaincy which his two prominent hosts had now offered him—along with suitable living quarters and a guaranteed emolument for his priestly services. Quite to the contrary, Padre Cícero expected to depart shortly for Fortaleza, the distant coastal capital of Ceará. There, on the shores of the Atlantic, at the diocesan seminary, from which he had been ordained in 1870, he planned to return to teaching. On the pretext of visiting his mother at her residence in Crato, Padre Cícero intended to leave the hamlet and travel directly to Fortaleza before it could be discovered that he had permanently left the region.

A dream, however, suddenly altered his plans.[4] Late one evening, after hours of confessing the men of the hamlet, the exhausted priest wearily crossed the dusty square from the chapel to the small schoolhouse where he was temporarily lodged. There, in quarters adjacent to the classroom, he fell asleep, and the fateful vision unfolded: Thirteen men in biblical attire entered the schoolhouse and took their places around the headmaster's desk in a fashion reminiscent of da Vinci's "Last Supper." The sleeping cleric dreamed that he then awoke and rose to spy unobserved upon the sacred visitors. At that moment, the twelve apostles turned to look upon their Master. According to the accounts of this dream, Christ appeared in the schoolhouse as he did in a popular nineteenth-century liturgical portrait—found in almost every devout Catholic home. In that portrait, the Nazarene's heart is visibly exposed and symbolically depicted as both set afire with his love for men and also torn and bleeding from the wounds inflicted by humanity's sins and indifference to the faith. Known as the Sacred Heart of Jesus, this portrait was at that time the object of great popular religious devotion throughout Europe, especially in France, and in Brazil—a devotion which assured its faithful practitioners of salvation from both hell's eternal fires and the world's endless adversities.[5]

As the imagined Christ rose to address his apostles, a host of impoverished peasants suddenly entered the schoolhouse. Carrying their scant possessions in bundles over their shoulders, the men and women were clad in rags, the children not at all. They appeared to have come from great distances, from every corner of Brazil's Northeastern backlands. Christ then turned to them to lament the evil state of the world and mankind's many offenses to His most Sacred Heart. He promised to make one last effort "to save the world," but if men did not soon repent, He would put an end to the very world He had created. At that moment, He pointed to the poor and turning unexpectedly to the startled young cleric, commanded: "And you, Padre Cícero, take charge of them."

"With that command," the priest recounted to a friend many years later, "I awoke and saw nothing; but I thought for awhile and decided, even if in error, to obey."[6] Later in 1872, Padre Cícero gathered up his few possessions in his native Crato, and with his mother and two spinster sisters moved to Joaseiro. There he took up residence in a small, thatch-covered house opposite the Chapel of Our Lady of Sorrows and began his life's ministry among the poor commended to him in the fateful dream by Christ.

This was neither the first nor last of the cleric's "visions." In 1862, his father had fallen victim to a regional cholera epidemic. Shortly thereafter he appeared to his son in a dream to assure him that he should "not abandon his books because God would find a way to enable him to study."[7] When the young student related this episode to his godparent, a wealthy merchant of Crato, the latter unhesitatingly aided the young man to pursue his religious vocation; in 1865 the youthful Cícero left to study at the seminary in Fortaleza. In later years, other "visions" occurred and in each there was the same discernible pattern: Figures of unquestionable authority appeared to him to decree and assure the devout cleric of his future course of action. Repeatedly, too, the priest was not averse to revealing these experiences to friends and relatives who, also compelled by a like piety and simplicity, came to revere him as a man with a singularly indelible calling to saintliness. It would be tempting to assert that Padre Cícero's extraordinary qualities and the deep impression these made upon those closest to him are sufficient to "explain" the miracle which was to take place in 1889. To do so, however, is to ignore the profound social roots from which there later sprung both a collective belief in a miracle and one of the most extraordinary popular religious movements in the history of the Brazilian Northeast.

The Cariry Valley

The area in which the movement at Joaseiro arose is the Cariry Valley.[8] It is situated in the southernmost corner of the present-day state of Ceará and

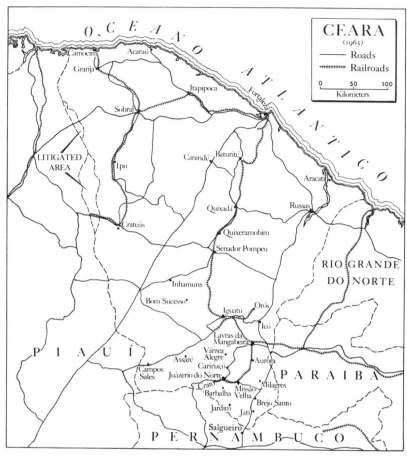

was settled in the opening quarter of the eighteenth century by cattle ranchers enticed there from Bahia and Pernambuco by fertile soils and perennial sources of water. Thanks to these natural resources, the Cariry Valley was a veritable oasis surrounded, as it was, on all sides by the endless expanses of barely productive and cyclically drought-stricken flatlands. Also because of the Valley's resources, agriculture, especially sugarcane, eventually came to predominate over pastoral activities. By the end of the eighteenth century many of the cattle herds had been forced northward into the less fertile zone of the Valley, as well as eastward and southward beyond the imposing plateau-topped Araripe Mountains and into the parched brushlands of the bordering states of Paraíba, Pernambuco, and Piauí. It was also at the end of the eighteenth century that the city of Crato, where Padre Cícero was born in 1844, had emerged as the most populous and important center of the Valley and was proudly called, "The Pearl of the Cariry." As it commanded some of the choicest soils of the Valley, Crato was the chief producer and on occasion supplier of surplus foodstuffs to the arid *sertão*. It increasingly became the hub of the Valley's commercial activities; as a major backland distribution center of imported European manufactures, its landed and merchantile elites were consequently more closely tied to Recife, the Northeast's principal Atlantic port and thriving colonial capital of Pernambuco, than it was to Fortaleza, the insignificant administrative seat of the Portuguese captain-generalcy of Ceará.[9]

These ties to Recife were of critical political importance during the first quarter of the nineteenth century. The port city was the hotbed of separatist and nationalist movements whose ideologies and political programs were transported into the Cariry Valley by many prominent Cratenses. As a result, Crato became the center of patriot armies which secured Brazilian independence in Ceará after a bitter struggle against the former Portuguese masters in Fortaleza and Icó, the only two other important centers of population and wealth in Ceará at that time.[10]

Crato's victory over the royalists, however, secured for the Valley neither expected province-wide political hegemony nor increased regional spoils. In part, the region's political leaders were too radical and quickly fell into disfavor with the conservatives who increasingly dominated the highly centralized power structure of the newly independent Brazilian Empire. More significant for the Valley's relative decline within Ceará between 1824 and 1850 were, however, the economic disadvantages which struck after independence. The Cariry, for example, did not yet produce the products, such as cotton, which Europe now demanded and more cheaply acquired from the newly cultivated and more proximate coastal regions of Ceará. There, the once somnolent colonial capital of Fortaleza was now in the throes of relative economic advance. Furthermore, from 1824 until 1850, communications between the Cariry and the coast went unimproved, while region-wide droughts in 1825 and 1845 proved so extremely severe as to promote widespread brigandage and wreak havoc on even the Valley's economy. Local political struggles also helped divert the region from its earlier aspirations to dominate the newly independent province of Ceará and to turn the Valley in on itself.[11]

Orthodox Catholicism in the Cariry was also in a state of disintegration as it was almost everywhere else in Brazil prior to to the 1860s. The number of priests was inadequate while clerical immorality was rampant. George Gardner, an English traveler who visited Crato in 1838, was shocked to observe that many clerics had mistresses and illegitimate children whom they shamelessly paraded in public. Even the churches, shrines, and cemeteries were in physical disrepair; and the imperial practice of holding elections in churches often led to their desecration and destruction, as armed political opponents battled each other in the sanctuaries on election day.[12]

Under these conditions, the collective religious life of the Valley deteriorated. The lower classes had only marginal contact with the official church, limited usually to the feast days of saints and important holy days when solemn processions and social celebrations took place in urban centers. Participation in the sacramental liturgies of the church was rare; even baptism and marriage were forsaken either because of the infrequent visits of the few priests to the rural areas or because clerical fees were beyond the reach of the poor. Only the occasional missions, usually preached by foreign priests—especially Italian Capuchins in the case of the Cariry—proved successful in bringing religion to the lower classes. However, the missionaries' emphasis on a wrathful God and man's imminent perdition due to sin tended to generate an array of superstitious beliefs. Not infrequently did the poor believe that the white European friars—thought to be racially and intellectually superior—were men of exceptional sanctity endowed with the gift of prophecy. Such was the case of the Italian Capuchin, Friar Vitale da Frascarolo, who preached around the Cariry in the early nineteenth century.[13] After his death, a prophecy foretelling of the destruction of the world was attributed to him; printed texts of that prophecy circulated throughout the Northeast for almost a century and its message was firmly believed in by rich and poor alike.

Among both classes, folk beliefs and para-liturgical practices prevailed over those of orthodox Catholicism; especially among the poor, the former were seen as efficacious means of controlling the harshness and adversities of life.[14] *Promessas,* or vows, were commonly made to saints in the hope of obtaining health, happiness, and fortune, while among rural workers, prayers often preceded the planting in an attempt to ward off evil spirits to whom all bad harvests were invariably attributed. Even among the Cariry elites, a mystical, superstitious mode of action was employed to achieve material amelioration. This was true especially in times of drought. Priests, perhaps the only recipients and dispensers of formal education in the Cariry until the 1850s, considered the cyclical, ravaging droughts to be a divine chastisement upon an erring people. As a result, priests and landowners practiced a complex and ancient liturgy in which the statues of parish patron saints were carried in public procession and supplicated to persuade the deity to provide rain. Novenas and other popular liturgical practices were also employed to right the wrongs of the world—a world that was for the Cariry Valley anarchic and dissolute until the mid-1850s.

Era of Economic and Political Revival

The mid-1850s and the decade of the sixties ushered in an era of revival and change in the Cariry.[15] The structures which began to take shape during this period eventually provided the context in which the movement at Joaseiro unfolded. Many of these changes were a result of demographic and economic shifts in several Northeastern states. Expanding urban centers such as Fortaleza and Recife as well as smaller cities in the interior increasingly demanded greater supplies of cheap foodstuffs. The growing European demand for raw materials, especially cotton during the sixties, gradually transformed the economies of many backland areas from subsistence to commercial export production.

The impact of these shifts was significant in the Cariry, especially in Crato where economic, political, and religious revitalization was most clearly under way. Agriculture, especially sugarcane production, rapidly expanded into all available lands within the *município.* In 1854, Crato's sugar producers won a decisive victory over the last remaining cattle ranchers: a protective municipal law obliged the ranchers to transfer their herds beyond the fertile fields.[16] In the neighboring *município* of Barbalha, sugarcane also flourished. Together, Crato and Barbalha possessed most of the Valley's two hundred *engenhos* (sugar mills), a marked increase over the thirty-seven which dotted the Valley a century before.[17] The chief produce of the region was not granulated sugar but rather *rapadura,* a rectangular block of coarse, brown sugar which has remained one of the most important staples in the diet of the lower classes. Then and now, it has been exported to the arid backlands of the adjacent states of Pernambuco, Paraíba, and Rio Grande do Norte, a factor which explains the strong political ties between these regions and the Cariry Valley. During the sixties, cotton also was cultivated in parts of the Valley, chiefly for export abroad. Cheaper grades of cotton were consumed domestically by incipient and short-lived cottage industries engaged in the manufacture of inexpensive cloth destined for local markets.[18] But the cotton boom, important as it was for the Valley, was short-lived; at the termination of the U. S. Civil War, Europe reduced its imports from the Brazilian Northeast and not until the 1920s were they resumed.

Therefore, sugar and the *engenho* were chiefly responsible for shaping the social hierarchy of the Valley.[19] At its apex stood the sugar planters who enjoyed unchallenged social and political prominence until the end of the nineteenth century. Far beneath them, with the sole exception of the intermediary liberal professions, there was a subservient labor force. But unlike the export-oriented sugar coast of Pernambuco, the Valley labor force was not comprised of slaves. The farm hands of the region were nominally free men while, racially, they were most often of *mestiço* rather than African origin. Nonetheless, they lived at the barest subsistence level and were, in fact, permanently "fixed" to the sugar producers' land as the Portuguese word for the workers, *agregados,* indicates. The tasks of the *agregados* were not limited only to production: In times of rivalry between landowners, the farm hands were given arms to defend dutifully their patrons' interests. Rebellion against the patron rarely occurred as religious and social ties, represented by the *compadrio* and *afilhadagem,* bound owner and worker into a network of mutual obligations and relations.[20]

A commercial upsurge also took place in the Cariry during the 1850s.[21] The influx of merchants and new capital into Crato was precipitated by a general decline in the once prosperous commercial city of Icó. Icoense capitalists, such as the elder Antonio Luis Alves Pequeno, whose son of the same name was Padre Cícero's godparent at confirmation and financier of his seminary education, had an immediate impact on Crato. Their arrival marked the establishment of the city's first *lojas* (large general stores) as well as the Valley's first permanent pharmacy. Shortly thereafter, the first *sobrados* (two-story homes of relative luxury) were constructed, usually by wealthier merchants. While the merchants did not acquire political power commensurate with their wealth for another half century—and then usually only with the support of landowners—they did stimulate a demand for greater municipal services such as improved transportation, medical services, and above all schools. Their presence in a community also attracted tax collectors, lawyers, and even journalists. Members of the fourth estate descended on Crato in 1855 where the weekly, *O Araripe,* was founded as the first regional newspaper and was to flourish for over a decade.[22]

These forward strides at mid-century rekindled the Valley's suppressed political ambitions. Momentarily, however, the conservative imperial court in Rio de Janeiro blocked Crato's hope of controlling the seat of provincial authority in Fortaleza. In 1856, therefore, the political leaders of Crato initiated a campaign to achieve political autonomy within the Empire.[23] That year, the *câmara municipal* (the city council) of Crato proposed to the imperial government and the provincial assembly a plan to create a new province with its political center in Crato, to be know as the Province of the Cariris-Novos. Crato aspired to extend its authority so as to embrace not only the entire southern region of Ceará, but also those areas of bordering Piauí, Paraíba, and Pernambuco where Cratense economic interests were becoming increasingly entrenched. Despite the generally favorable mood in Rio de Janeiro, the plan failed. Throughout the next hundred years, however, various proposals for autonomy were presented, usually as tactical ploys to bargain more effectively with existing structures for regional advantages.[24] Indeed, the vision of the greater Cariry did not die easily; in fact, in the early twentieth century Padre Cícero was responsible for rekindling this objective, although his reasons for doing so were less political than they were religious.

Religious Revival in the Valley: "Padre Mestre Ibiapina"

It is not surprising that the religious life of the Valley was also revitalized at mid-century. The most important changes to take place in the Cariry's religious structures did so during the sixties and were primarily due to the efforts of one of the Northeast's best known personalities, the zealous native-born missionary, "Padre Mestre Ibiapina."[25] Born near Sobral, Ceará in 1806, José Antônio Pereira Ibiapina had studied law at Olinda and was embarked on a promising career in Cearense politics when political and personal misfortunes forced him in 1837 to leave Ceará. Returning to Recife, he practiced law and soon became renowned as a defender of the poor. Then, in 1853, at the age of forty-seven, he abandoned the toga for a cassock. His "conversion" and ordination are both shrouded in mystery. A significant clue to his devout spirit, however, was his decision to change his family name Pereira, to Maria, in honor of the Virgin Mother of Christ to whom a rash of miracles was attributed in France during the 1830s and whose Immaculate Conception was decreed a dogma of faith by the Roman pontiff in 1854.

In 1862, the cholera epidemic, in which Padre Cícero's father perished, prompted Fr. José Maria Ibiapina to return to Ceará, where the compassion he once showed for the poor in the courts of law could now be expended in the cause of his God. Church authorities granted him permission to preach a mission in Sobral, an afflicted city near his own birthplace. There, his biographer curiously notes, he became the object of popular veneration and introduced "the innovation of calling all the faithful by the Most Holy Name of Maria." In turn, his admirers ceased "using their patronimic and surnames by which they were known—these being disdained—and placed before their Christian names that of Maria." It also seems that Ibiapina proceeded to establish a religious congregation of nuns. Towards the end of the year, he recruited young women of the city, issued them a religious habit and accepted from them a solemn profession of vows to labor in the Lord's vineyard. This step, however, far exceeded the narrow limits of his license to preach and as such was an affront to episcopal authority. In January 1863, Ceará's bishop personally traveled to Sobral. There, he publicly condemned the practices instituted by Ibiapina and, despite the public's solidarity with the missionary, ordered him to leave the diocese posthaste.[26]

Ibiapina repaired to the arid backlands of the Northeastern *sertão*. There, distant from his ecclesiastical superiors, he seemed inspired by the single-minded objective to win the people back to the church and to found a congregation of nuns to aid him in this task. For the next two decades (until his death in 1883) Ibiapina traversed six Northeastern states. Everywhere, he preached with the enthusiasm of his Sobral days; everywhere, he was received with veneration by rich and poor alike. The missionary's efforts did not neglect to encourage material improvements. He mobilized submissive and credulous laborers, not only to repair churches and cemeteries, but also to construct dams, open wells, and lay out new roads—improvements profoundly welcomed by backland elites, who especially after 1865 were eager to cash in on the prosperity which cotton exports would provide for at least five more years.

This, at least, was the case in the Cariry Valley, where Ibiapina made two lengthy visits from October 1864 until February 1865 and from July 1868 to June 1869. It was during these two sojourns that Ibiapina constructed his most durable, and for our story, important legacy, the *Casas de Caridade* (Charity Houses) of the Valley's four chief *municípios,* Crato, Barbalha, Milagres, and Missão Velha.[27] Like eighteen others built elsewhere throughout the arid Northeast, the Charity Houses were destined to serve simultaneously as schools for the daughters of wealthy landowners and merchants, as orphanages for children of the lower classes, as centers for the manufacture of cheap textiles, and, in line with Ibiapina's own ambition, as a "convent" for his own congregation of nuns.[28] The Valley's elites, whose daughters would be educated in the *casas,* eagerly endorsed the missionary's efforts by endowing the convent schools with land and income; the poor, for their part, generously gave of their labor in the not uncommon belief that Ibiapina, like the eighteenth-century Friar Vitale, was a prophet and a healer.

Ibiapina's persuasiveness was no less unique than the religious congregation of women he had founded. First, most of the women who entered the "sisterhoods of charity" and took the title of *beata* came from the lower classes of the Brazilian backlands. Second, although neither Rome nor any Brazilian bishop had granted approval, Ibiapina required the *beatas* to wear the habit and make a profession of vows just as if their calling and religious congregation had been canonically approved. Third, each house, although independent, lived according to a single "rule" authored by the missionary, a rule in which labor and pious practices were combined.[29]

Indeed, Ibiapina's work in the Valley was not short of extraordinary: He had founded perhaps the first national religious congregation of women in the Northeast of Brazil, which, despite its canonical illegality, was to be a significant precedent for later generations of Cariry priests intent on establishing genuinely Brazilian religious orders. He had provided in the Charity Houses the first educational institutions for women in the interior;[30] finally, he had brought together rich and poor alike in common ventures for the glory of God and the material progress of man. Ibiapina's example would not be lost upon the Cariry's inhabitants, as we shall see, but it was not well received and was, in fact, put into question by an equally devout and militant ecclesiastical hierarchy.

The "Romanization" of Brazilian Catholicism

In 1854, Rome created the Diocese of Ceará, an ecclesiastical jurisdiction coterminous with the territorial boundaries of the imperial province. In 1861, Dom Luis Antônio dos Santos, a native of Rio de Janeiro province, was installed as Ceará's first bishop.[31] The state of the diocese could not have been worse: in an estimated population of 720,000 inhabitants, there were only thirty-three priests of which more than two-thirds had reportedly constituted families and whose prestige among the laity was consequently at the lowest possible ebb.[32] It was this state of affairs which sharply determined Dom Luis' basic policy objectives in the new diocese. Those objectives, to be shared later by other militant, reform-minded bishops, were twofold: (1) to restore the prestige of the church and the orthodoxy of its faithful; and (2) to mold anew a zealous, exemplary clergy through whom religious beliefs and practices in Brazil might be made to conform to the Roman, Catholic, and Apostolic faith of which Europe was the standard-bearer. In another sense, Dom Luis sought to initiate a new era in which the church and her clergy were to take the lead in shedding Brazil's "colonial Catholicism" for the "universalist Catholicism" of Rome with all the doctrinal, moral, and hierarchical rigidity which that transition implied. In doing so, Dom Luis was a precursor of the hierarchy's long-term efforts to "romanize" Brazilian Catholicism.[33]

Shortly after his arrival in Ceará, Dom Luis set to work to establish the diocese's first seminary, a major step towards the "romanization" of the Brazilian Catholic Church. As a former student of the French Lazarist fathers at the Mariana seminary in Minas Gerais, Dom Luis invited his teachers' successors to staff and direct his new enterprise. In 1864, Fr. Pierre Chevallier arrived in Fortaleza with a small band of French compatriots.[34] Appointed to the post of rector, Fr. Chevallier and his colleagues began the arduous task of training new and zealous Brazilian priests for the salvation of souls in Ceará. While the imposition of European standards on Northeastern pupils later inspired dissension within the seminary, the Lazarists succeeded in 1867 in graduating their first class of twelve zealous, pious, and obedient priests.

Obedience was an essential ingredient to the success of Dom Luis' reforms. For that reason, the bishop would brook no defiance from Fr. Ibiapina whom he had ordered out of Sobral in 1863. In 1869, reports from the Cariry prompted the bishop to take new steps against the celebrated missionary. Ibiapina, it seems, had become the object of popular veneration. During his mission in Barbalha that year, he had advised an ailing woman, who beseeched him for a cure, to bathe in the waters of the Caldas spring, located outside the city. When the woman returned to Barbalha three days later, fully healed, Ibiapina was hailed as a "miracle worker." A grateful people erected a chapel to Bom Jesus dos Pecadores over the site where the woman was cured; shortly thereafter, pilgrimages to this and other sites in the Valley where similar episodes had occurred became commonplace.[35] The matter might have rested there were it not for the publicity given Ibiapina in a Crato newspaper. Edited by José Joaquim Telles Marrocos, a cousin of Padre Cícero's, Crato's A Voz da Religião no Curiri, created to encourage popular participation in Ibiapina's work, repeatedly publicized the "miraculous" cures attributed to the missionary.[36] In July 1869, five months after A Voz's articles appeared, Dom Luis ordered all missionary work in the interior to a halt. While not referring to Ibiapina by name, Dom Luis could only have had him in mind when he wrote in his decree that the backland missions had provoked "not a few inconveniences, with detriment to ecclesiastical discipline and to that peace and harmony which must reign between the flock and its shepherd. . . ."[37] Ibiapina left the Cariry, but his legacy continued to be an irritant to a "romanized" bishop.

In September 1872, just five months after Padre Cícero arrived in Joaseiro, Dom Luis descended upon Crato. The bishop had ostensibly come on a pastoral visit, his second to the region. A chief objective, however, was to bring the Charity Houses of the Valley under episcopal control. While it was clearly impossible to suppress the Casas after so many prominent Valley citizens had contributed to their erection and while the bishop had no intention of granting canonical approval to the self-styled congregation

of *beatas,* he did seek to restrain their reported spiritual excesses. Not only
were the pious women staunchly devoted to the Sacred Heart of Jesus, as
was Dom Luis himself, but also, as it was widely known, to Ibiapina whom
they praised in their prayers and in their public works of charity as a
prophet and healer.[38] This considerable deviation from orthodoxy and the
beatas' lack of any formal theological training could only be detrimental
to a romanizing church.[39] For that reason and also in order to ensure
episcopal control in the Valley, Dom Luis, it seems, demanded that Ibiapina
relinquish control of the Charity Houses. This conclusion is confirmed by
a letter which Ibiapina wrote to the Mother Superior of the Crato *Casa* in
September 1872 shortly after Dom Luis arrived in the city.[40] In that farewell
letter, the missionary pledged never again to return to the Valley. To those
devoted followers in the Cariry *Casas* who chose not to join him in Paraíba
he recommended total submission to the bishop. Upon this victory, Dom
Luis immediately placed the four *Casas de Caridade* of the Valley under
the direct jurisdiction of his priests, some of whom were not only to be
natives of the region but also among the twenty or more zealous clergymen
by then ordained in Fortaleza. The bishop believed that orthodoxy would
now prevail in the Valley, although he could not foresee that even his
zealous priests were admirers of Ibiapina and took to heart the missionary's
prophecy that as long as the Charity Houses survived, God would do no
harm to his people. It is understandable then how both the *beatas* of the
Cariry and their new-found directors from among the zealous, reforming
clergy might play a significant role in the miracle at Joaseiro.

Dom Luis' visit to Crato also had a second objective, namely, the
erection of a minor seminary in Crato, the "Pearl of the Cariry."[41] Now
that Ibiapina's activities could no longer divert the energies, resources, and
good will of the Valley's prominent citizens, the prospects for a backland
seminary improved. Padre Cícero, whom Dom Luis so admired that he
ordained him over the misgivings of Fr. Chevallier, was said to have urged
the seminary project upon his bishop.[42] Moreover, the region itself was
relatively prosperous and both the local merchants and landowners stood
to benefit greatly from the establishment of a boarding school of higher
education in Crato. In 1874 and 1875, the foundations of the minor seminary
were erected on the bluff overlooking Crato, a terrain donated to the church
by Padre Cícero's godfather, Col. Antonio Luis II. Padre Cícero, himself,
was said to have dispatched several hundred laborers from Joaseiro to aid

in its construction.[43] The seminary's subsequent life was precarious. The drought of 1877–1879 forced it, among other results, to close its doors. However, it was reopened in 1888—one year before the miracle at Joaseiro. As one of the only two superior schools in the entire province (exclusive of the Fortaleza seminary) it was a most prestigious institution which secured for Crato a monopoly over education in the Valley. More important, its rector had always been considered a man of learning and prominence; in 1888, Msgr. Francisco Rodrigues Monteiro, a distant relative of Padre Cícero's, a childhood friend and a recently ordained priest, held that post. He was also to play a leading role in the events of 1889.

The Faith and the Nation

The erection of the Crato seminary in the 1870s obeyed a logic which extended beyond the dreams of a single bishop and the intense pride of the Catholic inhabitants in the leading backland city of Ceará. Indirectly, the event reflected the growing tensions between a "romanizing" church and the secular forces of Brazilian society. Those tensions had partly been inspired by changes in Europe where troops of a liberal Italian monarchy overran the papal states and in 1870 captured Rome. Throughout the Catholic world, churchmen condemned the audacious violence against the See of Peter; symptomatically, in Ceará, Dom Luis issued a Pastoral Letter of protest against the invasion of the papal states.[44] Then, in 1872, the first significant conflict between the Brazilian church and the nation erupted. Referred to as the "imperial religious question," the conflict arose when Brazil's reigning monarch, Dom Pedro II, had had two of Brazil's bishops arrested, prosecuted, and sentenced for their "unauthorized" stand against Masonry.[45] The emperor, although himself a leading Mason, had not taken action because of the bishops' substantive attack against Masonry, but rather over their failure to obtain royal permission to do so. Such permission was required by the *Padroado Real,* the ecclesiastical privilege granted by Rome to the Brazilian emperor by which he, rather than the nation's bishops, was the titular head of the Brazilian church.

The bishops' attack, it is true, had its roots in the Vatican's intensive, world-wide campaign against modernism, signaled by the 1864 Syllabus of Errors, and directed against all its enemies, among which Masonry was considered to be one of the most hostile. While Brazilian Masonry had been but dimly anticlerical by comparison with its European counterpart,[46] the 1872 conflict foreshadowed the increasing "romanization" of Brazilian Catholicism; indeed, shortly after this episode, Catholics in Brazil, once indifferent to their own permissive national variant of Masonry, soon became—like their ultramontane coreligionists of Europe—the avowed opponents of Masonry. In addition, the 1872 conflict, which lasted for three years, provoked a growing disenchantment within the church hierarchy towards the very imperial structure it had blindly supported. For the first time in the history of the Empire, Brazilian churchmen openly questioned a governing system which now appeared to them to chain the church in bondage to the state.[47]

Churchmen, it is true, did not then advocate the overthrow of the Empire which occurred in 1889. That option was closed to them for many reasons but especially because the national proponents of that change had been inspired since the 1870s by republican and other doctrines which the churchmen believed to be equally or even more antagonistic to Catholicism. Such had also been the case in Europe, where liberalism and republicanism everywhere had put the church and even the Vatican itself in chains. It is for those reasons that when the Republic was proclaimed in Brazil in November 1889, the Catholic hierarchy hailed the *fall* of the Empire as a divinely inspired liberation of the church. But, at the same time, the church could not officially welcome the Republic, whose underlying ideologies it and Rome had long opposed. The political dilemma facing the church was only resolved in 1890, when the carefully worded Collective Pastoral of the Brazilian hierarchy swore allegiance to the new government, but demanded from it total liberty for the church to act in society as any other free citizen or corporate body of the nation, and, by implication, to continue to oppose those doctrines which were contrary to the Catholic faith.[48]

Those doctrines became manifest in Brazil after 1870.[49] The Masonic affair of 1872–1875 was especially felt in Ceará. While few bishops elsewhere in Brazil expressed immediate support for their two arrested confreres, Dom Luis proved to be one of their staunchest defenders. When prominent Catholics spoke in the national parliament in defense of the two bishops, Dom Luis encouraged them to take an adamant stand. Meanwhile, he supported the circulation of a petition throughout Ceará to protest the emperor's arrest of the anti-Masonic churchmen.[50] Thereafter, Ceará became particularly alerted to the "diabolic" plans of Masons to undermine the Catholic faith of Brazil.

Positivism, especially the doctrine of Auguste Comte, long since forgotten in Europe, had just begun to take root in Brazil. Its impact upon intellectuals and especially the young military officers who later deposed the Emperor has been said to have been a major factor in the founding of the Republic. Despite this exaggerated view, positivism was inherently at odds with Catholicism. When an insignificant number of adepts in Comte's religion of humanity erected a positivist church in Rio de Janeiro in 1875, the Catholic response was to look askance at this heretical religion and its subsequent republican pretensions. In Ceará, positivists had little influence, although there and in the Cariry, positivism was often synonymous with republicanism.

Republicanism, whose proponents created Brazil's first republican party in 1870 and saw it enshrined as the system of government after 1889, posed a threat to the church because of its advocacy of civil marriage, and its avowed policy of religious toleration. Those proposals were considered, prior to 1890, to be serious and iniquitous curtailments of the church's monopoly over religion in Brazil. Of related and equal concern to the churchmen of the Northeast was the growth of Protestant sects in Recife, Fortaleza, and elsewhere along the coast of the region. Often protected by Masons and republicans, welcomed by middle-class merchants, Protestants were even able to proselytize through the newspaper columns of some of the Northeast's leading newspapers.[51]

All these forces—Masonry, positivism, republicanism and Protestantism —were adamantly opposed by the churchmen Dom Luis' attitude in regard to the Masonic affair has already been seen. That of his successor, Dom Joaquim José Vieira, second bishop of Ceará, was by far more celebrated.[52] Born in 1836 in Itapetininga, São Paulo and educated, trained, and ordained in the South, the future bishop of Ceará (and later the chief opponent of the miracle at Joaseiro) had reportedly refused to greet Dom Pedro II at a reception in his honor because of the emperor's order to arrest the anti-Masonic bishops. Despite the affront, Dom Joaquim was consecrated as bishop of Ceará in 1883; ten years later, and but four after the proclamation of the Republic, Dom Joaquim, moreover, issued a celebrated pastoral letter warning his flock against the evils of positivism, republicanism, and Protestantism.[53]

In the backlands of Ceará there was much less sophistication about these doctrines, and perhaps as a result even greater opposition. In the Cariry, for example the words "Republican and Mason were almost synonymous

and both were associated with the idea of an assault upon the Catholic
Church and of a persecution against Christians." It was not difficult to
envisage in such an environment, as one journalist from the Valley assures
us existed, "the tenebrous perspectives of cruel privations for the followers
of Our Lord [and of an imminent martyrdom to be] inflicted upon all
believers."[54] This crisis mentality, however, was generated only in part by
the political anxieties of the church and conveyed to its faithful by devout
and zealous clerics. In the case of the Cariry, many of the popular anxieties
were reinforced by recurrent droughts and prophetic priests. In 1877–1879,
the Northeast, for example, was ravaged by one of the most devastating
droughts in its history; Ceará was declared a national disaster area. Then
in September 1878, the worst year of the afflication, Dom Luis Antônio dos
Santos dramatically consecrated the entire province to the Sacred Heart of
Jesus, just as bishops everywhere throughout the Catholic world had done
in 1875, in a solemn act of public reparation for man's sins. He furthermore
vowed that should the drought abate, he as bishop would erect a great
church in Fortaleza in honor of the Sacred Heart.[55] In the Cariry, the
clergy followed his example; devotions to this particular effigy of Christ
were everywhere held, while in Missão Velha and Barbalha the local curates
arranged to carry in solemn procession to each other's church the life-size
statues of their cities' respective patron saints.[56] It was in such times of
local, regional, and national crisis that Padre Cícero began his ministry in
Joaseiro and the surrounding Cariry.

Prelude to a Miracle

At the time of Padre Cícero's arrival, Joaseiro was an nondescript hamlet
at the Northeastern edge of the *município* of Crato. It had been settled in
1827 by a Fr. Pedro Ribeiro da Silva whose residence and sugar mill were
more impressive than the rustic chapel he ordered built and dedicated to
Our Lady of Sorrows.[57] In 1875, the hamlet had all but retained its essential
features as a sugar plantation; its population numbered no more than 2,000
inhabitants.[58] Five families—the Gonçalveses, Macedos, Sobreiras, Landims,
Bezerra de Menezes—were all that could be counted among the prominent
landowners. The remainder of the population consisted of the hands attached to the sugar *fazendas* of these families. Many of these workers were
descendants of Father Pedro's slaves, both mixed bloods and poor whites

who had since come to work the small and unassuming sugar plantations
in the vicinity. The hamlet boasted the chapel, one schoolhouse, and thirty-
two one-story dwellings of thatched roofs. There were only two streets. The
Rua Grande (later, Rua Padre Cícero) paralleled the length of the chapel
and met at a perpendicular with the Rua dos Brejos. Commercially, the
hamlet offered little to its inhabitants. Occasionally, tradesmen stopped at
Joaseiro en route from Missão Velha to Crato. On those occasions the dusty
praça (square) in front of the chapel became a fair in which coffee was
exchanged for some local produce. There was no moneyed economy to
speak of. The poorer members of the community were completely marginal
to the barter economy, and at the time of Padre Cícero's arrival had begun
to show signs of discontent. Those who had invited the priest to the hamlet
clearly believed that his presence would do much for the progress and
stability of the vicinity.

Unfortunately, there is much fiction and little fact about Padre Cícero's

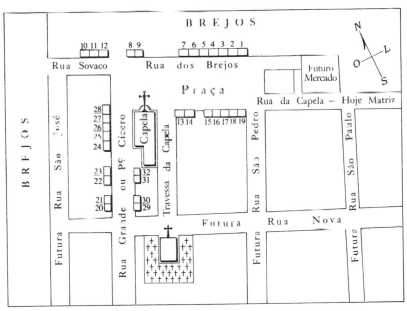

Joaseiro in 1875 (shaded area) with its original chapel and thirty-two dwellings, from
a map executed in January 1965 by the late Octávio Aires de Menezes at the author's
request. (*Brejos*, marshland; *capela*, chapel; *futura*, future; *hoje*, today; *mercado*, market;
ou, or; *rua*, street.)

life from the time of his arrival in 1872 until the miracle of 1889. Judicious use of all extant sources, however, can convey if not a portrait at least a sketch of this unquestionably devout, selfless, and zealous curate of souls.

Factual are the accounts of Padre Cícero's success in bringing the disorderly elements of Joaseiro's population back into the church. Several authors, including native sons of the city, affirm that lascivious and criminal elements abided in the hamlet.[59] They were given to drink and dancing the samba, which at the time was viewed as sensual and degenerate, owing to its origins in the slave population of Brazil. There is even a hint that several prostitutes had become permanent fixtures of this crossroad hamlet. Padre Cícero was not averse to punishing sinners in public. He prohibited their dances, stopped the men from drinking, and forced the prostitutes to confess their sins, do public penance, and amend their lives. In a relatively short time, it is said, Joaseiro had been brought to order by the efforts of its chaplain.

Also factual, in some respects, is Padre Cícero's emulation of Fr. Ibiapina, whom he resembled in zeal, single-mindedness, and independent action.[60] Like Ibiapina, Padre Cícero began early to recruit a number of single women of the hamlet into a sisterhood under his own authority. Some of the women had been *beatas* in the Charity House of Crato, while others took the veil for the first time in Joaseiro. Some were widows and women of some education, such as Isabel da Luz who became one of the hamlet's most prominent teachers of the young.[61] Others of lesser social standing and intelligence simply gave themselves over to a life of piety and prayer, occasional catechetical instruction, and exuberant participation in the annual Holy Week services and Christmas pageants which, under Padre Cícero's guidance, were designed to edify the population and inculcate in them a devotion to the church and her doctrines. Several of these *beatas* lived under the cleric's roof in the company of his widowed mother and two spinster sisters along with many orphans for whom he provided support.

Accurate also is Padre Cícero's renown as a selfless and impoverished priest.[62] Very rarely did he accept money for the administration of the sacraments among the inhabitants of the Cariry. As a result the young priest was so poor that wealthy friends and benefactors in Crato usually had to provide him with cassocks, shoes, and even the coppers to pay for his haircuts. It is also said that his mother, sisters, and their innumerable charges frequently lived on the brink of poverty; from time to time it was necessary for his mother to send someone through the town to beg villagers for food enough to sustain her charges.

Padre Cícero's integrity and devotion as a priest were similarly above reproach. Dom Joaquim José Vieira, his new bishop since 1883, had full confidence in him as did his episcopal predecessor. In issuing the cleric's annual license to celebrate mass and administer the sacraments, the bishop frequently granted Padre Cícero extensive discretionary powers to suspend, whenever necessary, the unessential rubrics of the church. In 1884, when Dom Joaquim visited Joaseiro to consecrate the altar of Our Lady of Sorrows chapel, then newly rebuilt by Padre Cícero, he hailed the cleric's enterprise as a "monument that attests to the power of the faith of the Holy Roman Catholic Apostolic Church."[63] After the miracle of 1889, however, there was a tendency to depict the cleric as having been during the previous decades a particularly overzealous and unexemplary priest. In this regard, much has been made of Dom Luis' 1870 decision to ordain Padre Cícero despite the objection of Fr. Pierre Chevallier who contended that the seminarian was often too mystical, strong-headed, and at times doctrinally audacious to make a good priest.[64] Little other proof, however, has been marshaled to justify the implicit charge that the backland chaplain had, prior to 1883, exceeded the orthodox norms of priestly conduct, devotion, and piety. Furthermore, in matters of zeal, he cannot, in fact, be compared with other Valley priests whose unbridled zealousness and pious excesses were renowned throughout the Valley.

For example, there was in Crato at this time a priest named Fr. Felix de Moura whose preaching reminded many of the old-time missionaries. Father Felix was also the founder or at least director of a society of Crato penitents.[65] These penitents—whose organizations and practices were not uncommon in Brazil—usually congregated in the streets of Crato late at night. Their faces and bodies were covered with hoods and capes, often marked with crosses. Under the direction of Father Felix, the penitents would march through the streets chanting hymns and prayers until they arrived, usually at midnight, at the local cemetery. There, they would strip the clothes from their backs and "discipline" themselves with leather whips at the end of which were sharp pieces of metal and other cutting objects. Father Felix's zeal was such that he was once reported to have stripped to the waist and flagellated himself while preaching a sermon in church.

Another priest of similarly overzealous inclinations was Monsignor

Francisco Monteiro, native of Crato and long-time friend of Padre Cícero, who in 1888 returned to Crato to become rector of the recently reopened seminary. While pastor of the parish of Iguatú, a city in central Ceará, Msgr. Monteiro established a reputation as a fiery preacher and prophet of the imminent castigation of mankind by God. In Iguatú he was also known to rant and rave from the pulpit, bringing tears of repentance to the eyes of his parishioners.[66] At the time of the "events of Joaserio," Msgr. Monteiro once again demonstrated his oratorical abilities and perhaps more than any other person was instrumental in proclaiming those events a miracle.

While Padre Cícero was known neither for his leadership of penitent societies nor his oratorical ability, the common people of Joaseiro, it is true, had continuously ascribed to him exceptional qualities of sanctity and prophecy.[67] Coupled with the public knowledge of the cleric's alleged visions, it cannot be denied that even his most ordinary actions were frequently thought to be of supernatural inspiration. When in 1877 he sent many drought victims who had fled to the Valley from the surrounding *sertão* to the unclaimed lands atop the Araripe Mountains and there obliged them to plant manioc to relieve their hunger, the grateful survivors later attributed their felicity to the priest whom they believed was holy.[68] During the drought of 1888, a similar but admittedly more dramatic episode took place which confirmed for the credulous their own conviction in Padre Cícero's sanctity. As the drought of 1888 proceeded to inflict great suffering on the Cariry Valley, Padre Cícero, Fr. Felix de Moura, and Fr. Fernandes Távora, then vicar of Crato, joined in prayer and in a *promessa* not unlike that of Dom Luis' in 1877. Should God grant their petition and bring the drought to an end, the three clerics would erect an enormous church in honor of the Sacred Heart atop the Serra do Catolé, at the northern edge of Joaseiro.[69] It is alleged that rains briefly inundated the Valley; not long after, the chaplain at Joaseiro set to work to fulfill his promise. Meanwhile, the Valley's temporary relief from the drought was attributed to Padre Cícero and his singular holiness. This further episode, too, was an opportunity for the credulous to embellish with myth a number of undisputable facts which greatly enhanced the backland cleric's fame as a devoted, selfless, and holy priest in the decades before the miracle at Joaseiro.

As the year 1889 unfolded, the drought of the "two-eights" (i.e., 1888) retrenched into the Valley. The people plaintively reverted to prayer to seek divine relief, while the Valley priests led them with renewed fervor. The circumstances were not unlike those of the devastating years of 1877–1879. One factor, however, was new: the presence of Maria de Araújo, a twenty-eight year old laundress, single, a native of Joaseiro, and a *beata* in the household of Padre Cícero.[70] Nothing in her stature or in her past indicated that this homely *mulata* would become an instrument of Providence, a stigmatic, and the object of veneration by the masses.

On 1 March 1889, Maria de Araújo was among several pious women who had come to the chapel of Joaseiro to attend the mass and rituals, celebrated on each first Friday of the month in honor of the Sacred Heart of Jesus.[71] She was among the first to receive communion. Suddenly, she fell to the ground and the immaculate white host which she had moments before received became red with blood. The extraordinary event was repeated every Wednesday and Friday of Lent for the next two months; from Passion Sunday to the feast of the Ascension of Christ into Heaven, a duration of forty-seven days, it recurred daily.

Finally on 7 July 1889, the solemn liturgical feast day of the Precious Blood, Monsignor Monteiro, Rector of the Crato seminary, led a pilgrimage of three thousand people, many from the most prominent families of Crato, to the hamlet of Joaseiro. Before an overflowing assembly, Monteiro mounted the pulpit and delivered a sermon on the mystery of Christ's passion and death that reportedly brought tears to the eyes of his listeners; then he dramatically thrust aloft a fistful of altar linens which were visibly stained with blood; that blood, he declared, had issued from the host received by Maria de Araújo, and it was, according to the Rector, the very blood of Jesus Christ.[72]

2

The Ecclesiastical Conflict

The Fatal Interlude

Only in early November 1889, eight months after the miracle had occurred for the first time, did news of it reach Dom Joaquim at the Diocesan Palace in Fortaleza. Even then his sources of information were most indirect: a letter from the curate of Crato and an article in a Recife newspaper.[1] The silence of Monsignor Monteiro who publicly proclaimed the miracle and of Padre Cícero who was its chief protagonist caused Dom Joaquim no small measure of indignation.[2] They had slighted episcopal authority and had audaciously given publicity to facts which were entirely unverified.

Despite this early but sparse publicity, the miracle of 1889 made little public impact on the Northeast until it recurred—nearly two years later—in Holy Week of 1891.[3] At that time, the ensuing coverage in the press of Ceará precipitated an ecclesiastical conflict that profoundly agitated the Roman Catholic hierarchy of Brazil and eventually led to a potential schism within the ranks of Catholicism in the Brazilian Northeast. However, it would be entirely erroneous to assume—as some authors have—that during

32

this interval of almost two years—November 1889 to March 1891—the so-called "religious question" of Joaseiro had lain dormant. Quite to the contrary, this was an interlude during which the policies pursued by Dom Joaquim, although out of the public eye, partly contributed to the open conflict that later erupted.[4] The details of this period, substantiated here by hitherto unpublished archival material, prove so important to Joaseiro's later history that they merit careful reconstruction and consideration.

Dom Joaquim reacted to the initial miracle of 1889 with greater restraint than might have been anticipated. It is true that he sternly reprimanded Padre Cícero for failing to advise him promptly of the "extraordinary" events and criticized his neglect as a breach of the clerical vow of obedience. But the tone of the bishop's letters of the fourth and fifth of November 1889 was hostile neither to the errant priest nor to the possibility that a miracle had indeed occurred. For the moment, the prelate's principal recourse was to demand a detailed report about the events and to prohibit Padre Cícero from preaching in public about miracles which had not yet been verified by the church.

The bishop could not have thought and acted otherwise. As protector of the Faith, it was his duty to watch over "the purity of Catholic doctrine"; but as a man of faith, he could not dismiss offhand a fact of reputedly divine origin. Moreover, Padre Cícero's long years of exemplary priestly conduct inspired a measure of confidence in the bishop. "I am a friend and admirer of Your Reverence," Dom Joaquim wrote in November 1889, "I trust in your sincerity and learning and therefore I judge you incapable of any hoax whatsoever."[5]

There may have been another factor which subconsciously influenced Dom Joaquim. At the time, the church had come under increasing attacks of the republicans. In 1888, the bishop had confided to Padre Cícero his own fears that the issue of "religious liberty" was becoming increasingly critical. The bishop believed that the nation's politicians "imbued with evil doctrines, wanted to dechristianize Brazil, but, thanks be to God, they will not succeed because there is still Faith to save the country."[6] Perhaps Dom Joaquim believed that the miracles of Joaseiro had been sent by God to "confound the unbelievers."

The lengthy conversations which Dom Joaquim subsequently held with Msgr. Monteiro in Fortaleza in either late December 1889 or early January 1890 did not illuminate to the Bishop's satisfaction the events in question.[7]

Then, Padre Cícero's long-awaited report finally reached Dom Joaquim on 7 January.[8] This report is one of the most curious documents of the "religious question" of Joaseiro. It reveals a pathetic self-portrait of the man who soon after became the central figure of the ecclesiastical conflict and one of the most controversial personalities in the history of Ceará.

Padre Cícero's account clearly underscores the religious fervor which prevailed in Joaseiro in the period preceding the first "miracle" of 1889. According to the cleric, the winter rains had not yet fallen. Famine and fear of an extended drought afflicted the inhabitants of the hamlet and the Valley. Prayers were offered in public and private: the priests of the Valley led the faithful in pilgrimages, novenas, and other devotions intended to stay God's hand from inflicting the "horrors of the drought" upon the people.

Those who gathered in the chapel of Joaseiro on the first Friday of March 1889, had clearly intended to make a profound act of reparation to the Sacred Heart of Jesus so that Joaseiro might be spared. Many persons had arrived the night before, especially the women who were members of Joaseiro's recently founded association of the Apostleship of Prayer, an organization which existed throughout the Catholic world and was dedicated to promoting the devotion to the Sacred Heart.[9] Six or seven of these pious women had kept an all-night vigil in the chapel, while Padre Cícero was confessing the men of the hamlet. At about 5 A.M., Padre Cícero wrote, he took compassion on the tired souls, among them Maria de Araújo; he decided to administer communion to them immediately so that they could return home and rest before the morning mass was to be celebrated. It was then that the alleged miracle occurred. Maria de Araújo was the first communicant. Padre Cícero placed the host upon her tongue; the *beata* fell to the floor in a trance. Blood streamed from the host, "a part of which she swallowed . . . while the other fell to the ground."

Padre Cícero's reaction is not clearly revealed in the document. He admits that at first he paid little attention to the incident. Perhaps he thought that the *beata,* infirm since childhood (a fact he only later confided to the bishop),[10] had suddenly fallen ill. Nonetheless he asserts unequivocally in his report—written ten months after the event took place—that the host received by Maria de Araújo had been transformed into the Precious Blood of Christ. In retrospect, however, doubt seems to have been his principal reaction. For example, even though the "transformation of the host" had recurred many times during Lent, he repeatedly demanded that Maria de Araújo ask for a divine sign to prove to him that the events in question were truly miraculous. Despite the *beata's* assurances, Padre Cícero made every effort to keep the "extraordinary" facts a secret. It was only after Msgr. Monteiro had mounted the pulpit in Joaseiro to proclaim that the host had been transformed into Christ's blood, that Padre Cícero assured the credulous that a miracle had occurred. Even then, however, he did so, as he states in his report, so as "not to give scandal [or show] any disrespect for Msgr. Monteiro,"[11] the prestigious rector of the Crato seminary.

Despite Padre Cícero's repeated assertions in the report that the event revealed Christ's "efforts to save men" and that he himself was convinced that it was Christ's blood which had issued from the host, the document conveys with clarity and force the image of a reluctant protagonist, of a zealous priest swept aloft by the conviction of his colleagues and by the tumultuous legions of credulous pilgrims who began ceaselessly to throng the hamlet in search of faith.

In Dom Joaquim's mind, Padre Cícero's report did not clarify the essential problem: from whence did the blood originate? If it issued from the host, Dom Joaquim assuringly reasoned, then indeed it was a "great marvel that merits to be spread throughout the entire world."[12] However, if the blood issued from the *beata's* mouth and spread to the host, then it would be illogical "to conclude that the host had been transformed into blood."[13]

Here was the crux of the problem which the bishop sought to clarify. Despite strong reservations, Dom Joaquim neither condemned the "miracle" nor his priests. It is true that he prohibited Padre Cícero from "qualifying as miraculous" the "extraordinary facts" which had occurred and forbade him to render public worship to the bloodstained altar linens. But the bishop did not prevent his priests from referring publicly to the events they had seen and taken part in. Furthermore, he specifically encouraged them to surround all future occurrences "with the testimony of witnesses who could swear under oath to what they had seen and heard."[14] This was the strategy called for by canon law, and in adopting it, the bishop had inadvertently encouraged the miracle's advocates to bestow upon the events of Joaseiro a procedural legality befitting the most revered miracles of Catholicism.

However, from January to March 1890, Dom Joaquim adopted a second strategy which alone, he believed, would put an immediate end to his own doubts. He suggested that Padre Cícero transfer Maria de Araújo from Joaseiro to the Charity House of Crato. If the priest and the *beata* complied, he conjectured, then their act of obedience would be a sign of their sincerity and sancitity. Furthermore, if the extraordinary events recurred in Crato in Padre Cícero's absence, while the *beata* was under the spiritual direction of some other priest, then all the speculation which had arisen in his mind about Padre Cícero's possible influence over the *beata* would be proven groundless.[15]

When in June the *beata's* mother requested that the bishop suspend the order, Dom Joaquim had received his answer. Disobedience to the bishop foreclosed the possibility of a miracle. Dom Joaquim withdrew his initiatives; his mind was made up. He now placed the burden of proof entirely upon Padre Cícero. Once again he forbade the priest to proclaim the events miraculous either from the pulpit or in the press. It was now up to Padre Cícero to prove to the bishop that what had occurred was a miracle.[16]

Dom Joaquim had spoken his last word, at least until May of 1891, when fresh publicity in the press of Ceará forced him to take public action. Until then he had remained aloof from the question, perhaps in the hope that it would disappear. From June 1890 until May 1891, it appears that not a single letter was exchanged between the Bishop of Ceará and the protagonists in Joaseiro. This official ecclesiastical silence, however, later proved to be detrimental to the bishop's position.

The Public Miracle and Its Doctrinal Implications

In the Cariry Valley, the subtle distinction which allowed Padre Cícero and other priests to speak publicly about "the extraordinary events" as long as they did not qualify them as miraculous was lost on the people. In Joaseiro, not a person doubted that a miracle had occurred. Its purpose had been allegedly revealed to Maria de Araújo in August 1889: the Lord had chosen Joaseiro as a center from which he would convert sinners and save mankind.[17] Furthermore, proof of the hamlet's divine mission lay in the endless waves of pilgrims who descended upon Joaseiro. There, Brazilian Masons and Protestants sought absolution and reembraced the church. The sick were cured and the faithful were made firm in their faith. Upon departure, believers took with them an amulet, a ribbon, or cloth strip that had been pressed against the glass container in which lay conserved the cloths and altar linens stained crimson by what was believed to be the Precious Blood of Christ.

In the neighboring city of Crato, almost the entire population, among them great landowners and wealthy merchants, remained firm in this belief. More than three thousand of the town's prominent citizens had made the first pilgrimage to Joaseiro in 1889.[18] A year later, again under the leadership of Msgr. Monteiro, they returned for the Holy Week celebrations held in Joaseiro. Their example was not lost upon the other cities of the Valley. From Barbalha, Milagres, and Missão Velha the faithful and their priests promoted the cause of Joaseiro, primarily by word of mouth and visits to the hamlet.

Contrary to the opinion that the miracle of Joaseiro originated among the lower classes, it was the priests of the Valley who played the most important role in spreading and justifying the popular belief in the miracles of Joaseiro. It is true that Padre Cícero's reputation as a zealous and pious priest remained as untarnished as ever and contributed to the credibility of events, but it has rarely been adequately emphasized that Msgr. Monteiro's prestige as Rector of the Crato seminary made it extremely difficult for the people to doubt. Other priests also played an active role: Fr. Quintino Rodrigues and Joaquim Soter, professors at the Crato seminary; Fr. Felix de Moura, director of the penitent association in Crato; and three curates from the cities of Missão Velha, Barbalha, and Milagres.[19] All these priests firmly believed at the outset that a miracle had taken place. As long as this belief was cloaked in secrecy, and as long as Dom Joaquim had not expressly condemned it, as Fr. Felix later confessed in a confidential letter to the bishop, they themselves believed without reservation.[20]

Furthermore, Dom Joaquim's inaction between June 1890 and May 1891 had greatly enabled the miracle to take root among the clergy and the faithful, both in the Valley and in the adjacent backland states. Moreover, his earlier request that Cícero produce witnesses "who could testify under oath" to the veracity of the miracle became a compelling reason for believers to rally witnesses to their cause. During the course of late 1890 and early 1891 there were few believers who hesitated to proclaim publicly the truth of the miracle.

Finally, on 24 April 1891, the Fortaleza newspaper *Cearense*[21] fired the first volley in the new round of the "religious question" of Joaseiro and the subsequent ecclesiastical conflict. Without comment, the newspaper published an eyewitness account of the transformation of the host. The author of the document was a noted physician in Crato, Dr. Marcos Rodrigues de Madeira. Madeira's credentials were extremely impressive. He had received his degree in Rio de Janeiro where he later practiced medicine in the Santa Casa de Misericôrdia. Under the monarchy he served a term as a Deputy in the Provincial Assembly of Rio de Janeiro. Further-more, Madeira had reputedly been an "unbeliever," a fact which gave even greater credibility to his testimony.

Madeira declared that he had been in Joaseiro on the solemn feast of Holy Thursday, 25 March 1891, when Padre Cícero called upon him to witness and evaluate the transformation of the host. The doctor undertook his inquiry in the presence of five priests, many notable citizens of the neighboring city of Crato, and a crowd which reached such proportions that he finally found it necessary to have Padre Cícero order the spectators to leave. After completing the examination—in conditions hardly considered optimum—Dr. Madeira concluded that the host received by Maria de Araújo had indeed turned into blood. He dismissed the notion that the *beata* was ill and asserted that the transformation "is a supernatural fact for which it was impossible . . . to find a scientific explanation."[22]

The publication of Madeira's weighty testimony, according to Dom Joaquim, profoundly "shocked the entire Diocese of Fortaleza and where-soever his testimony reached."[23] The educated Catholic population of the Northeast clamored for an explanation and their bishops' veredictum. In-deed Madeira's declaration had forced Dom Joaquim's hand; it was no longer possible to cope with Joaseiro from a distance. As a result, Dom Joaquim urgently ordered Padre Cícero to come to Fortaleza.

Meanwhile, in Crato, the curate of the parish reminded his parishioners that "no Catholic was obliged to believe in the events that had taken place inasmuch as the competent authority . . . [the bishop] had neither initiated an investigation nor verified the fact. . . ." He concluded his sermon by urging caution and prudence since, as the Church knew, it was not un-common in such matters for "the devil to make sacred things appear marvelous in order to distort the true religion of Jesus Christ."[24]

But this personal initiative of the only dissenting clergyman of the Valley had, of course, come too late. In Joaseiro and Crato few believed the devil had a hand in the miracles that had taken place since 1889, and of which so many reputable priests were witnesses and advocates. Now that a prominent physician had clearly stated that science could not explain an evidently supernatural occurrence, there was no reason for others to doubt. Wealthy landowners and merchants from Crato, who were present in Joaseiro during the solemn Holy Week services of 1891, supported Dr. Madeira's view. So too did several additional priests who had come on pilgrimage from the neighboring states of Pernambuco, Paraíba, and Rio Grande do Norte.[25] One of them immediately dispatched an article to Recife's prominent Catholic weekly, *Era Nova,* proclaiming the events a miracle.[26]

Shortly after Easter, a second prominent physician and a well known pharmacist made public their professional opinions. The physician was Dr. Ildefonso Correia Lima, a prominent politician in Ceará. His declaration concluded that the transformation of the host was due to some "outside agent, which I conclude to be—God."[27] The pharmacist was Joaquim Secundo Chaves of Crato, better known as Secundo, a devout Catholic and a lifelong friend of Padre Cícero's. Secundo offered a new perspective on the events of Joaseiro. He alleged that Maria de Araújo was a stigmatic, that is, that she bore Christ's wounds on her body. The implication of this observation was clear: if the *beata* so intimately emulated Christ's Passion then there could be no doubt of the divine origin of the transformation of the host.[28]

Many of these declarations rapidly found their way into the secular and religious press of the Brazilian Northeast. In May, in an effort to give them even wider publicity, the *Vanguarda* printing house in Crato collected them into a pamphlet entitled: *The Miracles of Joaseiro or Our Lord Jesus Christ Manifesting His Real Presence in the Divine and Adorable Sacrament of the Eucharist.*[29] It bore no ecclesiastical license and contained a number of startling theological propositions.[30] These propositions were found in the declarations of a few "professional men" but especially in those of priests and laymen alike, and provide some idea of the issues over which the ensuing ecclesiastical conflict developed.

The first of these propositions asserted unequivocally that the hosts had been transformed into the Precious Blood of Christ. This indeed had been the view of both Padre Cícero and Msgr. Monteiro from the start.

However, the force with which other priests had also adhered to this conviction presented a clear threat to the integrity of the Church's doctrine. For if the blood was indeed Christ's, shed again in Joaseiro "to convert sinners and save mankind," then the idea of a *second Redemption* could be clearly implied. This of course was contrary to the Church's teaching that the Redemption could and did occur but once.

A second proposition found in the pamphlet was equally audacious. In a public letter in which a certain Henrique Figueiredo Filho described the events of Joaseiro to relatives, he asserted "we are nearing the Day of the Last Judgment."[31] This prescience of the imminent advent of the apocalypse was said to have been confirmed to the author by Padre Cícero who himself declared that "all will be called and few will be chosen."

Both of these doctrinal innovations speedily gained currency in the backlands as Brazilian political life underwent its most profound change since independence: on 15 November 1889, the nation's army deposed the emperor and proclaimed the Republic. The decision of the new regime to disestablish the Catholic Church confirmed the worst fears of the militant hierarchy. To prevent further losses at the hands of the republicans, churchmen swiftly moved in 1890 to create a nation-wide political party, the Catholic party, to defend the church's interests. The party, however, soon perished from its own weaknesses but only after it had succeeded in mobilizing a handful of militant faithful in every nook and cranny of Brazil, including Crato and the neighboring cities. Among the local militants were several priests and laymen who were among the leading proponents of the miracles—which perhaps they now more readily embraced in order to take comfort in the midst of Catholicism's political defeat.

While the political condition of the nation seemed most propitious for the spread of the two new beliefs which began to emanate from Joaseiro, it is important to point out that each of these new beliefs appealed to distinct social groups. Belief in the second Redemption, with its sophisticated theological implications, took root chiefly among the clergy and highly educated laity. Belief in the advent of the millennium, intrinsically traumatic, had particular resonance among the superstitious and illiterate masses. Understandably then, it was the priests and their audacious theology of the second Redemption that raised the threat of a schism, while it was the masses, who in their expectancy of the millennium at any moment, would make it possible for that potential schism to win adherents.

Action and Reaction: The Legal Basis for Conflict

In mid-July 1891, Dom Joaquim moved swiftly to curb his unruly flock in the Cariry. In response to two summonses from the bishop, Padre Cícero had just arrived in Fortaleza amidst the jubilation and curiosity of the capital's population.[32] On 17 July the Diocesan Palace was the scene of the first formal inquiry into the "facts of Joaseiro." Two days later, after the lengthy interrogations and written reports were completed, Dom Joaquim issued an interlocutory decision.[33]

The heart of the canonically provisional decision was the bishop's unqualified rejection of the claim that the host had been transformed into the blood of Christ: "It is not nor can it be according to the teachings of Catholic Theology."[34] Dom Joaquim tried to demonstrate to Padre Cícero that the Thomistic view of the transubstantiation clearly negated such a contention. Any claim to the contrary implied, in the bishop's mind, an offensive innovation of doctrine, namely, that of the second Redemption, inasmuch as Thomistic theology infallibly taught that the Redemption was a unique historical event that could not recur. In a personal letter to Padre Cícero, before his departure on 22 July, Dom Joaquim again reproached the cleric for giving vent to the false doctrine, and vehemently criticized him for also insinuating to the faithful that the Last Judgment was at hand: "Did the Church authorize you to preach this novelty?"[35] The bishop's decision applied equally to his other disobedient priests. He forbade them once again to declare publicly that the "facts" were "miraculous" and called for the immediate halt to public veneration of the bloodstained cloths. As a final measure, he promised to establish an episcopal Commission of Inquiry to visit Joaseiro and investigate the "extraordinary facts" which had taken place there.

Why Dom Joaquim promised to dispatch a Commission of Inquiry, why he did not impose more severe sanctions upon his priests, and indeed why he did not act more vigorously to suppress the very beliefs whose veracity he himself appears to have denied are important questions. One possible explanation of his tolerant stance may have rested on his own conviction that Catholicism was the one, true religion, while miracles were God's own proofs of the divine origin of both the Faith and the church. As long as no one in the Cariry flouted episcopal authority in doctrinal matters by claiming that the blood issued from the host was Christ's and, once proven that it was not the *beata's*, then, Dom Joaquim patiently explained to Padre

Cícero, the facts of Joaseiro would constitute "a great marvel and a unique blessing for Ceará."

Another explanation, however, may be linked to Dom Joaquim's natural proclivity towards caution and a bureaucratic inclination to abide by the well-established canon laws governing such an extraordinary case. For that reason, a commission of inquiry not only could best resolve *in loco* all existing doubts, but also could best render its findings in a canonically binding manner. In addition, his interlocutory decision—that the blood "is not and cannot be" Christ's—assured Dom Joaquim that neither he nor his zealous priests in the Cariry would incur Rome's wrath for altering the inalterable teachings of St. Thomas and the church.

While the bishop had taken recourse to canon law, his interlocutory decision was hotly contested in the Cariry. Nine days after it reached the Valley, five priests and thirty-four citizens formally petitioned Dom Joaquim to rescind it.[36] The decision, they argued, had "wounded [Joaseiro's cause] to the death," even before the commission of inquiry had been dispatched to conduct its investigation. As a final measure, the appellants reminded their bishop of their canonical rights, established by the Council of Trent, which permitted them to appeal directly to Rome should Dom Joaquim refuse to rescind his fatal decision.

Known as the "July petition of appeal," the document was dispatched to Fortaleza in September 1891. To it was appended a personal letter from Padre Cícero who wrote that the enclosed appeal expressed not only his own views but also those of "many priests and thousands of persons who have come from many parts to this hamlet."[37] Correctly aware that Dom Joaquim might consider this but another act of disobedience, Padre Cícero justified his stand by recourse to a higher source of authority than that of Dom Joaquim's. The cleric solemnly explained that on three consecutive days in August, Christ had revealed to him in a series of visions the significance of the events in Joaseiro. "In view of testimony of this order," Padre Cícero asked, "should I stop believing and affirming that the blood manifested here in the sacred species is the Blood of Christ?"[38]

Dom Joaquim rejected the appeal outright, but promised not to prevent the appellants from carrying the case to Rome. The bishop was anguished and dismayed. But in Joaseiro, a chosen people was born. United in Christ, Who had chosen Joaseiro to defy the impious, the inhabitants of the hamlet prepared to receive the commission of inquiry.

The First Commission of Inquiry
and Brazilian Clerical Nationalism

The Commission of Inquiry reached Joaseiro in early September 1891.[39] It was composed of two members: Fr. Clycério da Costa Lôbo, Chief Commissioner, and Fr. Francisco Ferreira Antero, Secretary.[40] Fr. Clycério was fifty-two years old and had been a priest almost thirty years. After his studies in Olinda and ordination in Bahia, he resided for a time in Rio de Janeiro. At the request of Ceará's first bishop, he returned to Fortaleza to serve as Dom Luis' personal secretary and chief organizer of the Fortaleza seminary. Under Dom Joaquim, Fr. Clycério was chiefly responsible for the planning of Ceará's first Diocesan Synod in 1888. His service to the church had won for him a nomination to the post of Archbishop of Bahia, the oldest and most important diocese in Brazil, an honor which he modestly refused.[41]

Fr. Antero came from a prominent family of Icó which had given several sons to the priesthood. He had studied in Rome and was ordained from the Colégio Pio Latino-Americano in 1878. For a man of thirty-six years of age, he had already shown marked ability as a doctor of sacred theology and, at the time of his visit to Joaseiro, was being considered by Dom Joaquim as a nominee for a vacant bishopric somewhere in Brazil.[42] From these facts, it is clear that Dom Joaquim had appointed two competent men whose piety, learning, and service to the church were beyond reproach. Any irregularity in the "facts of Joaseiro" would not escape them.

The commission began its inquiry on 9 September 1891, after three days of meditation and prayer. Their objectives were twofold: to witness the transformation of the host and to interview the leading personalities in the question. Two weeks later, on 24 September, they left Joaseiro with Maria de Araújo, whom they transferred to the Charity House in Crato.[43] This was done upon the bishop's request in order that they might conduct their investigation in the absence of Padre Cícero. In all, the commissioners had personally witnessed the transformation of the host several times; they had questioned ten *beatas*, eight priests, and five prominent civilians; they also recorded the names of twenty-two persons who allegedly had been "miraculously cured" through their devotion to the "Precious Blood of Joaseiro."

On 13 October, Fr. Clycério brought the inquiry to a close. He returned to Fortaleza within the month and on 28 November submitted his report to Dom Joaquim. The bishop could hardly believe what he read; he concluded that the "business at Joaseiro" had set in motion a "church within a church."[44]

Each page of Fr. Clycério's report, entitled "The Proceedings of the Inquiry"[45] proclaimed the "miracles at Joaseiro" to be of divine origin. The document was, at once, a partisan defense of the "extraordinary facts" and the manifesto of a "church within a church." As a defense, the "Proceedings" clearly intended to refute every objection previously raised by Dom Joaquim. Twenty-three witnesses attested to the good health of Maria de Araújo, thereby ruling out natural causes which might have effected the transformation of the host. One witness assured the commissioners that the *beata* had borne the stigmata of Christ ever since 1885, implying, of course, that this prior sign of sanctity precluded any doubt about the divine origin of the transformation of the host. In order to dissipate the growing contention that Padre Cícero had exerted undue influence upon the *beata*, one witness specifically pointed out that "hypnotism" or "psychic suggestion" had not been employed by the priest. To further prove that it was God and not Padre Cícero who worked the miraculous transformation, the commissioners themselves testified that this "marvel" had occurred six times in their very presence and, more importantly, in Padre Cícero's absence.

The "Proceedings," moreover, also proved to be the manifesto of a "church within a church," the judgment imposed upon Joaseiro by Dom Joaquim himself. From the "Proceedings," it was clear that a potential sect was emerging, a sect which claimed as its chief source of authority the revelations of Christ to Padre Cícero and the *beata*. The revelations, in their turn, appear to have been tailored justifications of the errant theology which the dissident believers of Joaseiro had earlier and audaciously sustained before Dom Joaquim and from which neither pride nor changing circumstances now permitted retreat.

Just before the commission departed from Joaseiro, Padre Cícero submitted "An Addition" to his previous testimony recorded in the "Proceedings."[46] In the "Addition," the cleric transcribed his most recent revelation from Christ in defense of the miracle of Joaseiro. According to the priest, Christ explained that:[47]

. . . in order to satisfy [My] ardent desire . . . to manifest Myself again to men, it was necessary that I . . . multiply the most startling marvels, coming *to shed again* My Blood among you. . . .

. . . As My word is infallible, so too are My works everlasting. Therefore, *there is nothing here in these new manifestations that is contrary to the teaching of the Church and [her] theologians,* rather it [*sic*] is as a sovereign light and a source of all divine perfections which will transport you through the veil that envelops your souls in this almost lifeless faith. . . . [italics mine]

Maria de Araújo's revelation is far less elusive about the unique significance of the transformation, but she, too, invoked Christ's authority over the bishop's. The Sacred Heart instructed her in a relevation:[48]

. . . that the priests and bishops should offer prayers and celebrate masses for the successful outcome of this cause, promising to all those who did so, abundant graces; *that they [the priests and bishops] knew not this mystery since [it is] a new mystery which theologians have not dealt with*; let them gather together in My Divine Heart where they will drink of the knowledge and belief of this mystery . . . . [italics mine]

The inconsistency between these two alleged visions is understandable. Padre Cícero, *as a priest,* was less inclined than the *beata* to assert that a *new* mystery had come to pass. But this was of little consequence to the believers, whose only concern was to establish the cause of Joaseiro on the bedrock of Christian authority, Christ Himself.

If the doctrinal content of the "Proceedings" led Dom Joaquim to fear that a potential schism was in the offing, the evident defection of the diocese's two ablest priests further reinforced the certainty of that dreaded perspective. The decision of Frs. Clycério and Antero to cast their lot with the "church within the church" was of momentous importance to both the bewildered Dom Joaquim and the believers in Joaseiro, whose hand was now immensely strengthened by the support of the two commissioners. For these reasons, it is important to examine the factors which may have motivated the two learned priests to abandon their bishop and embrace the chosen people of Joaseiro.

There is no evidence that either Fr. Clycério or Fr. Antero had at any time undergone a psychological breakdown. Moreover, their learning and long service in the highest echelons of church administration seemed clearly to attest to their fidelity to the church. Perhaps the intensity of popular pressures in Joaseiro on the two commissioners to produce a favorable report may have weakened the priests' resolve as well as their critical faculties.[49] Here, however, there is insufficient evidence. Two other factors seem to offer a more satisfactory explanation of the commissioners' defection.

The first concerns the attitude prevalent within the Brazilian Catholic hierarchy towards the changing context of national politics. It must be remembered that both Fr. Clycério and Fr. Antero were, like many of their colleagues including Dom Joaquim, sensitive, alert, and distrustful of the untoward impact of "liberal" doctrines and politics upon the church and religion in Brazil. As ranking "romanized" administrators in the Diocesan Palace, they had closely followed the anticlerical ferment among Brazilian Masons, republicans, positivists and "materialists." They witnessed the proclamation of the Republic in 1889, the subsequent separation of church and state, and finally the utter failure of the Catholic Party in 1890 to galvanize the faithful into a political force capable of serving the church's interests. Then, in 1891, Protestant missionaries, under the protection of the law and with the support of the elites of Fortaleza, began to proselytize actively in Ceará.[50] These events seemed to have compelled the two commissioners to believe that God had intervened in Joaseiro at precisely the right moment to save men, the Faith, and the nation. Such is the inevitable conclusion that must be drawn from a letter written by Fr. Antero in August 1892, to the presiding officer of the Holy Office (the Inquisition) in Rome:[51]

If you only knew of the state of our unhappy Brazil where the powers of Satan are working to destroy religion [and where] Positivism and materialism are making progress, seeking to destroy dogmas, mysteries and all that is most holy in our religion.

I and others admire the victories of our religion against such dangerous and audacious enemies, victories that only came about through this miracle of the transformation of the consecrated hosts into the flesh and blood [of Our Lord Jesus Christ] in the hamlet of Joaseiro.

For his part, Fr. Clycério repeatedly exclaimed that "religious indifferentism" was running rampant in Brazil against which the miracle of Joaseiro had occurred as a holy antidote.[52]

The second factor is linked to the latent conflict between the Brazilian secular clergy of the diocese and the French Lazarist fathers who directed and staffed the seminary in Fortaleza. When this conflict originated is difficult to determine. Nonetheless, an explicit source of tension lay in the Brazilians' distaste for the rigid "European standards" which since 1864 had been imposed upon seminary life and were continually held up as the yardstick of perfection. This was such a serious issue that it remained alive for more than half a century. In 1914, for example, the *Album Histórico,* the commemorative volume of the Fortaleza seminary's fiftieth anniversary, repeatedly alluded—amidst generous praise for the Fernch Lazarists—to their foreign tutors' frequent incomprehension of Brazilian conditions.[53] Beneath the surface of these charges, however, lay the latent but growing national consciousness of the Brazilian seminarians which became manifest after the proclamation of the Republic.

In 1890, the long-standing and repressed tensions spilled over into the full-fledged "revolt of the seminarians."[54] On 13 May of that year, the second anniversary of the abolition of Brazilian slavery and a national holiday, Rector Chevallicr refused to suspend classes and summoned the students to their studies. His act deeply wounded the national pride of the students, especially those from Ceará whose native state was the first to abolish slavery in 1884. The students retaliated. For three days they rioted within the seminary compound, refused to attend class, and rebelled against every call to order. A priest-historian, who was a junior colleague of several of the participants in these events, recalled that not a single professor ". . . dared to pacify the 'ruffled spirits.' "[55] On the third day, Dom Joaquim was obliged to intervene. He assembled the student body and ordered the organizers to confess. None did, and no one else betrayed them. As a result, the bishop declared the seminary closed, but after three months, the result of the revolt proved a decisive victory for the students. Dom Joaquim reopened the seminary and not only removed Fr. Chevallier from the rectorship which he had held for a quarter of a century, but also, at the close of 1890, ordained as priests the three seminarians who had played decisive roles in the revolt.

Animosity towards the Lazarists had also arisen earlier in Crato during the great drought of 1877–1879. The foreign priests had arrived there in 1875 to inaugurate and staff the Crato seminary. With the onslaught of the drought in 1877, however, they fled the interior for the safety of the capital— to the dismay of the Valley inhabitants. A native of Crato has described their flight "as the desertion of soldiers in the face of the enemy."[56] an attitude which perhaps explains why a native Brazilian, Msgr. Monteiro, was later appointed as rector when the seminary reopened in 1888.

The long-standing tensions between the native Brazilian clergy and the French Lazarists in Ceará were sharply heightened by (if they were not themselves a major cause of) the "religious question" of Joaseiro. Fr. Clycério, for example, was deeply convinced that Fr. Chevallier had been primarily responsible for sowing seeds of doubt among his fellow clergymen about the validity of the miracles of Joaseiro. In fact, Fr. Clycério, bitterly denounced the French priest's "pretensions of being a theologian" as the chief reason why Dom Joaquim had so negatively prejudged the "extraordinary events" of Joaseiro.[57] Fr. Antero, himself a graduate of the Colégio Pio Latino-Americano in Rome and a doctor of sacred theology, proved to be the more stringent critic of the French Lazarists. In 1893, he wrote to a friend, then the Bishop of Pará, and unequivocally accused the foreign prelates of ". . . adulterating everything, lying and even calumniating [the miracle of Joaseiro]." In Fr. Antero's opinion, the Frenchmen's hostility to Joaseiro was rooted in their myopic European view that " 'Our Lord does not leave France to work miracles in Brazil.' "[58]

Furthermore, Antero was convinced, the French Lazarists notwithstanding, that by the miracle of Joaseiro, Brazilian Catholicism had come of age, and that the Brazilian church was now comparable to any in Europe. This is clearly the intent of his 1892 letter to the Inquisition. In that missive, he observed that should Rome *not* authenticate the miracles of Joaseiro then it would be faced with the task of invalidating "identical miracles [which had] already been approved by the Church . . ." and in which the peoples of France, Portugal, and Italy had long and faithfully believed.[59]

It might be argued that the preceding viewpoints of Frs. Clycério and Antero are of questionable value since they were formulated either sometime after the events in question had taken place or in the heat of a partisan conflict. Perhaps they are no more than rationalizations conjured up by two prominent churchmen whose prestige began to ebb once they had become irreversibly involved in the miracle of Joaseiro. Even at that, however, it is most revealing that the two priests had unmistakably cast an ecclesiastical and theological problem in terms of Brazilian nationalism.[60]

The "Church within a Church"

Both Fr. Clycério and Fr. Antero remained central to the "cause of Joaseiro," a phrase that refers to the subsequent legal attempt of the believers to appeal directly to Rome in their campaign to authenticate the miracles of Joaseiro. That campaign had its origin in the "July petition of appeal" dispatched directly to Dom Joaquim in September 1891, and summarily rejected by him because of the document's "impromptu" qualities. However, when the bishop returned the rejected July petition to its authors, he did not expressly forbid them from preparing another. In fact, he even encouraged them to do so provided that it met with the requirements of canon law. Moreover, he specifically promised the appellants not to "deny them recourse from [his] decisions to the Holy See."[61]

As a result of Dom Joaquim's adherence to canon law, the believers at Joaseiro reformulated their earlier petition, embroidered it with proper canonical usages and, in accordance with the bishop's earlier instructions, submitted it to Fr. Clycério in October 1891, just before his departure from Joaseiro. The October "Memorandum," as it was called, was formally presented in the name of Secundo Chaves, the Crato pharmacist and intimate friend of Padre Cícero's, and also in the name of sixty-one additional signatories from Crato, Joaseiro, and other Valley cities. Like the July petition, the October "Memorandum" insisted on the appellants' right to appeal directly to Rome over any and all of Dom Joaquim's objections.[62]

More surprising to Dom Joaquim than the new appeal was the petitioners' decision to name Fr. Antero in the document as one of Joaseiro's three "procurators," empowered by the appellants to represent their cause in Rome. Dom Joaquim needed no further proof of Fr. Antero's defection. Despite efforts to dissuade the young priest from advocating Joaseiro's cause, Fr. Antero gladly accepted his new position and in 1892 even sailed to Rome on the hamlet's behalf.[63]

In addition to Fr. Antero, two other "procurators" were named: one was Padre Cícero; the other, a Crato schoolteacher, José Joaquim Telles Marrocos, whose role in the early history of the "religious question" of Joaseiro is of such importance that some brief biographical remarks about him are in order.[64] José Marrocos was the illegitimate son of a priest, a relative and intimate friend of Padre Cícero's. Before the miracle of Joaseiro, he had already won a place in Ceará's history as one of Brazil's crusading abolitionists. As a journalist in Rio de Janeiro and later in Fortaleza, he had helped bring down the hated institution of slavery. This, moreover, was but a brief episode in a lifelong career, dedicated primarily to teaching and journalism in the Cariry where he was a founder of both schools and newspapers. Marrocos, however, was a frustrated man. His original ambition, like that of his cousin, Padre Cícero, was to enter the priesthood. But for disciplinary reasons, Fr. Chevallier expelled him from the Fortaleza seminary and thus put an end to Marrocos' deepest ambition.

Marrocos, it seems, compensated for this failure by a lifelong dedication to religion and the church. His contemporaries noted both his perennial habit of praying the Roman Breviary, the collection of prayers said each day by Catholic priests, and his frequent acts of piety. He befriended the poor as well as the clergy. He even constructed at his own expense a cemetery near Crato and a chapel in Fortaleza for the exclusive use of the capital's slave population. In 1890, at the request of Fr. A. E. Frota, the Vicar-General of the Diocese of Ceará, Marrocos organized in Crato the ill-fated Catholic Party for the purpose of "protesting the iniquitous laws of the government against our Holy Religion."[65] This was not the first occasion in which the ex-seminarian had demonstrated his enthusiasm for the special causes of his church. Three decades earlier, it was Marrocos who mobilized Crato in support of the venerable "Padre Mestre" Ibiapina. During the missionary's visit in 1868–1869, it was Marrocos who edited *A Voz da Religião no Cariri* and gave publicity to the "miraculous cures" attributed to Ibiapina at Caldas and elsewhere in the region.[66]

In view of Marrocos' past—his piety and politics—it is not surprising that he was to play a leading role in the miracle at Joaseiro. There is no doubt that he was among the first to be made privy to the initial miracle of March 1889. Three months later, he was secretly urging Padre Cícero to prepare Joaseiro for a most solemn celebration of the liturgical feast of the Precious Blood, the celebration which in fact took place in July and to which Msgr. Monteiro led three thousand pilgrims from Crato.[67] Moreover, Marrocos quietly put his journalistic talents to the task of propagating the Cariry's latest miracle. There is some evidence that the few articles which did appear in 1889 in Rio de Janeiro and Recife were authored by him.[68]

Only in July 1891, did Marrocos at last discard his cloak of anonymity. He did so in order to affix his name to the celebrated July petition. Then, in October, he personally submitted to the Commission of Inquiry a lengthy testimony in which he persuasively argued that the events of Joaseiro were truly divine.[69] In fact, after mid-year 1891, Marrocos, the intellectual, never spared his efforts on Joaseiro's behalf. He continued to write for the press of the Northeast, while, unknown to all but his most immediate colleagues, he began to dispatch to the bishops of Brazil and Portugal lengthy *consultas* (inquiries) in search of a sound theological defense of the miracles of Joaseiro.[70] By the end of 1891 it was alleged that Marrocos had completely eclipsed Padre Cícero as the "archpriest" of the "church within the church."

Indeed, Dom Joaquim had good cause for alarm. The participation of Marrocos now provided Joaseiro with new vigor, while the defection of the bishop's two ablest priests unexpectedly sounded for the miracle a crescendo of credibility. By the end of 1891, the impact was evident: Thousands of pilgrims descended each day on Joaseiro while the number of priests who came to support the "church within the church" had risen from five to almost twenty. At that point, Dom Joaquim concluded that a full-fledged schism had arisen on the horizon.

3

A Movement in the Making

Defiance and Protest

It is important to examine Dom Joaquim's charge of schism. It originated in a moment of anger and frustration. On the one hand, two of the diocese's most promising priests—Frs. Clycério and Antero—had cast their lot with Joaseiro; so too had eighteen other priests and thousands of pilgrims from Ceará, Pernambuco, Paraíba, and Rio Grande do Norte. On the other hand, one of Brazil's most prominent bishops, Dom Joaquim Arcoverde— later the nation's first cardinal—had laid the blame at Dom Joaquim's doorstep. In Arcoverde's hitherto unpublished and confidential opinion, Joaseiro had become a national "scandal, that merits removal or destruction and nothing more." For Arcoverde, Dom Joaquim had been tolerant in the extreme; for the future cardinal, there was only one course of action: suspend the priests, burn the evidence, prohibit loose talk, remove Maria de Araújo from Joaseiro, and submit the ludicrous "Proceedings" to the Inquisition in Rome.[1]

While the bishop's charge of schism reflected his anxiety and fears for the diocese, it was technically incorrect. It was incorrect because the back-land dissidents had neither formally rejected Catholic doctrine nor ceased to recognize papal supremacy. To the contrary, they invested all their hopes for the recognition of their miracle in Rome's benevolence. In circumventing their bishop's authority the dissidents had properly invoked their canonical rights to appeal to Rome. Furthermore, even Dom Joaquim had recognized this right, laid down by the Council of Trent, and had promised not to place obstacles in their way.[2]

Indeed, the dissidents *could not* abandon the church unless they wished their cause defeated. In their minds, the miracles of Joaseiro were provi-dential signs, divine proofs of two important assertions. First, God had responded to Brazil's "time of troubles"; by deigning again to redeem sinners He proclaimed Catholicism's national supremacy. The Catholic faith alone was the antidote to the inroads of Protestantism and Spiritism, to the erroneous republican ideology infused with positivist and materialist, Darwinist and Masonic doctrines. Second, Joaseiro's miracles were claimed to be identical with those that had occurred in Italy, France, and Portugal in centuries past and which had been subsequently sanctioned by the church. For the dissidents, Joaseiro's miracles had made Brazilian Catholicism equal to the traditional faith of Europe. Only Rome could legitimate these two assertions, by declaring the miracles true; schism could only result in their defeat.[3]

Nonetheless, the appeal to distant Rome appeared to Dom Joaquim as an act of defiance and protest against his more proximate authority. Such audacity, however, would have been inconceivable were it not for the dissidents' overwhelming support among the backlanders.

The elites of Crato, Barbalha, and other *municípios* of the Cariry Valley unanimously closed ranks behind the dissidents, due to both the prestige of Padre Cícero and the social stature of Msgr. Francisco Monteiro, Rector of the Crato seminary.[4] The presence of the Commission of Inquiry months earlier in Joaseiro and Crato, the endless influx of pilgrims and the public declarations of support of countless priests were all tangible proofs to the elites that the events of Joaseiro merited credibility.

It was the lower classes, however, who were the true enthusiasts of the miracles. Their faith in them and in Padre Cícero never waned. In fact, when Dom Joaquim later succeeded in stimulating defections among the elites and clergy, the lower classes became intransigent supporters of the cleric, even after his struggle with the Cearense hierarchy led to fresh governmental suspicions as well as ecclesiastical censures. This twofold hostility of church and state saw the lower classes of Joaseiro resort on several occasions to outbursts of violence and armed defense on behalf of Padre Cícero. These acts of protest against the dominant authorities of Brazilian society fell short, however, of revolution. Indeed, Padre Cícero never endorsed their aggressive expressions of solidarity; to the contrary, he did everything to contravene and prevent them. The cleric's personality and his profound desire for the success of his appeal to Rome required that his followers retain their docility, subservience, and apoliticism. How the lower classes—peasants, sharecroppers, and farm hands attached to the surrounding estates—became the backbone of the popular religious movement at Joaseiro merits consideration.

Popular Religion

For the lower classes, Joaseiro's chief attraction was the popular religion that began to manifest itself there early in 1891 and 1892 and not the theological imponderables that lay at the center of the debate among Ceará's divided clergy. The *beatas* of Joaseiro and Crato eventually became the key propagators of the popular religion. At first, only the lowly born laundress, Maria de Araújo, had shared the limelight of Joaseiro with Padre Cícero and Msgr. Monteiro. From 1889 until late 1891, she was proclaimed a "living saint." She alone had transformed the host into Christ's blood and she alone was sought out by the masses as a divinely inspired oracle whose power to intercede before the Godhead was considered omnipotent. In late 1891, however, other *beatas* from Crato and Joaseiro suddenly appeared on the scene. Encouraged by Padre Cícero and Msgr. Monteiro, nine such *beatas* had testified before the Commission of Inquiry in September 1891. Shortly thereafter, their self-proclaimed "visions, ecstasies and relevations" reported confidentially to the commission became widely publicized throughout the Cariry Valley. It was then that several of these *beatas,* discontent to live within the obscurity of the Charity House of Crato or the family residence of Padre Cícero began publicly to emulate Maria de Araújo.[5] Quickly, they overshadowed the taciturn, retiring, and reticent laundress-saint. Claiming to share her "supernatural powers," the new *beatas* became the popular oracles of Joaseiro. Drawn from the same social class as were most of the estimated four hundred pilgrims who arrived each day during 1891 and 1892, the new "saints" of the people articulated the religious credo of Joaseiro with resounding success. In the very shadow of the sophisticated theological dispute of the clergy, the *beatas* gave vent to the emerging popular religion.[6]

The crux of the popular faith propagated by the *beatas* was an apocalyptical vision of the imminent destruction of the world. Like the dissident priests of the Valley, the *beatas* pointed with alarm to both the recent overthrow of the Brazilian monarchy and the Republic's newly decreed authority over marriage, formerly the domain of the church alone. These two changes were considered to be signs ushering in the "last days."[7] As proof, one *beata* repeated the admonition of the Mother of God, allegedly conveyed in an earlier "apparition" to Maria de Araújo: "All these facts that have occurred here [in Joaseiro] are graces reserved for the last days. My divine Son deigns to punish mankind and put an end to the world . . . despite my fervent prayers on behalf of the world, He replies that He can no longer desist, that the time has come for Him to punish mankind."[8] Another *beata* reported that since the miracles of Joaseiro were divine gifts to redeem men, those who disbelieved would be damned![9] Indeed "neither bishop nor Pope nor all the earth was greater than God" who had elected Joaseiro to restore man's faith, "already on the wane."[10]

In addition to the apocalyptic vision, the "new religion" offered the believers relief from their temporal adversities. By October 1891, it was alleged that twenty-seven men and women who had come to Joaseiro from the states of Rio Grande do Norte, Pernambuco, and Ceará had been "miraculously" cured: The lame walked, the blind saw, and a barren woman was at last with child.[11] As a consequence, Joaseiro—like many orthodox religious centers of Brazil—was deluged by pilgrims in search of remedies to their earthly problems. Many came to make a *promessa*,* others to acknowledge *promessas* of the past. Unlike other popular Brazilian shrines, the pilgrims to Joaseiro did not venerate a powerful saint, but rather a small glass urn located on the main altar of the Chapel of Our Lady of

---

* *Promessa* (pl. *promessas*) is a vow or pledge made to a saint in order to obtain a spiritual or temporal remedy. Or, when such a "grace is obtained" (*graça alcançada*), the believer may also fulfill a *promessa* by some specific act of gratitude promised in advance. This may consist in a financial donation to the church, taking part in a public religious procession, walking on foot with a heavy burden, etc.

Sorrows. Inside the urn there were unconsumed hosts and a variety of cloths used in the celebration of mass. Both the hosts and the cloths bore visible stains allegedly made by the Precious Blood of Christ during the communions of Maria de Araújo. Despite the expressed prohibition of Dom Joaquim, the urn had fast become the central object of worship. For the pilgrims, the veneration of the urn and its sacred contents had taken priority over the orthodox liturgical practices of Catholicism. At the conclusion of each service, anxious pilgrims approached the glass container and pressed against it ribbons, tassels, and strips of cloth, which were instantaneously transformed into relics of the miracle of Joaseiro. For relatives and friends, either too old or too infirm to make the pilgrimage, these charmed relics were harbingers of temporal and spiritual salvation.

A final ingredient of Joaseiro's rising popular religion was its contagious spiritual euphoria. It prevailed throughout 1891 and 1892 and turned the hamlet into a frontier revival camp.[12] Each day there arrived fresh contingents of pilgrims: men, women, and children, laymen and clergy, rich and poor, the celebrated and the unsung. They crowded the chapel to hear mass, confess their sins, venerate the sacred urn. Among them were Masons and Protestants who, in public declarations, repented for their sins and converted to Christ. Meanwhile, several *beatas* ran through thronged streets holding aloft bronze crucifixes that bled "miraculously" while others fell into "ecstasies" and trances amidst the crowd.

Presiding over the hamlet was the cleric, Padre Cícero. He assured the rich and poor alike that what they saw and heard was true.[13]

The Hoax

For Dom Joaquim the reports from Joaseiro could only signify an incredible and sacrilegious hoax. The religious "fanaticism" of Joaseiro and the growing defiance by its people of episcopal authority prompted him to retaliate vigorously as he believed he ought to have done in 1889. However, convinced that Padre Cícero was "incapable of any hoax"—although stubborn, guillible, and rebellious—the bishop increasingly came to believe that Maria de Araújo was to blame.[14]

But it was not easy for him to uncover the suspected hoax. To his knowledge, not a single political chief, professional man, or landowner of the Cariry Valley had yet uttered a word in disbelief.[15] In addition, prominent clergymen in Fortaleza had yet to discount the varacity of the events in Joaseiro, as Dom Joaquim expected them to do.[16] Finally, all but two of his priests in the Valley were enthusiastic believers.[17]

Under these conditions it was necessary for the bishop to appoint an outsider to the vicariate of Crato. Msgr. Antonio Alexandrino de Alencar, the affable and devoted pastor of Quixadá (Ceará), arrived at his new post on 4 February 1892.[18] For the next eight years he uneasily assumed the most difficult assignment in the diocese: executor of the church's policy in Joaseiro. Because of his indecisiveness and uncertain sympathies he soon found himself caught in the cross fire of the disputants. First the bishop and then the dissidents believed he had betrayed their confidence. In turn each side blamed him for supporting the enemy. It is ironic that when his repeated request for a transfer was finally granted in 1900, both bishop and dissidents hailed him for advancing their respective goals.[19]

Within two months of Alexandrino's arrival, Dom Joaquim's drive to obtain evidence against the hoax—thought to be perpetrated by Maria de Araújo—was well underway. In April 1892, Alexandrino and several priests and laymen met in Crato, according to the bishop's orders, to conduct a second inquiry. After isolating the *beata* in the Charity House of Crato, Alexandrino administered communion to her at mass on three successive days. Not once did the transformation of the host occur! It was clear that the "miracles of Joaseiro" were nothing less than a ruse.[20]

Days later, however, a startling occurrence took place in Crato that obliged Dom Joaquim to look beyond the *beata* as the originator of the hoax. In early March, a month prior to the Crato inquiry, the celebrated glass urn containing the hosts and cloths stained with the alleged blood of Christ was ordered removed from Joaseiro by Dom Joaquim. For Dom Joaquim the veneration of the urn had constituted both an unauthorized liturgical innovation and the perpetuation of unbridled fanaticism. By removing the urn from Joaseiro the bishop hoped to put an end to the liturgical abuses. Furthermore, he could later submit the urn's contents to a thorough scientific examination. Reluctantly but obediently, Padre Cícero personally delivered the urn to Msgr. Alexandrino, who immediately locked it in the tabernacle centered on an altar of the Crato church. After Alexandrino concluded the second inquiry, he went to examine the urn and discovered the tabernacle empty. The urn had been stolen! In Crato, suspicion fell fast and heavily upon José Marrocos, the intellectual champion of Joaseiro's

cause, even though only circumstantial evidence indicted him. Only when
the urn was discovered among Marrocos' personal effects, shortly after his
death in 1910, did the eighteen-year mystery of its whereabouts finally
come to a just end. But its very discovery was to play as dramatic a role in
Joaseiro's subsequent political history as its sudden disappearance did in
the hamlet's earlier religious controversy.[21]

At the time of the theft Dom Joaquim immediately concluded that
Marrocos and not the *beata* was the mastermind of the hoax. Furthermore,
the assumption that Marracos had tried, at all costs, to prevent a thorough
examination of the urn's contents led swiftly to the unavoidable conclusion
that the bloodstains were of man-made, not divine origin. Another immediate consequence of the theft was the first significant breach in the hitherto
solid ranks of the Cariry Valley clergy. The two priests who had assisted
at the April inquiry—Fr. Quintino Rodrigues da Silva, vice-rector of Crato's
seminary, and Fr. Manoel Cândido dos Santos, curate of neighboring
Barbalha—totally abandoned the ranks of the dissidents for the orthodox
files of Dom Joaquim. Their example partly encouraged three prominent
political figures of the Cariry Valley to follow suit later that year.[22]

However, the boon to the bishop's mounting evidence against the dissidents came only in July 1892. That was the month annually dedicated
throughout the Catholic world to the pious liturgical veneration of the
Precious Blood of Christ. It was a propitious moment, in the eyes of the
dissidents, for divine Providence to repudiate the April findings of Alexandrino's second inquiry. However, an uncanny succession of "miraculous"
events in the cities of Joaseiro, Icó, Aracaty, and União more readily created
the impression of "diabolical" coordination rather than divine ordination.[23]

In each of the four cities, a similar spectacle occurred: *beatas* ran
through crowded streets holding aloft crucifixes of bronze that bled "miraculously." In Joaseiro, altars turned crimson as crosses and religious
statutes high above the tabernacle effused the blood of Redemption. In
distant União, similar events were singularly punctuated by millenarian
revelations of three *beatas*. The city's resident curate, Fr. Clycério da Costa
Lôbo—the ill-starred chief of the first Commission of Inquiry to Joaseiro
in 1891—proceeded to transmit to neighboring towns, including the port
city of Aracaty and the capital city of Fortaleza, the ominous prediction of
their imminent, divinely decreed destruction. During the next fortnight,
as the citizens of Aracaty and União awaited their biblical fate, the ensuing

exodus and public disorder warranted, in some minds, immediate police intervention.[24]

Whether these simultaneous occurrences originated from a single plan or independently of each other is unknown. The consequences, however, are known. On 5 August 1892, Dom Joaquim swiftly imposed the severest penalty yet employed: he suspended Padre Cícero from preaching, hearing confessions, and counseling the faithful. Only the faculty to celebrate mass was left to him. A similar action against Fr. Clycério, who shortly departed for another diocese, was aimed at preventing a second Joaseiro from emerging in União.[25] Seven months later, after the bishop had confidentially obtained additional testimony and after events in Joaseiro continued unabated, Dom Joaquim issued his first major public statement on the question. In his celebrated first Pastoral Letter of March 1893, Dom Joaquim admonished the faithful "against the vices opposed to our Most Holy and Divine Religion." He explicitly discredited, although he did not condemn, the "miracles of Joaseiro" and exhorted the members of his diocese to ignore them completely.[26]

Politics of Expectation

To Dom Joaquim's dismay, neither Padre Cícero's suspension in 1892 nor the Pastoral Letter of March 1893 settled the matter. His only recourse was to dispatch the case to Rome's Sacred Congregation of the Holy Office— the Inquisition.

Understandably, Dom Joaquim had been reluctant to do so earlier. In 1891, the only evidence in his possession was the biased and apologetic "Proceedings" of the first Commission of Inquiry. Had he dispatched this alone, the stern Cardinal Inquisitors might have been as critical of his "tolerance" as Dom Joaquim Arcoverde had been. Had Dom Joaquim condemned the report outright, the dissidents could have accused him of reneging on his earlier promise to allow them every recourse to Rome. Regardless of the bishop's tactic, Rome would demand to know Dom Joaquim's stand. Thus, in April 1892, he ordered the second inquiry and in August suspended Padre Cícero. The following March, he issued the Pastoral Letter whose theological ponderings were calculated to undo Joaseiro's unorthodox claims that the "miraculous blood" was Christ's. Finally in May 1893, Joaquim remitted his findings to Rome and waited.[27]

In contrast to their bishop's attitude, the dissidents had shown eagerness to repair to Rome. In 1891, it will be recalled, they established a three-man committee to advocate their cause before the Holy See. In August 1892, their representative, the learned theologian and Secretary of the first Commission of Inquiry, Fr. Francisco Antero, sailed to Rome without Dom Joaquim's permission. There he presented a purloined copy of the 1891 report to eminent churchmen, and argued that the "facts of Joaseiro" were proofs of divine solicitude for his native Brazil, ravaged and besieged, in his opinion, by the evil doctrines of materialism and positivism.[28] In June 1893, the dissidents reacted to the first Pastoral Letter by barraging the Holy Father with requests to reinstate Padre Cícero to the priesthood. In September, they dispatched Msgr. Monteiro, the Rector of the Crato seminary, to Petropolis with fresh documents for the papal nuncio to remit to Rome.[29] Finally in December 1893, in retaliation against a partial interdict imposed on Joaseiro by Dom Joaquim, José Marrocos wrote the Holy See. Ingeniously, he beseeched her to appoint, at the dissidents' expense, a curate to Joaseiro. As an emissary of the Papacy and therefore independent of Dom Joaquim's authority, the new pastor, Marrocos contended, could freely bear witness to Joaseiro's miracles and the faith of her people.[30]

Behind their enthusiastic recourse to Rome lay, of course, the conviction that Rome would favor the dissidents. There was also the assurance that everywhere in the backlands there were many who unquestioningly supported the dissidents—financially, politically, and, in the crudest sense, ideologically.

For example, throughout 1892 prominent regional figures contributed to Joaseiro's cause. In May, the Baron of Pajehú (Pernambuco) donated 300$000 reis and 300 head of cattle; in October, a member of the prominent Feitosa family of Inhamuns (Ceará) deposited another 500$000 reis into the dissidents' coffers.[31]* In addition, it was rumored that impoverished pilgrims from distant Northeastern states collectively contributed as much as half a conto (500$000 reis) per day. Joaseiro's finances multiplied so quickly that it was not uncommon for Padre Cícero to purchase in Crato as much as twenty contos of foodstuffs at a time.[32] The hamlet's economic potential was dramatically demonstrated in May 1892. After deciding to send Fr.

---

* The basic monetary unit of imperial Brazil was the *milreis* (1$000). One thousand *milreis* make a *conto* (1:000$000). The value of the *milreis* fluctuated widely during the 1890s.

Antero to Rome, Padre Cícero ordered several persons to solicit alms for the journey. One such beggar arrived the next day in Crato to exchange his paper currency for four gold contos![33] These sums were enormous for the day. In 1892, for example, the entire annual tax revenue of the neighboring *município* of Brejo dos Santos was a mere 600$000 reis; not until 1908 did it slightly exceed one and a half contos.[34]

Politically, the majority of the Cariry Valley elites continued to defend the priest despite the confidential testimony of a few locally prominent figures who denounced the miracles as a hoax. In fact, Msgr. Alexandrino reported that in August 1892, the overwhelming majority of his parishioners had become "thoroughly indignant" over Padre Cícero's suspension. Only through Alexandrino's mediation, it was contended, were several important citizens dissuaded from attacking the suspension in the press.[35] In October, however, their lingering resentment over Padre Cícero's suspension was rekindled; a prominent landowner of Joaseiro traveled throughout the Valley to muster support on the priest's behalf.[36] At last, in December 1892, the leading political chiefs and citizens of seven Valley cities—Crato, Barbalha, São Pedro, Jardim, Icó, Várzea Alegre, and Umaury—signed public protests in opposition to Dom Joaquim and in defense of Padre Cícero. They reasserted their right to believe in the "miracles" until Rome commanded to the contrary. They unanimously asserted the innocence of Padre Cícero from any role in the theft of the urn, and, finally, denied that he was a threat to public order.[37]

It was the last clause of the 1892 protest that gave the document its profound political significance. First, it implicitly demanded that the "religious question of Joaseiro" continue to remain a purely ecclesiastical, and not a civil matter. Second, it offered secular political support to Padre Cícero in his dispute with the ecclesiastical hierarchy. Finally, it implicitly presumed that, in exchange, Padre Cícero would not convert his massive "religious" following into a weapon against local political structures. In the future, this implicit agreement was repeated in essence if not in form. Each time, it increasingly wed the cleric and his movement to the existing political system in the backlands. Unconsciously, the religious movement at Joaseiro was becoming an integral part of Brazilian patrimonial politics, despite the intense defiance the movement generated against the institutional authority of the church.

That the followers of Padre Cícero constituted a movement was clear to the *coronéis* of the interior. But it is one of the more difficult realities to demonstrate to the contemporary observer. Indeed, not until 1895 was any formal organization constituted, and that only in the garb of *irmandades* (parish-wide religious associations of the laity). However, by 1893, a very crude ideological communion—a major component of any movement—slowly began to emerge. The principal tenet, of course, was belief in the divine origin of the miracles of Joaseiro. After Padre Cícero's suspension and especially after the publication of the 1893 Pastoral Letter, the continued belief in the discredited miracles necessarily required an even greater degree of militancy than in the past. Most characteristic of this militancy was the common people's increasing refusal to recognize Dom Joaquim's authority. Towards the end of 1893 the most abusive stories circulated about the bishop among Joaseiro's inhabitants and pilgrims: some accused him of fathering an illegitimate child, others portrayed him as a Mason.[38] Such stories illustrated and rationalized the people's defiance of the ecclesiastical hierarchy. In contrast, the people transformed Padre Cícero into a great miracle worker and the arbiter of their souls. "The ordinary people of Joaseiro are always like that," remarked Msgr. Alexandrino despondently, "[they] don't recognize any authority except that of Padre Cícero, *our Pope.*"[39]

Joaseiro's cohesion was further advanced in December 1893, when Dom Joaquim placed the hamlet under partial interdict: henceforth no religious function could take place in the chapel of Joaseiro.[40] The entire population of Joaseiro was thereby obliged to endure collectively spiritual privations for their unorthodox beliefs. José Marrocos aptly characterized the population's awareness of itself as a persecuted minority: they are condemned to "a spiritual ostracism . . . as if they had been ousted and had fled beyond the rim of the Catholic faith and the flock of the Good Shepherd. . . ."[41]

Treated as if they were a sect and deprived of celebrating religious festivals, the people readily substituted other practices to manifest their allegiance.[42] They decorated their homes with photographs of Padre Cícero and Maria de Araújo whom they valued as *"new saints, the discoverers of new mysteries"*; they wore around their necks medals coined in Europe which bore effigies of their heroes. While these practices, too, were condemned as "gross superstition," they were in reality acts of defiance.[43]

Throughout the early months of 1894, Alexandrino's reports monotonously documented both Joaseiro's continuing defiance of Ceará's hierarchy and its exuberant expectation of Rome's imminent approval.[44] Then on the last day of July 1894, the verdict of the Holy Roman and Universal Inquisition was at last made public:[45]

The Most Eminent and Most Reverend Fathers of the Holy Roman Church, the Cardinals Inquisitors-General, proclaimed, rejoined and decreed the following:— that the sham miracles and similar supernatural facts that were made known by Maria de Araújo are vain and superstitious prodigies and imply a most grave and most detestable irreverence and impious affront to the Most Holy Eucharist; therefore, the Apostolic Judge damns them and all must damn them and as damned and condemned so let them be acknowledged.

Dom Joaquim, perhaps remembering Arcoverde's advice, elaborated upon Rome's proscriptions—designed to eradicate the cyst—in his second Pastoral Letter. In his appendix to the published Roman decree, he ordered that: (1) all pilgrimages to Joaseiro must henceforth cease; (2) all vows and promises be declared null, void, and superstitious; (3) all written documents and publications defending the persons and facts cited, as well as the medals and photographs, be collected and burned; (4) neither priests nor laymen could henceforth speak or write about the sham occurrences without automatically incurring the respective penalties of suspension from orders and privation of the sacraments; (5) finally, the stolen urn and its contents were to be returned to the church authorities within thirty days to be burned; if the thief did not comply in time, let him be excommunicated *ipso facto*.

Accordingly, in July 1894, the bishop concluded his second Pastoral Letter publicizing the above decree and sanctions with the time-honored formula: *Roma locuta est; causa finita est.*[46]

Vox Populi

Two months had passed. Dom Joaquim's plan of action to implement the Roman decree and silence Joaseiro forever now went into effect. In early September 1894, Padre Cícero and four of his dissident colleagues-in-the-cloth arrived in Fortaleza, on orders from the bishop.[47] During their absence, Msgr. Alexandrino proceeded, as agreed, to Joaseiro. This mission would be the most difficult of his career. Not only was he to read the 1894 Pastoral Letter, but he was also to obtain the removal of Maria de Araújo from

Joaseiro and to obtain the public recantation of the nine other *beatas*, in compliance with an unpublished clause of the Roman decree. The gravity of the mission was confirmed by Crato's request for forty troops from the capital. Most were stationed in Crato, while part of the contingent preceded Alexandrino to Joaseiro.[48] Here is his account of that mission submitted to Dom Joaquim on 20 September 1894.[49] Hither to unpublished, it reveals more than any other document the militancy of Joaseiro's inhabitants:*

I went to Joaseiro on 13 September to advise Maria de Araújo of your instruction to retire to the Charity House of Barbalha for six months. "She said that she was ready [to comply]," but wanted to consult her family. In accordance with your order, I allowed her only four days to come to a decision. Then, I returned to Crato.

I proceeded to prepare for my return to Joaseiro on the weekend in order to read the Pastoral Letter. But, "at every moment, *I received threats of all sorts,* should I have the audacity to read the mentioned Pastoral." I left for Joaseiro on Saturday afternoon.

Sunday morning [16 September] "I mounted the pulpit and undertook the reading in inverted order." First, I read the Pastoral of 1893 *since this had never been read in the chapel of Joaseiro*. Then I read July's [1894], beginning with the decree of the Holy Office. It took me an hour and a half.

During this reading and as I preached to the people of the obligation to obey their bishop and the curial decree, "many women began to shout: *It's a lie, it's a lie.*" Not a small number of men and women left the chapel in order to avoid hearing the Pastoral and the sermon.

At 5:30 P.M. I returned to the chapel to celebrate benediction and preach another sermon that I had announced that morning. The theme of my sermon was the parable of the Pharisees and the Publicans, "pictures of the true and false believers; I censured with total indignation the hoaxes of Joaseiro, the sacrileges, the profanations and the irreverences against the Most Holy Sacrament . . . in the clearest terms, *I declared that everything in Joaseiro was a hoax.*"

That very day, two of Maria de Araújo's brothers came to tell me she was sick and thus couldn't leave for Barbalha. They asked that her departure be delayed for a month, to which I agreed, in the hope that it would meet with your approval.

The next morning, however, as I was preparing to leave Joaseiro, the *beata's* older brother abruptly summoned me to their home.

". . . I entered the house replete with women, perhaps some two hundred, and in the yard and adjacent properties [there were] *more than five hundred men, several of whom were armed.*" Only with difficulty did I enter the room in

* For the sake of brevity, the following text is a faithful paraphrase of Alexandrino's letter. Quotation marks indicate the actual text. Italics are mine.

which Maria de Araújo lay sick. When I asked for her definitive answer about withdrawing to Barbalha, she responded, "but I couldn't hear her answer."

A third brother and a younger sister interrupted us and in a loud voice shouted: *"she isn't going, she isn't going, because we don't want it."* They slammed the door closed and *I suppose that her three brothers wanted to do me in.* I banged on the door. It was opened immediately. I left the house and "I reproached the conduct of the people gathered there." A brother of the *beata* came up to me and said, "She isn't going because I won't let her." I pushed him aside and left for Crato. A short distance outside Joaseiro I heard them shout 'vivas'— I don't know for whom; perhaps for Padre Cícero and Maria de Araújo." Later I learned that they had jeered me and called me *"hypocritical (vigário de pau ôco) and other insults* of that sort. I continued on to Crato, disheartened by the anger they caused me."

Just yesterday (19 September) two uncles and a cousin of Araújo arrived in Crato for the court hearing in which they were charged with murder. Indeed, her brothers are *"quite capable of killing me."*[50]

"Ever since I read the Pastoral, Joaseiro has been in a state of complete conflagration so that it is impossible for me to go there any more. Many in Crato have advised me to stay away, even in the event of an emergency to confess the dying. I don't know how I shall continue to live here if things continue this way. Such is my depression that it has occurred to me to request a transfer."

Overcome by profound distress, Alexandrino added this postscript:

"The people of Joaseiro, almost in their totality, do not accept the decision of the Holy See [arguing against it with] sophisms.

"They are awaiting the return of Padre Cícero in whom all confide. They believe neither in Pope, bishop nor in any other ecclesiastical authority.

"For them, Padre Cícero is everything, and after him Maria de Araújo. When I went to her home, the people who stood about, believing her to be a saint, contemplated her full of admiration.

"This ignorant mob, composed of criminals and men of every ilk are capable of anything."

Furthermore, I am told that the merchants have incited the pilgrims and new inhabitants of Joaseiro against me so that they [the merchants] might stave off the disaster which would inevitably result from the decision of the Holy See.

In view of all this "presented without order and incoherently because of my state of mind, it strikes me that *it is necessary to place the church of Joaseiro under interdict.*

"They say in Joaseiro that if the doors were shut, they will tear them down and will pay no heed to the interdict.

"The spirit of revolt is planted there. . . ."

On 23 September, Padre Cícero finally returned to Joaseiro. It was a traditional backland reception. A half a league outside the hamlet he and Msgr. Monteiro were met by a large welcoming committee on horseback. There were countless others on foot. The riders formed an honor guard around the priests. Slowly they paraded along the principal thoroughfare, Rua Grande, to the center of Joaseiro. The entire route was festooned with hundreds of triumphal arches fashioned out of palm and *carnauba* branches. A display of rockets, roman candles, pinwheels, and other pyrotechnic devices hailed the returning heroes. An eyewitness called it a "most thunderous" reception. The following day, two leagues beyond the hamlet, in the fallow sugarcane fields of São José, Padre Cícero celebrated mass. More than three thousand followers from Joaseiro attended.[51]

Only after the priest's jubilant return did the military contingent withdraw from Joaseiro. Maria de Araújo finally left for Barbalha two days later, thanks only to Padre Cícero's intervention.[52] But there was little cause for rejoicing. Rome and Fortaleza seemed less intent on reclaiming Joaseiro for orthodoxy than they were on forcing it into extinction. Secret clauses of the decree and the bishop's plan of action sought to put an end to the movement's financial, political, and ideological supports.[53] For example, Padre Cícero was obliged not only to "make restitution for all [the money] received in the name of the sham miracles" but also, in the future, to refuse to accept offerings from pilgrims under any circumstances. Laymen who did not renounce their belief in the superstitions of Joaseiro would be deprived of the sacraments. As a result, the political chiefs of the Valley who had supported Padre Cícero in 1892 were, after September 1894, temporarily reluctant to do so.

In respect to the ten *beatas* of Joaseiro and Crato, Msgr. Alexandrino was empowered to exact from them both a written declaration of acceptance of the Roman decree and a full confession of guilt. Should they refuse, they could not continue to reside in the Charity House of Crato nor to wear their religious habit.[54]

In the following months, the dissidents suffered their severest blow: under the unrelenting pressure of Northeastern bishops, the remaining clerical supporters of Joaseiro recanted. Their formal declarations of loyalty to Rome were immediately published in the secular and religious newspapers of the region.[55] Henceforth Cícero's only recourse was the people itself. In the absence of clerical supporters, it became necessary to call upon the masses and later upon the political chiefs.

Then, just as the movement appeared on the verge of collapse, both Padre Cícero and Fr. Antero—the only two clerics who refused to recant—decided to appeal again to Rome. In their mind, it was rumored, "the decision of the Holy See was not infallible."[56] They contended that Dom Joaquim had altered the original report of the "Proceedings" of 1891. They also believed that the additional documents he dispatched to Rome in May 1893 had prejudiced the dissidents' cause. Padre Cícero himself declared, "I cannot deny what I saw, and indeed these facts [of Joaseiro] could be true because . . . although . . . the Congregation [of the Holy Office] cannot approve an error it can condemn a truth that is not well proven."[57]

As the new appeal got underway, the populace of Joaseiro, under virtual interdict within the hamlet's borders, responded to the new campaign with extraordinary solidarity. They immediately boycotted the priests and the religious services of Crato. Secretly they sought out one or two priests, who despite the Roman decree, appeared to the populace as sympathetic to their beliefs. These "underground" priests did not exact from the inhabitants of Joaseiro explicit denunciations of the "facts of Joaseiro" as the bishop's "agents" in Crato required. Joaseiro's church went "underground" while it publicly boycotted the official church. This boycott struck a sharp blow at the coffers of the "bishop's church," since the faithful of Joaseiro had accounted for two-thirds of the revenue of Crato's priests.[58] The protest, despite its financial success, was nonetheless inadequate for the tasks ahead. Indeed, if the new appeal to Rome was to succeed, Padre Cícero would need to find more effective ways of organizing his loyal but amorphous following.

4

The Movement
Organizes

The Brotherhoods

While the intellectual task of drafting the new appeals to Rome fell as usual upon the enigmatic José Marrocos, whom the hierarchy now considered to be excommunicated from the church for his failure to return the stolen glass urn, the more immediate and urgent task of mobilizing the followers of Padré Cicero was avidly assumed by the elderly lieutenant colonel of the National Guard, José Joaquim de Maria Lôbo. Lôbo, whose extreme piety and devotion later earned him the epithet of "fanatic," was a prosperous landowner from Lavras da Mangabeira, a backland *município* that lies at the northern gateway to the Cariry Valley. His earlier visits to Joaseiro and his wife's wholehearted belief in the miracles had prompted him to take up permanent residence in the "holy city." His entry into Joaseiro on 8 December 1894 could not have been more propitious for Joaseiro's resurgent cause.[1]

Lôbo set to work immediately. His principal task was to organize the dispersed and politically unconscious inhabitants of the hamlet and region into a viable instrument on Padre Cícero's behalf. Interestingly, the key vehicles upon which Lôbo relied were Joaseiro's *irmandades* (brotherhoods), parish-based religious organizations of the laity that included both men and women.* At least two of these lay associations—the Apostleship of Prayer of the Sacred Heart of Jesus and the Conference of St. Vincent de Paul—came into existence prior to the "miracle" of 1889 and, as was seen, played no small part in generating belief in the "miracles of Joaseiro." Four other brotherhoods were either reactivated or established under Lôbo's initiative and guidance: the Conference of Our Lady of Sorrows (patroness of the Joaseiro chapel); that of the Most Blessed Sacrament; that of the Precious Blood, and the last, founded on 7 July 1895, the Legion of the Cross.[2]

In general, the formal objectives of these six associations, like those of their counterparts established in parishes throughout the state and nation during the last half of the nineteenth century, were twofold: (1) to instruct the laity in church doctrine and improve the spiritual lives of its members; (2) to congregate the human and material resources of the faithful for the specific tasks of local parish life—these might range from the liturgical celebrations of holy days to the acquisition of funds for the repair of church facilities. Some brotherhoods, like the St. Vincent de Paul Society, were also engaged in works of charity and almsgiving on a local, state, and nation-wide basis.

Joaseiro's brotherhoods, like the parish unit itself, operated with considerable local autonomy, even though they were subject by canon law to varying degrees of hierarchical control. With the exception of the Legion of the Cross, Joaseiro's five lay associations had to and did in fact receive full canonical approval at the time of their establishment. All were formally recognized by Dom Joaquim and by the clerically controlled diocesan Central Council of Ceará whose headquarters was in Fortaleza. Parish brotherhoods could theoretically send representatives to the Central Council's annual meetings. In the case of the St. Vincent de Paul Society, each local unit also formed part of a national organization with intermediary units at the diocesan level.

These observations about the purposes and structure of the parish associations or brotherhoods make it clear that in Joaseiro: (1) large-scale

---

* The term parish does not accurately apply to Joaseiro at this time since the hamlet was canonically designated as a *capellania*, a smaller district of worship within a parish.

mobilization of Padre Cícero's followers was greatly facilitated by existing institutions authorized earlier by the church hierarchy; (2) that Joaseiro's brotherhoods potentially provided the dissidents with access to national institutions of the laity and clergy; and (3), that the brotherhoods offered a financial base for most of the activities conceived by José Lôbo on behalf of Joaseiro.

Under Lôbo's guidance Joaseiro's brotherhoods became, in reality, the "political" structures of the dissidents' cause. As long as they sustained the possibility of persuading Rome to reverse its 1894 decree, the brotherhoods did not want for members. For example, by 1898 the Apostleship of Prayer in Joaseiro claimed to have 125 officials and more than 5,000 active associates on its rolls.[3] That other brotherhoods simultaneously claimed an equally high membership indicates that there might have been considerable duplication of membership. However, even if all six brotherhoods in Joaseiro enlisted the same 5,000 persons, this probably represented almost the entire adult population among Joaseiro's inhabitants. In this case, the religious structures of the hamlet achieved an extremely high degree of mobilization, in contrast to the political parties of the region. In that same period, for example, the entire Cariry Valley had less than 2,000 voters while Brazil as a whole had enfranchised only slightly less than 2 per cent of its total population.[4]

The meetings of the brotherhoods, like the religious services of Joaseiro, often had more in common with "political rallies" than with catechism classes. For example, at one meeting of the Legion of the Cross, after 1895 Joaseiro's most important brotherhood, an important letter of protest was under discussion. An addendum to the minutes of this meeting regretfully notes that there were so many members present, 5,467, that not everyone was able to sign![5] Clearly, this massive "rally" may not have been typical of brotherhood activities, but it points to the wide-scale activism in which Joaseiro's population was engaged on behalf of Padre Cícero.

Two Minor Setbacks

The vitality of the brotherhoods was directly attributable to José Lôbo. He, not Padre Cícero nor José Marrocos, was the commander of the hamlet's "political" weapons in the struggle against the Ceará hierarchy. Garbed in a somber black suit with colored ribbons and other religious medals pinned to his lapels, he could be see almost every day toting from one meeting to another the thick, leather-bound volumes containing the minutes and correspondence of the brotherhoods.

In the short time since his arrival in Joaseiro, Lôbo had assumed a very prominent role in the hamlelt's St. Vincent de Paul Society.[6] In fact, it was on its behalf that he embarked on an important mission to Rio de Janeiro and Petropolis in March 1895. The voyage was prompted by a minor setback that had developed in the preceding months. On two occasions between December 1894 and January 1895, Padre Cícero had unsuccessfully directed an appeal to Pope Leo XIII to revoke the Holy Office's decree of 1894.[7] Cícero insisted that while he had not profaned the church's teachings neither could he deny the "true and sincere . . . facts of Joaseiro." The priest then petitioned the Holy Father to invite Cícero and other priests to Rome to explain their case personally before the pontiff, and to dispatch from Rome au "Apostolic Commission" to Joaseiro in order to study, verify, and witness for itself the "facts of Joaseiro." On both occasions the suspended cleric naively urged the Holy Father to "pronounce and substantiate nothing regarding the facts of Joaseiro until the petition of your servant arrives at your feet."[8] When it did, Rome swiftly reproached her servant: "Adquiescat decisis," ordered the telegram of 7 January 1895—"Submit to the decree!"[9]

It was Lôbo's mission to counter this defeat. Upon his departure for the South, Joaseiro was buoyantly hopeful that Lôbo would succeed in lifting the atmosphere of persecution that had engulfed the hamlet. His plan was to mobilize one of Brazil's largest Catholic associations of the laity upon Padre Cícero's behalf.

When Lôbo arrived in Rio de Janeiro in late March 1895, he proceeded to the headquarters of the Superior Council of the Conference of St. Vincent de Paul. Armed with credentials designating him as the official representative of the Conference's Joaseiro chapter, Lôbo appealed to the national Council to make Joaseiro's goals its own. To his misfortune the request that the Council offer its "good offices" before the Holy See fell on deaf ears. So too did his nationalist argument that the miracle of Joaseiro was comparable to those of Western Europe in centuries past. Even his impassioned attempt to convince his confreres that the miracle was a providential counterattack against the desecration of Brazilian Catholicism inflicted by the Republic was to no avail.[10]

Rebuffed by the Superior Council, Lôbo proceeded empty-handed to

Petropolis. There, during April 1895, he met three times with the papal nuncio to Brazil, Dom Jeronymo de Maria Gotti.[11] Lôbo reiterated the supplications contained in Padre Cícero's appeals to Pope Leo XIII earlier in December and January. The nuncio seems to have offered little encouragement to Lôbo, because several months after his return to Joaseiro he was still pursuing his case with Petropolis by mail.[12]

The Legion of the Cross

When Lôbo returned to Joaseiro in May 1895, it was clear that his mission to the South had ended in failure. However, he did not despair of achieving the two implicit goals of that mission: namely, (1) the intervention of a prestigious organization of Catholic laymen on Joaseiro's behalf, and (2) the renewed advocacy of Joaseiro's cause directly before the Holy See. In July 1895, these goals became the tacit objective of Joaseiro's newly established chapter of the Legion of the Cross.

The Legion was a national organization of Catholics founded in 1885.[13] It was inspired by a worldwide papal directive aimed at stemming the tide of the Holy See's financial and political crisis brought on by the Italian struggle for unification and independence. The purpose of the Legion was to raise funds from Catholics of all classes and all nations. Designated as the "obulo de São Pedro" or Peter's Pence, these contributions were, and still are, annually remitted directly to the Holy Father to be disposed of according to his needs and desires.[14]

Lôbo contended that the founding of the Legion chapter in Joaseiro was suggested to him and authorized by Rio de Janeiro's archbishop, Dom João Esberard, during Lôbo's earlier visit in April 1895.[15] However, Lôbo's failure to obtain canonical approval in Ceará later provoked Dom Joaquim to condemn Lôbo and the Legion in 1898. At that time, Ceará's bishop contended that the Legion was a "specious ruse" instigated to promote the false causes of Joaseiro.[16] Nonetheless, during its three-year existence (1895–1898) the Legion overshadowed all the other religious brotherhoods of Joaseiro and became the chief promoter of the dissidents' cause. Momentarily, Lôbo succeeded in linking Joaseiro's cause to a national institution whose prestige in Rome was known. Under Lôbo's guidance, it was to grow throughout the backlands.

By, 1897, membership in the Legion's Joaseiro branch had surpassed

5,000.[17] Extant minutes and documents allege that elsewhere there were an additional 10,000 active adherents. This latter were organized into nine *mesas,* or chapters, throughout Ceará and one in Paraíba. Most of the *mesas* were located in rural districts bordering on larger *municípios* in the interior of the state. Most of the members were farm hands.[18]

New members received a certificate of membership signed by José Lôbo. The certificates were dispatched to the president of the local chapter and distributed to each member, who was then expected to contribute the monthly sum of 100 reis. (Between 1895 and 1898, 1$000 reis was worth between $0.15 and $0.19 U. S.).[19] Theoretically, the Legion's total membership could potentially raise and remit to Joaseiro the annual sum of 18 contos, a figure equivalent to the total taxes paid to the state government of Ceará in 1894 by the *municípios* of Jardim, Brejo dos Santo, Milagres, Missão Velha, Porteiras, and Várzea-Alegre.[20] Extant though incomplete records of the Legion in Joaseiro indicate, however, that 20½ contos were raised during the entire three years in which the organization functioned. Of this, about 25 per cent was collected in Joaseiro alone; of the total, more than 14 contos were faithfully remitted to either the Rio de Janeiro office of the Legion or Rome directly.[21]

Although the Legion succeeded in raising only slightly more than twenty contos between July 1895 and September 1898, its financial capacity was in some respects as potent as that of the entire diocese of Ceará, at the time coterminous with the state of Ceará. For example, in 1898 Dom Joaquim authorized a diocesan-wide collection to honor Pope Leo XIII Slightly more than eleven contos were subsequently remitted to the Holy Father. In the same year, Joaseiro's Legion of the Cross—comprising less than 2 per cent of the diocese's population, and at that only the poorest farm hands—succeeded in remitting just under seven![22]

How the Legion propagated itself beyond Joaseiro's borders is difficult to reconstruct. Perhaps in the course of his many journeys across the state, José Lôbo established local chapters. A more plausible explanation, however, must consider the endless waves of pilgrims that flocked to Joaseiro, the "holy city." Between 1893 and 1898 Dom Joaquim had incessantly attempted to put an end to the pilgrimages. These, in his mind, only served to inculcate "the belief in the alleged [and condemned] miracles among innocent people of good faith, especially the *sertanejos* of the neighboring dioceses. . . ."[23] Indeed, after the establishment of the Legion in 1895, there was a noticeable increase in the number of pilgrimages as the gullible and clerically abandoned peasantry of the Northeast sought out the cures dispensed at Joaseiro. It is likely that the Legion actively encouraged this, one of the most extensive demographic movements in the history of the Brazilian Northeast. It is also likely that returning pilgrims, like pollen borne by the wind, founded Legion chapters wherever there was a desire to recreate the redemptive atmosphere of Joaseiro.

It was this increase in the number of pilgrimages to Joaseiro, inspired by the Legion in late 1895 and early 1896, that led Dom Joaquim to conclude once again that Padre Cícero and his followers were brazenly flouting the decree of the Holy Office. Consequently in April 1896, the bishop suspended Padre Cícero from all orders. Deprived four years earlier of the privilege to preach and confess, the dissident cleric was finally stripped of his only remaining prerogative, that of celebrating mass outside the walls of Joaseiro.[24]

In September 1896, José Lôbo went to Rome. As the backland delegate of Brazil's Legion of the Cross, and the bearer of the growing income of its Joaseiro chapter, Lôbo crossed the Atlantic on the first of four journeys to the Holy See. There he personally sought to obtain both the reversal of the 1894 decree and the full reinstatement of Padre Cícero. He appealed to Joaseiro's last resort, the Roman pontiff.[25]

Capangas and the Curia
The wheels of curial government grind even more slowly than those of secular regimes. The time-honored convention of the Inquisition to discuss matters of heresy and schism only on the Wednesday of each week, contributed further to delay consideration of the appeal submitted by Lôbo.

In Joaseiro, however, the long pause served to enliven the hopes of the dissidents and persuade them that Pope Leo XIII could only view their appeal with favor. Their militancy against the ecclesiastical hierarchy of Ceará continued. The boycott of the Crato clergy caused Msgr. Alexandrino to remark that the parochial income from Joaseiro was reduced to naught. At the same time, Joaseiro's parishioners continued to approach only those priests who, in defiance of Dom Joaquim's command, did not require them to confess their disbelief in the miracles of Joaseiro. To those priests, the financial rewards were more than ample.[26]

An unsavory incident toward the end of 1896 not only intensified Joaseiro's repudiation of the "official" church at Crato, but also raised the threat of a peasant revolt in the Cariry Valley. One evening in November, as Padre Cícero preached his illicit but customary homily before the enormous crowd that gathered outside his residence, five unidentified men attempted to approach him. Suddenly, they drew knives. Immediately the crowd jostled them and prevented their advance; four escaped and the fifth was taken prisoner. Padre Cícero had narrowly escaped death.

Joaseiro was outraged by the attempted assassination. The hamlet cast the blame on the official church of Crato and on its vicar, Msgr. Alexandrino. In the days and weeks that followed, the clergy and the wealthy landowners and merchants of Crato lived in fear of an imminent invasion of their lands and properties. They claimed that Joaseiro could muster four to five thousand armed *capangas* in less than an hour, should Padre Cícero sound the alarm. Panic struck so deeply in Crato that Msgr. Alexandrino, on the city's behalf, urged Dom Joaquim to request the immediate intervention of the state government. The vicar proposed that the government forcibly remove the growing population of Joaseiro to internment camps beyond the borders of the State! Apparently, the Governor of Ceará did not accede to this extreme request, but the threat of a potential peasant uprising in the Valley would not easily be forgotten.

Joaseiro continued in its militancy. Then in June 1897, their long-awaited reply from Rome arrived. To their astonishment and grief, the Holy Office not only rejected Lôbo's appeal but also threatened Padre Cícero with excommunication, should he not permanently withdraw from Joaseiro within ten days! If the suspended cleric had anything more to add, let him go personally to Rome.[27]

Padre Cícero's reaction was immediate and predictable: He departed for Salgueiro, a backland town in Pernambuco State, thirty leagues from Joaseiro.[28] There for several months he lived out his "exile" imposed by Rome, which in his own mind he had never disobeyed. During the next months, José Lôbo was dispatched again to Rome to appeal the new decree. In Joaseiro, José Marrocos proceeded to obtain the support of local political leaders on the cleric's behalf and hastily prepared Italian translations of important documents that Padre Cícero might take with him on his eventual trip to Rome.[29] In Salgueiro, Padre Cícero increasingly withdrew into himself, convinced that he was being persecuted by men from whom God and Our Lady of Sorrows would eventually deliver him.[30] It was during his exile, however, that the threat of excommunication was overshadowed by the startling accusation that the cleric was conspiring against the state.

Canudos and Joaseiro: Revolution and the Status Quo

This charge arose at a moment of national hysteria. The chief cause of this republican panic was the inglorious rout, in November 1896, of a federal army detachment by a motley band of peasants in the distant interior of Bahia State. The victory immediately focused national attention on the peasant band's leader, the celebrated, peripatetic mystic, Antonio Conselheiro.[31] Since 1882, the Counselor, as he was known to his followers, had been the object of ecclesiastical hostility because of his preaching of unorthodox religious beliefs among the ignorant backlanders. Since 1893, he was also the center of a national political controversy because of his purported advocacy of the recently deposed monarchy. With the Counselor's recent victory over republican troops, some political leaders accused him of being the fanatical guerrilla chieftain of a monarchist plot to overthrow the Republic. Subsequently, successive military detachments advanced against the Counselor in his isolated redoubt at Canudos. Only in October 1897 did republican forces at the cost of many lives finally succed in annihilating Canudos, as the last of its 8,000 defenders went to his death.

It was midway in the 1897 military campaign against Canudos, when national interest was at its apex, that Padre Cícero withdrew to Salgueiro. Almost immediately he came under fire as "another Antonio Conselheiro." The bishop of Ceará was among the first to take aim. In late July 1897, Dom Joaquim issued his third Pastoral Letter with regard to Joaseiro, advising the diocese of Rome's threat of excommunication. In this latest condemnation, the bishop inevitably alluded to the similarity between the fanaticism of Canudos and Joaseiro. He noted especially the propensity of the ignorant masses to accept blindly "any novelty apparently marvelous" and admonished Cícero not to emulate Antonio Conselheiro.[32]

Within a fortnight, Dom Joaquim's gratuitous analogy echoed in the political and ecclesiastical capitals of the Brazilian Northeast. Now Padre Cícero's long dispute with the church hierarchy of Ceará was transformed into a national political issue: A new conspirator had arisen against the Republic! In Bahia, Governor Luis Vianna charged that "a phalanx of fanatics" under Padre Cícero's command was marching to reinforce the peasant ranks of Canudos. In Maceiô, the capital of the neighboring state of Alagôas, the Governor, responding to rumors, ordered military precautions to be taken in the event that Padre Cícero and his "great escorts" should pass through the Alagôan city of Água Branca en route to Canudos. From Fortaleza, press reports, which later proved to be of partisan political inspiration, estimated Cícero's contingent to number over eight hundred armed *capangas*.[33]

In Pernambuco, where the cleric was now in exile, there were ample reasons for accepting these accounts as true. Months before, when the military episode at Canudos had just erupted, the respected Northeastern daily, the *Diario de Pernambuco*, had reiterated that in Joaseiro, the "metropolis of backland superstition," the fanaticism "created by Padre Cícero will sooner or later foster serious disruption of public order. . . ." Then, referring to Canudos, the Recife daily proceeded to demonstrate that superstitious beliefs among the ignorant masses had spurred them on in their "conquest of power and status [and] the obtaining of wealth and the material advantages of life." Critical of government indifference to the increasing fanaticism in the backlands, the *Diario* reminded its readers of the urgent necessity "to react against all superstitious practices" before "malefic" leaders might utilize them "to sow anarchy within society."[34]

While the press continued to portray these backland rebellions as the harbingers of destruction of the urbane civilization of the coast cities, Pernambuco's Governor and bishop cautiously moved against the "malefic" leader in Salgueiro. The Governor eventually accused Padre Cícero of "searching out Canudos in order to aid Antonio Conselheiro!" The bishop sternly admonished him to desist from stirring up the local populace.[35]

But the coastal elites had utterly misread the man and the situation. Unlike the Counselor, Padre Cícero's cause was not social revolution, but each man's personal redemption. He was an unwilling messiah, to whom his God had entrusted the conversion of sinners. Suddenly and involuntarily he was cast in the role of an archconspirator. To him, this new charge, like the threat upon his life and the enduring hostility of his bishop, was but one more inscrutable persecution imposed by Providence. Ultimately, he believed, this same Providence would deliver him and proclaim his cause true.

The crisis passed as quickly as it had appeared. Within hours after the communiqués of the Governor and bishop of Pernambuco reached Salgueiro, the backlands spoke up in defense of the exile. *Coronéis,* judges, curates, and police chiefs without hesitation declared that Cícero was "a force for order," the defender of authority and the pacifier of the unruly masses. He had come to Salgueiro in obedience, not defiance, of Holy Mother the Church and he would soon travel to Rome in compliance with the order of the Holy See.[36]

Cícero's prompt pledge of loyalty to Rome and Brazil's republican Constitution, as well as his immediate recourse to the political potentates of the backland had once again deflected the twofold hostility of church and state. Indeed, ever since his dispute had begun with Ceará's ecclesiastical hierarchy in 1891, Padre Cícero, unlike Antonio Conselheiro, had often sought, obtained, and cultivated the protection of the local political hierarchy.[37] Now in Salgueiro, he reasserted this perhaps unwitting policy of nonpartisan respect for the established order. This predictable yet nonetheless timely action may have forever spared his "holy city" from the total annihilation of which Canudos proved the Republic so capable.

So persuasive was the cleric's declared allegiance to the state and public order that he quickly won the confidence of one of his chief accusers, Dr. Joaquim Correia Lima, Pernambuco's Governor. Thanks to his influence, Padre Cícero embarked for Europe at Recife in February 1898. Indeed, without the Governor's personal financial assistance, the cleric's journey to Rome might never have occurred.[38]

Rome and Fortaleza: At Odds

It is ironic that despite his alleged fortune, Padre Cícero spent the next nine months (from March to October 1898) in Rome with few funds to spare. Only through the kindness of a Roman cleric and subsequent aid from his influential benefactors in Recife, was Padre Cícero able to remain in the Eternal City as long as he did.[39] It is nonetheless true that he arrived in Rome with a cache of more than 22 contos ($3,300.00 U.S.) just less than half of the lifetime income of an ordinary backland curate. But this sum was not his own. It represented the stipends offered by Brazilian pilgrims for the celebration of more than 10,000 masses. Respectful of canon law which required the celebration of each mass, the suspended cleric scrupulously distributed the mass-stipends among several priests and religious institutions in Rome.[40] Not even the arrival of José Lôbo on his third trip to Rome, in April 1898, offered any significant relief. Lôbo dutifully presented Pope Leo XIII all seven contos collected earlier by the Legion of the Cross, and had little left to rescue the priest.[41]

Padre Cícero's financial straits were insignificant in comparison with his frustrations. The constant memory of his recent "persecutions" and the failure to obtain an immediate audience with the Holy Father led him at times to contemplate never returning to Brazil. But his unquenchable longing for his family and lifetime friends in the backlands ultimately persuaded him to dismiss the idea.[42]

Unfortunately most of Padre Cícero's subsequent steps in Rome have been untraceable, and because of this they became subject to various interpretations by contemporaries upon his return. Nonetheless, it is known that the Sacred Congregation of the Holy Office finally granted him several audiences prior to August 1898. That month the Holy Office concluded its hearings of his personal appeal by declaring all previous decrees in force.[43] It dismissed Padre Cícero and José Lôbo, who apparently interceded on Cícero's behalf during the hearings, "with grave warning and the prohibition to speak or write about the facts of Joaseiro." In addition, it suggested that Cícero abandon Joaseiro forever and reiterated his suspension, imposed by Dom Joaquim in 1892, from preaching, hearing confessions, and counseling the faithful.

In one sense, the decision momentarily closed Rome's books on the alleged miracles of Joaseiro and produced no significant change in Padre Cícero's priestly status. Some concessions, however, were granted. First, the Holy Office considered both Cícero and Lôbo "absolved of any censures that they might have incurred in any way" in light of previous decrees. Therefore, it required no "explicit and formal declaration of guilt" to be made in public as the bishop of Fortaleza had insistently demanded. Second, it granted Padre Cícero permission to celebrate mass in Rome and, contingent on the approval of Dom Joaquim, in Ceará as well. Finally, it withdrew any future change in Cícero's clerical standing from the jurisdiction of Dom Joaquim and placed it solely within the Sacred Congregation of the Holy Office of the Roman and Universal Inquisition.

In Padre Cícero's mind, these concessions were a partial victory. Perhaps in the future, Rome might reinstate him, whereas Dom Joaquim, he was convinced, never would. Furthermore, he could return to Joaseiro, since

Rome had only *suggested, not ordered,* that he abandon the hamlet. Finally, he again could celebrate mass, a privilege which he expected Dom Joaquim to ratify in view of the Holy Office's generosity. Indeed, in his eyes, the journey to the Eternal City was a success. After celebrating mass in Rome for the first time since 1896, he wrote to the backlands of his imminent return and confided his joy that Rome had relieved him of "the mountain which weighed heavily upon me." Three weeks later, he recorded in his breviary a perfunctory audience with Pope Leo XIII that nevertheless crowned his visit with triumph.[44]

It appears, however, that even this limited victory took the Cearense hierarchy by surprise as Cícero reached Fortaleza in November 1898.[45] Had the vast sums of money distributed by José Lôbo and Padre Cícero among high Roman dignitaries influenced events there? There is no conclusive evidence to warrant this charge of bribery, implied by Dom Joaquim in a Pastoral Letter later that year.[46] Nonetheless, this suspicion would continue to influence the already hostile relations between the hierarchy and the "miracle worker."

When Padre Cícero finally reached Joaseiro on 4 December 1898, the animosity toward Dom Joaquim had not subsided, especially in view of his refusal to allow the cleric to celebrate mass in Joaseiro until Rome officially communicated its decision to the bishop. Immediately rumors began to circulate that Dom Joaquim had stripped Padre Cícero of the victory he had obtained from the Holy Office. Loyal to the prohibition to desist from speaking or writing about the facts of Joaseiro, neither Cícero nor Lôbo tried to deny these rumors.[47]

Indeed, neither Cícero's exile in Salgueiro nor his extended stay in Rome appeared to change the relations between Fortaleza and Joaseiro. Outside the hamlet, the lower classes continued to rally behind the "miracle worker" and in Joaseiro there was growing resentment against Dom Joaquim and his agents in Crato.

During the next decade and a half Joaseiro remained to most observers "a center of religious fanaticism." But behind this façade important political and economic developments were taking place.

An unpublished and undated photograph of *Beato* Francelino who testified in 1891 before the first episcopal Commission of Inquiry sent that year to investigate the "miracles" of Joaseiro. (*Courtesy of D. Amália Xavier de Oliveira, Juàzeiro do Norte, Ceará.*)

Crowds encircling Padre Cícero's funeral cortege en route to the Chapel of Our Lady of Perpetual Help, where the cleric was buried on 21 July 1934. (*Courtesy of D. Amália Xavier de Oliveira of Juàzeiro do Norte, Ceará.*)

Padre Cícero Romão Batista at the age of eighty-nine in the company of some members of his household and several neighbors. The woman in the black dress standing behind Padre Cícero is Joanna Tertuliano de Jesus, better known as "Beata Mocinha," the celebrated majordomo of the cleric's residence. (*Courtesy of Fr. Azaria Sobreira of Fortaleza, Ceará. Date: ca. 1933.*)

Padre Cícero at the inauguration of the airfield in Joaseiro on 17 February 1933, thirteen months before his death at the age of ninety. (*Courtesy of Fr. Azarias Sobreira, Fortaleza, Ceará.*)

Undated photograph of *romeiros* (pilgrims) congregating outside Padre Cícero's residence on the Rua Nôva in anticipation of the cleric's daily *consagração* (homily). (*Courtesy of D. Amália Xavier de Oliveira of Juàzeiro do Norte, Ceará.*)

Pilgrims visiting site of the incompleted Church of the Sacred Heart of Jesus atop the Serra do Catolé, called the "Hôrto," just north of Joaseiro Padre Cícero initiated the construction in 1890 to fulfill a *promessa* made by him and two other priests in 1888. The bishop, Dom Joaquim José Vieira, banned the project in 1896 and 1903. The ruins were demolished in the 1940s by the cleric's heirs, the Salesian Fathers, who used the building materials for other purposes. Behind the ruins Padre Cícero's summer residence can be discerned. It still stands today, but in a state of considerable disrepair (*Courtesy of D. Amália Xavier de Oliveira of Juàzeiro do Norte. Date of picture is unknown.*)

A view of workers and pilgrims during the course of the reconstruction of Our Lady of Sorrows. It was probably taken in late 1924 or sometime shortly thereafter in as much as both bell towers appear completed. (*Courtesy of D. Amália Xavier de Oliveira of Juàzeiro do Norte, Ceará.*)

Two photographs of the celebrated *beata*, Maria de Araújo, taken at the height of the "religious question" of Joaseiro, ca. 1891–1898. (*Courtesy of D. Amália Xavier de Oliveira of Juàzeiro do Norte, Ceará.*)

The sepulchre of Maria de Araújo, who died in 1914. It was located in the Chapel of Our Lady of Perpetual Help but was demolished after Padre Cícero's death in 1934 by order of the ecclesiastical authorities intent on eradicating it as a source of pilgrimages and other "fanatical" devotions. (*Courtesy of D. Amália Xavier de Oliveira of Juàzeiro do Norte, Ceará.*)

An extremely rare photograph of Padre Cícero taken during the heyday of the "religious question of Joaseiro," ca. 1889-1898. He was then between forty-five and fifty-four years of age. The woman standing to his side is allegedly his younger sister, D. Angêlica. (*Courtesy of Fr. Azarias Sobreira of Fortaleza, Ceará.*)

AO POVO.

Alerta Joaseirenses ! Apresenta-se, tirando de tudo a mascara. como inimigo do Rev.mo Padre Cicero e dos romeiros—o ZÉ ANDRÈ—do sobrado

Diz elle querer espulsar, desta terra, o vosso venerando chefe, amigo e pae esperitual, com toda a canalha dos romeiros.

Vós, briosos romeiros e mais amigos do Padre Cicero, não consintaes em tamanha monstruosidade!

Expulsar o Padre Cicero do Joaseiro, é tirar-lhe a vida! deportar os seus romeiros, é desolação!

Não ! Não mais façaes compra de especie alguma em sua loja; fujaes delle como de um contagio !

Está em vossa dignidade não mais fazer negocio algum com—o ZÉ ANDRÈ—que é inimigo, inimigo do Padre Cicero e de vós!

Joaseiro—Janeiro de 912

Photocopy of an original handbill circulated during a political crisis in Joaseiro in January, 1912 (and referred to in Chapter VIII, p. 137).

TRANSLATION:
On your guard Joaseirenses! ZÊ ANDRÈ, "the old moneybags," has finally showed his true colors as an enemy of Rev. Padre Cícero and the *romeiros* [pilgrims].

He says he wants to expel your venerable chief, friend and spiritual father from this land along with the dirty clic of *romeiros*.

You, courageous *romeiros* and other friends of Padre 'Cícero, do not consent to such an outrageous monstrosity!

To expel Padre Cícero from Joaseiro is to take away his life! to deport his *romeiros* is an utter crime!

No! Buy nothing whatsoever from his shop anymore; flee from him like the plague!

It's beneath your dignity to do business any longer with—ZÊ ANDRÈ— who is an enemy, Padre Cícero's enemy and yours!

JOASEIRO, JANUARY, 1912

Source: A copy of the handbill was presented to the author by the late Sr. Odílio Figueiredo of Fortaleza, Ceará.

Dr. Floro Bartholomeu da Côsta in a rare photograph taken in Crato probably shortly after his arrival in the Cariry Valley in May, 1908. (*Courtesy of D. Amália Xavier de Oliveira, Juàzeiro do Norte, Ceará.*)

A grieving Padre Cícero surrounded by mourners. The deceased was originally identified as D. "Quinou," the cleric's mother, which would date the photograph in the first week of August, 1914. However, the aged appearance of the cleric, bearing a strong resemblance to other photographs taken of him during the early 1920s, gives reason to believe that the deceased woman is probably his sister, D. Angêlica, who died on 6 October 1923. (*Courtesy of the Instituto do Ceará, Fortaleza, where the author accidentally found the original glass negative.*)

The visit of Ceará's Governor, Dr. João Thomé de Sabôia (seated front row, center), to Joaseiro in 1917. Seated on the governor's left is Padre Cícero, then seventy-three years old. Standing behind the Governor is Dr. Floro Bartholomeu da Côsta, at the time, the Caríry's *deputado* to the State Legislature. To one side is Sr. José Ferreira de Bezerra de Menezes (standing, third from right), Dr. Floro's long-time political associate in Joaseiro. To the other side is the French nobleman, Conde Adolpho van den Brule (standing, fourth from left), who came to Joaseiro with Dr. Floro in May, 1908. (*Courtesy of Sr. José Ferreira de Bezerra de Menezes of Juàzeiro do Norte, Ceará.*)

A typical souvenir photograph taken in August, 1964 by one of Joaseiro's innumerable *lâmbe-lâmbes* (street-photographers). Against the background of the Church of Our Lady of Sorrows, whose original two bell towers have long since disappeared, the composition includes: the author and members of his family (lower right and left); a representation of "Our Miraculous Lady of Sorrows who is venerated in the Chapel of Juàzeiro Ceará" (upper left); a popular depiction of Padre Cícero engulfed by the clouds upon which he is purportedly returning to earth (upper right); the Italian Capuchin missionary, Frei Damião (center foreground), who has been prohibited from preaching in many parts of the Brazilian Northeast because of the alleged belief of the lower classes that the foreign friar is the reincarnation of Padre Cícero. (*Source: Photograph in author's possession.*)

5

From Religion into Politics

The New Jerusalem

Joaseiro's transition from a center of religious "fanaticism" into an important economic and political force within the Cariry Valley took place almost imperceptibly. In fact, even today, the atmosphere of a mecca has not fully vanished; it prevails during the September festivities in honor of Our Lady of Sorrows, Joaseiro's patroness, and the November commemoration of the feast of All Souls. On these occasions as many as forty thousand pilgrims converge upon the city, as happened in November 1965.[1]

At the turn of the century the view of Joaseiro as a center of "fanaticism" was particularly pronounced. Several factors contributed to this impression. One was the policy of Ceará's ecclesiastical hierarchy: It continued to brand Joaseiro as a cancerous sect within the church (and within the body politic as well). For example, when Dom Joaquim publicly condemned the Legion of the Cross in December 1898, he cited not merely José Lôbo's deliberate failure to obtain episcopal approval to establish the Legion but, more significantly, the heretical religious practices of its members. The bishop singled out the peasant "Legionnaires" near Sobral and Ipú; he accused them of creating their own ministers and sacraments in defiance of the local curates. These "fanatics" had also defied the local landowners who did not hesitate to call for police intervention. In Ipú, for example, a local peasant leader of the Legion chapter had "in the name of Padre Cícero and Maria de Araújo" armed his confreres for the purpose of assassinating a prominent political chief.[2]

While in Joaseiro itself no open conflict between the civil authorities and the followers of Padre Cícero had yet erupted, the hamlet had succeeded in attracting many marginal social elements whose fanatical beliefs and practices greatly contributed to justify the impression that Joaseiro was a "citadel of sectarianism and fanaticism." This was the view that prevailed in a confidential report written in 1903. Submitted apparently to Fr. Quintino Rodrigues de Oliveira e Silva, who three years earlier had succeeded Msgr. Alexandrino as Vicar of Crato, the report provides a valuable, if somewhat exaggerated, description of the burgeoning "New Jerusalem."[3] "Today in Joaseiro," the document begins, "rare is the person . . . who follows Catholicism; everyone has a religion as it suits him, Cícero being its Minister, its Chief, a god. Many deny him mortal qualities, saying that he was not born and that if he has a mother, that is merely *a comparison*." Everywhere, the document contends, superstition was rampant: the ignorant masses attributed miraculous cures to plants found on the outskirts of the city and also to the water of a certain well in the center of town simply "because its location was chosen by Padre Cícero"; pilgrims, for example, refused to drink from any other.

The *beatas* continued to play as important a role in 1903 as they had in the 1890s. The report records the widely rumored attempt of Maria de Araújo and other *beatas* to restore the life of Maria's dead father. For two days they stood in vigil before the corpse praying for its resurrection on the third day. The document summarily dismisses these women as "dangerous, evil-tongued and ignorant. . . ."

Beatos, the male counterparts of the self-styled nuns, had by 1903 made their appearance in Joaseiro. There was "friar" Francelino, a mulatto, who conspicuously wore a crown of thorns and was renowned for his earlier denunciation of Dom Joaquim's authority before the priests of Crato. There was also the "*beato* da Cruz," who wore a long, black robe adorned with cabalistic designs, religious medals, rosaries, and amulets and who carried everywhere an enormous wooden cross.[4] These and other *beatos*, who numbered about a dozen, spent their time in prayer, visiting the sick, burying the dead and serving as personal messengers of Padre Cícero. On some occasions they led the rhythmic chants to which brigades of workers labored during the periods of planting and harvesting. Some *beatos* distributed *orações fortes*[5]—prayers to which both gullible pilgrims and orthodox Catholics commonly attributed special curative or intercessory powers; others conducted religious services in the Chapel of Our Lady of Sorrows whose doors in 1903 "were open day and night," but where by order of Dom Joaquim, no priest was to set foot from 1895 until 1916.

It is not surprising that during these two decades the deeply rooted antipathy towards the "official church" prevailed. The confidential document of 1903 boldly reveals that "there was great prejudice against the bishop of Ceará"; it singled out the aging José Lôbo as "perhaps Padre Cícero's most ardent partisan and as such the Bishop's greatest adversary." Moreover, it shows that Padre Cícero's followers, who continued to boycott the clergy of Crato, held most of the Valley priests "in low esteem [and considered] those who did not believe in the Miracles of Joaseiro and the sanctity of Padre Cícero [to be] atheists, Masons and Protestants. . . ."

It is also not surprising that in 1903, perhaps the apex of the hamlet's isolation from the official church, the most fanatical elements in Joaseiro, abandoned to their own religious inclinations and imagination, believed the terrain of Joaseiro to be the Holy Land and anxiously waited for Christ to appear. Padre Cícero had indirectly contributed to this belief. It happened in the following manner.

During the 1890s he had begun to construct a chapel in honor of the Sacred Heart of Jesus in fulfillment of a vow made—it will be recalled—by the priest and three colleagues in the drought year of 1890. By 1895 the chapel's foundations had been laid atop the Serra do Catolé, the mountain range that rises abruptly at the northern edge of the hamlet. A year later, however, Dom Joaquim ordered the "blasphemous" work to a halt! But since his vow had been made prior to Rome's condemnation of the miracles, the cleric maintained, it was in good faith that he recommenced building after his return from Rome. There he had obtained blueprints to convert the modest structure into perhaps the largest "cathedral" in the interior of the Brazilian Northeast. Transepts rose fifty feet into the air, their brick walls extended six feet in width. This renewed audacity provoked another

ban in late 1903, after which the empty shell remained unaltered until a
decade after the cleric's death in 1934.[6] In Joaseiro Dom Joaquim's new
prohibition was denounced as "a futile pretext to stop the spread of
fanaticism" at a moment when—in Padre Cícero's mind—Brazil's " 'free-
thinkers' were undertaking an enormous campaign against Roman
Catholicism."[7]

In the course of constructing the "cathedral" the people "transformed"
Joaseiro into the Holy Land.[8] The Serra do Catolé was renamed the Serra
do Hôrto, or "garden," and was identified with Gethsemane, where Cícero,
like Christ, now endured his agony. Similarly the sharply inclined, rock-
hewn road from the hamlet to the Hôrto became known as the route to
Calvary: here miniature chapels constructed under the supervision of Elias
Gilli, an Italian fugitive turned *beato,* housed the stations of the cross.
Even the winter stream of Salgadinho, that flows from the Hôrto to the
marshes west of Joaseiro, was dubbed the River Jordan. In this New
Jerusalem, according to the confidential document of 1903, Christ was
eagerly awaited. Twice people converged in expectation; twice his arrival
was postponed.[9] It hardly mattered. Pilgrims continued to come to Joaseiro,
for it was here, in the words of one priest, that "there was revealed the
imminence of a new Redemption, . . . out of Joaseiro new Apostles will
march as they had marched out of Jerusalem; for this reason Joaseiro would
be called the new Jerusalem. . . ."[10]

The Patriarch and His Pilgrims

Thousands of pilgrims continued to converge upon Joaseiro each year.
Many remained to settle in the hamlet. Between 1890 and 1898, Joaseiro's
population more than doubled to over 5,000 inhabitants; by 1905 it rose to
12,000; by 1909 to about 15,000.[11] Data (sparse and often of questionable
accuracy) allow only a cursory analysis of this significant migratory movement and of the motivations of those who came to Joaseiro.

The pilgrimage was the chief vehicle that accounted for Joaseiro's rapid
demographic expansion. Yet it is important to distinguish between the
pilgrimages which took place during the heyday of the "miracles" (prior to
Rome's condemnation of 1894) and those that occurred during the next
four decades. The former, as seen earlier, were principally initiated by the
"dissident" priests who believed in and propagated the "miracle of Joaseiro."

Under clerical auspices, these pilgrimages originated largely in the *municípios* of the Carity Valley and in the Pernambucan towns just across the Ceará state line. Contingents from Paraíba and Rio Grande do Norte were less frequent. The pilgrims themselves were drawn from among all social classes; there was no scarcity of wealthy landowners, political chiefs, and prominent civil servants, nor of merchants, doctors, lawyers, and educators. There were also large numbers of landless rural workers who accounted for most of the hamlet's permanent population by 1894.

Under the impact of Rome's 1894 decree and the subsequent recantation of Padre Cícero's clerical supporters, the pilgrimages to Joaseiro altered in several respects. First, they became "spontaneous," unorganized movements. While perhaps encouraged by the Legion of the Cross and the newly established merchants of Joaseiro, they were nevertheless undertaken in opposition to repeated episcopal prohibitions, and without clerical participation.[12] From this period dates the practice of carving crosses on trees to mark the most frequently traveled Northeastern routes to Joaseiro.[13] Second, the Carity-based pilgrimages diminished sharply and yielded to those originating in distant areas. The poor from the interior of Maranhão and Bahia as well as from the drought regions of Pernambuco, Paraíba, and Rio Grande do Norte greatly surpassed the decreasing trickle from Ceará, as if to prove the maxim that a prophet is never welcomed among his own. The greatest numbers, however, came from the distant São Francisco river region of the poverty-stricken state of Alagôas. Their impact has always been considerable. Even today, for example, Alagôanos and their descendants make up a large percentage of Joaseiro's 80,000 inhabitants.[14] Third, the composition of the post-1894 pilgrimages revealed little of the earlier social heterogeneity: most pilgrims were impoverished rural farm hands, *vaqueiros* (cow hands), and landless *rendeiros* (tenant farmers), and a scattering of artisans. Merchants, educators, and lawyers, in this latter period, came for commercial, professional, and political reasons but seldom religious as had frequently been the case prior to 1894.

In considering why pilgrims came to Joaseiro between 1894 and 1934, it would be an oversimplification to insist solely upon their "religious" motivation.[15] Most of these "pilgrims" or "fanatics" were illiterate, impoverished, and politically inert. Beneath their unorthodox or heterodox religious impulses was their often fruitless search to control the adverse environment and overcome social injustices which made their life a misery.

Such at least is the conclusion that can be drawn from the moving contents of several hundred letters addressed to Padre Cícero during the years 1910 through 1913.[16] Written mostly by semi-literates these letters constitute a rare historical indictment by Brazil's poor of the social iniquities prevailing in the Northeastern *sertão* during the early part of the twentieth century.

The most common plight of these poor was their chronic infirmity. Recovery, however, was entrusted to the saints, or *rezadores* (healers) rather than to physicians who were as rare in the backland villages as their fees were high. The fortunate *município* might boast of a self-taught pharmacist, but his assistance to the poor was also uncommon. Even home-remedies were unknown to them. Under such circumstances, Padre Cícero often dispensed medical advice, often simple suggestions of hygiene, which, when effective, were hailed as "miraculous." His fame as the people's physician was ridiculed in Crato where it was cynically claimed that "he had set himself up as a doctor for every disease and issues written prescriptions to the plebe."[17] For the infirm, however, a cure was proof of Padre Cícero's sanctity. Here is a typical request from a blind woman of Sertãozinho: "I implore my Padrinho [godfather] and I have Faith that when this [letter] reaches my Padrinho my sight will return and he will remove the pain from my legs I beg my Padrinho by the Holy powers and virtues he possesses to be my Padrinho in all my trials and dangers. . . ."[18] The litany of requests to cure dizziness, paralysis, blindness, rheumatism, infertility, and scores of other ailments and deficiencies reads like a catalogue of regional pathologies. One woman addressing herself to the "Son of Holiness, Sirsáro [*sic:* Cícero] Romão Batista" even requested a cure to restore a mad woman to sanity.[19]

An equally common plight was the breakdown of family life. From Alagôas, a mother of five children confided that her husband had deserted her after twenty-five years of marriage.[20] Another, whose husband and elder son had abandoned her with a brood of younger children requested the cleric's advice whether she should wait for their return or set off with her children in search of her breadwinners.[21]

The endemic want of justice in Brazil led both criminals and the victims of crime to seek out Padre Cícero's protection and counsel. A widow with five children wrote that her husband had been assassinated in 1906 by the notorious bandit, Antonio Silvino. Now she, her children, and her two sons-in-law could no longer remain, for fear of their lives. Her one hope:

"I avail myself of your Rev. that you may protect me and my seven children through your great powers and virtues of God and the Holy Virgin."[22] Even Chico Pereira, one of the Northeast's most celebrated *cangaceiros* (bandits), took momentary refuge in Joaseiro in 1922 where he went with his family in the belief that "Padre Cícero had God-given power to make a man go straight."[23]

The chronic poverty of the Northeast and the desperate quest of the poor for a subsistence wage seemed to account significantly for the readiness of thousands of "pilgrims" to uproot themselves and search out Joaseiro, "the oasis where all human sorrows would die." A mother of five children, too poor to own even a small statue of a saint, desperately declared: "I have nothing here, not even a piece of land . . ."; may she come to Joaseiro?; "My help is first in God and second in Yr. Rev. to work a miracle that would transport me from here to there. . . ."[24] From many parts of the Northeast and even from distant Minas Gerais,[25] men and women implored him for work and the right to come to live in what one Pernambucan called "Holy Joaseiro."[26]

Indeed, Joaseiro was a "holy city" presided over by a saintly Patriarch* who was the *padrinho* (godfather) of the sick, the homeless, the oppressed, the hungry, the criminal, and the sinner. Branded as "fanatics" by the cultured coastal society of Brazil, these pilgrims, on the contrary, perceived themselves simply as the *afilhados* (godchildren) of Padre Cícero.[27] The cleric, moreover, willingly assumed the roles of physician, counselor, provider, and confessor imposed upon him by his followers and, in his own mind, by God himself. In 1918, while urging an errant fellow priest to amend his life, Padre Cícero offered one of his rare explanations of the "theology of Joaseiro":[28]

Joaseiro has been a refuge for the shipwrecks of life. It [harbors] people from everywhere who humbly come to shelter themselves beneath the protection of the Most Holy Virgin.

And as it is sure that all Good, even the smallest Good, comes from God and that from all evil it is God who delivers us . . . then the coming to Joaseiro of those in search of the Most Holy Virgin is a Good because it is God who brings them.

* The term Patriarch is used here figuratively and not as a title of ecclesiastical rank. It gained currency only after Padre Cícero's death primarily among writers and intellectuals. It is used here because it aptly conveys the paternal and religious authority which he exercised over his followers.

The Economy of the Northeast

Clearly, neither the will of God nor the backlanders' passive rebellion
against injustice entirely accounts for either the massive influx of pilgrims
into Joaseiro or the hamlet's ensuing economic growth. A fuller explanation
of Joaseiro's development after 1894 must be set against the significant
changes that were simultaneously taking place in the economy of the
Brazilian Northeast and the nation as a whole.

The four decades from 1877 to 1915 were a critical period in the
economic history of the Northeast. During this time one minor and four
major droughts struck the region, crippling agriculture during twelve of
the thirty-eight years.[29] Ceará's earlier decade of prosperity had come to a
halt. That prosperity was begun in the 1860s when traditional American
cotton exports to England declined sharply after the eruption of the U.S.
Civil War. To supply her textile mills with raw cotton England quickly
sought other producers, among them Brazil. Between 1862 and 1877, the
arid Northeast, especially the states of Ceará, Maranhão, Paraíba, and
Pernambuco, entered upon an unheralded period of growth, as former
cattle lands were rapidly and extensively converted into the production of
cotton.[30] In supplying the international need for cotton the Northeast
integrated itself into an expanding world market. In Ceará, for example,
several English- and French-owned commercial houses were established
as well as a direct maritime link between Fortaleza and Liverpool (1866).
The influx of capital stimulated production of cotton, hides, and other raw
materials even in distant cities of the *sertão*. Nationals, too, opened ware-
houses and trading companies in Fortaleza to reexport to the backlands
foreign and Brazilian foodstuffs and manufactures in exchange for the
exportable produce of the land.[31]

This decade and a half of economic growth was abruptly curtailed by
the calamitous drought that began in 1877. In 1878 alone, famine claimed
57,000 lives among the *flagelados* (drought migrants) who had fled from
the interior to the makeshift shelters in Fortaleza; another 55,000 fell victim
to a government-financed emigration program and were obliged to embark
for other states. When the drought terminated in mid-1880, approximately
300,000 persons, more than a third of Ceará's population, had either emi-
grated or died of hunger and disease.[32]

The subsequent droughts of 1888, 1898, 1900, and 1915 were equally
disastrous for Ceará's economy. Collectively they set in motion the emi-

gration of almost half a million backlanders.[33] But this loss of Ceará's labor force cannot be attributed to drought alone. The massive exodus of labor was made possible in large measure by the concurrent rise of coffee production in the South and, after 1888, the opening of the vast rubber-tree forests in the under-populated provinces of Amazonas and Pará. Both regions required a large, inexpensive, and highly flexible labor force in order to meet the expanding demand for coffee and rubber, of which Brazil became the world's largest producer. While European immigrants increasingly satisfied the manpower requirements of the Southern coffee plantations, the forests of the Far North depended almost entirely on the labor reserves of the more proximate Northeastern region. Each drought enabled "rubber agents" to recruit larger and larger numbers of workers. Ample federal subsidies financed the outward passage to the Far North, while Ceará's state government collected a "head tax" for each able body that departed.[34] Ironically, the policy of substituting human exports, capable of remitting earnings home, for the export of raw materials soon resulted in the real crisis of the Northeast: That crisis was not the drought alone, but clearly the consequently rapid depletion of human capital syphoned off to the South and, especially, to the Far North. Indeed, without cheap and abundant labor the traditional agriculture of the arid Northeast—cotton and cattle—was incapable of recovering in nondrought years and, in fact, was threatened with extinction. When Ceará's state government realized the contradiction inherent in trafficking in manpower, it hastily attempted to protect the region's labor supply and prevent it from emigrating.[35] But its meager measures came too late; not even the collapse of the Brazilian rubber boom around 1913 alleviated the Northeastern labor shortage. It remained chronic until the early 1920s.[36]

The Economics of the New Jerusalem

In the midst of this chronic labor shortage, Joaseiro and the surrounding Cariry Valley emerged as one of the few regions of the arid backlands that gained rather than lost human capital. It is true that the Valley's fertile soils and perennial water sources defied all but the worst droughts. It is also true that since the mid-nineteenth century its uninhabited lands had traditionally provided a haven for the drought victims of the surrounding arid backlands.[37] However, there is no doubt that Padre Cícero's fame as a "saint" and "miracle worker" did as much as the natural fertility of the Valley to attract scarce laborers to the Cariry. Furthermore, the devoted loyalty he inspired among the newcomers significantly enabled the Patriarch to emerge as the undisputed "labor czar" of the arid Northeast. No pilgrim, for example, undertook any task or employment without his counsel or command; furthermore, neither the agricultural enterprises of the Cariry Valley nor the subsequent public works programs financed by the federal government in the Brazilian Northeast would have progressed as they did without the labor force dispatched by the priest.[38]

Undeniably, the influx of pilgrim-workers had virtually transformed several Valley towns. In nearby Barbalha, for example, the production of sugarcane and *rapadura* had expanded rapidly. By 1903 or 1904, Barbalha rose to challenge the economic supremacy of Crato, the "Pearl of the Cariry."[39]

The Valley's less populated mountain plateaus were also subjugated quickly by the hoe of the pilgrim. Under Padre Cícero's initiative and direction, both the Serra do Araripe near Crato and the Serra de São Pedro, to the northeast of Joaseiro, were cleared, parceled out, and made to yield abundant harvests of manioc, the "wheat flour" of the backlands. So numerous were the newcomers in the Serra de São Pedro that they transformed the dormant *município* of São Pedro into a thriving town. Even today it is acknowledged as the "city of Padre Cícero's *afilhados*."

Steadily after 1900 and increasingly after 1914, the hitherto neglected *serras* and the labor-intensive agriculture on the Valley floors accounted for the Cariry's impressive surpluses of foodstuffs. With their export on a large scale to other parts of Ceará and the surrounding states of Pernambuco, Paraíba, and Rio Grande do Norte, "the Cariry won the title of the 'granary of Ceará.' "[40] A prominent Cariry Valley historian, a contemporary chronicler of these events, offers the following assessment of the impact of the pilgrims and Padre Cícero upon the region's economy: "The Cariry profited eminently from the immigration of pilgrims. From this point of view, Padre Cícero was—there isn't any doubt—one of the greatest forces of progress in the economic life of Southern Ceará. In addition to the cultivation of manioc in the *serra*, there took place in the Cariry Valley a considerable expansion in the production of corn, beans and sugar cane, until then cultivated in reduced quantities because of the scarcity of manpower."[41]

Joaseiro, too, "profited eminently" from the influx of pilgrims. By 1909, its limited rural area (less than half of the district's 219 square kilometers) contained twenty-two sugar *engenhos* engaged in the production of *rapadura* and alcoholic by-products.[42] Eight years later, there were two more *engenhos* as well as sixty localities equipped to process manioc flour. In addition to the cultivation of rice, beans, and corn, Joaseiro excelled in the production of *maniçoba* rubber and cotton. Rubber was introduced into the region by Padre Cícero during the first decade of the twentieth century and was cultivated extensively throughout the *serras*.[43] Thanks also to the Patriarch, cotton, long neglected, made its comeback in the Cariry between 1908 and 1911 shortly after the priest purchased one of the first motor-driven cotton gins ever used in the Valley.[44] Both products—rubber and cotton—were primarily responsible for linking Joaseiro's economy to the export trade of Fortaleza's great commercial houses, namely the French-owned firm of Boris Frères and the Brazilian company of Adolpho Barroso.

Joaseiro's urban growth was even more notable than its agricultural expansion. On 1 January 1909, 15,050 inhabitants were thickly settled within Joaseiro's urban center, comprised of twenty-two streets and two public squares that were illuminated by kerosene. To service the town there were two bakeries, three barbershops, fifteen tailors, two pharmacies, twenty primary schools (only two of them public), one printing house, a telegraph station, a post office, a public notary, and a state tax collection agency.[45]

The hamlet's commerce was lively. In addition to a weekly fair, held each Sunday in the church square, Joaseiro boasted ten large permanently fixed dry-goods stores, an equal number of general stores and about thirty small groceries, bars, and sundry shops. Most of the merchants had immigrated to Joaseiro from neighboring towns and distant states prior to 1910. One of the wealthiest was the Pernambucan-born merchant, João David da Silva, who had accompanied Padre Cícero to Rome in 1898.[46]

Joaseiro's principal economic activity, however, was derived from its flourishing artisan industries. These arose not merely to meet the consumer needs of the burgeoning hamlet, but also as a timely response to the inability of Joaseiro's limited rural areas to absorb the immigrants into agricultural activities as quickly as they arrived. At first these industries were engaged primarily in house construction, as well as the manufacture of a variety of domestic articles made from local raw materials: crockery, pots, cutlery, shoes, leather goods, hats and mats of plant fibers, cord, twine, sacks, and other receptacles for storing and shipping foodstuffs. At the same time the steady influx of "pilgrim tourists" (those who returned home after a brief visit) stimulated the manufacture of both fireworks—traditionally set off by each pilgrim upon his arrival in Joaseiro—and religious articles and mementos: wooden and clay statues of the Virgin, the Saints and, above all, of Padre Cícero; crucifixes and medals of tin, silver, and gold; rosaries, scapulas, holy pictures—the gamut of religious trinkets that quickly found a market throughout the entire Northeast.[47] Eventually local skills and backland needs led to the manufacture and export of typical rural utensils: hoes, shovels, knives, daggers, rifles, shotguns, bullets, and gunpowder.

By 1909 Joaseiro's artisans had moved out of their homes and into sizable, machine-equipped workshops, located in the center of town easily accessible to the growing ranks of employees and buyers alike. At that time the city contained forty master builders, eight blacksmith and seven tin-smith workshops, fifteen manufacturers of fireworks, twenty shoe factories, two jewelry works (there were fifteen in 1917), thirty-five carpentry shops, five cabinetmakers, and even one foundry that produced churchbells and tower clocks for export throughout the Northeast.[48]

These industries were linked to a specialized sector of commerce "that at first only distributed their products and later came to finance and control them, resulting in a growing division of labor among the artisans: work-shop owners, some independent, others reliant upon commercial financiers and a greater number of salaried workers. . . . [As one historian exclaimed] One can imagine what this mercantile, artisan activity came to signify for the liberation of a considerable number of men who until then lived sub-jugated to the large landowners."[49]

The effects of Joaseiro's economic growth were clearly visible in the hamlet's increasing share of taxes paid to the federal and state governments: Federal taxes grew from 2 contos 444 milréis in 1916 to 36 contos 550 milréis in 1923; state taxes, from 29:800$000 in 1912 to 52:100$000 in 1922.[50] Furthermore, Joaseiro's growth continued to have an impact on the Cariry Valley. In 1921, both the region's first bank and an association of com-mercial farmers were established in Crato. Five years later, the main line of the Fortaleza railroad (*Rede da Viação Cearense*) reached Joaseiro and Crato.[51]

In the decade-and-a-half after 1894 Joaseiro's economic structure was forged: it helped to set the stage for the hamlet's bid for municipal autonomy around 1909 and 1910. That bid, however, might have been impossible had it not been for a number of significant changes that had started to take place earlier in the political system of the nation, state, and region. Those changes began under the administration of Manuel Ferraz de Campos Sales (1898–1902), the second civilian to assume the presidency of Brazil after the overthrow of the Empire.

The Politics of the Governors

Campos Sales took office at a time of internal political dissensions and turmoil that resulted from the transition from monarchy to republicanism. The nation's ensuing economic instability had seriously prejudiced its foreign markets and credit sources. The new president's principal goal was to restore Europe's confidence in Brazil by adopting an austere financial program whose chief objective was to secure a balanced national treasury.[52] To execute this policy Campos Sales readily made broad political concessions to diverse regional interests. This not only proved a boon to the powerful coffee exporting states of São Paulo and Minas Gerais, where half the national electorate resided, but also resulted in the immediate consolidation of "oligarchies" in less powerful states. There "the groups that had gained control [after the proclamation of the Republic] were made up mainly of former members of the monarchic parties. They calmly went about setting up powerful machines devoted to graft, bribery and violence."[53] This presidential readiness to allow local interests to gain total control in exchange for their support of national policies was dubbed "the politics of the governors."

In Ceará, the political holdovers of the Empire were led by the former imperial Senator, Comendador Antonio Pinto Nogueira Accioly; they regained control of the state in 1892. Four years later, under the banner of the *Partido Republicano Conservador-Ceará* (PRC-C), Accioly himself was elected governor of Ceará. Twice reelected (in 1904 and 1908), he personally retained control of the state machinery as well as the PRC-C until 1912 (not excepting the period from 1900 to 1904 when a hand-picked successor assumed the governorship).[54]

Accioly ran the interior of Ceará much in the same fashion as the federal government did the states. He willingly accorded to the local *coronéis,* or political chiefs, full control over municipal government: political recognition, fiscal control, and the distribution of state and federal patronage. In return, he exacted electoral support and party solidarity. This system, known as *coronelismo,* predicated that political power in the interior was the tradition-bound prerogative of the great landowners, a fact that was not altered radically by the fall of the monarchy.[55] But it also recognized the structural changes introduced by the Republic: each state was now made responsible for education, public services, administration, and its own financial solvency. As a consequence, the *município* became a critical thread in the web of government: it was the chief source of revenues, necessary to maintain the essentially bureaucratic expansion of state government. To assure the steady flow of "legal tribute," the state oligarchy would reward municipal chiefs not only with federal and state employment and local patronage, but also with a larger share of local revenues.[56] It was this marked increment of local power and wealth, rather than the mere continuation of time-honored local rivalries between prominent families, that unleashed throughout the backlands the violent struggles for municipal power in the first decades after the proclamation of the Republic.[57]

Nowhere was political violence more intense and frequent than in the Cariry Valley. There both the "politics of the oligarch" as well as the region's accelerated economic growth made municipal government a desirable plum. Between 1901 and 1910 political chiefs of eight Valley *municípios* were violently deposed by rivals, several others were theatened with deposition.[58] Neither faction hesitated to seize or retain power by arming its rural workers (*campangas* or *cabras bons*) or recruiting hired gunmen (*jaguncos* or *cangaceiros*) from the backlands of Pernambuco and Paraíba.[59] (In fact, the metamorphosis of the Cariry Valley into a refuge of *cangaceiros* protected by the local *coronéis* dates from this period.)[60] Interestingly enough, each faction claimed to be loyal to the "partido acciolino" as the PRC-C was more popularly known in the backlands). Accioly, for his part, did not intervene in local disputes other than to confer recognition upon the local victor. One contemporary critic of the "oligarch" summed up the workings of the backland political system in Ceará as follows.[61]

In each locality of the *alto sertão,* in the perpetually tumultuous region of the Cariry, there almost always exist two *chefes* who [presiding over their bands of] *cangaceiros* claim to be tied to the *partido* of the oligarch, struggling against each other for power.

These men, the wealthiest, maintain at their own cost armed and disciplined troops for their personal protection and for the conquest of [political] positions. In the end, it is the strongest who obtains the favors of the despot [i.e., Accioly].

[The despot] doesn't intervene in these struggles. Indifferent, passive, he watches over the bloody battles, the violent incursions, the depradations and the pillaging. . . . The entire territory of the State could be set aflame; the oligarch does not interfere in these disputes between rival *chefes*. . . . To the strongest the despot confers the palm-leaf of triumph and the dominion over the locality by the massive firing of the deposed authorities.

The Politics of the New Jerusalem

While the Cariry enmeshed itself in a decade of political struggles, Joaseiro and its Patriarch purposely stood aloof. The cleric's chief concern was not politics but the restoration of his clerical orders. Attesting to this priority are the successive petitions dispatched either to the papal nuncio in Petropolis or the Pope in Rome—in 1900, 1902, 1903, 1905, 1906, and 1908.[62] Hardly a year passed when the cleric did not encourage the innumerable initiatives of friends to restore him to holy orders. Business associates in Fortaleza, but especially the political chiefs of the Valley, increasingly intervened on his behalf before the ecclesiastical authorities. For example, between 1905 and 1906, the *coronéis* of Crato, Barbalha, Santana do Cariri, and Brejo dos Santos officially appealed to Dom Joaquim in the name of their local municipal governments and in behalf "of the popular soul of the Cariryense" to reinstate the Patriarch.[63]

Primarily for this reason, Padre Cícero showed no partisanship in the Valley's political rivalries. He sought at all costs to remain in the good graces of all the political chiefs. For example, in 1904 when Crato's prominent merchant-landowner, Col. Antonio Luis Alves Pequeno (the son of Padre Cícero's godfather and the third successive descendant to bear this illustrious name), violently deposed that city's prefect of fourteen years— both of whom were related to the cleric by the sacraments of the church— Padre Cícero took no sides; in the past both the vanquished and the victor of Crato had consistently lent their prestige to the Patriarch's personal cause. The necessity to retain the continued solidarity of the Valley *chefes* in order to win reinstatement from Rome undoubtedly justified his "politics of neutrality."[64]

It is important to note that neutrality did not preclude the Patriarch's efforts to pacify the political disputes within the Cariry. In fact, important

Valley figures repeatedly beseeched the priest to exercise willingly or not his "uncontestable authority . . . to avoid . . . conflict[s] that would otherwise result in sad consequences. . . ." Between 1903 and 1909 petitions such as this came from interested parties of Missão Velha, Lavras, and Aurora, three *municípios* on the verge of conflict. In 1911, even the Governor of Ceará, Comendador Accioly, helpless to retain the support of Barbalha's political chief, appealed to Padre Cícero to win back the recalcitrant *coronel*.[65]

Upon reflection, the Patriarch's neutrality (understood *latu sensu* as a refusal to join either of the conflicting sides but a readiness to conciliate adversaries) was thoroughly consistent with both his hope for clerical reinstatement and his vision of Joaseiro as a city of God. In fact, during this period of incessant political turmoil, the Patriarch converted the hamlet from a "refuge for the shipwrecks of life" into a political haven for rival Valley chiefs, irrespective of their politics. José Lôbo, never lacking in tribute to Padre Cícero, recalled in his political testament how the Patriarch threw open Joaseiro's doors to the "families and fortunes" of feuding *coroneis* during the first decade of the twentieth century:[66]

> During the ill-fated and turbulent times through which this region has passed, many persons entrusted [Padre Cícero] with their fortunes and families as happened in July, 1904, on [the occasion of] the strife in Crato; his residence on the *serra* known as the "Hôrto" and other houses in this hamlet belonging to . . . Padre Cícero could be seen crowded —[so crowded that] it was impossible to walk around . . . with the wives, daughters and children of the principal families of Crato, without regard to their political colors. . . .
>
> Upon the . . . deposition of Col. Nêco Rebeiro, ex-*chefe* of Barbalha [February–March 1906], the dolorous scene was identical, [whereby] the fathers of families of those cities provided a testimony that they confided more . . . [along with] their treasures and families . . . in the defenseless Padre Cícero than in their armed henchmen and partisans who surrounded them. . . . All were witnesses to these scenes, and [if] two reliable eyewitnesses constitute full proof, how much greater [proof do] the many.

Clearly the policy of neutrality kept Joaseiro at peace with its neighbors and at the same time enabled the hamlet to progress rapidly towards economic prosperity. In addition, the Patriarch's recorded benevolence and conciliatory efforts in five of the eight cases of armed municipal conflict unforeseeably endowed him with even greater *de facto* political authority than that of the very *coronéis* at conflict. Indeed, at the close of the first decade of the twentieth century the Patriarch's New Jerusalem found itself populous and powerful enough to rival its potent neighbors, Crato and Barbalha. However, none of the above conditions entirely accounted for Joaseiro's subsequent campaign for municipal autonomy, won only in 1911, or the Patriarch's later transformation into the most powerful *coronel* in the political history of the Brazilian Northeast.

6

Padre Cícero
Enters Politics

The Patriarch's Politics and the Two Joaseiros

Joaseiro's bid for municipal autonomy was gradually formulated during the years 1908 to 1910. In the end, this bid met with Padre Cícero's whole-hearted approval and consequently marked the Patriarch's irrevocable entry into politics. This decision, or more correctly a series of decisions, forced him to abandon the decade-long policy of neutrality, an abandonment which on the surface could only appear as an ill omen for his quest to win priestly reinstatement. Moreover, this momentous decision to enter politics resulted in the Patriarch's rapid ascent into the governing circles of the state and nation, but unfortunately it has never been satisfactorily explained. On the one hand, the cleric's adversaries contended that he lusted after power and wealth and branded him an "oriental despot," a megalomaniac, and a paranoiac. On the other, his admirers panegyrically defended his political actions as either well-intentioned deeds or the inevitable result of circumstances. Clearly, these "hypotheses" primarily serve to illustrate the intensity of the lifelong public controversy in which his political decision inextricably embroiled him; they do not explain that decision.[1]

Any attempt to do so must begin by examining the Patriarch's own avowal that he "never wanted to be a politician," and its formal contradiction when he took office as Joaseiro's first prefect in late 1911. The cleric explained that, just prior to Joaseiro's elevation to municipal status, he "was forced to collaborate in politics . . . in order to prevent that another citizen— [because of his] lack of knowledge or capacity to keep up the delicate balance of order until then maintained by me—might compromise the salutary progress of this land [Joaseiro]. . . ."

This retrospective justification was contained in the Patriarch's last will written in 1923.[2] But it corresponds in substance and chronology to an earlier declaration made by the prelate in a hitherto unpublished letter. That missive, addressed to Ceará's Governor in June 1911 (one month before the State Assembly granted municipal autonomy to Joaseiro), substantiates that the prelate had actively sought to nullify the attempts of "another citizen" to become the city's first prefect. Here are the cleric's reasons as he confided them to Governor Accioly:[3]

I must tell Your Excellency, before it is too late, that he is totally unacceptable to the people, against whom he has always assumed a determinedly hostile attitude. I make such a statement because I am his friend and I don't want to see him undergo the pain of grappling with this truth which perhaps he neither can nor wants to face. . . .

Furthermore [the rejection of his candidacy will in the long run] aid me in preventing unnecessary disturbances.

Fortunately, the 1911 letter, unlike the 1923 will, revealed the "mystery-citizen" to be Joaseiro's wealthiest landowner, Major Joaquim Bezerra de Menezes, a direct descendant of the Cariry's founding family and a native son of Joaseiro.[4] Equally unknown until now, was Major Joaquim's audacious sponsorship of Joaseiro's first political meeting in August 1907—an event to which Padre Cícero lent neither his consent nor presence.[5] In a handbill circulated "to the People of Joaseiro," the Major summoned local "patriots" to his home to discuss "the betterment of this blessed and much beloved birth-place." While proclaiming the event to be a "civic meeting without political hue," the Major did not conceal his intention to promote the elevation of Joaseiro to municipal status, and, in retrospect, his own designation as the hamlet's first prefect.[6]

Although Major Joaquim's role in Joaseiro's history is today all but forgotten, it raises two important questions about Padre Cícero's actions. First, why did the Patriarch "boycott" Major Joaquim's call for Joaseiro's municipal autonomy in 1907? Second, why in 1911 did the cleric continue to oppose the great landowner's personal political ambitions?

To answer the first question, it must be recalled that Joaseiro was an administrative sub-unit (*distrito*) of the *município* of Crato. Its elevation to municipal autonomy would require Crato to cede its rights to territorial and political jurisdiction over the hamlet. While the State Legislature might legally grant autonomy, the action would most likely alienate Crato's political chief, Col. Antonio Luis Alves Pequeno, one of the most powerful *coronéis* of the Cariry. However, in 1907 the Patriarch's "politics of neutrality" was in full force; just a year earlier, for example, Col. Antonio Luis had lent his political prestige to a petition urging Dom Joaquim to authorize the cleric's reinstatement.[7] Furthermore, at this time, the Patriarch's closest advisors, José Marrocos and José Lôbo were primarily concerned with Padre Cícero's struggle against the ecclesiastical hierarchy. In politics, moreover, Marrocos had advocated conciliation and cooperation among regional chiefs, not rivalry and dissension. Lôbo, for his part, had remained a monarchist and branded cooperation with republican institutions as a betrayal of the Catholic faith.[8] Clearly then, Major Joaquim's 1907 plan for Joaseiro's autonomy came at the wrong time. For Padre Cícero, there was reason neither to scrap his successful policy of neutrality nor alienate friends such as Marrocos, Lôbo, and even Col. Antonio Luis, a would-be defender in future pleas for reinstatement.

Why, however, did the priest also oppose Major Joaquim's bid for prefect on the eve of Joaseiro's inauguration as a *município* in 1911? The Patriarch had reasoned in his letter to Accioly that the Major "was totally unacceptable to the people, against whom he has always assumed a determinedly hostile attitude." In his will of 1923, he had also added that Major Joaquim lacked both the knowledge and capability "to keep up the delicate balance of order" that until 1911 had been maintained by the Patriarch.

Both reasons clearly point to the profound change that had taken place in the social composition of Joaseiro, a change perfectly understood by the cleric and without which no understanding of Joaseiro's political history is possible. Over time, the inhabitants of Joaseiro had become divided into two increasingly hostile groups: the *filhos da terra* (native sons) and the *adventícios* (newcomers).[9] The *filhos da terra* were not only those born in Joaseiro but also some who had come there from either Crato or other parts of the Cariry. On the whole, their social status had always been assured by their lineage, property, or simply, birthright. The *adventícios,* in time the majority of Joaseiro, included most of the recent immigrants from more distant regions. The term referred equally to prominent merchants, such as the Silva brothers from Alagôas and João Batista de Oliveira of Pernambuco, as well as to the lowly born *romeiros* (pilgrims) who settled in Joaseiro.[10] The prestige of this group was determined far less by their origins or newly acquired wealth than by their social proximity to the Patriarch.

The distinction between native sons and newcomers first became apparent in 1894, when Rome's condemnation prompted several native sons, especially the independently wealthy landowners, to discredit the miracles; as a consequence, many privately undid the ties of intimacy that had bound them earlier to the priest.[11] Some *filhos da terra,* it is true, especially merchants and the religiously zealous, retained the Patriarch's friendship for economic or religious reasons. They unstintingly supported the cleric, as did, for example, Pelusio Macêdo, the clever craftsman of church bells and tower clocks, who remained throughout his life a high official in Joaseiro's brotherhoods.[12] However, the 1894 decree led the Patriarch to rely increasingly on Joaseiro's newcomers. It was José Lôbo who engineered the Legion of the Cross; it was pilgrims' alms that financed the pleas to Rome; it was the business-minded merchant immigrants who became the cleric's steadfast supporters. It was not a coincidence, therefore, that it was João Batista de Oliveira, the hamlet's Pernambucan-born cloth merchant, who accompanied Padre Cícero to Rome in 1898. As the Patriarch favored the newcomers, resentments among the *filhos da terra* grew deeper.

The cleavage between the groups became wider as Joaseiro entered the twentieth century. In 1905, Pelusio Macêdo, then in charge of soliciting donations to pay the costs of one of the recent telegraphic appeals to Rome astutely observed an underlying economic aspect of the cleavage: "The

population of the new Joaseiro (I say new because among the old inhabitants one gets only a cold shoulder) . . . was astir in the streets having
just raised the enormous sum necessary to pay for the cost [of the telegram].
. . . Never before have people given money with such punctuality and
pleasure . . . those not accustomed [to doing so] appear to give more
gladly. . . ."[13]

Another economic aspect of this cleavage was the competitive spirit of
newcomer merchants who frequently proved more successful in business
affairs than did the native sons.[14] By 1907, the division between the "new"
and "old" Joaseiro had begun to harden as evidenced by the mutually disrespectful nicknames that had come into vogue. Native sons called the
newcomers *fanáticos, rabos de burro*, and most pejoratively of all *romeiros*,
the otherwise ordinary Portuguese word for pilgrim. In turn, the newcomers labeled the native sons *cacaritos* or simply *nativos*, which nonetheless bore a most disrespectful connotation.[15] Marriage was rarely contracted
between "new" and "old" inhabitants and even membership in Joaseiro's
religious brotherhoods became increasingly drawn from one or the other
group.[16]

As hostility drove a wedge between native sons and newcomers, the
Patriarch alone was able to bridge the gap; and for several decades he
alone held together "the two Joaseiros" in uneasy coalescence. This tenuous
unity also accounts for his rejection of Major Joaquim's 1907 bid to better
"this blessed and much beloved birth-place." Had the cleric approved, he
would have shifted "the delicate balance of order" in favor of the *filhos
da terra* minority. In 1911, when the *adventícios* clearly constituted Joaseiro's
majority, the Major had understandably become, in Padre Cícero's words
"totally unacceptable" as a candidate of the "people," that is, the newcomers
"against whom [the Major] had always assumed a definitely hostile attitude." As a result, the Patriarch "was forced to collaborate in politics" and
shortly thereafter became Joaseiro's first prefect. This act, however, was a
tacit admission that the cleric himself had come full circle in favor of the
"people." The cleric's 1911 alignment with the newcomers had been brought
to maturity during the previous three years. During that time, the most
astute *adventício* ever to come to Joaseiro, Doctor Floro Bartholomeu da
Côsta, rose rapidly to the apex of the "new Joaseiro." His overwhelming
influence over Padre Cícero has been widely argued by several authors as
the chief reason for the Patriarch's entry into politics.[17]

Copper and the Cariry Bishopric

Dr. Floro Bartholomeu da Côsta, a Bahian-born physician, came to Joaseiro in May 1908.[18] Prior to his arrival he had worked as a journalist, public notary, and itinerant doctor in the backlands of Bahia and Pernambuco. In 1907, he abandoned his full-time medical practice to join an expatriate French nobleman, the mining engineer Conde Adolpho Van den Brule, in the search for diamonds and semiprecious metals.[19] Later that year, Conde Adolpho decided to return to the Cariry Valley where he had earlier promoted a Paris-incorporated firm to exploit recently discovered copper deposits at the Coxá fields, not far from Joaseiro. Prompted by rumors that unfriendly landowners intended to lay illegal claim to the area, the two adventurers made haste to the Valley.[20]

Their first encounter with Padre Cícero in May 1908 was not arbitrary. Sometime before, the Patriarch had acquired property rights to most of the Coxá copper deposits.[21] But, the adventurers argued, neither they nor the Patriarch could develop the deposits until the ownership of the Coxá fields could be clearly determined. Impressed by the intelligence and persuasiveness of Dr. Floro and the technical skill and European contacts of Conde Adolpho, Padre Cícero soon agreed to petition the district court for the right to demarcate Coxá, and thereby settle the question of ownership.[22]

At the same time the Patriarch appointed Dr. Floro his legal proxy. During the next months, the energetic physician scavenged the real estate records of Crato and other Valley towns. In order to defend Padre Cícero's interests more effectively, he took up residence in July in Milagres and traveled often to Missão Velha, the two *municípios* under whose jurisdiction the Coxá mines fell. When in mid-December 1908 the district court at Milagres finally approved the priest's request to demarcate the lands, no rival claim to Coxá had yet been filed. But Dr. Floro's satisfaction was shortlived. En route to Coxá on 15 December, the Patriarch's representatives (a lawyer, surveyor, and fellow priest), led by Dr. Floro, narrowly escaped death by ambush.[23] To retaliate, the Bahian adventurer immediately enlisted the support of the political chiefs of Milagres and Missão Velha, with whom he and the Patriarch had become increasingly friendly. Provided with over fifty armed *capangas,* Dr. Floro boldly routed the band of assassins whose aim it was to prevent Coxá from falling into the hands of the Patriarch.

The armed conflict brought an abrupt end to Padre Cícero's politics of neutrality: the Patriarch was held responsible for Floro's counterattack. That armed action proved, furthermore, to be an unwanted declaration of war against Crato's powerful chief, Col. Antonio Luis Alves Pequeno, because it was with his tacit approval that his close relative, Col. J. F. Alves Teixeira (who long and guardedly coveted Coxá) had dispatched the band of assassins to stop Floro. Within months, these circumstances would force-fully contribute to the Patriarch's decision to enter politics.[24]

In sharp contrast to that decision, Padre Cícero's original entry into partnership with Floro and Conde Adolpho over Coxá was *not* motivated by political considerations. Rather, behind his eagerness to exploit Coxá lay his perennial obsession to regain priestly status. The failure of his repeated petitions led him to adopt a new strategy in 1908 with regard to the recalcitrant church hierarchy. That strategy arose after reports had reached Padre Cícero in 1907 that Rome intended to establish a new bishopric in the interior of Ceará State, a cause which the cleric claimed to have cham-pioned before the Holy Father in 1898.[25] However in 1908 the likely choice for the seat of the new diocese was nearby Crato from whence ecclesiastical censures and sanctions against Joaseiro had emanated ever since 1892. Indeed, a bishopric in Crato might forever dash Padre Cícero's hopes of clerical reinstatement, unless, of course, the new See could be erected in Joaseiro![26] Immediately the cleric set to work to lay the founda-tions of the "Diocese of the Cariry." In the press and before influential church friends in the South he argued that Joaseiro, not Crato, was the very heart of the Northeastern *sertão,* the principal center of convergence "from Alagôas to Maranhão." So sure was the Patriarch of success that he ordered an old house on Rua Grande rebuilt as the future residence of the Cariry's first bishop.[27]

Meanwhile, under pressure from the aging Dom Joaquim, Fr. Quintino, the Vicar of Crato, moved swiftly to win the honor for the "Pearl of the Cariry." On 8 December 1908, the feast of the Immaculate Conception, prominent Cratenses solemnly met to plan a fund drive for the patrimony of the new diocese, with its seat in Crato.[28]

This challenge, which contributed much to the later resentments be-tween Crato and Joaseiro, did not pass unnoticed. On 10 December 1908, the Patriarch telegraphed an influential contact before the Apostolic Nuncio in Petropolis: "Spare no effort for the chancery seat in Joaseiro, Ceará."[29] Five days later—exactly one week after the fund-drive meeting in Crato—

Dr. Floro set out to demarcate Coxá. There is no doubt that the Patriarch had earmarked the copper fields as the patrimony of the "Bishopric of the Cariry"—with its seat in Joaseiro![30] So convinced was the Patriarch that it was God's will to elevate Joaseiro to an episcopal see—not a *município*— that the ominous political implications of Dr. Floro's armed struggle at Coxá were totally lost on him. Instead, as the vision of the new diocese, and perhaps his own reinstatement, grew brighter, the sexagenarian decided to travel secretly to Rio de Janeiro to promote the cause in person. On 23 April 1909, he left Joaseiro believing, "Divine Providence wants me to make the journey."[31] On the eve of his departure he wrote to José Marrocos, whose unsung labors on behalf of the new diocese were as great as any he had ever undertaken: "Pray for me to the Most Holy Virgin that we may meet with success."[32]

The Journey into Politics

Two months later, *Unitário* (Fortaleza's libelous opposition daily to the Accioly oligarchy) reported Padre Cícero's hasty return from Rio de Janeiro. The Patriarch had disembarked in Salvador, Bahia—rather than Fortaleza —and proceeded to the interior via the São Francisco River R.R. As *Unitário* noted, the cleric had chosen "the shortest possible route" to the Cariry, whither he had been suddenly and "expressly summoned to put down a rebellion."[33]

In his absence, the events at Coxá had become a cause and pretext of a new and "serious threat to the peace of the Cariry": in May 1909, Dr. Floro's friends, the political chiefs of Milagres and Missão Velha, entered into *coligação* (a coalition) with nearby Barbalha for the purpose of deposing Crato's Col. Antonio Luis Alves Pequeno.[34] His "behind-the-scenes" role in the Coxá ambush of Dr. Floro in 1908—the origin of which was now attributed directly to him rather than to his relative, Col. Teixeira Alves—was quickly converted into the nominal "cause de guerre" by his trio of enemies.

Chief among these enemies was Col. Domingos Furtado, *chefe político* of Milagres. The real cause of Furtado's feud with Antonio Luis began in 1904. That year, the wealthy apolitical merchant, Antonio Luis, in a "marriage of convenience" with Crato's otherwise hostile landowners, violently deposed the city's prefect, also a merchant, Col. José Belém de

Figueiredo. Belém—as an outsider who was born and raised in Milagres—was intensely disliked in Crato, because neither his unmerited rise to power in 1892 nor his subsequent control over the *município* would have been possible without the prompt and continuing support of Furtado, his political mentor. In the following decade, after Belém became Third Vice President of Ceará State, the Crato–Milagres axis saw to it that political power and wealth were evenly fed back into the predominantly commercial- and pastoral-based economies of the two respective cities. When Antonio Luis and his landowner allies of Crato decided to move against Belém, Furtado rushed to the side of his protégé with several hundred armed *cabras*. After Belém's bloody defeat on 29 June 1904, the vanquished ex-*chefe* and Furtado regrouped their forces to invade Crato with eight hundred men. But news of the secret plot leaked out. Crato's victorious new prefect, Antonio Luis, hastily mustered an "army" more than a thousand men strong and forced Furtado into shameless retreat before even a single shot was fired. This humiliation, greater than defeat itself, and the subsequent cutback of power and wealth to Milagres once Belém was ousted, gnawed deeply at Furtado who now sought revenge. Thus, *vingança* (revenge) and the desperate desire for Milagres' economic comeback at any price, clearly accounted for Furtado's readiness to support Dr. Floro at Coxá in 1908 as well as to assume the leadership of the three-sided *coligação* of 1909.

Furtado's counterparts in Missão-Velha (also a former ally of the ex-chief Belém) and Barbalha no less resented Antonio Luis' immense political power in Valley affairs. His supremacy, the trio alleged, could not be attributed to Crato's more numerous electorate nor to the powerful post of deputy to the State Assembly which Antonio Luis inherited from Col. Belém and had assumed and held in full regalia since 1905. To the contrary, contended the trio, the Crato chief's power as the state oligarchy's patronage broker for the entire Cariry was due primarily to the special favors extravagantly accorded him by his first cousin, the Governor of Ceará, Dr. Accioly.[35] In addition, the traditional pastoral interests in the Cariry Valley, typified by Col. Domingos Furtado, attributed their declining fortunes to the growing wealth, power, and competitive expansion of Crato's merchants, symbolized by Col. Antonio Luis, into many sectors of the Valley economy.[36] Furthermore, the merchant forces in the primarily agriculture-based *municípios* of Missão Velha and Barbalha entered the triple alliance with a view to increasing their own shares of mercantile profits, once Crato was whittled down to size.

These factors lay behind the three-sided *coligação* that planned to attack Crato in May 1909 in the name of Coxá and the absent Patriarch. Each contender, the trio and Crato, summarily proceeded to recruit more than a thousand armed *capangas* from its usual sources of supply in the neighboring backlands of Pernambuco and Paraíba. As each faction made ready for the showdown, Padre Cícero was urgently summoned to return. However, the conflict never erupted. Thanks to the conciliatory initiatives of three Barbalha merchants, probably instigated at Governor Accioly's request, immediate violence was averted. However, a most tenuous and uneasy truce set in.[37]

The prevailing enmity was not the only change to greet the Patriarch upon his arrival in Joaseiro on 18 July 1909. The first edition of *O Rebate*, the hamlet's first weekly newspaper, rolled off the press that same day sporting a front-page portrait of the cleric.[38] Under the editorship of Fr. Joaquim de Alencar Peixoto, a maverick Crato priest and bitter political enemy of Col. Antonio Luis, who had come to Joaseiro in 1907, *Rebate's* debut marked the yearnings of Joaseiro's merchants for municipal autonomy.[39]

The appearance of *Rebate*, like the political consequences of Coxá, had occurred without the Patriarch's awareness, and indeed, during his absence. Nonetheless, these two circumstances—"faits accomplis"—were portrayed to Padre Cícero by Fr. Peixoto and Dr. Floro as irrevocable signs that only municipal autonomy could secure peace for Joaseiro, the Coxá fields for the Patriarch, and full satisfaction for the hamlet's merchants whose expanding trade had placed them on an almost equal economic footing with Crato. The arguments evidently had merit because within the week of his return, the Patriarch confidentially telegraphed Governor Accioly to request the hamlet's elevation to municipal status. The oligarch cautiously deferred the decision to Crato's Antonio Luis who, in turn, summarily refused to deal with the issue, but tactically and tactfully promised to consider it the following year.[40]

Perhaps lost upon the Patriarch was the fact that his exchange of telegrams with Gov. Accioly marked his first steps into politics. But, once again motivations other than political lay at the root of this decisive action. On the one hand, his journay to Rio de Janeiro had not met with the success which he expected Providence and the Virgin to accord him. To his dismay, the ailing and aged Dom Joaquim who had sworn to defeat the cleric's goal, unexpectedly arrived in Rio de Janeiro during the Patriarch's stay. Once in the "marvelous city," the bishop earnestly and defiantly campaigned against the erection of a bishopric in Joaseiro.[41] On the other hand, despite Dom Joaquim's encouragement, Crato had not yet succeeded in raising sufficient funds for the patrimony. Since Rome would not likely grant a benefice to paupers, there was a slight chance that Padre Cícero might still succeed. These two considerations seem to have led the Patriarch to believe that Joaseiro's political independence might conceivably increase his influence both in bringing the see to Joaseiro and ultimately winning back his clerical status.[42]

The "Satan of Joaseiro" and his "Alter Ego"

Shortly after the Patriarch's return, however, new hostilities between him and the hierarchy erupted. On 26 August 1909, Dom Manuel Lopes, Ceará's coadjutor-bishop and aide-de-camp of the ailing Dom Joaquim, arrived in Crato on a pastoral visit.[43] The following day orthodoxy fired the first volley in its new campaign. One of the priests in the bishop's entourage, known to be of intelligence and education, mounted the pulpit erected in the public square in front of the Crato church. Before thousands of persons assembled there for the week-long outdoor mission services, he "began his sermon in the following manner: 'Proud and noble people of Crato, I beg your permission to speak about the filthy rabble of Joaseiro who live guided by Satan.' "[44] Thus, under the guise of a holy mission and pastoral visit, the hierarchy went to war against the "Satan of Joaseiro" intent on defeating his bid for the "Bishopric of the Cariry."

But the virulent diatribe did not go unchallenged. Under the *nom de plume* of Manuel Ferreira de Figueiredo, Dr. Floro, the one-time journalist, took to the pages of O Rebate. In three combative articles, impeccable in their logic, rhetoric, and militancy, the Bahian physician roundly denounced the hypocrisy of the hierarchy and stoutly defended the Patriarch of Joaseiro.[45] The effect of this *"justa defesa"* was the immediate ascent of Dr. Floro into public prominence: Until his death in 1926, he was to be the most important single figure in Joaseiro's history, second only to Padre Cícero. Understandably, his enemies, whose own political ambitions were frustrated because of the favors showered upon him by Padre Cícero, denounced his ascendency over the Patriarch and denigrated the newcomer as the cleric's "alter ego." As such, Dr. Floro was depicted as an ambitious, self-seeking adventurer who, it was claimed, rose to glory and national political prominence "behind the shadow of the most ancient cassock of the Cariry."[46] Dr. Floro's influence over the Patriarch is an undisputed fact. However, it cannot be accounted for simply in terms of Dr. Floro's ambition or Padre Cícero's gullibility. Floro's ascent as the *de facto* political chief of Joaseiro until 1926 was possible only because of a variety of circumstances that it is important to recall here.

First of all, while Floro's multiple role in the Coxá enterprise—lawyer, researcher, and when necessary, armed defender—certainly made him indispensable to the Patriarch intent on erecting a diocese, it was not the sole cause fostering the early intimacy and friendship between the two unlike personalities. Perhaps of greater significance was Floro's little-known first defense of the priest against the church hierarchy during the course of 1908. It was prompted by the following circumstance.

Shortly after his arrival in Joaseiro, Dr. Floro made the acquaintance of D. Hermínia Marques de Gouveia, a young woman from nearby Jardim whose childless marriage had earlier drawn her to Joaseiro in expectation of a miracle.[47] Her excessive piety and devotion had quickly made her one of the Patriarch's favorite spiritual daughters. When the cleric was taken gravely ill, in either 1905 or 1906, D. Hermínia and other devout women made a *promessa* to the Virgin under the invocation of Our Lady of Perpetual Help: In return for Padre Cícero's recovery, a chapel would be erected at the new cemetery on the western edge of the hamlet.[48] In October 1906, after Padre Cícero was fully recuperated, he himself, convinced that the Virgin had answered the petition, ordered the construction of the chapel promised by Hermínia.[49] Shortly thereafter, however, Crato's vicar, in the name of Dom Joaquim, ordered the work to a halt. So it remained for almost two years. Then Floro arrived; Hermínia asked him to sponsor the construction and Padre Cícero agreed to finance it should Floro, as an outsider to the region, obtain the necessary ecclesiastical license. Oddly enough, the physician was granted approval, provided Padre Cícero "in no way intervened" in the matter, a condition which Floro later condemned as pure "episcopal caprice."[50] Then in mid-November 1908, as the chapel was nearing completion, D. Hermínia died.[51] In order to reward justly the holy woman's efforts and virtues, the Patriarch, with Dr. Floro's consent, decided to bury her in a sepulchre inside the new chapel. When Fr. Quintino, vicar of Crato, learned of this, he tried unsuccessfully to stop the burial.

Days later he issued a new prohibition to stop the construction of the chapel. At that point the exasperated Dr. Floro took matters into his own hand. Later, he recollected: "On that occasion, considering all that [to be] nothing but buffoonery, I resolved to finish building [the chapel] without listening to any further considerations of Padre Cícero nor of anyone else . . . I just went ahead with great satisfaction, quite ready to assume the responsibility of any consequences which, for me, no matter how serious they might be, wouldn't bother me in the least."[52]

Several months later, when the Patriarch requested permission from Dom Joaquim to consecrate the chapel, the bishop refused "because he had been informed on good authority that Padre Cícero had buried [there] the body of a prostitute."[53] That development cut deeply into the Patriarch. He turned increasingly to Floro whose audacity and loyalty, whose utter unwillingness to temporize with the "calumny and chicanery" of the men of the cloth, seemed the only antidote to their relentless persecution of the Patriarch.[54] In a word, Floro, whose evident anticlericalism ironically dovetailed with Padre Cícero's unshakable conviction in his own innocence, became from this moment in 1908 until his death, the forceful and faithful advocate of the Patriarch against the church. Whether in fact Floro's attacks against the hierarchy more often jeopardized Padre Cícero's cause is not in question here; they were sufficient proofs of fidelity for the Patriarch to bestow upon the newcomer his lasting trust, friendship, and gratitude.

A second factor helps explain Floro's increasing intimacy with the priest: Padre Cícero's two surviving friends and defenders, José Lôbo and José Marrocos, were becoming less evident in his life. It is difficult to determine whether Floro subtly promoted that rupture or whether the Patriarch's bygone associates decided to keep their distance out of resentment towards the newcomer who now enjoyed the aging cleric's favor; but the signs of that rupture are indisputable.

José Lôbo, for example, increasingly lived at home in seclusion. There, the one-time founder of the Legion of the Cross devoted his time to answering the hundreds of letters that daily arrived for the Patriarch from the poor and clergyless *sertanejos* of the Brazilian Northeast. But as more and more of the region's destitute came to Joaseiro on pilgrimage, Lôbo's tasks became less numerous and significant.[55] Shortly after Dr. Floro took up residence in the Patriarch's household in 1908, old Zé Lôbo either fabricated or indeed experienced a bitter coldness in his friendship with Padre Cícero.

One day Lôbo confronted the priest and threatened that unless his supposed coldness thawed, he would never again cross the Patriarch's threshold. The cleric, unaware of any change in his affections toward Lôbo, strongly denied that their friendship had altered. Days later, rumors, perhaps prompted by the jealousy of newcomers, alleged that Zé Lôbo had tried to poison the Patriarch. Padre Cícero publicly condemned the accusation as false and libelous; but Lôbo saw this as the "last straw." Thereafter, until his death in 1918, he never again set foot in the Patriarch's home.[56]

In the case of José Marrocos, the souring of an old friendship was as sudden as it was strange and unexepected. Before the Patriarch's journey to Rio de Janeiro, it was Marrocos who had labored long, hard, and hurriedly to prepare the cleric's defense of the new diocese in Joaseiro. It was to José Marrocos that Padre Cícero had confided his hope for success on the very eve of his departure. Then, on 19 July 1909, the day after the Patriarch returned and *Rebate* made its debut, Marrocos plaintively wrote his long-time friend from neighboring Barbalha:[57]

All day Saturday [17 July 1909] I waited for the invitation to attend the inaugural celebration of Joaseiro's newspaper: I wanted to seal with my presence the new progress of a place that I have always admired and for whose prosperity I have labored to the small degree that it was possible for me [to do]. I waited in vain, . . . disappointed if not most distraught, I accepted other obligations. . . . How deeply I regretted not to witness this latest advance of Joaseiro: but believe me that neither am I nor can I be indifferent and so right from here, I exclaim: Viva Joaseiro!

Deeply wounded, Marrocos nonetheless attempted to regain his influence over the Patriarch. Later in 1909, he completed a scathing attack against Dom Joaquim which he intended to publish in the newspapers of Fortaleza.[58] But his bid to win the Patriarch's favor by recalling the "past struggle against a common enemy" and by rekindling the controversy over the validity of the miracles of 1889–1891, was anachronistic by comparison to Floro's more persuasive tactics of contrasting the Patriarch's personal integrity to the hierarchy's hypocrisy, avoiding completely the old thorn of the miracles. As a consequence, Marrocos' last unsung diatribe, cryptically entitled "Joaseiro: The Open Letter of Snr. Nicodemos—The Reply of José de Arimatea" only went to press as a pamphlet with a most limited circulation.[59]

Marrocos, however, stubbornly persisted. In early 1910, the famous educator of the Cariry closed down his private *colégio* in Barbalha and opened its doors in Joaseiro. In greater proximity to his old friend, Marrocos, it appears, may have regained some of his bygone influence: at least, on 15 August, a political rally was scheduled to take place at his new *colégio* in Joaseiro. The rally was never convened: on the afternoon of 14 August, José Marrocos died suddenly. The coroner's report listed the cause of death as pneumonia, but Marrocos' state of reputed good health the previous morning later gave rise to rumors that Dr. Floro had poisoned the venerable professor.[60] This accusation seems groundless since Dr. Floro was in Missão Velha the day Marrocos died; only on 16 August did he return to Joaseiro for the sexagenarian's burial and on that occasion the doctor delivered the principal funeral oration.[61] The motive attributed, many years later, to Floro was that Marrocos' repeated counsel had kept Padre Cícero from entering politics and the ranks of Governor Accioly's *Partido Republicano Conservador*.[62] Whether this be true or not, it clearly illustrates that Floro's ascendancy caused or coincided with the rupture between the Patriarch and his former intimates;[63] thereafter, politics rather than miracles became the order of the day.

A third and final factor accounting for Floro's ascendancy was inherent in the structural changes that were engendered by the marked penetration of modern capitalistic forms into the *sertão* and especially into the Cariry Valley with the dawn of the twentieth century. Despite frequent economic setbacks caused by droughts, Europe's demand for *maniçoba* rubber, hides, and cotton, as well as for markets capable of absorbing its exports of credit, financial services, and manufactures sparked new economic life into the backlands between 1880 and 1920.[64] As the new-found riches of rural landowners helped stimulate the rise of a new class of aggressive, money-oriented, small-town merchants, the latter's growing profits soon enabled the *commerciantes* to vie with the *fazendeiros* for local political power. As we have seen, during the "politics of the governors," the Republic, too, had initially invested the *município* with greater autonomy, new fiscal prerogatives and an increased number of bureaucratic posts which precipitated, even within the same political party, often violent and bloody factional strife for control of local government.

The "new era" of republicanism and capitalist penetration necessarily altered the style of backland politics. The traditional methods of political coercion, intensified by the growth of regional political spoils, were increasingly out of step with the times. The land-based *coronéis* had now to legitimate their power in terms of new republican laws. They were increasingly forced to contend with the new "rules of the game," the scattered pockets of "public opinion" in the coastal cities, and the growing demands for material advances that began to emerge even among the small literate sectors of backland society. Increasingly, then, the backland *coronel* came to rely on the services of the rising numbers of the rhetoric-prone but talented *bacharéis,* the graduates of the coastal university faculties of law and medicine. To these middle-class *bacharéis,* whose omnipresence and ambition marked the politics of the republican period and whose opportunism and corruption later led critics to equate the decadence of republicanism with the "plague of the *bacharéis,*" service to the *coronel* opened the avenues to power, prominence, and success.[65]

The Cariry typified this social and political transformation of the *sertão* during the Old Republic (1889–1930).[66] Lawyers such as Raimundo Gomes de Matos and Raul de Souza Carvalho became the spokesmen of local political chiefs; while in Crato, the young physician, Dr. Irineu Pinheiro, served Col. Antonio Luis Alves Pequeno in economic matters as founder and director (in 1921) of the city's first bank. Frequently, the intimacy between the *bacharel* and the *coronel* led to the *bacharel's* marriage to a close relative of the *coronel*: matrimony not only enhanced the professional's rise to success, it also guaranteed the artless political chief of his ambitious aide's loyalty.[67] In the first decade of the twentieth century, the principal task of the *bacharéis* was the verbal defense of their political chiefs. Everywhere throughout the Cariry, newspapers proliferated in lucid testimony to recent economic advances and as political combat became increasingly rhetorical and thus less bloody, less costly, and more emulative of the values of the urban coast: Between 1904 and 1909 more than eleven newspapers appeared in just three cities of the Valley. Of these, two in Crato, two in Barbalha and *O Rebate* in Joaseiro achieved considerable longevity and rarely missed the weekly publication date.[68]

Dr. Floro, a graduate of the faculty of medicine in Bahia, was a *bacharel* who had arrived in the Cariry in the moment of transition. His profession gave him access to the homes of Joaseiro's rich and poor; his clinic and pharmacy ingratiated him to the villagers and the Pariarch, who also welcomed him not only as the hamlet's first resident doctor, but as a sure sign of the *sertão's* overdue right to progress.[69] Dr. Floro followed the same road to political success that was typical of all other backland physicians and lawyers of this period.[70] In addition, his earlier experience as a journalist and public notary, as well as personal qualities of ambition, audacity, and loyalty were to serve himself, the Patriarch and Joaseiro admirably in its political struggle for independence from Crato.

7

Joaseiro
Bids for Autonomy

A Tale of Two Cities

Understandably, Joaseiro's bid for autonomy from Crato unleashed a most bitter rivalry between the two cities.[1] This rivalry nominally originated with the "religious question" of Joaseiro, but at its roots lay a series of basically economic attritions between the two towns that dated from 1896. That year, the "fanatical" squatters of Padre Cícero were reported to have made ready for an armed invasion of the fertile lands of Crato. That threat, it will be remembered, prompted Crato's then Vicar, Msgr. Alexandrino, to urge Gov. Accioly to dispatch troops in order to protect the "Pearl of the Cariry."[2] The Coxá events of 1908 and the pastoral visit of August 1909 now served to rekindle that deeply rooted enmity. The pastoral visit, it must be noted, not only embittered relations between the hierarchy and the Patriarch, as we have already seen, but also, and more significantly, completed the economic rupture between Crato and Joaseiro. Apparently the missionary's attack on the people of Joaseiro as "rabble" and blind "followers of Satan" resulted in the calling of a total strike against Crato's economy. The *romeiros* who tilled the fields and, as domestics, staffed the homes of well-to-do Cratenses returned to Joaseiro. Furthermore, the entire population of Joaseiro boycotted Crato's weekly fair: Joaseiro's artisans refused to sell their wares there while all Joaseirenses refused to buy there. Only upon Padre Cícero's command did the situation return to a short-lived normalcy in September 1909.[3]

The economic boycott, moreover, underscored the fundamental cause of cleavage between the two cities: on the one hand, an autonomous Joaseiro would seriously undermine Crato's regional hegemony; on the other, the merchants and, to a lesser extent, the artisans of Joaseiro believed that their economic growth merited them commensurate political power.[4] Crato's fears were articulated in November and December 1909. Col. Antonio Luis' political journal, the weekly *Correio do Cariry,* accused Joaseiro of planning to withhold payment of municipal taxes. Such action, the *Correio* argued, was a clear threat to overthrow the legally constituted authorities of both Crato and the state government. *O Rebate* retorted immediately, denouncing the charge as a "libelous, incredible and monstrous rumor" designed to indispose the government of Gov. Accioly against Joaseiro, and to provide him and Col. Antonio Luis with the pretext to "invade Joaseiro with soldiers, inundate it with blood, sack, rob and reduce the [hamlet] to nought." *Rebate,* however, remained silent about whether Joaseiro would refuse to pay its taxes.[5]

The omission was evidently purposeful. For in early 1910, Joaseiro ceased speaking guardedly of its aspirations. In a May article of *O Rebate,* Flavio Gouveia, another of Dr. Floro's *noms de plume,* if not *nom de guerre,* bitterly denounced "the detestable, petty, egoistic and idiotic" politics of Antonio Luis. This unparalleled attack against the Valley "king-maker" had been provoked by the arrival of a state police battalion in Crato earlier that month. Floro alleged that Col. Antonio Luis clearly intended to deploy the battalion against Joaseiro as the first step in the campaign to liquidate Crato's traditional enemy, Col. Domingos Furtado of Milagres. By linking Joaseiro's destiny to the fate of Milagres, Floro clearly resurrected the old threat of a Milagres-Joaseiro alliance, whose foundations, in retrospect, he had carefully laid at the time of Coxá. Dr. Floro then astutely proceeded to champion, not his own political ambitions, but the aspirations of the hamlet's merchants, who, like himself, were on the whole *adventícios* in Joaseiro:[6]

This is a great city yet due to the irrationality of fate Joaseiro still remains in the lowest category of a village. [This is due to the despicable politics of Col. Antonio Luis Alves Pequeno.] . . .
Such politics will send him groveling into the mud. Yes! . . .

Why, if Joaseiro is twice as large as the city of Crato, which reputedly is the first among the cities of the arid *sertões* [encompassing] four or five states, [and why, if it] provides the tax collector with an income larger than [Crato's, why then must Joaseiro remain] in the shadows of disregard with the status of a hamlet?

What a sad antagonism of fate! . . .

[If there is any explanation to this irony], it is because Crato is the octopus that keeps sucking the very lifeblood of Joaseiro. *(Bracketed material is my own paraphrase.)*

Crato was indeed in a dilemma. The threat of both a tax boycott and a Milagres–Joaseiro alliance was now complicated by Padre Cícero's repeated request that Col. Antonio Luis fulfill his 1909 promise to support Joaseiro's request for autonomy at the opening session of Ceará's Legislative Assembly in July–August 1910. That June, Crato responded with a last-ditch effort to scuttle the bid by trying to divide the population of Joaseiro over the issue of municipal independence. The split in Joaseiro between the *filhos da terra* and the *adventícios* entered into Crato's strategy. On 12 June, the *Correio* accused *O Rebate's* editor, Fr. Joaquim de Peixoto Alencar, the maverick Cratense priest and enemy of Col. Antonio Luis, of seeking the prefecture of Joaseiro.[7] There was much truth in the charge and considerable political wisdom in raising it at that moment. The *adventícios* of Joaseiro strongly disliked Peixoto whose renegade status in Joaseiro did not entirely absolve him of strong links to his native city of Crato. The *filhos da terra*, for their part, were resentful that a Cratense should become Joaseiro's first prefect. Furthermore, both factions had little respect for the priest because of his questionable integrity and allegedly unbecoming liaisons with lower class women.[8] Even Gov. Accioly was horrified at the prospect of Fr. Peixoto as Joaseiro's first prefect. While the oligarch seemed willing to grant the hamlet autonomy, he could hardly add insult to injury by handing over the prefecture of Joaseiro to a maverick priest who was the renowned enemy of the Governor's first cousin, Col. Antonio Luis.[9]

The *Correio's* divisionary tactic was hotly repudiated by Fr. Peixoto himself: It was an infamy to spread rumors that Joaseiro's editor-in-chief plotted to stir up the newcomers to the point of expelling the native sons of Joaseiro. Nonetheless, the *Correio* forced Peixoto to deny publicly his own ambitions.[10] Furthermore, he was obliged to back in the press as Joaseiro's candidate for the prefecture Col. José André de Figueiredo, a native son, and for the intendant of the future city council (*câmara municipal*), Col. Cincinato Silva, a newcomer, both merchants. Fabricated under pressure from Crato, the new ticket cemented an alliance between newcomers and native sons.[11]

A Second Bid: A Declaration of Independence, Come What May!

Peixoto's forced withdrawal and the proclamation of the conciliatory Figueiredo-Silva ticket cleared the way for Joaseiro's second bid for autonomy. In late July 1910, the Patriarch moved to mollify the hesitant Accioly by yielding to the Governor's viewpoint that the police battalion, recently stationed in Crato, was intended to rid the area of *cangaceiros* and not to attack Joaseiro.[12] Despite this and other concessions—including one which assured Accioly of Joaseiro's electoral support for future PRC-C candidates—it was still uncertain whether the Governor was willing to grant Joaseiro autonomy.[13] To precipitate a formal decision, plans were made for massive public rallies in Joaseiro, a tactic clearly aimed at putting pressure on the indecisive oligarch. The first of these was scheduled for 15 August 1910 at José Marrocos' *colégio*.[14] His sudden death the day before transformed a rally into a burial.

Marrocos' death, however, was a boon to Col. Antonio Luis. His political aides, led by his youthful nephew-in-law, Raul de Sousa Carvalho— Crato's interim district judge and key political journalist of the *Correio*— entered the deceased's long-time residence in Crato. Under the legal guise of taking inventory of Marrocos' estate, the *bacharéis* adamantly prevented entry to the emissaries of Padre Cícero who had claimed the right to take possession of Marrocos' effects. The Patriarch became further irate when Antonio Luis' aides made off with the late professor's most valuable possession: an apparently worthless wooden box. In it were the "miraculously" bloodstained cloths once conserved in the glass urn in Joaseiro and subsequently stolen from the Crato tabernacle in the distant year of 1892. That theft, which had conferred *ipso facto* excommunication upon Marrocos, now provided Col. Antonio Luis with the strongest possible weapon against Joaseiro.[15]

The rediscovery of the cloths could not have come at a more propitious moment. Just five days after Marrocos' death, Ceará's governor, apparently pleased by the Patriarch's agreement to accept the police battalion in Crato and support the PRC-C's candidates, had now telegraphed Padre Cícero of the Legislative Assembly's intention to elevate Joaseiro to municipal status.[16] When Col. Antonio Luis, who went to Fortaleza to take his seat in the Assembly learned of Accioly's decision, he refused to consent. He alleged that he was unprepared to settle the boundaries of the would-be *município,* and in deference to him, the Assembly agreed to postpone Joaseiro's bid.[17] The Crato chief's obstinacy and apparent readiness to risk a severe reaction in Joaseiro were clearly based on his control over the police battalion stationed in Crato, and, more significantly, on his possession of the little wooden box. That "find" loomed large in Padre Cícero's mind: Whether the cloths' state of conservation would prove the twenty-one year old miracles to be a hoax or a truth was only incidental to the Patriarch's fear that his nemesis, Dom Joaquim, might in some way come to possess them.[18] As a consequence, the Patriarch might well exchange the proverbial kingdom for the wooden box; at least he might resign himself more readily to the second consecutive postponement of Joaseiro's autonomy if he could possess the "find." Later that August, an unsigned telegram from Fortaleza undoubtedly penned by Col. Antonio Luis, reached the Patriarch: "Padre Cícero, Joaseiro: stop the useless quarrel in the press; what you are looking for is in safe hands."[19] The Crato chief was true to his word: shortly after his return from Fortaleza, he secretly met with the Patriarch at a rendezvous halfway on the road between Crato and Joaseiro. There, the Patriarch re-possessed the treasure that he was parted from only at death.[20]

But Col. Antonio Luis had badly miscalculated: first he overestimated the Patriarch's ability and willingness to contain Joaseiro's wrath after it became known that the Crato chief had forced Accioly into an about-face. Second, he underestimated the political repercussions of his stubbornness upon Joaseiro. The Patriarch, in truth, proved no longer able to restrain Fr. Peixoto, Dr. Floro, and the hamlet's merchants from defiantly opting for independence, regardless of Accioly's reversal. On 30 August—the same day on which news reached Joaseiro of the Assembly's contravention—fifteen thousand persons assembled in Joaseiro's *Praça da Liberdade* (Freedom Square). They marched on the chapel of Our Lady of Sorrows to pray for victory, then paraded to the offices of *O Rebate* to hear the inflammatory

declaration of independence unleashed by Pexito and Floro and finally
snaked their way to the homes of José André, Cincinato Silva, and Padre
Cícero amidst songs and cheers of defiance against Crato. On the following
day, at the very moment in which Col. Antonio Luis had arrived from
Fortaleza, fifteen thousand persons reassembled and marched again in favor
of independence. Then, on 3 September, the Crato chief tactlessly dispatched
the police battalion into Joaseiro under the pretext of collecting taxes. Elec-
trified, the entire hamlet emptied itself into Freedom Square, went on the
alert and stood in armed vigil throughout the night to repel the imminent
attack.[21] If Padre Cícero had previously hesitated to allow his followers to
vent their vengeance on Antonio Luis, the threat of an armed attack dis-
abused him of his pacific inclinations. Although a native son of Crato,
steeped in its history and local traditions, the Patriarch now unequivocally
asserted that Joaseiro was his homeland: "I am a son of Crato, that is certain,
but Joaseiro is my son."[22]

Another equally important factor accounted for his sudden willingness
to take a political stand. Two days earlier, the Patriarch had learned that
Joaseiro's most prominent landowner and *filho da terra* had, unknown to
the cleric, attempted to champion Joaseiro's autonomy in Fortaleza. Maj.
Joaquim Bezerra, intensely disliked by Col. Antonio Luis and the *adventícios* of Joaseiro, had tried to outflank the Patriarch and rekindle his 1907
bid for the prefecture of the future *município*.[23] News of Maj. Joaquim's
"betrayal" left the Patriarch no alternative. Immediately he personally demanded that Gov. Accioly now render justice to Joaseiro.[24] When the
oligarch feigningly replied that the lack of agreement over the new *município's* borders had obliged him to pigeonhole the promised autonomy
legislation, Padre Cícero sanctioned the use of the hamlet's sole weapon:
Henceforth, he telegraphed Accioly, Joaseiro will no longer pay taxes to
the city council of Crato; moreover, he asserted, either the oligarch must
immediately order Col. Antonio Luis to withdraw the police battalion from
Joaseiro, or else "assume full responsibility for the dire consequences of
Snr. Antonio Luis' misplaced capriciousness and political adventurism."[25]

Joaseiro's Independence:
Backland Coronéis and the Tottering "Simpleton"

The Patriarch's decisiveness had now set the stage for several months of
bitter controversy. The relentless invective of Crato's *Correio* and Joaseiro's

Rebate set a new low in political libel. No one was sacred—Antonio Luis and Padre Cícero, bishops and *bacharéis,* priests and politicians—all fell victim to political vituperation, as the "journalist—*bacharéis*" churned up and wallowed in the muddied sties of republican politics. New Year's Day 1911 ushered in the frightful prospect that the verbal attacks might soon be turned into armed aggression: Crato, rankling under the tax boycott, threatened to raze Joaseiro.[26] On reflection, it seems unbelievable that only six months later, on 22 July 1911, Ceará's Legislative Assembly should have promulgated Law No. 1,028, by which Joaseiro was granted municipal autonomy. Credit for this success has usually gone to the Patriarch and his adamant stand against Antonio Luis. Lesser laurels were bestowed on the other momentary heroes such as Fr. Peixoto, Dr. Floro, José André, and Cincinato Silva.[27] However, in reexamining this important event in Joaseiro's history, the interplay between the regional politics of the Cariry and the changing political fortunes in Ceará State, now appear to have been of equal, if not greater, significance in Joaseiro's triumph.

As far as the political chiefs of the Cariry were concerned, Antonio Luis' success in twice reversing, at the last minute, Accioly's pledge to grant Joaseiro independence offered one more proof that "blood was thicker than water." To defeat the protected *"oligarcha mirim"* (the "little oligarch") of Crato, it was clearly necessary for Crato's rivals to unite the Cariry. For this reason, Joaseiro's defiant freedom rallies of 30 and 31 August 1910 were conspicuously attended by the political chiefs of Milagres, Missão Velha, and Barbalha,[28] the very same *coligação* (coalition) that had attempted in early May 1909 to depose Antonio Luis during Padre Cícero's journey to Rio de Janeiro. All three now stoutly defended Joaseiro's claim to autonomy. Those of Barbalha and Missão Velha, whose boundaries were contiguous to Joaseiro, readily agreed to yield a portion of their territory to the aspiring *município* in a clear attempt to pressure Antonio Luis to concede some of Crato's vast terrain to the future jurisdiction of Joaseiro.[29] Indeed, their loss was small in comparison to the gains expected. The merchant communities of thriving Barbalha and declining Missão Velha contemplated by their concession greater access to the growing market of Joaseiro, until then manipulated by the rival superior commercial thrust of Crato.[30] In the case of Col. Domingos Furtado, chief of the predominantly agro-pastoral *município* of Milagres, pure political revenge against Antonio Luis clearly motivated his support. The *coligacão's* renewed alliance with Joaseiro was not lost on other Valley chiefs. Friendly *coronéis* of Aurora,

whom Antonio Luis had allegedly tried to depose two years earlier because
of Coxá, came to the Patriarch's door in September 1910 and declared their
solidarity with Joaseiro's independence. Their visit proved an occasion for
the chiefs of Barbalha and Missão Velha to issue a second declaration of
support.[31]

The formation of the little "big four" (Barbalha, Missão Velha, Milagres, and Aurora) against Crato posed an imminent threat to many
vested interests within the "Pearl of the Cariry." Even if Crato, surrounded
by enemies, were spared from armed attack, the Patriarch's hand was now
greatly strengthened by the unwavering support of the four neighboring
municípios. Should Joaseiro's dogmatic refusal to pay taxes be seconded
by another economic boycott, Crato's agrarian and mercantile economy
would unduly suffer. For the moment, however, the dissident agrarian
interests in Crato did not diverge openly from Antonio Luis' position and
as a result the hostilities between the two cities continued to mount during
the next five months. Tensions indeed ran high as the *Correio* and *Rebate*
carried on their reckless feud (which seems, in retrospect, to have been
inflamed more by the enmities between the respective cities' ambitious
bacharéis than between their patrons). Nonetheless, two journalistic disputes
were to bring dissident agrarian forces within Crato to action. The first,
launched by the *Correio,* renewed an earlier charge that Fr. Peixoto had
commissioned his brother to disfigure a *Correio* reporter who had slandered
O Rebate's chief editor. As the name of Alencar Peixoto was slandered, a
veritable flood of invective cascaded from *Rebate*. Then, in January and
February 1911, after *Correio* countered with accusations against Padre
Cícero's integrity, Dr. Floro ignited the second round with a series of five
articles, entitled "De Àgus Abaixo, Não Irá o Joaseiro," his most celebrated
defense of Joaseiro's right to independence, at any price![32]

At this point, Crato's most prominent citizen called a halt to Antonio
Luis' folly. Col. Nelson Franca de Alencar, the uncle of Fr. Peixoto and
Crato's wealthiest landowner, mobilized Crato's agrarian faction and demanded an end to hostilities. The rich *fazendeiro* was not to be crossed,
nor his proud family name, borne by Fr. Alencar Peixoto, sullied in Crato's
"bacharelesque" press. Col. Nelson, an ardent and intimate friend of Crato's
ex-*chefe* Belém, had supported Antonio Luis' 1904 coup only with reluctance. Family pressures had accounted for his ultimate decisiveness, after
which Col. Nelson's dozens of armed henchmen won the day for Antonio

Luis.[33] But now, after seven years of an expedient union between Crato's richest *fazendeiro* and an equally well-to-do *commerciante*, Col. Nelson and Antonio Luis once against stood in opposing camps. The Crato chief notwithstanding, Col. Nelson's brother, Col. Abdon Franca de Alencar, was dispatched to Joaseiro on 18 February 1911, at the head of a four-man delegation; it included two of Crato's most respected merchants.[34] For its part, Joaseiro was represented by the Patriarch, Fr. Peixoto, and the hamlet's prospective prefect, the powerful merchant José Andé. Both parties—in tune with each city's vested interests—quickly came to a three point agreement:[35] (1) Joaseiro would become a *município* and *comârca* (an autonomous judicial district) with agreed upon territorial limits to be set by fiat of the State Assembly at its next session in July 1911; (2) Joaseiro would pay its back taxes to Crato immediately after autonomy was granted; and (3) the feud between the *Correio* and *O Rebate* would cease immediately. (To the last issue, Col. Abdon's presence was tantamount to his nephew's consent.) Although Antonio Luis strongly opposed the terms of surrender, Cols. Nelson and Abdon Franca de Alencar adamantly held out their continuing support of the "little oligarch" in exchange for his consent. After March 1911, when Joaseiro finally agreed to barter its claim for the *comârca* in return for both *termo status* (a sub-court dependent on the Crato *comârca*) and Crato's guarantee to yield adequate territory, the feud between the two cities ceased.[36]

However, Joaseiro's victory cannot be solely attributed to the division inflicted on Crato's landowners and merchants by the hamlet's alliance with the little "big four." That regional alliance literally dislodged Ceará's Governor from his calculated temporizing on behalf of his first cousin in Crato. In fact, the month after the four chiefs publicly took Joaseiro's side, Accioly hurriedly promised the Patriarch (in October 1910) "to exert myself to harmonize the interests of Crato and Joaseiro in order to see the aspirations of the inhabitants of those localities soon satisfied."[37] Political astuteness rather than altruism motivated the oligarch. In his letter to the Patriarch, Accioly repeatedly lamented the evident political fission that had developed in the Cariry, the traditional stronghold of the PRC-C. His preference was to see "all friends united in the advancement of our common cause," a veiled allusion to the need for electoral solidarity within local PRC-C ranks. Accioly, however, was clearly aware of the alternative: his continued support of Antonio Luis and a failure to resolve the Crato–Joaseiro feud could conceivably cost the PRC-C the electoral loss of five Valley outposts. Furthermore, the combined electorates (traditionally manipulated by the local chiefs) of Joaseiro, Milagres, Missão Velha, Barbalha, and Aurora surpassed that of solitary Crato. Should the five towns seek vengeance against Antonio Luis—who since 1905 was the kingpin of Accioly's political empire in the Cariry—the PRC-C and the oligarch might easily suffer defeat in the Valley.

This fear of political defeat was neither premature nor unfounded. Congressional elections were only three months away, while the gubernatorial race was to be decided at the polls just four months after that, in April 1912. What disturbed the Governor about those forthcoming contests was the likelihood that they would galvanize his opponents into a serious threat to his authority. Indeed, such a threat had been only a feeble one in 1907. That year, Accioly bulldozed through the Assembly a state constitutional change that would allow him to succeed himself as governor after the fixed elections of 1908.[38] When the oligarch in fact won his third term as governor, the middle-class professionals in Fortaleza were compelled to close ranks behind the new moneyed merchants and dissident traditional landowners in open opposition to Accioly whom they increasingly dared to mock as "The Simpletion," (*O Babaquara*).[39] By late 1911, Accioly's long and singular control over Ceará's politics and political machinery since 1888 had been finally put into question; moreover, the system's senile weakness had finally united Accioly's enemies—not as yet into a formal political party—but rather as an influential nucleus under the banner of Fortaleza's cantankerous and muckraking eight year old daily, *O Unitário*.[40] Its clarion call for the defeat of the "oligarchia acciolyno" had been greatly enhanced by the nationwide "civilianist" presidential campaign of 1910. Although army Marshal Hermes da Fonseca then triumphed at the polls, it was his opponent, the renowned Brazilian statesman, Rui Barbosa, who had championed in 1910 the cause of the urban coastal populations throughout Brazil in their "latent revolt against old abuses, vices and errors . . . which had persisted since the downfall of the monarchy."[41]

In view of the concrete possibility that an *Unitário*-backed slate on the coast might now expediently ally itself with Cariry's anti-Crato forces in the elections of 1912, Accioly quickened his pace to resolve the Valley feud. Although only indirect documentary evidence has been found, there can be little doubt that the oligarch had had a hand in splitting Crato's ranks to the detriment of his own cousin Antonio Luis! It was not accidental that one of the four members of the Crato peace delegation was Pedro Gomes de Mattos, the brother of Accioly's favorite son-in-law, the celebrated Cearense lawyer, Raimundo Gomes de Mattos.[42] Also, Crato's physician-banker, Dr. Irineu Pinheiro, a blood relative of both Accioly and Antonio Luis, had played an important "behind-the-scenes" role in sending the peace mission to Joaseiro.[43] That family ties should have played such a significant role was typical of Brazilian society and politics; however, such ties clearly did not prevail over the overriding political and economic realities which consciously motivated all the parties in question.

Padre Cícero, Coronel of the Biggest Bailiwick in Ceará

After February 1911, the peace was rigidly enforced. *Correio* and *Rebate* strictly abided by the agreement and refrained from printing any political news whatsoever. Only the April publication of *polyantheas* to commemorate Fr. Peixoto's birthday and Dr. Floro's sixth anniversary as a physician offered any indication that a power struggle for the prefecture was taking place in Joaseiro.[44] In May, *Rebate's* extensive coverage of the PRC-C's platform hastily issued eleven months before the scheduled 1912 elections, was symptomatic of both Accioly's deteriorating position in Fortaleza and the growing ties between the oligarch and the Patriarch.[45] Beneath the deceptive Cariry calm, an issue critical to Joaseiro and Fortaleza, alike, remained unresolved, Joaseiro's choice for prefect.

On 27 August 1911, the storm broke. *Rebate's* lead article was addressed "To the Public." Having secretly set the type, Fr. Peixoto, editor-in-chief and aspiring prefect, adamantly denied rumors that he had broken with Padre Cícero. Bitterly resentful, the maverick cleric contended that it was the Patriarch who now reneged on an old promise to make him Joaseiro's first prefect. The return of the "little wooden box," Peixoto alleged, had been made contingent on his political liquidation. In ironic fulmination, he denied that Padre Cícero had now favored the "political goldminer," Dr. Floro because, should he do so, wrote Peixoto vengefully, the Patriarch would thereby "negate everything he has ever stood for."[46]

Whether Padre Cícero really intended to make Floro prefect is unimportant. Peixoto's revelations had now equally ruled out Floro's selection as well as his own. Of the remaining two possible choices, Maj. Joaquim

Bezerra's betrayal as well as his unpopularity with Col. Antonio Luis and Joaseiro's *adventícios* necessarily eliminated him; Padre Cícero had firmly seen to that in June 1911.[47] There remained only Col. José André, Joaseiro's wealthiest merchant whom Peixoto had ostensibly championed as prefect as early as 30 August 1910. But his subsequent elimination is wrapped in mystery. Three probable causes for his demotion from prefect to chairman (*intendente*) of Joaseiro's city council seem plausible.[48] First, the choice of José André, a prominent *filho da terra*, would very likely cause deep resentment among Joaseiro's merchant community which was overwhelmingly composed of *adventícios*. Indeed, Padre Cícero alone was capable of preventing the detrimental split. Second, with José André in control of the new *município*, Floro's ambitions would be sharply delimited. For the *Bahiano*, whose fine and fearless hand was present, if not fully made public, in every phase of the struggle against Crato and in the negotiations with Accioly and local Valley chiefs, the only alternative left was to have Padre Cícero himself assume the post. Then Floro's influence over the Patriarch could clearly guarantee his own ambitions. Finally José André, the merchant, was not the optimum choice for the "Simpleton" of Fortaleza. There, the Commercial Association of Ceará, a voluntary organization of merchants throughout the state had swiftly become a major component of the anti-Accioly forces.[49] Unless the Patriarch himself retained control of Joaseiro, Accioly's strength both there and in the Cariry might be easily put into question. Shortly thereafter Padre Cícero assumed the prefecture of Joaseiro. Under the insistent prodding of Dr. Floro and the Governor, the Patriarch wrote to Accioly's son, then state Secretary of Interior: "Personal ambitions here allowed that I, in response to the wish of the people, officially assume the political direction [of Joaseiro] in order to prevent setbacks in the forward march of political affairs."[50]

Indeed, Accioly's interest in Padre Cícero's ascent to the prefecture and the "forward march of political affairs" cannot be underestimated. The long delay between the State Assembly's vote to grant Joaseiro autonomy in July 1911 and the formal inauguration of the new *município* only in October 1911, strongly hints at the oligarch's feverish maneuvers to heal the wounds of Valley chiefs. Indeed, a united Cariry represented about a third of the state electorate; its unity in the 1912 elections might well outweigh the sharp factionalism that was mounting elsewhere throughout the state.[51] Cleverly, the oligarch planted the initiative for the signing of a collective pact in Joaseiro in order to secure the Valley chiefs' support of the PRC-C with Col. Joaquim Sant'Anna, the *chefe* of Missão Velha and one of Crato's leading rivals.[52] In Sant'Anna, Accioly had found a ready agent to prevent Col. Antonio Luis from rejecting the oligarch's initiative. The obstinate Crato chief bluffingly held out until seven days before the *pactuantes* (signatories) met in Joaseiro. But upon Padre Cícero's pledge "to put an end to this period of hostility" and reaffirmation of his personal solidarity with the Cratense chief whose father had financed the Patriarch's seminary education, Antonio Luis consented.[53]

On 4 October 1911, the new *município* of Joaseiro was pompously inaugurated. *Coronéis* and their representatives from seventeen Cariry towns attended. Content to triumph over Antonio Luis and secretly anxious to restrain Joaseiro from dominating the region, the political chiefs issued the now celebrated "Pact of the *Coronéis*."[54] This formal agreement—unique in the annals of Brazilian regional politics—collectively affirmed the intent to maintain the status quo in Valley politics—that is, to oppose any further depositions. It further pledged to renew and strengthen the personal and political ties of the participants. Finally, in an effort both to enforce the pact and guarantee the region's stake in the political spoils of state power, the delegates pledged "to maintain unconditional solidarity with H. E. Doctor Antonio Pinto Nogueira Accioly, our honored chief, and as disciplined politicians [to] obey unconditionally his orders and determinations."

This pact, sealed at the meeting of the *"Haya-Mirim"* or "Little Hague" —to use the Patriarch's naive, yet apt phrase—was a triumph for Gov. Accioly.[55] How great a triumph only became apparent on 20 December 1911. Then, in the face of mounting political opposition to Accioly, PRC-C delegates met in Fortaleza at the up-dated convention brusquely summoned just four days earlier.[56] There, Padre Cícero Romão Batista, Prefect of Joaseiro was unanimously nominated as the PRC-C's candidate to the office of Third Vice-President of Ceará State.[57] As a man of his word and genuinely beholden to the oligarch for Joaseiro's newly won autonomy, the politically disinterested cleric reluctantly accepted the nomination in order to keep his pledge delivered publicly in the October pact. In return for Joaseiro's autonomy, "The Simpleton" of Fortaleza had sagaciously co-opted into his party's ranks the *chefe* of one of the largest bailiwicks in Ceará and unquestionably the most popular vote-getter in the political history of the Northeastern *sertão*. It could not have come at a more momentous time: in January 1912, just six days before the scheduled congressional elections and three months before the gubernatorial election, the tottering "Simpleton" was violently deposed.

8

The Cariry Bids
for Statewide Power

The Fall of Accioly and National Politics

During the two decades after the fall of Accioly, Padre Cícero became one
of the most important political chiefs in the history of the Brazilian Northeast. His movement, once religious, became eminently political and a main-
stay of the conservative political forces. To trace the transition, it is necessary
to review here a number of events during the latter part of 1911 and early
1912, the period in which the Accioly oligarchy met its downfall.

The revolt against Accioly, his deposition and forced flight to Rio de
Janeiro took place in rapid succession between 21 December 1911 and 24
January 1912. Unlike the previous three decades of oligarchic rule, this
single month of popular triumph has been chronicled in minute detail in
the celebrated work of Rodolpho Theophilo, *Libertação do Ceará*.[1] Representative of Fortaleza's politically ambitious but long-frustrated professionals and merchants, Theophilo understandably attributed victory over
the oligarchy almost entirely to Fortaleza's local elites. In contrast, the
present account stresses the changing context of Brazilian national politics.

National politics seem, in retrospect, to have been of greater significance in Accioly's defeat than contemporaries such as Theophilo were willing to admit.[2]

First of all, it must be remembered that anti-Accioly forces, confined principally to the capital city of Ceará, were powerless for almost a decade. Loosely organized in 1903, when PRC-C dissidents rallied behind João Brigido and when Fortaleza's *Unitário* first rolled off the press declaring war upon the oligarchy, it was only in 1910 that this local opposition proved capable of consolidation. Their renewed vigor clearly coincided with the nation-wide "civilianist" presidential campaign of 1910. That campaign, it will be recalled, had pitched Rui Barbosa as spokesman for the disenchanted middle classes against the Brazilian army Marshal Hermes da Fonseca. In turn the Marshal's candidacy was supported by the army and decadent state oligarchies which symbolized for the nation's urban middle classes "not only military imposition, but also the irritating dominance of the republican [state] oligarchies."[3] In Ceará, Rui's campaign and Hermes' later victory, the latter made possible by Accioly's fraudulent electoral machine, did more to forge the unity of opposition forces in Fortaleza than all previous local efforts against the oligarch.[4]

Secondly, the later reversal of local political situations clearly stemmed from internal contradictions which wracked the Hermes administration from the outset. One source of contradiction was the Brazilian army which the Marshal's victory had transformed into "the new dominant political party" of the nation.[5] At first, the military rallied behind the recently inaugurated Hermes. In old-fashioned military tradition, reminiscent of the one-time army president, Floriano Peixoto (1891–1894), the army helped Hermes crush the remnants of middle class, "civilianist" opposition in the Rio de Janeiro state legislature in November 1911. But the ease of their success, the unleashing of their ambitions, as well as the reassertion of the army's essentially middle class origins and sympathies, quickly turned many officers into vengeful opponents not of Rui's "civilianist" supporters, but rather of the very state oligarchic regimes which had secured the presidency for Hermes.[6] Between December 1910, and December 1911, the victorious middle-class military forged a new alliance with their originally anti-Hermes "civilianist" counterparts that led to the overthrow of oligarchical machines in Pará, Bahia, and Pernambuco states. Their victories were deliriously acclaimed as *"salvações"* (rescues), while the newly imposed military governors were hailed as *"salvadores."*[7]

The reversal of Hermes' stand towards the oligarchies was not solely due to the middle-class sympathies and ambitions of the army for political power. The reversal also stemmed from another important contradiction: the growing cleavage between the army officers and Hermes' chief civilian supporter, José Gomes de Pinheiro Machado. As senator from the Southern *gaúcho* state of Rio Grande do Sul, Pinheiro Machado was the leader of the nominally nation-wide *Partido Republicano Conservador,* the party of the state oligarchies. It was the *gaúcho* who engineered Hermes' candidacy after a momentary split over the choice of the presidential successor in 1910 had developed in the dominant Minas Gerais-São Paulo axis which alternately controlled the presidency since 1894.[8] It was Pinheiro Machado who also forged the unholy, fragile but triumphant electoral alliance between professional soldiers and the state oligarchic forces. Once the Marshal took office, however, Pinheiro Machado's influence over him grew enormously—to the detriment of the military's ambitions. Moreover, when affairs of the heart increasingly turned the widower Hermes away from the affairs of state, the *gaúcho* emerged as the *de facto* president of Brazil. Pinheiro's national prestige encouraged him after 1912 to seek the presidential nomination for himself. But the "strong-man's" political future clearly rested on his continuing alliance with the oligarchic state chiefs of the PRC. As a result, Pinheiro's reluctance to promote additional *"salvações"* drove the military men into hostile opposition.[9]

The Failure of "Continuismo" and "Conciliação"

The rift between the strong-man and the military had sharply widened by December 1911. With three *"salvações"* to their credit, in Rio de Janeiro, Pernambuco, and Bahia states, the military now sought to depose Accioly. For his part, Pinheiro Machado realized that his presidential ambitions required him to preserve intact Accioly's electoral machine, even if Accioly himself might be sacrificed to the rising middle-class hostility in Fortaleza. Accioly, of course, had no intention of not continuing to direct the destiny of Ceará. When Hermes and the *gaúcho* strong-man momentarily agreed to try to force Accioly to name a suitable successor, the oligarch hastily convoked the PRC-C Convention on 16 December 1911. Four days later, even before party representatives from the interior could reach Fortaleza, the hand-picked delegates overwhelmingly approved Accioly's gubernatorial slate (which included Padre Cícero as the candidate for the Third Vice-

Presidency). However, the oligarch's aged choice for governor, who impoliticly avowed to continue Accioly's policies to the letter, proved totally unacceptable to Pinheiro Machado. Anti-Accioly forces in Fortaleza immediately seized upon the disapproval of Cattete (the presidential palace in Rio de Janeiro): Without regard to principle they proposed a conciliatory candidate from among several of the oligarch's cronies who might prove simultaneously acceptable to both Accioly and Pinheiro Machado. Accioly, however, would brook no conciliation with his opposition and the prospective candidates publicly refused the dubious honor.[10]

At this point, the military *"salvadores"* persuaded the anti-Accioly forces in Ceará's capital to propose a candidate of their own to be chosen from within the officer corps of the Brazilian army. Under the prompting of the federal army officer assigned to the Fourth Military Inspectory located in Fortaleza, a mammoth political rally was held in the capital on the evening of 21 December 1911. From that moment on, Accioly's local opponents, thanks to military promises of support, found their "saviour": the candidacy of Lt. Col. Marcos Franco Rabelo was jubilantly launched. Leaflets inundated the city: *"Ecce Homo!"*[11]

Franco Rabelo was a native son of the *"terra do sol"* who had not set foot in Ceará for almost two decades. A one-time professor at Fortaleza's defunct military academy and currently stationed in Rio de Janeiro he was best remmbered, if at all, as the son-in-law of Gen. José Clarindo de Queiroz, a one-time Governor of Ceará whose term of office had come to an abrupt end in 1892 when Accioly's supporters helped to depose him. Despite Franco Rabelo's anonymity he was quickly endorsed by the former Minister of War, Gen. Dantas Barreto, who had recently resigned from his high federal post to become the *"salvador"* and then Governor of neighboring Pernambuco state. Within Ceará the choice of Franco Rabelo was widely applauded by Fortaleza's merchants and middle class.[12] The merchants indeed proved to be the little-known officer's most ardent supporters. With Ceará's economy yielding spectacular profits in 1910, thanks largely to the Amazon rubber boom, the merchant community of Ceará had grown increasingly dissatisfied with their lack of political power, with Accioly's continued support of his friends within the traditional agrarian sector, and with the oligarch's alleged failure to improve public works that, according to the merchants, ought to benefit their state capital. These and other grievances, presumably stemming from Accioly's nepotistic and peculatory policies, galvanized the merchants into moralistic crusaders without whose financial and political support no state government could long remain stable.[13] Too weak alone to depose Accioly, the merchants, with recent promises of military support from Rio de Janeiro, were now assured of a chance to triumph. Without delay, they prepared for the showdown, which like similar *"salvações"* in Pernambuco and Bahia, where the middle class had taken an active role, also symbolized the slow but irreversible penetration of modern capitalism into the Brazilian Northeast and the total inadequacy of a traditional agrarian-backed oligarchy to function effectively under the new world-wide conditions of modern commerce and industry.[14]

Clientele Politics: "Rabelismo" and the "Marretas"

The immediate cause of Accioly's fall was the imprudent shooting and the consequent death of an innocent child by his mounted state police in the midst of nearly ten thousand middle class demonstrators who took part in the merchant-financed *"passeiatas"* (rallies and marches) on 29 December 1911, and 14 and 21 January 1912.[15] Resentment against police brutality was further inflamed not only by the crudeness of Accioly's rural recruits, but also by their absorption of more than a third of the annual state budget.[16] Middle-class hostility could no longer be contained. While the powerful Commercial Association of Ceará demanded federal troops to protect them, small shopkeepers, clerks, artisans, railroad workers, train conductors, and self-employed mechanics voluntarily took up arms. *Suo moto,* these lower-class elements captured government buildings, set up roadblocks to starve out Accioly's police and finally bombarded the governor's palace where Accioly and his family were holding out.[17]

In the final analysis, the oligarch's surrender on 24 January 1912 must be attributed less to the merchants than to Fortaleza's embryonic proletariat. Their consciously terroristic retaliation against Accioly and his police was never authorized by the merchants and, in fact, was condemned by them.[18] Nonetheless, their decisive action and their banding together into a 500-man militia enabled Cattete's pro-Rabelo military inspector in Fortaleza to plead total inability to defend Accioly, alleging that his limited fifty-troop federal garrison was, in his opinion, grossly outnumbered by the 500-man workers' militia.[19] Furthermore, when Hermes, under Pinheiro's influence, ordered the restoration of Accioly the day after he was deposed—fully aware of his inability to enforce it and not intending to try—the workers' militia rose up against their middle-class leaders and threatened to revolt if Accioly were restored. Only after the leadership promised to exile Accioly, who departed for Rio de Janeiro on 25 December, did the worker-soldiers disband.[20] However, the concession of the workers to abide their bourgeois leaders promptly put an end to their inarticulate political aspirations just as a similar concession in 1890 quickly ended in the dissolution of Ceará's first proletarian political party; not until 1930 were the workers of Ceará to be heard from again.[21]

With the oligarch in exile and the proletariat suppressed, Ceará's political "ins" and "outs" eyed the national congressional elections scheduled for 30 January 1912 as a first test of strength. Ten seats were at stake.[22] Anti-Accioly forces united under the banner of *"rabelismo."* But the new party label could hardly conceal the three principal factions which had joined Rabelo's bandwagon: first, there were the traditional anti-Accioly agrarian interests identified with the Paula Pessôa and Paula Rodrigues families. (This clan had earlier supported Franco Rabelo's father-in-law, the then governor Clarindo de Queiroz whom Accioly forces successfully deposed in 1892.);[23] second, there were the dissident-Acciolystas who had broken from the PRC-C in 1903 and had united under the leadership of *Unitário's* editor João Brigido; third and finally, there were the nouveau-riche merchants of Fortaleza, their *"salvacionista"* allies within the officer corps of the army, and recent *"aderista"* merchants (recent party adherents) in the interior.[24] Against these *"rabelistas"* stood the remnants of Accioly's PRC-C, represented in Fortaleza by Dr. José Accioly, the oligarch's son, who in previous administrations had served as Secretary of the Interior. Forced to remain in Fortaleza as a "hostage" to placate the angry workers' militia, Dr. José nonetheless was allowed full liberty to telegraph the PRC-C's backland *coronéis*. He even received their delegations in Fortaleza while under "house arrest." His presence in the capital, however, proved inadequate to prevent one-time Accioly appointees in the lower echelons of the state bureaucracy from deserting party ranks in favor of *rabelismo* and its promise of job security.[25] In fact, despite Dr. José's efforts, the results of the January federal congressional elections were a disaster for Accioly's candidates: *rabelista* influence in several coastal cities and their control over the regional election-verifying committees (*mesas de apuração*) in the backlands gave eight of the ten contested seats to *rabelismo*. Exuberantly, Accioly's PRC-C was pronounced dead on the urban coast. However, *acciolysmo* was not yet politically finished: in the backlands, many *coronéis* had willingly rigged the elections in testimony of their devotion to the deposed oligarch. Moreover, the Acciolys still held an important trump: Most of the thirty incumbent deputies in the State Legislature, elected in 1908 and constitutionally empowered to approve the results of the gubernatorial elections scheduled for April 1912, were still nominally loyal to the oligarch.[26]

The loyalty of backland chiefs to the PRC-C and the anticipated solidarity of incumbent PRC-C deputies within the State Assembly convinced Pinheiro Machado, his eye on the Brazilian presidency, of the political value and necessity to preserve the old PRC-C and its electoral machine. On 19 March 1912, Col. Marcos Franco Rabelo made his first triumphal entry into Ceará clamorously greeted by 20,000 supporters after almost two decades of absence; just four days later, however, Cearense federal Senator, Thomas Cavalcante,—Pinheiro Machado's hatchet man—quietly arrived in Fortaleza to stop the Rabelo bandwagon and to regroup Accioly's PRC-C into an *acciolysmo* without Accioly.[27]

Cavalcante had come to Ceará to champion the anti-*rabelista* gubernatorial candidacy of Gen. Bizerril Fontenele. Armed with financial support from Rio de Janeiro, Pinheiro Machado's agent proceeded to buy the support of former Accioly supporters. But Bizerril Fontenele was subsequently defeated in the April elections; moreover Cavalcante's blatant attempt to preserve the PRC-C without Accioly was perceived by the ex-oligarch and his fellow PRC-C exiles in Rio de Janeiro as an unscrupulous move. They immediately charged Pinheiro Machado with treachery.

The *gaúcho's* betrayal of the one-time oligarch quickly caused a radical realignment of Ceará's political forces. Fearful that the Pinheiro Machado-Cavalcante axis would succeed in depriving the Accioly dynasty of its power-base, José Accioly—who had just returned to Rio de Janeiro—opened talks in May with Rabelo's emissaries! Finally, in June, the Acciolys expediently agreed to an alliance with *rabelismo*! In exchange for two of the state's three vice-presidencies and half of the thirty seats in Ceará's Legislative Assembly (to be elected in November 1912), the Acciolys promised to deliver their share of the votes of incumbent state legislators in support of Rabelo's installation as governor scheduled to occur in July. When news of the June pact reached Fortaleza, the dissident *acciolystas* of 1903 (led by *Unitário's* João Brigido) indignantly broke their earlier alliance with the *rabelistas* and joined forces with Cavalcante. Together, Brigido and Cavalcante established a new political party, later dubbed *"marreta."*

Clientele politics, notorious throughout Brazil during the "old republic," spoke only the unideological tongue of opportunism and "catch as catch can." Its fruit in Ceará was a new, unstable political potpourri: *rabelismo*, originally conceived in the moralistic womb of military and middle-class ambition and anti-Accioly hatred now openly embraced its former enemies. In opposition to *rabelismo*, there now arose Cavalcante's newly formed *marreta* party whose leadership was entrusted to Accioly's long-time enemy and one-time *rabelista*, the unpredictable João Brigido.[28]

The upshot of this new political division in Fortaleza led expectedly to Franco Rabelo's installation in July 1912 as Governor of Ceará for the 1912–1916 term.[29] Contrary to the expectations of the June pact, however, his support in the Legislative Assembly was less than unanimous. The incumbent thirty-man legislature whose constitutional task it was to confirm the Governor in office was torn asunder: most of the one-time *acciolysta* deputies deserted to Cavalcante-Brigido's *marretas*, but were forbidden to enter the assembly by armed *rabelistas* who correctly feared that the "new" *marretas* would refuse to recognize Rabelo as governor. Of the twelve deputies who did approve Rabelo's installation, only five were true *rabelistas* while seven were relatives of Accioly, who thus proved faithful to the June pact. Rabelo's failure to receive the required majority of sixteen votes did not prevent him from taking office on 14 July 1912. Momentarily, even President Hermes and Pinheiro Machado publicly accepted Rabelo's victory and expediently had the federal congress approve the credentials of some of the new Governor's hand-picked candidates who had been elected to the lower house in January. But Rabelo's failure to obtain the legislative majority made his administration constitutionally stillborn; his illegal accession to the governorship would later serve as a constitutional pretext for his enemies to depose Ceará's new "*salvador*."[30]

"Clientelismo" in the Cariry

The political crisscrosses and double crosses from Rio de Janeiro to Fortaleza reached deeply into the backlands. Significantly, the Cariry Valley did not abide these zigzags in pristine and primitive abandonment, nor did it respond to outside impulses as if it were a partially isolated "rustic" community whose style of politics, as some authors have implied, was essentially different from or at variance with the "civilized" or "modern urbanized" political culture of the coast.[31] To the contrary, the Cariry kept itself abreast of every distant and tortuous political turn; not surprisingly each new turn saw its political leaders maneuver with consummate skill in the defense of both their respective local interests and the maintenance of the larger political network into which, for more than a decade, backland political structures had been integrated.

In Joaseiro, for example, the proclamation of Franco Rabelo's candidacy resulted in the establishment of a local *rabelista* faction as early as January 1912. It was led by the *município's* former aspirant to the prefectship, Col. José André de Figueiredo, a native son and prominent merchant. This was the same Col. José André who in late 1911 had been forcibly demoted from the prospective post of prefect to that of the presidency of the city council in order that Padre Cícero might mitigate former Governor Accioly's antipathies towards his rising merchant adversaries on the coast. Floro, of course, did not view Col. José André's renewed bid for power with favor. Under Floro's probable influence, harassments were directed against José André to dissuade him from seeking office. In January 1912, handbills circulated in Joaseiro condemning the native son, who was then in Fortaleza, "as an enemy of Rev. Padre Cícero and the *romeiros* [pilgrims or newcomers]." Alleging that José André planned "to deport the pilgrims," the handbills urged the populace to boycott the merchant's store. One contemporary source has even claimed that José André's wife and children were held as hostages until he finally withdrew his nomination. A recent history of Joaseiro, however, suggests that José André continued to receive support from the native sons for the prefectship well after this January crisis, an assumption which the present account follows.[32]

What is indisputable about the January crisis, however, is the manifestation of Floro's design to win political power for himself. After Accioly's fall, Floro took it upon himself to extirpate *rabelismo* from Joaseiro and assume the self-imposed mission of restoring PRC-C hegemony in the Cariry. Anxious to gain the confidence of party leaders in Fortaleza and *in loco*, he assiduously proceeded to buoy the spirits of the Valley's disillusioned political chiefs whose friendship he had continuously cultivated since the days of Coxá and Joaseiro's campaign for autonomy.[33]

Two additional events beyond Joaseiro's borders, however, intervened to alter the local political spectrum. The first occurred in early June 1912. That month, a bomb exploded in the Fortaleza home of Sen. Thomas

Cavalcante, whom Pinheiro Machado had entrusted with the preservation of *acciolysmo* without Accioly.[34] Shortly afterwards, under the probable influence of Dr. Floro, Joaseiro's city council was convened for the purpose of expressing sorrow over the attempted assassination. The resolution, designed to keep Joaseiro's links open to Cavalcante and Pinheiro Machado, the self-appointed heirs to Accioly's PRC-C, was about to pass unanimously. Then, three of the council's eight members refused to vote in favor of an amendment which denounced the alleged assassins for being *rabelistas*. The three dissenters were the brothers Cincinato and Manuel Victorino da Silva, wealthy "newcomer" merchants from Alagôas, and Col. João Bezerra de Menezes, a prominent landowner and native son.[35] The Silva brothers obviously chose not to risk their thriving business in Joaseiro: condemnation of Cavalcante's alleged assassins as *rabelistas* would only incite the wrath of the Commercial Association of Ceará (CAC) against them. Col. João Bezerra, for his part, had little to fear from Fortaleza's CAC since his wealth lay in land; however, as a member of one of Joaseiro's traditional families, his resentment towards Dr. Floro could no longer be contained: this was the moment for Joaseiro to unite against Floro. The break of the three dissident councilmen had clearly salvaged Col. José André de Figueiredo's flagging candidacy. More consequential, even if short-lived, was the channeling of anti-Floro sentiment into the local *rabelista* party which had at last united both native sons (under the leadership of two traditional families: the Figueiredo's and the Bezerra's de Menezes) and a portion of the city's "newcomers" (in the persons of the Silva brothers) willing to defy Dr. Floro.

Floro's own ambitions now hung in uncertainty when a second event radically shifted Joaseiro's party alignments. This was the late June pact between José Accioly and the *rabelistas* to oppose the Pinheiro Machado-Cavalcante axis. The effects of Accioly's subsequent order to loyal PRC-C deputies in Fortaleza to recognize Franco Rabelo's claim to the governorship at the opening session of the State Assembly fell "like a bomb of dynamite" upon many of the oligarch's traditional PRC-C supporters in Fortaleza.[36] Interpreting the expedient switch as a betrayal by Accioly, some PRC-C diehards refused to recognize Rabelo's installation as governor and "adhered" immediately to Sen. Cavalcante's newly created *Partido Marreta*.[37] Led by João Brigido and the anti-Accioly dissidents of 1903 ,the new party's first circular was dispatched to backland *chefes* of the PRC-C on 30 July 1912.[38]

Its arrival in Joaseiro in early August proved a boon to Floro's ambitions. He immediately assumed the leadership of Joaseiro's *Partido Marreta* in opposition to *rabelismo* led by Col. José André and his supporters. Floro, however, did not propose his own candidacy for prefect. Instead, he decided to drive a wedge in Joaseiro's *rabelista* constituency by offering the nomination to the newcomer merchant Manuel Victorino da Silva,[39] who had earlier declared his support for the native son, José André. With Silva's acceptance, *marretismo* in Joaseiro momentarily became concentric with the newcomer population, while *rabelismo* encompassed only the native sons. The long-feared threat of dividing the *município's* inhabitants according to birthplace once again posed itself; its economic and political consequences could only be disastrous for Joaseiro. The threat, however, never materialized; at some unspecified time before the municipal elections, Dr. Floro realized that Manuel Victorino da Silva's candidacy was totally unviable and he adopted a new strategy. Joaseiro's late historian, Octavio Aires de Menezes, describes the ensuing political events in Joaseiro, thus:[40]

Meeting in convention, the *Marretas* under Floro's leadership and other friends' of Padre Cícero, concluded that only another *filho da terra* could compete with the *rabelista* candidate, Col. José André. [Then] the *filhos da terra* organized a dissident wing of the *Marreta* Party and presented as their candidate, Citizen João Bezerra de Menezes, another *filho da terra*. The upshot of this political maneuver, *conjured up by the partisan political brilliance of Dr. Floro*, was immediately evident: the *filhos da terra* split into two antagonistic groups. The entire Bezerra de Menezes family came over to support their candidate-relative [and] along with them *the entire [newcomer] electorate under the orders and orientation of Dr. Floro*. In this way, the candidacy of Snr. José André was liquidated without any possibility of victory. [Italics mine.]

Aires de Menezes' incomplete account poses several questions; unfortunately, the scarcity of incontrovertible documentation permits only tentative replies. Floro's initial decision, for example, to bestow the *marreta* candidacy upon Silva was probably not intended to divide Joaseiro in two. Rather, by bribing Silva to abandon José André, Floro in fact succeeded in reassembling all the newcomer population once again under his own wing. It was from this position of strength that Floro proceeded to negotiate with the native sons. Silva's candidacy was then withdrawn (after he and his brother Cincinato were promised key posts in the post-electoral municipal government);[41] Floro then convened the meeting of the "dissident wing" of the *marreta* party, offered the prefectship to João Bezerra, and thereby forged a new alliance between newcomers and one sector of the *filhos da terra*.

Also important to explain is the willingness of Col. João Bezerra de Menezes to join his enemy Dr. Floro and, in so doing, guarantee the defeat of Col. José André, a fellow native son.[42] The quiet rivalry between these two traditional Joaseiro families, (one merchant, the other chiefly agrarian) seems to have been less at issue than the tempting opportunity presented to Col. João Bezerra to become prefect. Indeed, Bezerra apparently accepted Dr. Floro's support only to obtain power. That power he secretly hoped to use later against Dr. Floro whom most of the native sons were intent on removing from Joaseiro. Subsequent events (to be recounted later) clearly confirm that Bezerra had an anti-Floro plan which, not insignificantly, won the support of many political *elements* in neighboring Crato. There too coastal *rabelismo* had earlier wrought alterations in the structure of local political power.

Shortly after Rabelo's victory, Crato's traditional agrarian interests, led by Col. Nelson da Franca Alencar who had proven so instrumental in forcing Col. Antonio Luis Alves Pequeno to grant Joaseiro autonomy in 1911, readily severed their alliance with Antonio Luis and aligned themselves with Col. Francisco José de Britto, one of the ex-*chefe's* merchant competitors. This new merchant-agrarian coalition became the local *rabelista* party. As in Joaseiro, the makeshift coalition's hope for victory rested on the promised municipal elections, made possible by the fulfillment of Franco Rabelo's campaign pledge to put an end to Accioly's long-time policy by which local prefects had been appointed by state governors, rather than popularly elected.[43] Unlike Joaseiro, where João Bezerra's victory aided by Floro had occurred under the banner of the nominal "dissident wing" of the *Marreta* party, the victory of Crato's merchant-agrarian coalition was hailed as a clean sweep for *rabelismo*. However, it was not elections but an earlier outburst of violence that had secured that victory. Impatient *rabelistas* took advantage of Antonio Luis' absence from Crato in mid-year 1912. After assembling a band of soldiers and *cangaceiros,* they marched on the municipal tax office, knocked down the doors, stole the city's archives and forcibly ordered the reins of government transferred to the vice-prefect. This act, rather than the subsequent election, had removed Col. Antonio Luis from the office he himself had won by armed violence in the distant year of 1904.[44] The lightning defeat of Crato's "little oligarch," no longer the regional "king-maker" in view of Accioly's fall, immediately set the *rabelistas* off on a mad scurry to consolidate their newly won power throughout the Valley. Barbalha, with its strongly competitive merchant class, rather than Crato where the new merchant prefect, Col. Francisco José de Britto, was as much a prisoner as he was an ally of the city's traditional agrarian interests, soon emerged as the key center of *rabelismo* in the Cariry. It was in Barbalha, several months after Rabelo came to power, that *rabelista* representatives from fifteen Valley *municípios* met—not in dissimilar fashion from the "Little Hague" convened in Joaseiro by Accioly supporters just a year earlier—to pledge their unflagging loyalty to Ceará's new "*salvador*."[45] However, *rabelistas* in the Valley were politically realistic. They realized that their chances of retaining power against the deposed but still powerful PRC-C *chefes* of the Cariry would be nil without strong military support. *Rabelismo's* urgent and almost desperate need to bolster recently won political power with military force was, in our opinion, one of the chief pressures behind Franco Rabelo's hastily declared campaign against *cangaceirismo* in the Cariry. That campaign was widely hailed in its day as a politically disinterested and humanitarian effort to rid the state of criminal elements. But in fact, it legally enabled Rabelo to send loyal state troopers into the Cariry and thereby secure his own and that of his supporters survival in an otherwise politically inimical region of Ceará.[46]

Cangaceirismo in the Cariry

The dispatch of 200 state police to Crato immediately after Franco Rabelo's inauguration in July 1912, has been traditionally justified by the alleged recrudescence of *cangaceirismo* in the Cariry Valley.[47] Indeed, the problem of banditry in the interior of the arid Northeast had come into sharp relief ever since the mid-nineteenth century. From about 1845 on, demographic increase and sporadic droughts consistently conspired to transform otherwise docile peasants into hungry highwaymen.[48] Then during the great drought of 1877–1879, individual highwaymen began to band together into groups of five to twenty, assumed terrifying *noms de guerre* by which history now remembers them and collectively prosecuted their adventures for personal gain but not infrequently for the welfare of their drought-stricken and helpless peasant compatriots. However, the incipient social goals of these primitive rebels, these Brazilian Robin Hoods, seem to have disappeared as quickly as the drought subsided. Then, with the proclamation of the Republic in 1889, backland politics in the arid Northeast altered significantly: Municipal politics increasingly became a ready avenue to riches and powers. As local *chefes*, like those in the Cariry, struggled against each other for local control, *cangaceirismo* reemerged. Absent, however, were its earlier embryonic social aspirations, its collective organization, and, of course, its implicit emphasis on the individual's liberation from and independence of the landowners.[49] On the contrary, it was now the land-owner himself (that is, the political chief) who for his own political interest became the captain, protector, recruiter, and promoter of *cangaceirismo*. In the late 19th century, Crato, for example, was relatively free from banditry, whether self-generated from among dissident peasants or politically organized from above. Then, in 1894, the oligarchic state government legally reserved to itself the prerogative of organizing a statewide police force. It withdrew from the municipal councils the right to retain their own armed forces and delegated only to the local prefect (then called *intendente,* who was appointed directly or sanctioned in office by the Governor) the sole authority to recruit and direct the local constabulary.[50] It was the con-stabulary in Crato, recruited from among criminals and bandits by the reigning *coronel,* during the administration of Col. José Belém (1892–1904), and its arbitrary, brutal, and politically inspired acts of aggression against Belém's opponents that led to his violent deposition in 1904.[51] The succession to the prefectship by Col. Antonio Luis Alves Pequeno in no way halted the pattern of increasingly reliance by political chiefs on hired *cangaceiros*. In 1904, Antonio Luis recruited more than one thousand of them in the neighboring states of Paraíba and Pernambuco, where earlier persecutions directed against them by government troops contributed to their readiness to enter the employ of Cariry Valley *coronéis*. These same *cangaceiros* stood guard over Crato and the "little oligarch" throughout the following year.[52] Several depositions and unsuccessful attempts in other Valley cities, the Coxá copper episode of 1908, and the later friction between

Crato and Joaseiro over the Joaseiro's autonomy all helped raise significantly the number of hired *cangaceiros* who resided in the Cariry under the protection of its local *chefes* at the time of Franco Rabelo's installation in July 1912.

These conditions, and Rabelo's obvious political interest in securing a firm political base in the Cariry with the aid of loyal state troopers only partially accounted for the dispatch of two hundred soldiers to Crato in mid-year 1912. A third reason was Padre Cícero's alleged role as the chief protector (*coiteiro*) of bandits in the Valley, a false charge that nonetheless continues to find exponents.[53] Floro's actions in Coxá in 1908 clearly contributed to that illusion, while the Patriarch's policy of tolerance and his pastoral theology which conceived of Joaseiro as a "haven for the shipwrecks of life," were purposely misinterpreted by many as a political ploy to attract criminals and bandits who sought refuge, into the Brazilian "New Jerusalem." However, the priest himself firmly believed, if somewhat naively, that once in Joaseiro these hardened refugees might repent and lead good lives. Ironically, the image of Padre Cícero as a protector of bandits was further enhanced in 1910, by a series of brutal criminal acts inflicted upon various members of Joaseiro's population by the hamlet's chief of police, Nazário Furtado Landim. In his pay there were a number of well-known bandits and criminals, it is true. However, often forgotten by Padre Cícero's critics is that Landim and his henchmen had been purposely hired and appointed to their posts by Crato's Col. Antonio Luis;[54] not until July 1911, it must be remembered, did Joaseiro cease to be a "district" within Crato over which the "little oligarch" not a little ruthlessly presided.

In 1911, moreover, a single episode did more to garb that illusion in the cloak of apparent truth than any other circumstance to that date. It has been a source of such endless controversy that a documented clarification is in order. In June of 1911, the prominent Paraíban political chief of Algôa do Monteiro, Col. Augusto Santa Cruz took refuge in Joaseiro.[55] With him there arrived a party of one hundred-thirty retainers including relatives, friends, political aides, and, of consequence, more than two dozen armed *cangaceiros*.[56] In flight from the Pernambucan and Paraíban interior police police (recruited, incidentally, from among criminals and bandits who, once uniformed and named *volantes*—or government posses—practised their arts with lawful approbation), Santa Cruz's presence was prejudicial to Joaseiro's interests. At the time, Crato's Col. Antonio Luis and Padre Cícero were nearing their accord to grant Joaseiro autonomy. But, Santa Cruz's armed henchmen, now under the Patriarch's protection, provided the Crato chief with a pretext to renege. To prevent this, Padre Cícero personally had Santa Cruz's entire retinue disarmed; had their rifles and munitions sold, and counseled the Paraíban chief and his retainers to migrate to the distant interior of Brazil where they could work the land in an honest livelihood. Finally, when the Patriarch promised to protect Santa Cruz's wife and children in Joaseiro, the Paraíban political chief agreed to depart from the city until a time when it was safe to return for his brood.[57] At the same time, the Patriarch dispatched twenty-five of Santa Cruz's *cangaceiros* to the Serra do Araripe where they were ordered to work "penitentially" the *maniçoba* rubber sites.[58]

The incident would have ended here without serious consequences to the Patriarch, had it not been for Santa Cruz's later decision to disregard Padre Cícero's counsel, return to Paraíba, and attempt to depose his enemies, among whom was the very Governor of the state. A month after Joaseiro's inauguration in October of 1911, the Patriarch, aware of Santa Cruz's plans, sent him this unequivocal advice: "I must frankly state [that it is] irrational to start a revolution in Paraíba; I see no favorable result. . . . Reflect carefully and don't jump [into it, thereby] ruining your entire future. I can never agree to a revolution and much less with you, a friend whom I wish every good. Think about it and may God direct and bless you."[59]

Neither the letter nor the Patriarch's enclosed plea that Santa Cruz return to the Cariry where the cleric proposed he purchase a cattle ranch then on the realtor's block and settle down were of any avail. In early 1912, Santa Cruz "jumped in."[60] When he did, Padre Cícero was immediately implicated in the plot as one of the chief conspirators despite all the evidence to the contrary. Just as in 1897 when vested political interests expediently linked the Patriarch, then exiled in Salgueiro, to the Canudos revolt of Antonio Conselheiro, so too in 1912 did similar interests in Paraíba publicly accuse the cleric of subversion. Paraíba's Governor, Dr. João Machado, telegraphed President Hermes charging that Padre Cícero planned to sack Paraíba with Santa Cruz.[61] Despite the Patriarch's denial, the illusion that he was a political subversive and protector of *cangaceiros* persisted. Rabelo, or perhaps his aides, quickly and carefully acted upon that image, although unflattering and untrue, for their own political purposes.

An Invitation to "Revolution," 1912

With the arrival of two hundred soldiers in Crato and the subsequent dispatch of a sizable contingent to aid Rabelo's faction then in power in neighboring Barbalha, the *rabelistas* of the Cariry felt their hand had been strengthened. Under the pretext of ridding the region of banditry, they and the state police systematically went about their eminently partisan political task.[62] For the record, they arrested a paltry fifty *cangaceiros* in the pay of the opposition; with greater diligence they obliged many of the Valley's PRC-C chiefs to stand trial.[63] Humiliated, even if not always sentenced, the *chefes* cautiously and momentarily laid low, while dreaming of vengeance.

While the euphoria generated by triumphant *rabelismo* still persisted, Joaseiro's new prefect, João Bezerra de Menezes, moved quickly to execute his secret plan against Floro. In late August or early September 1912, Col. João Bezerra ended all pretenses of being a "dissident *marreta*" and loyal coreligionist of Floro. His confrontation with Floro, without whom political victory would have been impossible, arose when the Patriarch's "alter ego" refused to turn over the fledging *município's* archives to the new prefect.[64] Bezerra then sent an emissary to Fortaleza. After talks with state officials, Franco Rabelo agreed to come to Bezerra's aid. Paying perfunctory homage to Padre Cícero's position as Third Vice-President of Ceará, Rabelo unabashedly appointed a loyal officer of the State Military Battalion, Capt. José Ferreira do Valle, as Joaseiro's chief of police (*delegado*).[65] Shortly after his arrival in September 1912, the *rabelista* military interloper proceeded not only to secure Bezerra's position as prefect, but also to complete the political encirclement of the Cariry by Rabelo's military police. The challenge to Padre Cícero's authority could not have been clearer. When Capt. Valle threatened some of Joaseiro's city councilmen loyal to the Patriarch with arrests and tried to force Floro to turn over the municipal archives to João Bezerra, Padre Cícero demanded his removal. Rabelo, however, only partially acquiesced; although Valle was transferred from Joaseiro, his substitute, Lt. Julio Ladislau, who had earlier been stationed in Barbalha, proved to be an equally loyal *rabelista*.[66]

Further proofs of Rabelo's designs to control the Cariry and counter the Patriarch's prestige were not wanting. First of all, shortly after Ladislau's appointment, a second strategic post in Joaseiro fell into *rabelista* hands. Pelusio Macedo, the self-taught bell and clockmaker and Padre's Cícero's oldest, most intimate friend since José Marrocos' death, was removed from his position as chief telegrapher of Joaseiro, despite Padre Cícero's repeated protests. As a result, *rabelistas* now not only controlled police headquarters but also had ready access to the cleric's personal and political correspondence (a fact which explains his prompt resort to employ a secret code for telegrams and trusted messengers to deliver his other correspondence). Pelusio's removal was a critical factor in convincing Padre Cícero that Franco Rabelo, not unlike the ailing Dom Joaquim (who shortly resigned his see to return to his native São Paulo), was intent on "persecuting" the Patriarch and his "holy city."[67]

A second proof of Rabelo's hostility seemed far more serious and irrefutable. In December 1912, Rabelo's government sent a representative to Recife, capital of Pernambuco. There counterparts from Pernambuco, Paraíba, and Rio Grande do Norte agreed with Ceará to the first interstate pact to suppress banditry throughout the Northeast.[68] From Rabelo's standpoint, this historic accord not only impeded the opposition *chefes* of the Cariry Valley from their traditional practices of recruiting and protecting *cangaceiros* in neighboring states. It also gave an aura of greater legitimacy to his policy of policing the Valley where the only serious opposition to his government remained potent, even if dormant on the surface. When rumors began to circulate in the Cariry that the real purpose of the interstate pact was to enable Rabelo to suppress PRC-C forces there, the Patriarch announced that as Vice-President of Ceará, he could no longer support the "*salvador's*" government![69]

The Patriarch's decision to chill relations with Rabelo was not an arbitrary one. It was based on his conviction that Franco Rabelo had become a creature of his political advisors, all fervent anti-acciolystas, and was himself no longer capable of restraining the acts of violence and aggression of his supporters. Proof of the incapacity had been made manifest in Fortaleza, in November 1912. There, the *rabelistas* (merchants, the middle classes, and some workers) gave cause for alarm after it was learned that the majority of the incumbent deputies of the Legislative Assembly (the sixteen *marretas* who had opposed the June pact and refused to approve Rabelo's installation) had intended to annul Rabelo's mandate as Governor. (This was legally possible since Rabelo's installation had never been ratified by a majority vote of the State Assembly.) When the sixteen incumbent *marretas* attempted to convene their meeting in November 1912, under the protection of army units recently sent by Pinheiro Machado, rumors spread among Rabelo's partisans in Fortaleza that Accioly might be reinstated as Governor. To prevent this, *rabelistas* barricaded the doors of the State Assembly, put a torch to the homes of Accioly and his most prominent supporters, burned the oligarch's textile plant to the ground, and demolished the editorial and printing offices of João Brigido's vitriolic *Unitário*. Ultimately, they forced the Accioly clan and their supporters to take refuge in an English ship that, anchored then in Fortaleza's port, finally took the party to Rio de Janeiro.[70]

As Rodolfo Theophilo observed in *Sedição do Joazeiro,* a sequel to his earlier account of Accioly's downfall in 1912, Rabelo could not and dared not prevent his supporters from venting their wrath on the Acciolys, whom the outgoing assemblymen allegedly intended to return to office after first annuling Rabelo's originally unconstitutional mandate. As Theophilo noted:[71]

To open fire on those who were defending themselves from the assault of the Acciolys, to kill those who [four months earlier] had chosen [Rabelo] for the governorship, was an absurdity.

If Franco Rabelo had given the order to put down the outburst, he would have been disobeyed, the police force would have taken the people's side and the disorders would have been endless and of greater gravity.

After these incendiary events, the expedient June political pact between Rabelo and the Acciolys also went up in smoke. Once again exiled to Rio de Janeiro the Acciolys had no alternative but to join forces with *marretas,* Sen. Cavalcante and João Brigido, as well as with a few other dissident elements who, through Rabelo's political myopia, had been excluded from his government.[72] Shortly thereafter, this united anti-*rabelista* front desperately presented a full slate of thirty candidates to run for the Legislative Assembly. However, the November contest saw none elected. *Rabelismo* had won a total victory; on the surface *marretas* and *acciolystas* stood no chance of ever returning to power.[73] Their one hope, however, now fell on Padre Cícero who, as one of Ceará's vice-presidents, was the leading oppositionist still to hold a high political office. In view of *rabelismo's* triumph, even that hope was a dim one. But it might have been all but extinguished were it not for the almost total success of Rabelo's politico-military policies. In the Cariry, that very success generated a sense of profound desperation among the political "outs." For them Rabelo's too complete success was tantamount to an invitation to "revolution," their last resort to return to power.

Planning the "Revolution," 1913

By January 1913, Padre Cícero and his followers were convinced that *rabelismo* was bent on destroying Joaseiro.[74] Previous events made that conviction inescapable: the appointments of two successive *rabelista* police-chiefs and a telegrapher in Joaseiro, and Rabelo's failure to punish the guilty arsonists in Fortaleza. Furthermore, the interstate campaign against *cangaceirismo* was considered a façade for Rabelo's campaign against the old-line *coronéis* of the Cariry. Indeed, if the "New Jerusalem" itself was to be delivered, the Patriarch must look elsewhere for support. Thus in early January 1913, in the interests of defending Joaseiro, Padre Cícero renewed his pledge of solidarity to the Acciolys, whom he nonetheless criticized for their earlier pact with Rabelo. Politically naive, he believed that the "ill-starred accord of June" was the cause of all of the Cariry's ills.[75]

Thereafter, Padre Cícero's antipathies toward Rabelo were fanned by an endless stream of correspondence from the PRC-C exiles in Rio de Janeiro and, above all, by the persuasiveness of Floro Bartholomeu and Crato's ex-*chefe,* Col. Antonio Luis, who together became the septuagenarian's absolute mentors and ministers in politics. Understandably, their differences originating over Joaseiro's autonomy quickly dissolved once *rabelistas* in Joaseiro and Crato had deprived both men of political office. The "alter ego" and the "little oligarch" rapidly became fast friends and political allies. Proof of their comradeship was Antonio Luis' important role in securing Floro's nomination for state deputy on the defeated *marreta*-PRC-C slate in the November 1912 elections.[76] Thereafter, relations between Floro and Antonio Luis became increasingly intimate; Floro frequently visited Antonio Luis at home in Crato. The one was the incarnation of ambition and audacity, the other of political expertise and love of power; together they galvanized the desperation of old-guard Valley chiefs into a commitment to revolt against Rabelo's government.[77]

Contrary to most contemporary as well as recent interpretations, it seems certain that Col. Antonio Luis was a chief architect of that plan in the Cariry; Floro was its chief executor and Padre Cícero, its bewildered and reluctant accomplice.[78] It is clear today that it could not have been otherwise. Antonio Luis, first cousin of ex-Governor Accioly, deposed chief of Crato, former State deputy, and one-time "king-maker" of the entire Cariry Valley, had most to gain by "revolution." Besides, he alone was the experienced politician, while Floro knew personally not a single political figure in Ceará and had never even been to Fortaleza! Only after reaching Rio de Janeiro in August 1913 did Floro at last make the acquaintance of the Acciolys, Senator Cavalcante, and Pinheiro Machado himself![79] As for Padre Cícero, he was the believing captive of growing rumors of Rabelo's innumerable deeds of hostility, the object of flattery from the powerful and self-seeking Rio de Janeiro exiles, and the trusting pawn of Floro and Antonio Luis. They, along with their subordinates, became the isolated cleric's chief interpreters of the deteriorating political crisis of 1913.[80] Just how sincere the Patriarch's implicit confidence in Floro and Antonio Luis was, can be adjudged by subsequent events, but, especially by his last will and testament. In that document, the cleric named Floro and Antonio Luis as executors of his estate, an indisputable sign of trust in a society where friends alone could guarantee the law's fulfillment.[81]

Admittedly, Antonio Luis and Floro were not lone conspirators. There was also the unpredictable João Brigido, editor of *Unitário*, who first departed for Rio de Janeiro in 1913 to plot against Rabelo's government. The attempted assassination of a *marreta* congressman in late 1912 gave Brigido the pretext to undo yet another government.[82] The chief conspirator, however, was the *gaúcho* senator and national chairman of the PRC, Pinheiro Machado. His public bid in early 1913 for the party's presidential nomination was violently opposed at the start by a coalition of São Paulo, Minas Gerais, and many of the Northeastern states which had earlier fallen to the military "*salvadores.*" General Dantas Barreto, the "*salvacionista*" Governor of Pernambuco and first advocate of Franco Rabelo's candidacy in 1912, emerged as the national spokesman of these opposition forces. In February 1913, it was Dantas Barreto who organized the celebrated "*Bloco do Norte*," the caucus of Northeastern states united against Pinheiro Machado's candidacy. The following month, Franco Rabelo publicly led Ceará into the "*bloco.*" Despite his protests of continued loyalty to Pinheiro Machado, Rabelo's entry into the "*bloco*" was an irreversable affront to the *gaúcho.*[83] Immediately thereafter, with the support of President Hermes, then planning to wed and oblivious to politics, Pinheiro Machado unhesitatingly "decreed Rabelo's deposition."[84] At that point, the exiled Acciolys could do little else but cast their political lot with the Brazilian strong-man and his *marreta* favorites in Ceará, Thomas Cavalcante and João Brigido.

As a result of Brigido's mission to Rio de Janeiro, military personnel loyal to Pinheiro Machado were shortly transferred to Fortaleza. The plan conceived by Cattete called for a "barrack uprising" of the federal army detachment garrisoned in Ceará's capital. However, the uprising, aimed at forcing Rabelo to resign, was uncovered before it could be executed. With its failure, a second and more sinister alternative was called for.[85]

That alternative was initiated in August 1913 when Floro Bartholomeu left for Rio de Janeiro under the pretext of obtaining urgent medical attention.[86] As far as the aging Patriarch was concerned, the confidential mission would enable Floro to inform Rio de Janeiro "bigwigs" of Joaseiro's desperate situation. Just six weeks before Floro's departure, Joaseiro's *rabelista* police chief had harassed several innocent inhabitants who were celebrating the traditional backland holiday in honor of St. John. The exact cause of the incident is lost to history. But efforts to determine it at the time led to mutual recriminations between the Patriarch and the police chief. Fortaleza wholeheartedly defended its appointee who had accused the cleric of lying. Irate, the Patriarch personally admonished Rabelo that he alone must bear responsibility for any future disorder or anarchy that might result from another affront to the priest's honor and Joaseiro's tranquility.[87] Nonetheless, to defend Joaseiro from attack (which now seemed imminent to him) Padre Cícero prevailed upon Rio friends to have Cattete authorize the creation of the National Guard in Joaseiro. Such a unit, loyal to the Patriarch was the only conceivable security against the local *rabelista* police force. This urgent task Padre Cícero entrusted to Floro to complete in Rio de Janeiro.[88]

Floro's journey to the South was equally important to the Patriarch for another reason. There, Floro was commissioned to contact a wealthy potential benefactor of the prospective "Diocese of the Cariry." Despite Dom Joaquim's devastating opposition in 1909, Padre Cícero persisted in his plan to erect the bishopric in Joaseiro. Since Rome had not yet disclosed the new diocese's location, the cleric had reason to hope that his "New Jerusalem" might still become an episcopal see. After that, the road to reinstatement into the priesthood might be cleared of obstacles.[89]

From August through October 1913, Floro stayed on in Rio de Janeiro, wined and dined by Pinheiro Machado, wheeling and dealing with *marretas* and *acciolystas,* sought after by pragmatists and opportunists who anxiously plotted the moment of their return to power.[90] In time, an accord was struck of which the main points were as follows: Floro was to return to Joaseiro; convene there a "rump" session of Ceará's

Legislative Assembly to which sixteen incumbent deputies of the 1908–1912 legislature would be invited; have himself elected its "legal" president; and then, after contesting the constitutionality of Rabelo's government, await the promised arrival of federal troops in Fortaleza to depose the *"salvador's"* illegally constituted administration. The parties to the sinister plan (for which Hermes' armed intervention in favor of one of the dual assemblies created in the State of Rio de Janeiro in 1910 served as a precedent), were Floro, Pinheiro Machado, the Acciolys, Sen. Cavalcante, and João Brigido. Most probably, Antonio Luis was early made aware of the plot, while Padre Cícero appears to have been informed by October of the intent to create the dual legislature. Only upon Floro's return to Joaseiro in November, however, were other details of the conspiracy revealed to the cleric and only at Floro's discretion. Even then, however, Padre Cícero seemed to have believed that the key issue was Floro's election and that this step conformed both to the law of the nation and the desires of Brazil's highest elected officials. Furthermore, Floro apparently told nothing of the planned dispatch of federal troops, which in any case, never materialized on schedule;[91] subsequent events unanticipated by the conspirators were to turn the sinister plot into a veritable holocaust. Nonetheless, when Floro left Rio de Janeiro, Rabelo's fate was sealed.

The "Revolution" of 1913–1914

Rabelo was first to open hostilities in September 1913, while Floro was still in Rio. The Governor had ordered fresh troops to Crato; these, he stated publicly, were to replace, not supplement existing units.[92] Most Joaseirenses, however, believed that Rabelo was about to invade Joaseiro.[93] Contrary to the Governor's denial, it can now be said with considerable certainty that the report of a proposed invasion of Joaseiro was well founded. The plan had originated with *rabelista chefes* in the Cariry. Their spokesman, Crato's *rabelista* prefect, Col. Francisco José de Britto, had personally proposed it in talks with Rabelo in Fortaleza; the influx of *cangeceiros* into Joaseiro, Crato's *chefe* contended, foretold of an imminent attack against *rabelista coronéis* throughout the Cariry. Britto's plan of invasion, for which he promised to supply an adequate number of armed men (doubtless, *cangaceiros*), "consisted in the military occupation of the *municípios* bordering on Joaseiro." Approximately two hundred armed men were to be stationed in each of those cities, namely, Crato, Barbalha, Missão Velha, and São Pedro (Caririaçu). "On a prearranged day, the combined forces would converge upon Joaseiro, penetrate it, disarm its entire population and arrest all of its criminal elements."[94]

Whether Padre Cícero really knew of or merely suspected Britto's plot is not certain. However, from the outset, he bitterly protested the intended invasion so that Rabelo was publicly forced to deny it and withdraw his support.[95] But tensions rose again when "seditious handbills" attacking the Governor mysteriously circulated in Joaseiro. Rabelo warned the cleric that his government would "know how to repel" any intended act of subversion.[96]

In Floro's absence the Patriarch took matters into his own hands (for the first and perhaps only time in his entire "political" career). Joaseiro's defense was his chief concern. To that end, he wrote in October to ex-Governor Accioly in Rio de Janeiro. Oblivious to most details of the conspiracy agreed upon there against Rabelo, the cleric reported that three hundred soldiers had arrived in Crato and that it was likely that they would forcibly prevent a meeting of the Assembly in Joaseiro. It was then that the Patriarch proposed his own solution:[97]

> Things are going badly here and any day now we expect a revolution [to break out] provoked by the governor of the state. It would be *most reasonable* if Sr. Marshal Hermes would personally invite Sr. Col. Rabelo to a conference in Rio and make him *pacifically and honorably resign his office.* . . .
>
> I ask Providence that [the Marshal] intervene *positively so as to direct and save us* . . . from the great dangers that threaten us with such a government.

In respect for the truth, the pacific tone of the Patriarch's letter, and its implicit rejection of violence clearly support Padre Cícero's lifelong affirmation that he "did not direct the revolution [that followed] nor in it took part, nor on its behalf contributed, nor did [he] have . . . directly or indirectly the slightest responsibility for the events which [later] occurred."[98] Indeed, when the letter reached Rio de Janeiro, it very probably confirmed the fears of the conspirators that the Patriarch's nonviolent and conciliatory stand towards Rabelo might undermine their sinister plan.[99] As soon as the letter was received in Rio de Janeiro, Floro departed in haste.[100]

Floro secretly returned to Joaseiro by a backland route via Bahia and Pernambuco. Rabelo was prepared to stop him, but important federal army officers in Fortaleza, loyal to Pinheiro Machado, refused to take any action against the conspirator. With Floro safely in Joaseiro by late November, loyal PRC-C deputies from various parts of Ceará began to trickle into the "New Jerusalem" to await the convocation of the "rump" Assembly.[101]

No date had been set for the conspiratorial "rump." That decision had been left to the trusted João Brigido who arrived earlier in Fortaleza. On 5 December 1913, Brigido sent a secret missive to Floro. In it, he recommended that the "rump" Assembly be convened only after 30 December 1913 and prior to the following May. During this traditional recess of the federal congress, the executive branch of government could support the "rump" Assembly in Joaseiro with complete public and congressional impunity. Brigido's letter, however, was intercepted en route to Joaseiro by *rabelistas*. Once Brigido advised Floro on 9 December 1913 of the letter's theft, the "revolution of Joaseiro," invariably called "sedition," erupted.[102]

It is clear that some of the other events which followed in Joaseiro were not entirely anticipated in Rio de Janeiro, but the deposition of Joaseiro's *rabelista* prefect, João Bezerra, and the arrest of the *rabelista* police force on 9 December 1913 were. Precipitous but also expected were the installation of the "rump" Assembly (although only five instead of the expected sixteen incumbent deputies had arrived) on 12 December and the "election of Floro Bartholomeu as President of the Provisional Government," three days later.[103]

However, the reactions to Floro's initiatives were unanticipated. First, Cattete, engulfed by protests from the federal congress still in session, refused to sanction military or political support.[104] Second, *rabelista* exiles from Joaseiro joined their local coreligionists in Crato and began to recruit *cangaceiros* from neighboring states to invade Joaseiro.[105] From Fortaleza, Rabelo sent new contingents of troops to the Cariry amidst premature victory rallies in the capital of merchants and the middle classes who voluntarily took up arms to defend the city. Last, although Joaseiro's fate was in the balance Padre Cícero himself still refused to sanction violence.

Then, on 15 December, Col. Ladislau Lourenço, commander of the state troops in Crato, sent a threatening telegram to Floro: "I have 600 men under arms. Get ready, old boy, because today or tomorrow I'm going to dine on the turkey you offered me. . . . Don't have a heart attack because your number's up."[106] The threat sent Joaseiro's population into the public squares. There, under Padre Cícero's incentive, men, women, and children began to dig with their hands miles of trenches around the city. Day and night, they piled the fresh earth, six feet high, to one side of the trench. Every few feet pipes perforated the protective embankment from which a handful of Mauser rifles and antiquated muskets (*bacamartes*) could be aimed against the enemy.[107] Four days later, the famous *vallados,* whose partial ruins still exist, were completed just in time for a new ultimatum. Recently arrived in Crato, Col. Alípio Lopes, Rabelo's hand-picked commander of the invasion cynically telegraphed Padre Cícero:[108]

Seeing that Joaseiro is invaded by armed *cangaceiros* contrary to legal orders, I suggest Y. Exc. disarm those *cangaceiros* to avoid spilling blood of our compatriots . . . [I guarantee] your life and properties according to the expressed determination of H. Exc., Sr. President of the State. Y. Exc. has twelve hours to deliberate. At the end of the above period I will energetically open fire.

On the following day, 20 December 1913, Col. Alípio's forces invaded Joaseiro but were repelled fifteen hours later. Padre Cícero's hope to avoid bloodshed had proved to be in vain. His earlier appeals to Pinheiro Machado and Marshal Hermes for a pacific solution were to no avail; in fact, these two men who held the highest responsibility to the Brazilian people, simply kept silent and thereby made the conflict inevitable. At that point the Patriarch could not and would not permit Joaseiro to be destroyed. In his last will and testament written ten years after the revolution Padre Cícero recalled that after he had failed to avert a war (and in the face of repeated aggressive acts against Joaseiro), "[I] considered my arduous task ended. [I withdrew from] the camp of political action leaving Dr. Floro to act in accord with his orders received [from Rio] in so far as it was not possible for me to spare this hard-working populace from its sad destiny of a defenseless victim."[109]

During the following days *rabelista* troops encircled Joaseiro: hunger became widespread; the populace possessed few arms and even fewer supplies of munitions. Col. Antonio Luis of Crato, who had escaped with his family to Joaseiro, set up a makeshift munitions plant in Freedom Square.[110] Food, however, remained in short supply. These two factors forced Floro to transform the "New Jerusalem" from a city on the defense to a city on the offense. In his favor, Joaseiro's morale was buoyant. Songs and poems denounced Rabelo, praised Floro, and elevated Padre Cícero to a divine protector of the city.[111] Among the fanatically religious, there were a few who believed that the Patriarch's blessing was a spiritual breast-plate against the death-sting of piercing enemy bullets.

After a month of defensive encounters and only after heavy reinforce-ments from Fortaleza inundated Crato, did Joaseiro counter-attack; only then did the Patriarch consent to a "defensive" offensive. On 24 January 1914, Crato fell; three days later, Barbalha. The politically inspired pillage and sacking of these two cities which ensued and were denounced by Padre Cícero were limited but would nonetheless leave bitter memories and open scars in the Cariry for many years to come. However, the seized granaries of Crato and Barbalha, then filled to the brim, helped stave off hunger and famine in Joaseiro.

The brutalities inflicted by *cangaceiros* in Floro's pay (frequently against *cangaceiros* employed by the *rabelistas*) were nonetheless bitterly denounced by Padre Cícero. In fact, when orders were given by Floro to attack Crato, the Patriarch clearly commanded the combatants to spare the city's families by keeping one of the prinicpal arteries to the city free for them to escape.[112] He specifically forbade any harm to come to Msgr. Quintino, vicar of Crato, even though he had been the relentless agent of Dom Joaquim in regard to the "religious question of Joaseiro," a role deeply resented by the "New Jerusalem's" faithful. As partisan good wishes for the victory over Crato were received in Joaseiro, the Patriarch, himself a native son of the "Pearl of the Cariry," became despondent. On a con-gratulatory telegram dispatched from a *coronel* of nearby Campos Sales, Pelusio Macedo, now restored to the post of telegrapher, entered this ob-servation in the station's archives: "Upon the arrival of this telegram, my *Padrinho* was so indignant about the thefts in Barbalha [committed against] the Sampaios [the city's most prominent merchants and long-time friends of the cleric, that] . . . he would not accept congratulations or congratula-tory telegrams in view of the unparalleled horrors."[113]

While the Patriarch struggled with his conscience, Floro's prominent military aides, two backland *chefes,* Pedro Silvino and José Borba de Vasconcelos, marched their bands of criminals and *cangaceiros* against Rabelo's forces. Victorious over state troops led by the heroic officer, Capt. J. da Penha, who lost his life on 22 February, the revolutionaries finally reached Fortaleza, by foot and train.[114] They entered the capital on 19 March, only after two federal decrees had earlier permitted Cattete to dis-patch several warships and three batallions of troops to Fortaleza. Pinheiro

Machado had at last fulfilled his promise of armed support to the conspiracy, and the state capital fell with little bloodshed.[115] On 24 March 1914, Rabelo embarked for Rio de Janeiro after Ceará's government had been assumed by the recently arrived federal interventor, Marshal Setembrino de Carvalho.[116]

The "revolution" of Joaseiro was over. Ironically it converted Joaseiro into the most important political bailiwick of the Brazilian Northeast; yet it left unresolved the political crisis of Ceará. It also transformed the Patriarch of the "New Jerusalem" into a potent *coronel* of national stature; yet his personal reputation never emerged from the political depths into which it had descended. In many ways, the triumphant "revolution" was but a Pyrrhic victory.

9

Joaseiro
in National
Perspective

The Balance Sheet of Power: Cattete and Fortaleza

If the goal of Cattete's "sedition" was to restore Ceará's traditional oligarchical interests to power, then the revolution of Joaseiro must be considered
a defeat. No sooner had the Rio de Janeiro conspirators agreed upon a
gubernatorial successor, when the scission of the Rabelo era inflicted itself
again upon Ceará's political system. Regardless of temporary realignments
and successive changes in party organization and nomenclature, the political
forces of Ceará divided themselves into the two very same camps that had
clearly come to the fore upon Accioly's deposition in 1912: the middle-class
and merchant interests of Ceará (supported by a faction of anti-Accioly
landowners), on the one hand, and the primarily traditional agrarian-based
interests, on the other. In fact, the two sides were so equally matched that,
until 1930, each was obliged to rule the state in uneasy and shifting coalition
with the other. Paradoxically, within this coalition framework, the interests
of Joaseiro and the Cariry benefited for some time almost as greatly as if
the revolution had fully triumphed. However, before taking stock of

Joaseiro and the Cariry after 1914, it is necessary to examine Cattete's political failure to regain control of Cearense politics.

After the revolution, Rio de Janeiro's military interventor in Fortaleza turned over, with Cattete's approval the reins of state government to Col. Benjamin Liberato Barroso in May 1914.[1] Like Rabelo, Barroso had not lived nor set foot in Ceará for two decades. Like Rabelo, he was an army officer whose career was made chiefly in the nation's capital, oblivious to Cearense politics and immersed in national military affairs. In fact, Marshal Hermes had demanded his appointment in order to assuage and assure other army officers that Lt. Col. Rabelo's deposition was not intended as an affront to the pride of the growing national military establishment.[2] In a third way, Barroso was like his predecessor; he was as though "conceived" in "anti-*acciolysmo*." Barroso, it ought to be noted, had briefly governed Ceará in 1892. It was he who had succeeded Rabelo's father-in-law, the deposed General Clarindo de Queiroz, a friend and fellow officer, in the highest office of the state. Both Clarindo's deposition and Barroso's interim term as government had been brought to an end by Accioly-dominated forces who in 1893 were to win and retain oligarchical power over Ceará until 1912.[3]

As Governor, Barroso chose not to deal with the deposed *rabelistas*. Unlike Rabelo, he was of a pre-*"salvacionista"* military generation and had, unlike the *"salvadores,"* little sympathy for the nouveau-riche middle classes. Rather, his administration—wracked by the rubber "bust" of 1913, the European war of 1914, and the drought which struck Ceará in 1915 (as horrendously as in 1877)—was to rest firmly, if momentarily, on the victorious conservative alliance of *marretas* and *acciolystas*.

This alliance, of course, was tenuous and unstable. Pinheiro Machado, for one, had no serious intention of favoring the Acciolys' return to power, despite their role in the revolution; wanting, however, to retain the political machinery of conservatism, the *gaúcho* strong-man decided to place all of the federal government's power behind his chief Cearense confidant, Thomas Cavalcante, founder of the *marreta* party in Ceará. For his part, Cavalcante had no use for Accioly. So he reminded the public that the Acciolys had agreed in June 1912 to a pact with Rabelo; the object of this treacherous propaganda was to deprive Accioly of his share of power in the Barroso government. More significantly, Cavalcante, desirous of winning the governorship at a later date, refused to disband his *marreta* party's local branches throughout Ceará, or merge them with the remnants of PRC-C units, the one time main line of Accioly's power. Governor Barroso, for his part, had little use for the Acciolystas who had deprived him and General Clarindo de Queiroz of power in 1892. Thus, Barroso, beholden to Cattete and surrounded by *marretas,* abandoned his policy of neutrality and threw his support to Cavalcante by naming only loyal *marretas* to high posts in his new government.[4]

Cavalcante's maneuver to retain his own party structures (now supported by Barroso) and his efforts to win all power for himself at the expense of both "recent" *marretas* such as Floro and João Brigido and the *acciolystas,* resulted in the immediate rupture of the unstable *marreta-acciolysta* alliance. The effects of this rupture were immediately visible in the Legislative Assembly. Elected in May 1914, with Cattete's protection, the thirty "revolutionary" deputies split in September into two camps: fifteen supported the *Partido Unionista,* a hodgepodge of *acciolystas,* led by Floro and the followers of João Brigido; the other fifteen closed ranks behind the *Partido Conservador Cearense,* in effect, those *marretas* who, financed by Pinheiro Machado, continued to follow Thomas Cavalcante.[5] Thus, equally divided, neither party had a majority (sixteen votes). The stalemate was further complicated when two *marreta* seats became vacant upon the death of one deputy and the selection of the other by Barroso for a top state government post. Barroso then proposed two more *marretas* to fill the vacant seats. But, Floro Bartholomeu, who as president of the "rump" Assembly in Joaseiro was chosen as the legitimate president of the new Assembly, refused to recognize the substitutes. Three reasons prompted Floro's defiance. First of all, he saw that a Barroso-*marreta* coalition, sanctioned by Pinheiro Machado, would effectively deprive the *acciolystas* of power, and as a result, curtail his own bid for a political career. Secondly, he was convinced that Barroso had personally betrayed him. Earlier, the Governor had vetoed a bill that would have compensated Floro for the 400 contos he had spent for the successful revolution.[6] Thirdly, if Floro could succeed in appointing an *acciolysta* partisan to but one of the two vacant legislative seats, then he would have obtained a working majority in the Assembly, loyal to *acciolysmo.* As a result, not only would he obtain his 400 contos, but perhaps even a congressional nomination on the old PRC-C (now *Unionista*) ticket.

As it was, Floro's break with Barroso confirmed the *marreta-acciolysta* rupture; with deputies divided equally in the assembly, the state government became immobile and inoperative. Despite a mounting economic crisis, now aggravated by the cessation of trade with war-torn Europe, Floro remained obstinate. The ambitious *bacharel,* archetype of an "old Republic" generation, was holding out for higher stakes: not only a congressional seat, but as leader of the revolution, a determining voice in national affairs. It was at this juncture that he and Padre Cícero nearly parted ways—a crisis never again repeated in their eighteen year friendship. At the time the Patriarch was in Joaseiro, far removed from the Fortaleza battleground in which Floro and his *marreta* opponents were locked in a war of political survival. Nonetheless, interested parties in Fortaleza and Rio de Janeiro (including Pinheiro Machado and Senator Cavalcante) deluged the priest with urgent telegrams petitioning him to intervene to end the rift created by Floro.[7] When these appeals to his patriotism, political naivete, and basically pacific inclinations prompted the Patriarch to urge Floro to heal party wounds, Floro resorted to a deadly weapon: the threat to end his friendship with the cleric. Fearing that a single impolitic move on Padre Cícero's part could end his career, Floro telegraphed the Patriarch. In this missive of 20 September 1914, Floro asked for the priest's trust and assured him that he was acting in Joaseiro's and the nation's interests; he concluded, however, with the following demands and admonition:[8]

> Convince yourself that Y. Rev. can achieve nothing from there except at the risk of further worsening the [present]situation. . . .
> I beg that you do not part from my orientation but should you desire or believe it [necessary] to do so, then be frank with me so that I may relieve myself of this [responsibility, thus] leaving myself free to act as it suits me best, no longer concerning myself with the desire of your enemies to do as they wish, especially in regard to Joaseiro.

The seventy-year old Patriarch had no alternative. His hope to return to the priesthood rested with Floro. So, too, did Joaseiro's security. With the return to the Cariry of Floro's "revolutionary" *cangaceiro* regiments from Fortaleza, Joaseiro's political enemies again charged the Patriarch with "protecting criminals." In turn, Barroso, like his predecessor, ordered a police campaign against banditry in the Cariry;[9] only Floro's political presence in the highest circles of state and nation could prevent the inimical Governor from transforming that campaign, as had Rabelo, into a political weapon against the faithful *acciolysta chefes* in the Valley. These considerations were paramount when the Patriarch submitted to Floro's leadership. Two months later, this submission was and would remain complete until Floro's death in 1926: Upon Floro's demand, the Patriarch agreed never again to act politically without Floro's prior approval.[10]

Despite Floro's complete political ascension over the Patriarch, the *marreta-acciolysta* stalemate continued unchanged well into 1915. That year, the onslaught of one of the worst droughts in Ceará's history further crippled the economy and almost depopulated the Cariry and the "New Jerusalem" whose unemployed *maniçoba* workers began to flee, often to the ranks of the São Paulo state police force, one of the few available jobs at the time. The worsening of the economic crisis, however, provided the impetus to ending the political stalemate. Deposed *rabelistas* (who held not a single political post in Barroso's government) met with their one-time *acciolysta* allies in Rio de Janeiro. Pledged to renew the fatal pact of June 1912, *rabelistas* and *acciolystas* decided at first on a legal tactic to depose Barroso and his *marreta* supporters. The new allies argued that the revolution of Joaseiro had illegally dissolved the 1913 Assembly which had been composed entirely of *rabelistas*. If the nation's Supreme Court could be persuaded to declare the *rabelista* assembly still to be constitutional, then under their renewed pact, both *acciolystas* and *rabelistas* would together return to power. But the Supreme Court refused and as a result the new pact was stillborn, and the government of Benjamin Barroso continued immobilized until its tenure drew to a close in 1916.[11] Only then, with the drought ended and the economy on the road to restoration, did Ceará find its political equilibrium. In essence, the *rabelistas* joined forces with the agrarian interests of one-time *marretas* in a "popular" democratic party. Then, with the return of José Accioly to Fortaleza, one-time PRC-C adherents, both representatives of traditional agrarian interests and some professionals, recomposed a new conservative party. Their equal strength led to coalition politics in most of the subsequent administrations until 1930.[12] The Cariry Valley *chefes,* for their part, most frequently sided with the younger Accioly's conservative party. However, the Cariry, united for a decade behind Padre Cícero, skillfully used its decisive political power more often in the interests of its own region than in Accioly's. The emergence of the Cariry as a "third force" in Cearense politics was a direct result of the revolution of 1914.

The Balance Sheet of Power: Joaseiro and the Cariry

It cannot be denied that Joaseiro had gained immediately from the "revolution." In late 1914, Ceará's assembly endowed the *município* with the status
of an autonomous judicial district (*comârca*). It also granted Joaseiro its
own justice of the peace as well as a public notary (*tabellião público* or
cartório), perhaps the most important legal institution in Brazil during the
"Old Republic."[13] In a word, the revolution of 1914 had at last completed
the process of Joaseiro's liberation from Crato: the notarial and juridical
autonomy achieved in 1914 confirmed the victory of total independence
that had begun with the granting of political autonomy in 1911. Now
on an equal footing, Joaseiro and Crato, despite recurring tensions, assumed
joint leadership of the Valley. Barbalha, which had aspired to the joint role
with Crato, entered upon a long decline which only reversed itself in 1960.
In Crato, Col. Antonio Luis also returned to power, as prefect and state
deputy.[14] Thereafter, his personal friendship and unwritten political alliance
with the Patriarch and Floro significantly prevented Crato's resentment from
spilling over, especially as Joaseiro slowly but certainly assumed the dominant position which it enjoys today in the continuing tale of these two cities.

From 1916 until 1926, the Joaseiro–Crato axis dominated the Cariry
Valley. Its conservative party units owed less to the Acciolys (as they did
in the early 1900s) than they did to the political prestige of Padre Cícero.
As Vice-President of Ceará (in the elections of 1914, he moved from Third
to First Vice-President), as real or imagined leader of the revolution, as a
distributor of political patronage and of cheap manpower throughout the
backlands, the Patriarch was showered with deference by Cariry *coronéis*.
Only with his advice did they appoint local officials, support state and
federal candidates; and only with his endorsement did they solicit government subsidies for public works and economic development. Indeed, until
1926 the Patriarch was granted by Ceará's unstable governmental coalitions
considerable local patronage in exchange for his electoral support and endorsement. In turn, the Patriarch—flanked by Antonio Luis and Floro
Bartholomeu—used his influence for the advancement of Joaseiro and the
Cariry Valley.

Indeed, the Cariry had at last achieved a considerable measure of
bargaining power within Cearense politics. For almost four decades, it had
received few benefits from Fortaleza. In contrast, its taxes were destined
for asphalting and illuminating the streets of the capital as well as providing

the merchant middle class of the coast with sewage, potable water, tramways, theatres, new churches, luxurious private clubs, hospitals, clinics, and cinemas.[15] This inequality was long decried in the Cariry, "the granary of the Northeast," and partly explains why Valley merchants historically preferred to do business with the *praça* of Recife. Indeed, Recife's port, closer to Europe and Brazil's industrial South than Fortaleza's, offered manufactured goods at a lower price, while the better transportation facilities within Pernambuco also reduced the costs for retail merchants in the interior. Despite the natural market that existed between the Valley and the Pernambucan coast, it was the political and fiscal power of equidistant Fortaleza that took much from the Valley and returned little.[16]

This disparity also seems to have been an important factor behind the Cariry's participation in the revolution of 1913–1914. In retrospect, that event must now be understood *not* as a conflict between a "retrograde backland culture" and the "civilized coast," but rather as the attempt of the Valley to increase its share of "civilization," power, and consequent material gains. The so-called "sedition," then, was not a revolt to destroy the power structure of the state, but rather a violent means purposely employed to obtain a greater share in that system, commensurate with the Valley's contribution to Ceará's progress. That this ambition was partially frustrated explains the persistence into the present of strong localist sentiment.[17] The origin and continued survival of that sentiment coincided with a significantly broader notion of "Northeastern Regionalism," which, beginning in the 1920s, represented the claims of the inhabitants of the arid Northeast for a greater share of the nation's increasing prosperity. In both the Cariry and the Northeast this movement paralleled the rise of nationalist sentiment throughout Brazil in which Padre Cícero was also to play a role.

For the moment, it is necessary to note that immediately after the revolution the Patriarch's influence, political and otherwise, extended rapidly both within the Cariry and into other states of the Northeast, thus justifying the repeated assertion that Joaseiro was the largest bailiwick in the Northeast. For example, in neighboring Pernambuco and Paraíba, even in distant Alagôas (from whence so many of Joaseiro's pilgrims hailed) there were few candidates for political office who did not request the cleric's endorsement.[18] The highest tribute to his influence was paid by Ceará's governors themselves. After 1917, three of the four governors elected prior to 1930 made a personal "pilgrimage" to Joaseiro after which photographs taken with the Patriarch formed an important ingredient of campaign literature. Even after Padre Cícero's death in 1934, candidates and politicians continued to visit the Patriarch's tomb; some have even called themselves *"romeiros do meu Padim,"* with an eye to capturing the vote of the followers of the "saint of Joaseiro."[19]

The basis of the Patriarch's political influence only partly derived from his religious prestige among the lower classes. In large measure, it stemmed from and was secured by the constant activity and ambition of Floro Bartholomeu. After Floro's brief stint as president of Ceará's legislative assembly (1914–1915), he was reelected state deputy for the 1916–1920 period. In 1921, he was sent as an "independent" (from the Cariry) to the lower house of the national congress, to which he had unsuccessfully aspired in 1916. Floro retained his seat in congress until his untimely death in March 1926.[20] His passing, it must be added, was the beginning of the Patriarch's political end—proof enough that without Floro, the cleric's honorific title as the "greatest *coronel* of the Brazilian Northeast" might never have been conferred.

Upon Floro's death, Padre Cícero desperately tried to appoint as successor Juvêncio Santanna, Joaseiro's first judge, the Patriarch's godchild (*afilhado*) and son of Missão Velha's prominent political *chefe*. But the Patriarch's failure rested upon the decision of both parties to end the Cariry's "third force" position in state affairs, for they refused their support. As a consequence, Valley interests, intent on retaining the Cariry's decisive advantage, obliged the Patriarch himself to succeed Floro, the true builder of the Valley's political kingdom. In May 1926, the Patriarch easily won election to the Brazilian congress. But, because of ill health, little inclination, and the stringent criticism which disappointed coastal *"políticos"* heaped upon his candidacy, the Patriarch never took his seat. Nonetheless, his decision to yield to Valley chiefs momentarily saved the Cariry from the decline intended for the region by the professional and ambitious politicians of the coast. Two years later, the Patriarch, despite ill health, oncoming blindness, advanced years (he was 86 years old) once again tried to rally electoral support behind Juvêncio, his own and the Cariry's choice for congress. But this too failed, while Juvêncio's appointment as.Secretary of the Interior of the State in the 1928 government was engineered in Fortaleza to placate the Cariry's loss of a post in the national congress.[21] However, in 1930 the Vargas revolution symbolically completed the rapid destruction (since Floro's death) of the cleric's and the Cariry's direct political influence: Joaseiro's new prefect, appointed by the revolutionary government, ordered the Patriarch's portrait removed from the city hall. This act, which deeply wounded the octagenarian, was the symbolic end of an era in the political history of the Brazilian Northeast. Padre Cícero's death in 1934, while truly an occasion for the apotheosis of the "saint of Joaseiro" by the poor, the humble, and the faithful, was in political terms an anticlimax.[22]

The Cariry: The Context of Regional Development

It is important to reexamine the Cariry's transformation and achievements during the fifteen years prior to the Vargas revolution. There is no intent here to vindicate the memory of Floro and the Patriarch, although without them these changes and advances might have been less successful and pronounced. Rather, such a discussion might help to illustrate the dimensions along which development and modernization of a sort did take place within a blackland region of the Brazilian Northeast, as well as to place this decade and a half of progress within the context of important national developments.

The political dimensions of change have been alluded to already, namely, a hierarchical system of political patronage in which an exchange for electoral support was the key to any one region's chances of growth. During the oligarchic period of Northeastern history (ca. 1896–1910) the states became the organizing units of patronage. During the subsequent "salvacionista" or bourgeois period of Northeastern history (ca. 1910–1930), the federal government—via its expanding federal bureaucracy and legion of military and political appointees—began to compete with the states as the source of patronage and by definition, the manipulation of the political system. In a sense, the Vargas revolution of 1930 established the completion of that process by which a centralized federal government finally displaced the state governments as the principal dispenser of the national largesse and the arbiter of the conditions under which any single region was to obtain its share. In the Cariry, the oligarchic period corresponded to the Cratense municipal administrations of both colonels Belém (1896–1904) and Antonio Luis (1904–1912), each of whom held high offices in the state government. The "bourgeois" period coincided with the state and congressional power exercised by Floro Bartholomeu (1913–1926). In each period, the development of the Cariry Valley depended directly upon the region's political ties now to the state, now to the federal government.

Since the earlier chapters have already examined those ties in detail prior to 1913, it is in order here to examine briefly how they developed in the latter period of increasing federal centralization. The high degree to which Floro, for example, was linked to the federal government has already been illustrated by his role in the revolution of Joaseiro, the execution of which directly originated with Cattete. In 1919, when Brazil's president, the Northeasterner, Epitácio Pessôa, allocated vast federal subsidies to the arid backlands for public works against droughts (dams, roads, wells, and railroads),[23] the Cariry's gains were to prove proportional to its federal political influence (even though the fertile region itself was not properly speaking a drought area). It was in that year (1919) that Floro Bartholomeu received a federal subsidy for the pavement of Joaseiro's urban center. Thousands of men and women, unemployed by the partial drought of 1919, were put to work under Floro's direction. Although the project was a limited one, it was federal—rather than state funds—that made it at all possible.[24]

In 1926, the Cariry's ties to the federal government proved even more reciprocal. Just four years earlier, the *"Tenentes,"* reform-minded junior officers of the Brazilian army, had revolted.[25] Under the leadership of Lt. Luis Carlos Prestes, they took to the interior on a forced march in flight from government persecution. During their backland peregrinations, they became for the urban populations of the coast a standard-bearer of greater democratization of the Brazilian political process; they also symbolized growing nationalist sentiments in Brazil. When the famous Prestes Column reached Ceará, in early 1926, it was congressman Floro Bartholomeu who, with the approval of then President Arthur Bernardes, organized Joaseiro's "Patriotic Battalion" to defeat the anti-government "rebels." It was then that the Patriarch, under Floro's influence, issued his celebrated letter to the *"revoltosos."* Although he asked them to surrender, he recognized their aspirations as just. No doubt, Floro's defense of Bernardes' government in the long run placed the Patriarch and the Cariry in frank and irreversible opposition to the *tenentes* and their widespread liberal supporters who, once awakened in 1922, went on to triumph nationally in 1930.[26] However, Floro's actions against the Prestes Column were from the Cariry's vantage point—as a "third force" within Ceará politics—a guarantee of federal patronage and continued regional gains. Unfortunately, with Floro's sudden death in March 1926, the Valley never really collected. Instead, for its "defense of the republic," Floro was posthumously rewarded with the honorific rank of general of the army. The twenty-gun salute above his bier was the political death-knell of the Cariry.[27]

Federal political patronage was not the sole key to development. Changes in the world economy also stimulated decisive gains in the Cariry after 1918, which, in turn, enhanced the region's bargaining power within state and federal political circles.[28] The drought of 1915, in which Padre Cícero's actions greatly spared Joaseiro from total collapse, came to end the following year, while postwar European reconstruction was soon to create a rising demand for Ceará's mineral and agricultural products. Signs of future prosperity were already in the offing in 1917. That year, for example, a Brazilian army officer joined forces with Joaseiro's resident engineer, the Frenchman, Conde Adolpho Van den Brule, to exploit iron mines recently surveyed in the Valley. At the same time, the Patriarch did not cease to use his political influence in Rio de Janeiro to resolve in his favor his disputed title to the copper deposits at Coxá. (Legal setbacks and counterclaims by the federal government delayed the final settlement of this celebrated question until two decades after the Patriarch's death.) Furthermore, in the 1920s, Europe's renewed drive to export capital to Brazil's emerging private industrial sector prompted Padre Cícero to sponsor a project for the development of coal deposits recently found in the Cariry. But the reason for the failure of these early efforts to industrialize the backlands was the greater abundance and higher profitability of the region's agricultural resources.[29]

Indeed, Europe's chief interest lay in the purchase of Brazil's cheaply produced agricultural raw materials. Cotton, once Ceará's key export during the American Civil War, again became "king."[30] Between 1916 and 1918, cotton represented half of the value of Ceará's total annual exports. Throughout the twenties, it consistently accounted for about 75 per cent of Ceará's total revenues, while taxes derived from various aspects of cotton production and export amounted to 55 per cent of the annual operating budget of Ceará's state government. One indicator of cotton's importance can be seen from the report issued in 1923 by a delegation of British textile manufacturers who visited Joaseiro and other production centers in the Northeast to promote increases in both the volume and quality of cotton exports to England.[31] Cotton's expansion, however, was not limited to Ceará but also occurred in other Northeastern states, especially Paraíba. There the city of

Campina Grande, situated in the *agreste* zone, began to emerge at this time as the chief sorting and exporting center of cotton destined for Europe and increasingly (to 1930), for the expanding textile mills of Recife and São Paulo.[32]

The reintegration of Northeastern production into the world economy after 1918, and the large-scale public works program undertaken in the arid *sertão* by the federal government with surplus coffee export earnings between 1919 and 1922 greatly increased Padre Cícero's influence as a manpower magnate. If during the earlier *maniçoba* "boom," the Patriarch had emerged as the "labor czar" of the Cariry, during cotton's revival in the twenties, he became the "labor czar" of the entire Northeast. English and American engineering firms hired to construct the federally subsidized dams, incessantly solicited the priest for the work brigades employed in Paraíba, Pernambuco, and Rio Grande do Norte. So, too, did the Brazilian engineers engaged in extending the Baturité Railroad from Iguatú to the Cariry. Without the Patriarch's labor brigades, the cotton industry in the Paraíban *sertão* "would have disappeared." According to Floro, "annually at harvest time, five thousand workers, mostly women," left Joaseiro to pick the crop of the chief cotton *municípios* in Paraíba, alone.[33]

But the Patriarch not only harnessed and mobilized labor, he also inculcated in these peasants the values requisite in a wage-earning economy. Every evening he preached to the multitude of workers that assembled before his residence. Invariably, these *consagrações* (since the bishop had canonically forbidden the Patriarch to preach and call his talks "sermons") dwelt upon honesty, hard work, and respect for the civil and ecclesiastical authorities, and ended with the injunction: "Whoever has stolen, steal no more; whoever has murdered, murder no more; whoever was dishonest, abandon your evil paths. . . . Go to your work and pray the rosary of the Mother of God each day at sunrise and at sundown."[34] Quite unintentionally, the cleric had become a key agent in the process of "modernization"— conservative, capitalist, and paternalistic in inspiration though it was—of the neglected Northeast.

Furthermore, as the modern economy extended its production, wage, credit, and banking systems into hitherto somnolent areas, it was the Patriarch who tried to prevent some of the "negative" consequences of this process from disrupting the social order. In the Northeast, a new wave of professional banditry was but one of the symptoms of the region's haphazard adaptation to a modern capitalist economy. Unlike the paid, political banditry engendered and protected by *coronéis* prior to 1914, professional banditry of the twenties gave rise to small bands of uprooted men in which leadership was invested in one of its own members. The archetype of this modern *cangaceiro* was the Brazilian Robin Hood, Antonio Virgulino Ferreira, the celebrated *Lampeão*. At times respectful of the lower classes, his insurgent career and wide-scale destruction of property incited terror among all social classes, backland *chefes* as well as government officials. Before *Lampeão* and others of his kind (whose significance to the modern social history of Brazil is beyond the scope of this study) the Patriarch preached against the use of violence and urged repentance. When *Lampeão* and his band entered Joaseiro in 1926, supposedly on the invitation of Dr. Floro to help put down the Prestes Column, the urban press of the Northeast seized the occasion to chastize Padre Cícero as a "protector of bandits." But, the priest retorted, his only interest was to convince *Lampeão* and his band to abandon their errant ways and retire to the inland state of Matto Grosso, where as farmers they could commence an honest life.[35]

The pacific counsels of the Patriarch were only sometimes heeded in such extreme cases of social disorder. For this reason, the cleric personally campaigned in the late twenties for the establishment of a federal army garrison in Joaseiro.[36] Its chief purposes were to keep the peace and enlist into military service the more recalcitrant elements of backland society. Floro, who in 1914 and again in the 1920s personally ordered the arrest of several professional bandits who had infiltrated Joaseiro,[37] perhaps best summarized Padre Cícero's efficacious acts on behalf of the conservative society in transition. In his defense of the Patriarch before the national congress in 1923, various congressmen interrupted Floro's speech to sum up the impression which Floro attempted to convey: "Padre Cícero is a force for order in that *sertão*. . . . Without him the government would be unable to maintain order there; this is the truth."[38]

The Cariry: The Impact of Regional Development

During the twenties, the Cariry was the scene of manifold economic changes and advances.[39] As the wage-labor system spread throughout the Northeast, the price of labor in the Valley (and throughout Ceará) rose. So too did the price of the less fertile land situated in the Araripe plateau. That became increasingly parceled out and sold in smaller lots that proved more manageable for the production by small farmers of foodstuffs, especially manioc, beans, rice, and corn. Growing consumer markets for this produce had been created elsewhere in the Northeast by large labor forces engaged in railroad and dam building. *Rapadura,* like manioc, a basic staple of the lower classes, continued as a major regional export of Crato and Barbalha, the traditional sugarcane centers of the Valley.

Cotton, or "white gold," rapidly came to dominate the local economy. One-time *maniçoba* fields no longer lay fallow or served as pasture for cattle; at harvest time, cotton turned the red earth into a blanket of snow. The rise of cotton in the Valley was spectacular enough that in the thirties it attracted extensive capital investment by the American-owned Anderson, Clayton Company and remains today, under Brazilian control, the chief product of the Valley.[40]

However, the Cariry's forward thrust is best attested to by the establishment of the first bank in the Northeastern *sertão* (in Crato in 1921) and of the first regional association of export agriculturists (*the Associação Agrícola do Cariri* also in Crato in 1921)[41] and, in 1926, by the arrival of the railroad in Joaseiro and Crato—for which Padre Cícero had worked since 1910, and for whose construction he had provided the major supply of laborers.[42]

Socially too, the integration of the backlands into both a national political system and an international economic network was beginning to have effect. In Joaseiro, for example, there were efforts to put an end not only to banditry, gambling, and other social vices, but also to the excessive manifestations of religious fanaticism. Floro, as in so many other questions, was chiefly responsible for this change, although neither his methods nor the consequent repression of the lower classes are at issue here. Understandably, as a *bacharel* and urban oriented professional man it was unpleasant for him to be scoffed at in the Federal Congress as the *"deputado dos fanáticos."* During the minor drought of 1919 he violently suppressed the recrudescence of a society of penitential flagellants, a religious institution which had existed in the Cariry even before Padre Cícero's arrival in 1872. Under Floro's orders, the *penitentes* were disbanded.[43] So, too, was a small millenarian sect known as "the celestial hosts" whose members took the names of saints and resided, in sexual deviance, in the Hôrto. The religious garb and ceremonial accoutrements of both the flagellants and "celestial hosts" were ordered burned in public by Floro, while the unrepentant were forcibly put to work in repairing the streets and sidewalks of Joaseiro.[44] Again in 1921, Floro acted decisively: this time against the Valley's most renowned *beato*, José Lourenço, caretaker of one of the Patriarch's prized breeding bulls. The *beato's* admirers had attributed curative powers to the animal's waste. Floro ordered the animal slain in the public square and its flesh sold for public consumption. (Unfortunately, the tale of José Lourenço has been recounted in a largely anecdotal and partisan manner. Only recently has the *beato's* role as initiator of a popularly inspired agrarian reform experiment been made evident.)[45]

Joaseiro's social life changed in other respects. Thanks to Joaseiro's urbane and cosmopolitan physician-deputy, the traditional religious feasts of the town slowly began to yield some of the limelight to secular celebrations. The pre-Lenten carnival, independence day, and even Joaseiro's anniversary of municipal autonomy now became festive occasions in the social life of a city whose sons and daughters were ever more educated and sophisticated.[46] Educational institutions, until now mostly private and sustained by the Patriarch, began to expand. In 1917, for example, Joaseiro's first normal-school teacher, trained in Fortaleza, organized the city's primary school system. Several years later, an eccentric *Paraíbano* (to whom Joaseiro owes one of its first recorded histories) founded the city's first secondary school. Its life, unfortunately was short.[47] Nonetheless by 1923, Joaseiro could take pride in its four state- and municipal-financed primary schools and a large number of private ones. More extensive educational facilities were not established, but not because of the Patriarch's hostility to learning, as one writer has claimed.[48] On the contrary, the Patriarch had helped establish dozens of private primary schools. As early as 1916 he personally founded one of the first orphanages of the interior, the *Orfanato Jesus, Maria e José*.[49] In 1932, it was the Patriarch who donated his own land for the government to erect the first rural teachers' training school, established finally in 1934 as the *Escóla Normal Rural,* the first of its kind in the Brazilian Northeast.[50]

If secondary education lagged in Joaseiro, as indeed it did, it was partly because superior educational institutions already existed in Crato, just 18 kilometers from Joaseiro. There many clergymen, not inclined toward pastoral duties, usually earned their livelihood by directing and teaching in their own private primary and secondary schools, often with boarding facilities (*internatos*). Indeed, until 1941, when Joaseiro's first permanent secondary school was built, most of its *município's* high school population matriculated in Crato's *internatos*. Moreover, Joaseiro not only willingly provided students to help keep Crato's superior educational institutions solvent, but also sufficiently respected Crato's clerical monopoly over instruction. As a result, rivalry in educational matters did not occur until 1941.

Not so in other fields of endeavor, where intensive rivalry between the two cities had very early become a major stimulant to reciprocal economic and social improvements. As such, town rivalry, not uncommon to neighboring cities in Brazil as the history of Olinda and Recife demonstrates, proved a key, even if unanticipated, determinant of modern economic development. That rivalry, it will be remembered, originated with the "religious question" in the 1890s and was intensified during the struggle for Joaseiro's autonomy (1908–1911). After almost a decade of cooperation (1912–1921) it reemerged in the twenties (although not on the political level), when Joaseiro bid to reduce, in a matter of decades, Crato's position of leadership in the Cariry that had dated from the late eighteenth century. In 1921, Crato became, for example, the first Valley city to establish an office of rural public health (*pôsto de profilâxia rural*); in 1924, Joaseiro followed suit.[51] In 1921, Col. Antonio Luis inaugurated a new public square in Crato; in 1925, Joaseiro's Freedom Square was totally refurbished and in addition was graced with a life-size statue of Padre Cícero erected by Floro.[52] Crato's banking system, begun in 1921, was only equaled by Joaseiro in 1932 (partly because Joaseiro's moneylenders resisted the changeover to a legal credit system and partly because Crato's banking system appears to have successfully resisted any attempts by investors in Joaseiro to establish their own credit institutions). Unfortunately, this intensive rivalry has, on occasion, resulted in a duplication of public services that has proven detrimental to the growing needs of the Cariry as a whole. For example, shortly after 1928, when airplanes began to traverse the Northeastern skies of the southern cross, airfields were constructed—first in Joaseiro, on land donated by the Patriarch, then in Crato.[53] Pride, however, has barred each city from taking the first step in proposing a single, more centrally located, airport that would serve both cities more efficiently than either of the existing ones does at present. Pride, too, continues to impede more efficient collaboration today in the experimental industrialization program which was begun in 1963 by the state government in collaboration with technicians from abroad. Finally, this same pride prevents Crato, long the "Pearl of the Cariry," from recognizing that Joaseiro may have at last become the leading city of the Valley. At least in one respect, such superiority may have recently been confirmed: in 1966, four decades after Floro's death, a former prefect of Joaseiro was returned to the Federal Congress as the elected deputy of the Cariry Valley.

Northeastern Regionalism and "Folkloric" Nationalism

The economic and social rivalry between Joaseiro and Crato during the twenties must not obscure their essential political unity when viewed from the perspective of the Cariry Valley as a homogeneous political region within Ceará state. That unity prevailed from the revolution of 1913–1914 until the Vargas victory in 1930. That unity was symbolized in the intimate friendship between the Patriarch, Floro, and Col. Antonio Luis.[54] Finally, that unity secured the leadership of the Cariry which, with federal support, cleverly and successfully converted the region into a "third force" within Cearense politics.

Why was Cariry regionalism so successful during the twenties? Some writers point to the mid-nineteenth-century efforts of the Valley to become an autonomous state. Others observe that, a century later (1955), a similar proposal to create a new "State of the Cariris-Novos" reconfirmed the strength of the region's sentiments. Indeed, both those movements, like the "revolution of 1913–1914," were important rallying points—rather than secessionist or revolutionary movements—designed primarily to increase the Cariry's relative strength within the existing conservative political structure of Ceará. However in our opinion neither the nineteenth century precedent nor twentieth century continuity of Cariry "localism" are alone sufficient to explain the success of the region's "third force" politics in the twenties. Two additional factors appear more fruitful. One, primarily political, has already been stressed: the expanding role of direct federal patronage in the Valley and the stalemate of Ceará's two-party system after 1916. The other concerns the forward thrust which the Valley's collective stand received from the concurrent political awakening of the entire Northeast.

Indeed, "Cariry localism" in the twenties coincided chronologically with the rise of "Northeastern Regionalism." This latter movement may be said to have originated quite unconsciously in the last quarter of the 19th century. The great droughts of 1877–1879 and of 1888–1889 profoundly dramatized to the entire nation the plight of fellow Brazilians in the abandoned Northeast.[55] When sporadic public and private charity proved inadequate to relieve this afflicted third of Brazil's populaion, more systematic aid at last appeared. In 1911, the federal government created the IFOCS, the Federal Inspectory of Works Against Droughts. Its jurisdiction over several chronically drought-stricken states not only provided a common institutional framework within which regional politics could unfold but also underscored an important common problem of the region with which its inhabitants might identify. Thus IFOCS and droughts came inadvertently to provide in part the coordinates within which a "Northeastern consciousness" took shape. In a word, a climatic condition and a federal agency contributed greatly to the development both of a Northeastern regional unity, and of a region-wide awakening to the right to share more fully in the fruits of the nation.

While the everpresent material backwardness of the Northeast, when compared to the industrial South, provided the basis for the region's demands for improvement, it was the local students of folklore who generated the common ideology of "Northeastern Regionalism." In 1912, the Cearense historian, Gustavo Barroso, (under the symbolic penname, João do Norte) wrote the first major work of Northeastern folklore, *Terra do Sol.*[56] This study of Ceará diverged considerably from the views of many contemporary intellectuals such as Rodolpho Theophilo. The latter contended that the Northeast's social stagnation was a consequence of the human inferiority of the racially mixed *sertanejo* or *cabóclo* (rural inhabitant) of the backlands. In contrast, João do Norte, while not entirely free of racist sentiments, depicted the backlanders as the very source of an ennobled people whose language and values constituted the very essence of Northeastern civilization. Their capacity to suffer, to endure hardships, to labor tirelessly, and their love of the backlands, of family, and of religion—all these were hailed as positive qualities which Brazilians, regardless of region, might learn, love, and emulate on the road to modernity.

If João do Norte was the most prominent pioneer of the folkloric base of Northeastern regionalism, it was another Cearense who was among the first authors to link the region's folklore to rising Brazilian nationalism during the twenties. Journalist and historian, Leonardo Motta devoted his life to interpreting and transmitting the values of the *sertão* to the literate and nationalistic middle classes of the urban coast. Motta made his debut

in 1921 with the classic work, *Cantadores*.[57] Its subject was the eight backland troubadours who, to the accompaniment of the guitar, sang and recited
their popular poetry at backland fairs. *Contadores* transcribed their tales of
geste, their heroism, sanctity, humor, as well as the innate backland cynicism
reserved for delinquent churchmen and unfaithful politicians; in time, the
sophisticated urban elites unhesitatingly appropriated these perspectives
as the special mark of their own "abandoned" region. As the "ambas-
sador of the *sertão*," Leonardo Motta consciously sought to be not only the
intransigent defender of "the forgotten, ridiculed and calumniated *sertão*,"
but also the nationalist propagator of the "acuity, spiritual vitality and
vivacity of the neglected *sertanejo*. . . ."[58]

Contemporaries of Leonardo Motta and João do Norte among Northeastern journalists, writers, and politicians were also enflamed by the desire
to redeem the Northeast. Prior to 1930, they launched new attacks against
old distortions, and put forth new claims for Northeastern economic advancement against the old reluctance of Southern Brazil to share the nation's
wealth with the impoverished Northeast. In literature, the prose of Rachel
de Queiroz later exemplified the fully awakened Northeastern consciousness,
while in political and economic studies, the earlier monumental study,
Parahyba e os Seus Problemas of José Americo de Almeida, was the most
articulate claim to the Northeast's dissatisfaction with its secular relegation
to an inferior place in the nation.[59] Even Floro Bartholomeu, a native-born
Bahian, played his small share. In an impassioned defense of the Northeast
in the Federal Congress, Floro denounced the attacks of urban dilettantes
against the Northeast; he concluded: "What is certain is that it is in the
sertão where the moral heritage of the country is to be found."[60]

In this anguished process of regional awakening (it has continued into
the 1950s and 1960s under the Northeastern leadership of both Francisco
Julião, the radical lawyer and founder of the Peasant Leagues, and Celso
Furtado, the economist and first director of the Superintendancy for the
Economic Development of the Northeast), it is not surprising that for some
sectors of the region, prior to 1934, Padre Cícero came to be a symbol of the
Northeast's cause. Three journalists wrote of the Patriarch and his "New
Jerusalem" as proofs that the Northeast was capable of progress and growth,
if just given the opportunity.[61] With relish, they favorably compared the
sertanejos' capacity for hard work to that of the European immigrants who
had inundated Southern Brazil; they shrilly condemned the federal govern-

ment for abandoning the *sertanejos* while offering preferential treatment, land, and better wages to the immigrants. They praised the Patriarch's paternalistic guidance of the poor while they denounced the political "big-wigs" for their self-interest and hypocrisy. One writer, in line with the growing nationalist fervor of the late 1920s and early 1930s, even hailed the Patriarch as an eminent Brazilian nationalist: Padre Cícero's opposition to the government's "give-away" of vast portions of the Amazon rubber forests to Henry Ford in 1928 was contrasted to the *entreguista* ("sell out") mentality of federal officials.[62]

In view of these considerations, it is not surprising then that the Cariry's political success as a "third force" partly lay in the synchronized rise of its own localist spirit with that of "Northeastern Regionalism." That senti-ment, shared by conservative backlanders and the liberal middle classes of the coast, momentarily overrode ideological differences. Similarly, the "regionalist" sentiments of the Northeast—while atangonistic to the wealthier South—more often than not coincided with the more radical as-pirations of the southern-based nationalists who also sought a more just integration of the vital forces of the whole nation and a more equitable distribution of Brazil's spiritual and material wealth—aspirations that have yet to be realized.

10

The Patriarch
and the Church

The Abdication of the Patriarch

There can be no doubt that Padre Cícero figured prominently during the twenties in both the material advances of the Cariry and the rise of Northeastern regionalism and Brazilian nationalism. However, it is also beyond any doubt that in many of these developments he had often been a passive participant. Paradoxically, while the revolution of 1913–1914 nominally endowed him with extraordinary political power, he himself had personally abdicated from exercising that power. Clearly, his act of abdication was one of the chief consequences of the revolution. Although the Patriach became a national political figure and in Joaseiro was transformed into the "eternal" prefect, a post which he held uninterruptedly from 1914 until 1927, it was Floro who, in fact, held power.[1] In 1914, it will be recalled, Floro issued his ultimatum to the cleric, who was to take no public stand without his "alter ego's" prior consent. After 1921, when Floro easily won election to the federal congress, the Patriarch's influence, like the seasonal rivers of the *sertão,* effectively disappeared. Floro's domination, however, did not entirely account for the cleric's abdication. It may be rightly argued that the Patriarch was never a "political man"; that role had been clearly forced upon him in 1908 when Joaseiro began its struggle for autonomy from Crato. Thus, his political withdrawal after 1914 might be seen as a return to a life-style that was more fitting to the Patriarch's taste and preference. Yet, two additional factors were clearly at play and more accurately accounted for the prelate's action. First of all, there was his perennial hope to return fully to the priesthood. Once the political battle of 1913–1914 ended, Padre Cícero readily directed his remaining energies to the single-minded goal of regaining clerical orders. In fact, that all-consuming task (as we shall see later) continued to occupy him until he died, in 1934. Secondly, it is impossible to ignore the cleric's increasingly ill health and advanced age as a major reason for his political and social withdrawal. Indeed, after 1924, when the Patriarch celebrated his eightieth year, repeated infirmities and the toll of longevity conspired to oblige him to live in virtual isolation within the walls of the very city he had endowed with life.[2]

There is no clearer indicator of the Patriarch's abdication and withdrawal than the profound changes which occurred within his own household.[3] Decades earlier, Padre Cícero's modest residence alongside the Chapel of Our Lady of Sorrows had been the spiritual oasis of a young, zealous, and disinterested priest. Its doors were never closed to the poor and to all in need of material and spiritual refreshment. It was also the hearth and home of the cleric's mother and sisters and of the *beatas* and orphan girls who resided there permanently under the protection of the priest and his kin. During the height of the "religious question," it became as much a center of pilgrimage as did the Chapel of Our Lady of Sorrows; it was the fortress of those enduring friendships with José Marrocos and José Lôbo who, with the cleric, defended their "miracle" against the church. It even became a refuge for fellow priests, like Frs. Alencar Peixoto and Quintino Rodrigues, who for political or other reasons, sought and obtained temporary asylum within the Patriarch's residence. Some years later, as Joaseiro's campaign against Crato intensified, it became the hub of politics from which enthusiasm and moral encouragement radiated; it was even briefly the home of Floro Bartholomeu who was initially welcomed by all as Joaseiro's first physician and later hailed as the architect of victory over Crato.

Then, in 1914, the victorious revolution abruptly altered the past. Under

Floro's influence, the Patriarch was obliged to move to more spacious quarters. A sister and a few *beatas* accompanied him; but his mother, his older sister, and the celebrated Maria de Araújo were now deceased; so too, his intimate childhood friends of another era.[4] The move to a more socially prominent residence coincided with a more radical change in the types of men who now graced the cleric's table. Under Floro's command, the Patriarch's kith and kin were replaced by governors and politicians of national repute, by military officers and federal officials. On their heels there came an endless train of foreign dignitaries who were received more readily than the endless train of pilgrims: British and American engineers, English cotton buyers, European botanists and museum curators, and even an emissary of the Rockefeller Foundation's Yellow Fever Commission.[5] During this new era, Padre Cícero apparently reigned while Floro in fact ruled. After the latter's death in 1926, those who aspired to replace him obliged the Patriarch to move once more to even more splendid quarters. But, the era of grandeur was at last on the wane as was the Patriarch's very life.

Indeed, the angel of death brooked no defiance; the Patriarch's declining health attested to that. Early in the twenties Cícero's physicians prescribed for him a strict diet and increased rest. As a result, the cleric's appearances at Floro's political banquets declined sharply; his other activities were also restricted. By 1924, the Patriarch's home became a sick ward and a virtual prison; he himself now had little contact with the world outside his walls. This change was signaled by the increased authority which was exercised over him and his affairs by the other celebrated *beata* in his life, D. Joanna Tertuliana de Jesus.[6] Known as *"Beata Mocinha,"* Joanna had come to Joaseiro in the 1890s, undoubtedly attracted by the miracles. At that time she was among the Patriarch's staunchest defenders, although her testimony before the bishop's commissions of inquiry revealed that she was not among the women who claimed supernatural powers. Unlike most of the witnesses who testified, Mocinha did not express belief in the miracles although she did fall subject to the penalties imposed on several *beatas* in 1894. Unlike most of the *beatas,* Mocinha was literate and intelligent besides and was devoted to the Patriarch. These qualities became evident after the death of Padre Cícero's mother, D. Quinou, in 1914. Mocinha then assumed the role of majordomo of the Patriarch's residence. With the subsequent illness and death (in 1923) of D. Angélica, Padre Cícero's sister, Mocinha had become the cleric's "alter ego" in most matters other than politics.[7]

It was she who cared for his health and personal affairs. In all business matters she acted energetically in the Patriarch's name: she bought and sold land, houses, and other properties; she invested in stocks of the first Brazilian-owned oil company; she opened the first model slaughterhouse in Joaseiro, and, in financial matters, borrowed money from local loan sharks in order that the aged priest could pay his medical bills.[8] She was the Patriarch's chief secretary; in this capacity she distributed mass-stipends to his fellow priests and supervised the receipt and dispatch of almost all his mounting correspondence which, eventually, required her to hire two full-time secretaries. Most important of all, Mocinha was, in effect, the Patriarch's warden. She arranged every detail of his life (especially during his last decade). Without her consent, few could pass the now locked doors of the priest's residence; neither *romeiro* nor the most respected figure of society gained entry to the citadel without Mocinha's approval.

Under these conditions, Mochina was invested with influence, the vastness of which she herself may have been unaware. But, others were; and they did their best to persuade the lowly born *beata* that their intentions in seeking out the Patriarch were of the utmost good. Two successful groups of petitioners clearly emerged in the last decade or so of the Patriarch's life. The one was comprised of "job seekers" and middle class *bacharéis* throughout Brazil intent on obtaining the Patriarch's electoral endorsement. There were also landowners and merchants, coastal businessmen, insurance agents, and industrialists; each was interested in some small favor, whether it be the obtention of workers and domestic servants or authorization to use the cleric's name or photograph in the publicity and sale of their products.[9]

The other group was comprised of the merchants of Joaseiro who sought some immediate financial gain. Chief among these were the *santeiros,* the city's craftsmen and venders of religious goods (now an important produce of Joaseiro artisans).[10] Through the *santeiros'* efforts, pilgrims were encouraged to come to Joaseiro; indeed the massive influxes of pilgrims which today occur twice annually date from the twenties when the religious goods merchants began to give publicity to the pilgrimage throughout the *sertão* and transform it into a lower-class backland variant of commercial tourism. It was during the twenties that the heavy influx of pilgrim-tourists made it impossible for the ailing Patriarch to see personally all his *"amiginhos"* (little friends, as he called them); organization was needed and the *santeiros* filled the need. With each sale of a rosary, saint's statue, or religious medal, the pilgrim was also offered a visit with the Patriarch. Each day, those *santeiros* who enjoyed the special favor of *"Beata* Mocinha" could be seen leading a regiment of their backland clients from any one of eight shops to the Patriarch's residence. Inside, a coterie of self-seekers often parted the pilgrim from his donation to the Patriarch despite the watchful eyes of the aging Mocinha, or so it was said.[11]

Another group of merchants, fewer in number and far more wealthy than the *santeiros* also availed themselves of the new era. They enjoyed the Patriarch's blessing, Floro's political munificience, and Mocinha's confidence; as a result, they enjoyed oligopolic control over the city's market for dry goods, hardware, foodstuffs, and other imported and locally made manufactures. It was this group that most feared the Patriarch's passing, believing that both newcomers and pilgrims would subsequently abandon the city. It is probably for this reason that the important merchants—under Floro's initiative—erected in 1925 the life-size bronze statue of the Patriarch in the center of Joaseiro.[12]

The Patriarch's abdication and his subsequent encirclement by the well meaning Mocinha and a coterie of self-seekers gave rise to profound resentments among the native sons. In 1925, they responded by making a bid for political power. That bid, however, might never have been possible were it not for a transitory modification in Padre Cícero's position vis-à-vis the ecclesiastical hierarchy after 1914.

The "Religious Question," 1914–1916

There can be no doubt that since his suspension in 1896, the Patriarch's paramount goal was to regain his orders. Neither the victorious revolution of 1914, nor the politicization of his residence under Floro's influence thereafter, nor his increased isolation in the twenties diminished this obsession. Obsession it was. No greater proof exists of the lengths to which the Patriarch would go than his frantic effort to establish the new ecclesiastical diocese of the Cariry in Joaseiro, even though Rome had already decreed Crato to be the episcopal seat! Crato's victory came in October 1914, when Pope Benedict XV issued the bull, *Catholicae Ecclesiae*.[13] According to this decree, Crato was made the episcopal see of the new diocese that was both to bear its name (instead of that of the Cariry, as Padre Cícero had proposed earlier) and to embrace twenty parishes scattered over the length and

breadth of the Cariry Valley. In December, news of the papal bull reached
Padre Cícero in the midst of the political rupture between Floro and Ceará's
Governor Barrosso. Momentous as that issue was, the Patriarch disregarded
the entire question. Instead, he moved swiftly and desperately to reverse the
papal bull! His archive of telegrams indicates that he urged friends in
Fortaleza to besiege the newly consecrated archbishop in the capital and the
papal nuncio in Petropolis with his appeal. To Rio de Janeiro, he dispatched
an urgent plea to his old friend, Comendador Accioly and to Floro, then
in the nation's capital to forge a second alliance between *acciolystas* and
rabelistas against Gov. Barosso. The text of that telegram clearly conveys
the Patriarch's audacious compulsiveness:[14]

Demonstrate [to the nuncio and others] my rights [to the new diocese] by
virtue of my endeavors in Rome in 1898 [and my continuing] efforts with the
aid of Dr. Leandro Bezerra [in 1908]. . . . Make [them] see this right [to erect]
the see here [in Joaseiro] where I offer them two properties [one in Coxá] of
sufficient value to constitute the patrimony, a house [that can serve as] the chan-
cellary, [and] land for a seminary whose construction I will facilitate."

Needless to say, the Patriarch's efforts were unsuccessful. Perhaps, his
offer of a generous patrimony even worked to his disadvantage because of
its apparent crassness. Indeed, *Roma locuta est, causa finita est:* the Diocese
of Crato was decreed.

Not even a less bold attempt to entice the Franciscan Order to erect a
school in Joaseiro met with success. Letters between Padre Cícero and the
head of the Franciscans in Brazil were exchanged throughout 1915.[15] But,
the Patriarch's intention "to save souls and teach Holy Doctrine. . . . [to]
a vast populace favorably disposed to the things of God"[16] was subject first
and foremost to the approval of his superior, the bishop. Indeed, no religious order could or would come to Joaseiro as long as the Patriarch
remained a "defrocked" priest and disobedient to the bishop. Ironically,
every time the cleric attempted to prove his orthodoxy and disprove that
he was a "fanaticizer," his effort was viewed with suspicion.[17] In turn,
refusal convinced him of the existence of a hierarchically inspired "persecution" against him and Joaseiro.

In 1916, the relentless tension between Joaseiro and the church abruptly
ceased. In December, Dom Quintino, Crato's first bishop and one-time
vigário, put an end to hostilities. On his first pastoral visit to Joaseiro at

Christmastime, he granted the Patriarch the privilege (rescinded in 1899) to celebrate mass, (although orders to confess and preach were still withheld).[18] One month later, Dom Quintino elevated Joaseiro's Chapel of Our Lady of Sorrows (until then under the ecclesiastical jurisdiction of Crato) to the status of a full fledged parish (*freguezia*) within the new diocese.[19] Joaseiro was doubly jubilant, at least momentarily. Unfortunately, its joy was short-lived, for the war between dissidence and orthodoxy continued to flare up and in 1921 the Patriarch was again fully suspended. Clearly the recrudescence of hostilities could hardly have been avoided; their roots were deep and had inevitably been allowed to grow deeper because of the very terms of the transitory truce, unilaterally imposed by Dom Quintino in December 1916 and January 1917.

It is therefore necessary to examine the reasons and motives which may have inspired the new bishop's policies. This task is difficult because the extant records are all-too-frequently silent.[20] However, it seems certain, that Dom Quintino's policies were in no way inspired by the Patriarch's repeated efforts to regain orders; rather, the new and sudden shift of policies responded to the needs and circumstances created by the erection of the new diocese in Crato. For the same reason, it is also necessary not to interpret the changes in 1916 and 1917 solely as an act of charity and friendship by Dom Quintino.[21] Indeed, Quintino may have been so motivated. After all, as a young priest in Crato he had himself ardently believed in the miracles of 1889. Only in 1891 did he renounce that belief to become a stalwart defender of orthodoxy. Perhaps this personal crisis enabled him— in contrast to Dom Joaquim—to suffer Padre Cícero with charity. Perhaps, too, their personal friendship was a factor. In 1904, Quintino had taken refuge in the Patriarch's residence after a political dispute with Crato's Col. Antonio Luis.[22] Then, ten years later, when the "revolutionaries" of Joaseiro invaded Crato, the Patriarch gave strict orders that no harm was to befall Quintino or any other clergyman, for that matter.[23] These personal factors, however, must not be overstressed in effecting Padre Cícero's partial reinstatement in 1916, if only because they were incapable of preventing Dom Quintino from fully suspending the Patriarch again in 1921.

Nor is it possible to attribute Padre Cícero's partial reinstatement and Joaseiro's elevation to parish status to the Patriarch's entry into politics— as one author has implied.[24] Certainly, it would have been anomalous to retain Joaseiro as a chapel (*capella*) dependent on Crato, when the city itself was already an autonomous *município* and, after 1914, the seat of a district court (*comârca*). However, although Dom Quintino took office as Crato's first bishop in January 1916, it was only in December that he granted Padre Cícero orders to celebrate mass; only in January 1917, did he grant Joaseiro full parish status. Obviously, the new bishop was in no way beholden to the priest-politician. This is not to affirm, however, that Padre Cícero's entry into politics and especially his alleged leadership of the revolution of 1913–1914 played no role in his partial reinstatement. Indeed, the revolution indirectly played a major role, but not in the manner which has hitherto been suggested.

Rather than enhance his prestige in the eyes of the church, Padre Cícero's participation in the revolution created new enemies for him. At first, the destruction and death inflicted by the revolution—although relatively insignificant according to one foreign observer, an Italian Capuchin missionary[25]—resulted in a storm of indignation against the Patriarch. Within the clergy, it prompted immediate and summary condemnation of their fellow priest. A telegram from an anonymous clergyman during the revolution clearly summed up the majority opinion: "It's time to save your soul and the people who surround you. . . . A warning from heaven [signed] Brother in Christ."[26] Furthermore, the Patriarch did not ingratiate himself to his fellow priests when, during the revolution, he decided to bury the celebrated *beata,* Maria de Araújo, who died suddenly, in a handsome sepulchre in the unconsecrated Chapel of Our Lady of Perpetual Help.[27] This, in the clergy's opinion, was but one more proof of the cleric's intention to encourage fanaticism in Joaseiro. Henceforth, the Patriarch and his city once again remained renegades and dissidents. For more than a year after the revolution, there was no visible change in the hierarchy's attitude, except, perhaps for increasing bitterness and resentment.[28]

Then, in the last quarter of 1915, a fresh incident rekindled animosities among the clergy. Dom Lucas Heuzer, a German Benedictine and Abbott of the Holy Cross monastery at Quixadá (Ceará), made a visit to Joaseiro. After conversing with the Patriarch, he continued his journey to Crato. There, he allegedly reported to Quintino that Padre Cícero planned to destroy the people of Crato! According to an unpublished letter written by D. Marôca, the wife of the trusted Pelusio Macedo, the Patriarch vehemently denied the charge. The Macedos then corresponded with Dom Lucas who attempted to deny transmitting the charge to Quintino.[29] The incident, however, did not die easily. On the contrary, throughout the year 1916, rumors spread through the Valley that Quintino and the new Archibishop of Fortaleza had—according to Floro—partisanly reported to the Holy See that "Padre Cícero had led a revolution in which many Christians went to their death. . . ."[30] It was also rumored that they concurred with Dom Lucas' opinion that the Patriarch was planning to do so again! Months later, it was widely believed that Rome had responded with an order to excommunicate Padre Cícero. Several years later, Floro publicly doubted whether the Patriarch's fellow priests were "capable of such an iniquitous act. . . ."[31] But, Floro, it seems, strongly suspected that they were; in one respect history proved Floro correct, because in June 1916, Rome had indeed decreed Padre Cícero's excommunication![32]

According to Dom Quintino, Rome's order reached him in December 1916 one month short of his first anniversary as bishop of Crato.[33] It also arrived, Quintino claimed, in the midst of a holy mission then being preached in Joaseiro by his order and in accordance with one of the demands of Rome's 1898 decree which his predecessor, Dom Joaquim, had never fully implemented. Furthermore, as the bishop later informed Rome, the excommunication order had arrived *only after* he himself had reinvested Padre Cícero with the canonical privilege to celebrate mass. Since Rome had granted the bishop discretionary power to implement and make the order public, Dom Quintino also claimed that he had chosen not to execute it at that time.

The bishop's account, however, is partly suspect. The absence of Rome's order of excommunication from his archives and the deliberate vagueness with which his later correspondence referred to the order's date of arrival leads us to believe that Quintino may have all along been well aware of Rome's intentions. As early as November 1915, he had indeed corresponded with the papal nuncio in Petropolis about the Patriarch's status.[34] Furthermore, the rumors about the possible excommunication, which dated from 1916, could not have been unknown to Quintino. Despite full documentary proof, it seems plausible to say that the bishop may have decided to reinstate the Patriarch before Rome's decree could reach him. In that way, it would be easier to ignore the decree and thereby counteract the growing animosity in Joaseiro against the church and the new see. For the same reason, Quintino never made the excommunication order public, and only revealed it to Padre Cícero in 1920. In retrospect, Dom Quintino's flexible reaction to Rome's decree and the implementation of his own policies were eminently pragmatic. Had he allowed Rome to press for Cícero's excommunication, a bitter struggle between orthodoxy and dissidence might have been rekindled. Had that occurred, the newly created Diocese of Crato would have been torn asunder as its largest parish, Joaseiro, returned to its bygone days of religious rebellion.[35]

The Aims of Reintegration, 1916–1917

Dom Quintino's goals, moreover, were not merely designed to prevent Joaseiro from reverting to its anti-orthodox militance. Even had there been no threat of excommunication in 1916, the new bishop would have eventually had to come to ecclesiastical terms with Joaseiro. This he did in January 1917, by making the city a full fledged parish. It was, after all, the most populous parish in the Cariry, if the seasonal influx of tourist-pilgrims were tallied along with its permanent residents.[36] As such it was among the wealthiest parishes of the new diocese whose see in Crato, incidentally, had still to succeed in raising an adequate patrimony.[37] Therefore, by partially restoring the Patriarch's orders, the bishop had done more than neutralize the city's potential hostility; he appeared as the Patriarch's champion and as such could count on Joaseiro's reintegration into the fold. Moreover, from the political viewpoint of the hierarchy, the creation of the parish of Joaseiro would afford Dom Quintino more effective administrative and financial control over Joaseiro than ever the church had hitherto enjoyed!

Administrative control was imposed in January 1917. That month the bishop appointed Fr. Pedro Esmeraldo da Silva as Joaseiro's first pastor (*vigário*).[38] The young priest was a talented orator and a hand-picked protégé. Through him, the bishop intended to harness Joaseiro's unbridled fervor into strict conformity with the dogma and practices of Brazil's "Romanized" Catholicism. Furthermore, in Esmeraldo, the bishop could count on a trusted agent within the walls of Joaseiro—the first permanent one since Padre Cícero's suspension in 1896.

Financial control over the new parish was also made more secure after 1917, although specific details of church finances remain impossible to obtain. In the case of Joaseiro, however, some aspects have either become public or may be presumed to have been operative. It is known, for example, that although the chapel at Joaseiro had been under interdict (prior to 1917), all alms and donations offered to the patron saint nonetheless became the property of the parish of Crato. Floro, who was always critical of the clergy, chided the hierachy in this matter: "there was no interdict [he declared] when it came to transporting the vast sums of donations . . . in large sacks to Crato."[39] This view was later confirmed by Fr. Azarias Sobreira, a native son of Joaseiro. The priest, whose sacerdotal career has been beyond reproach, noted more objectively that while Joaseireneses did not resent the outflow of church funds to Crato, they did protest that "from there, nothing ever returned."[40]

Now that Joaseiro was a parish (and as long as it remained in good standing with the diocese), it theoretically retained all donations as part of its own patrimony. However, in 1921, Dom Quintino founded the Bank of the Cariry in Crato.[41] By episcopal order, Joaseiro and all parishes within the diocese were thereafter obliged to employ the bank as the chief depository for their patrimonies and collections.[42] Much of Crato's development, it must now be suggested, may have very likely been the result of the ready credit made available through the church-sponsored Crato bank by forced savings of all twenty Cariry parishes.

Unfortunately the one area where diocesan financial control may have been most critical cannot be documented. This concerns the income the diocese may have derived from the countless thousands of mass-stipends received by the Patriarch from his pilgrim-tourists. According to canon law each priest is permitted to celebrate one mass each day from which the stipend received may be used for his personal sustenance. Also, according to canon law, all requests for masses and their corresponding stipends in excess of the number of masses a priest can normally celebrate must either be celebrated by another priest or submitted to his bishop. Elsewhere, it has been shown that during the years of the miracles the Patriarch had scrupulously channeled these excess masses and stipends to various priests and to religious orders in Brazil and Rome. Even after the creation of the Crato bishopric and the granting of parish status to Joaseiro, the Patriarch's archives reveal that he continued to distribute both mass "intentions" and their stipends to many priests in Brazil and abroad.[43] Foreign missionaries in Brazil such as the Franciscans, Benedictines, and Salesians continued to receive mass offerings from the Patriarch. Charitable institutions of the Catholic Church in Italy, Lebanon, and the Holy Land were also recipients. After World War I, a few priests in Germany and France were able to support themselves and the reconstruction of their parishes thanks to excess mass offerings sent them by the Patriarch.

It may be assumed that the partial reinstatement of the Patriarch probably brought about closer episcopal supervision in this matter. In that case, it would seem likely that most excess mass intentions were no longer transmitted abroad. Certainly, the extant archives of Padre Cícero confirm this, although they in no way specifically indicate that the bishopric was subsequently made the recipient. There is, however, a possibility that this indeed occurred. If it did, canon law might have also permitted Dom Quintino to "reduce" the mass requests received from Joaseiro. "Reduction" is the canonical right of a bishop to celebrate fewer masses which are nonetheless valid for the larger number of requests.[44] In such a case, the surplus stipends revert to the diocese and, at the bishop's discretion, may be used to finance *obras pias* or the charitable works of the diocese. This method of "financing" is increasingly used today in dioceses whose patrimonies are inadequate to support the local church's work. It is presently in force in the Diocese of Crato where, in 1965, over a million cruzeiros ($500.00) in mass stipends— collected in Joaseiro in a single day—were transmitted to the bishop.[45]

Should this system have been operative in Crato during Dom Quintino's tenure, it would signify that the mass requests received by the Patriarch had then (as now) indirectly contributed to the development of Crato. It was there that the diocese administered the best educational institutions of the Valley, its only seminary, a weekly newspaper and, of course, the Bank of the Cariry. In a word, if the church was a factor in the development of the Valley, in the manner described above, then it is ironic that it was partly made possible by the mass offerings and stipends of the "fanatics" loyal to the Patriarch, but unfavorably viewed by the hiearchy.

The Renewed Religious Conflict, 1917–1923

There seems no doubt that practical goals lay beneath Dom Quintino's decision to grant Padre Cícero partial reinstatement. However, the bishop's additional needs to assert his own ecclesiastical authority within the Valley and to offer proof of his fidelity to Rome in regard to Joaseiro obliged him to demand the Patriarch's unconditional surrender. That demand left little room for leniency, understanding, and compromise. As a result, the very terms on which the Patriarch was granted partial reinstatement engendered an atmosphere of mutual suspicion which prevailed from 1916 until 1921, when the Patriarch was again suspended.

In retracing the steps which led from the renewal of Padre Cícero's suspension to the reopening of the ecclesiastical conflict, it is necessary to return to December 1916. That month, Quintino granted Padre Cícero partial reinstatement in return for a written declaration about past and future relations. Chief among the pledges exacted from the Patriarch were: (1) an "unconditional acceptance" of Rome's decrees of 1894, 1897, and 1898; (2) a disavowal of any personal participation in the revolution of 1913–1914 as well as an unequivocal denial of any intention to lead "a second [armed] political movement"; (3) the cleric's promise "not to interfere in the administration and activities of the [newly created] diocese [of Crato]."[46]

Of equal importance to the strengthening of episcopal authority, was Dom Quintino's attempt to put an end to both the pilgrimages to Joaseiro and, by definition, to the Patriarch's chief source of personal income.[47] Rome had repeatedly sought both objectives since 1894. In fact, the Patriarch's alleged refusal at that time either to return the countless "personal gifts" received by him in kind and specie to their respective donors or to entrust the full sum to charitable institutions of the church (*obras pias*) as Rome had commanded, was a source of constant irritation and ill will. Indeed, the latter command was only executed in 1923, when the Patriarch bequeathed his vast estate of lands, houses, and other properties to the Salesian Order in return for their pledge to build a vocational school and church in Joaseiro. However, in 1916, when Quintino ascended to the mitre, the issue of "personal gifts" was still outstanding as was the Patriarch's continuing reception of pilgrims and the "gifts" they offered him. In an effort to implement Rome's order, Quintino banned all pilgrimages to Joaseiro. When the bishop chose to implement this command by prohibiting Padre Cícero from receiving pilgrims in his residence, the Patriarch protested. He argued that many of the pilgrims had come as personal friends. As such, the Patriarch claimed, it was impossible for him to treat his friends with discourtesy. This argument, however, easily led Quintino to view the Patriarch with suspicion. Thereafter, his actions came under the scrutiny of his fellow priests who, like their bishop, appeared to put the Patriarch's integrity in doubt.

Such was the case in February 1917. Fr. Esmeraldo had yet to complete one month as Joaseiro's new vicar. Nonetheless, he replied to one of Dom Quintino's inquiries about the Patriarch's conduct and the attitude of Joaseiro's inhabitants towards the church.[48] The young vicar, perhaps unconsciously, portrayed the Patriarch as guilty of duplicity: according to Esmeraldo, Padre Cícero did not "bless" religious articles, in accordance with the bishop's order, but indeed the vicar had spied the cleric making some "sign" over them. Yes, Esmeraldo noted, the sale of sacrilegious medals bearing the Patriarch's effigy had ceased; however—as if to find fault with Padre Cícero—the vicar added that the use of these medals remained widespread. Finally, the young curate observed that, it could be said that the inhabitants of Joaseiro had treated him with respect only "if one bears in mind the lamentable ignorance of the great majority of [these] poor fanatics."[49]

Indeed Esmeraldo's unsympathetic attitude was typical of the "more respectable" clergy of the Valley (and in retrospect, his selection as Joaseiro's first vicar was unfortunate for all parties concerned). As a native son of Crato and descendant of one of its most prominent and orthodox Catholic families, the young vicar continuously demonstrated the aversion with which most of the recently ordained priests regarded Joaseiro's "fanatic" masses. Esmeraldo's disdain did not endear him to the town's inhabitants, just as his equivocal reports to Dom Quintino about the Patriarch had contributed to heightening tensions between the recently reinstated priest and the church hierarchy.

In April 1917, a new decree from Rome was issued; its arrival in Crato further contributed to the tense situation.[50] For reasons still unknown, Rome was dismayed that its 1897 decree ordering the Patriarch to abandon Joaseiro forever had not been obeyed. Thus, in 1917, it reiterated its earlier decision and observed that until the Patriarch did so, the "Holy See declares [Padre Cícero] excommunicated. . . ." For reasons known only to Dom Quintino, the bishop chose not to implement Rome's new order; perhaps Quintino feared the outburst of a popular revolt if the Patriarch were forced to abandon Joaseiro.

However, from the numerous pledges and declarations signed by the priest between June 1917 and December 1918, it appears that Dom Quintino's more lenient policy was tantamount to forcing Padre Cícero into exile—within the very walls of Joaseiro.[51] The bishop adamantly insisted that the Patriarch receive no pilgrims at his residence, that he not bless them or any religious articles without authorization, that he not baptize children even if they were in danger of death. To all of these demands, the Patriarch acceded, as well as to an endless round of secret conferences in Crato, and in December 1918, to the humiliation of mounting Joaseiro's pulpit to denounce again publicly the miracles of the 1890s.

These events in turn enraged Dr. Floro.[52] The physician alleged that the eighteen-month ordeal had physically harmed the Patriarch. Furthermore, according to the *bahiano,* the bishop's harassment was really aimed at making the Patriarch's life in Joaseiro so unbearable as to oblige him to depart "voluntarily" from his "new Jerusalem." Perhaps fearing Dom Quintino's success and, as a result, the loss of his own political base, Floro conferred with the bishop sometime in late 1918. At that meeting, Floro hotly denounced the bishop's alleged intentions. He added that, should the Patriarch be forced to withdraw from Joaseiro, he, Floro, "would morally rehabilitate [the Patriarch] before the Catholic and secular world. . . ."[53]

This showdown between Dr. Floro and Dom Quintino presaged the Doctor's denunciation of the clergy in 1923; however, in 1918, its immediate effect was to force Dom Quintino to act with greater moderation. At least this conclusion seems justified by the relative surface calm which prevailed during 1919 and 1920 in the relations between the church and Padre Cícero. In 1920, however, Rome again attempted to force Dom Quintino's hand. In November, the bishop traveled to Rio de Janeiro. There and in Petrópolis, he met with the papal nuncio in an attempt to obtain a more conciliatory attitude from Rome. Unfortunately, the motives and events of this period remain obscure. Extant drafts of a letter from Quintino to the Holy See at this time indicate that the outstanding problem was the conflict between the bishop's readiness to renew Padre Cícero's partial reinstatement and Rome's insistence that its earlier decrees of excommunication be publicized and implemented.[54] In December 1920, Dom Quintino returned to Crato. Perhaps, in an effort to placate Rome, he again ordered Padre Cícero to mount the pulpit in Joaseiro from whence the cleric reiterated his acceptance of Rome's condemnation of the miracles.[55] Then in March, 1921, Rome repeated its earlier demand: excommunicate Padre Cícero unless he abandon Joaseiro forever.[56] In June, Rome's decree reached Crato. Dom Quintino fully suspended the Patriarch, while in the interests of preventing a rebellion, the order to publicize Rome's decree was conveniently ignored.[57]

Despite Quintino's caution, news of the Patriarch's suspension immediately stirred up widespread indignation in Joaseiro. Understandably, Fr. Esmeraldo was singled out as the target of popular resentment. During his tenure as vicar, he was unfavorably seen as the bishops' agent; in recent months, he had furthered that hapless image by zealously condemning most Joaseirenses as "fanatics." Indeed, a fellow clergyman noted that Esmeraldo's invectives "had deeply wounded the *romeiros* in what they held to be most sacred—their love for Joaseiro and for Padre Cícero. . . ."[58] In retaliation, the *romeiros* wounded Esmeraldo in what he considered to be the landmark of his five year's labors as vicar—the reconstruction of the east bell tower of Our Lady of Sorrow's church. Persuaded by vested business interests which feared the new suspension would put an end to the pilgrimages, the *romeiros* surrounded the church; they stood guard over a statue of the Virgin which, they believed, Fr. Esmeraldo was planning to remove to Crato. Reconstruction of the bell tower ceased while tensions rose sharply.[59] At last, Esmeraldo resigned his pastorate and departed for Crato. In Dom Quintino's mind, this incident sealed the Patriarch's fate. Indeed, while Quintino lived, the prospects of regaining orders seemed forever dimmed.

11

The Last Days

Religion and Politics: The Two Joaseiros

For nearly a year and a half, Joaseiro was a parish without a vicar. Then, in January 1923, Dom Quintino finally named Esmeraldo's successor. It was Fr. Manuel Macedo, the son of the inventive telegraphist of Joaseiro, Pelusio Macedo, one of the Patriarch's ardent supporters and oldest friends.[1] The choice of Fr. "Macedinho," as he was affectionately called, was most satisfactory to all the parties concerned.

For Padre Cícero, Macedinho, who had visited Joaseiro during 1920 or 1921, was a boon. Unlike Esmeraldo, Fr. Macedo wanted to be assigned to Joaseiro, his home-town. Furthermore, he brought with him the rigorous training of the São Paulo seminary where he had studied for ordination; he also held a doctorate in sacred theology acquired in 1920 in Rome where he had been sent on scholarship by Brazil's future prince of the church, Rio de Janeiro's Archbishop Sebastião Cardinal Leme. These qualities, the Patriarch thought, might alter the religious atmosphere of Joaseiro. In addition, Fr. Macedo's personal friendships in Rome, with Dom Quintino, and

with members of the Brazilian hierarchy might prove helpful to the Patriarch's quest for reinstatement. Evidence of Padre Cícero's utmost confidence
in the young vicar is, in our opinion, indicated by the suspended cleric's
unpublished first will (1922).[2] Although contravened in 1923, the earlier
will had bequeathed the greater part of Padre Cícero's possessions to the
Premonstratensian Order, whose priests at the Pirapora Seminary in São
Paulo had trained "Macedinho" for the priesthood.[3]

For Dom Quintino, too, the new vicar of Joaseiro was a model priest:
A doctorate in theology from Rome was indeed an invaluable credential.
Furthermore, Quintino knew well that the Macedo family enjoyed Padre
Cícero's esteem and friendship. Perhaps, he may have thought, those ancient
ties would enable the eager curate to exert a salutary influence upon the
aged Patriarch and eventually lead Joaseiro back to orthodoxy.

There may have been another reason for Dom Quintino's choice, a
reason that bears upon the growing nationalist outlook of the Brazilian
clergy during the twenties. For all of Dom Quintino's emphasis upon
episcopal authority and strict adherence to "Romanized" liturgical norms by
his fellow priests, Crato's bishop appears as an ardent Brazilian nationalist
within the ecclesiastical hierarchy. As a young priest in the Valley, he had
witnessed foreign missionaries desert the interior during the droughts, the
very moment when the church should have been present in the midst
of its suffering flock. Also, as an early believer in the miracles of Joaseiro,
he may have shared for a while in the nationalist justification of those
events which his fellow clergymen at the time put forth. Later, in 1919,
Quintino wrote to a fellow priest one of the clearest expressions of his
nationalist sentiments: "We are not in agreement in regard to [your] preference for French, Belgian or Spanish nuns over Germans. *Much better
would that we had competent Brazilians. . . .*"[4] Quintino's strong desire
for a "Brazilian" clergy actively led him in the twenties to propose the
creation of an entirely Brazilian religious order, (*"uma congregação de
padres nacionaes"*).[5] These Josephites, as he planned to call them, would
be recruited only in the backlands, especially in the Cariry. After appropriate
training, they would "direct the seminaries of the *sertão* of Brazil." Once
their ranks expanded, the native-born Josephites would then replace for-
eigners in order to take sole charge of the Holy Missions in the rural areas
of the *"sertão* still so wanting in religious instruction." For many reasons,
Quintino's dream never fully materialized. But shortly before his untimely
death in 1929, Rome did grant him permission to establish an organization

for Crato's seminarians, known as the *Pia União Josephita*, on which he intended to build his backland order.[6] It is not a coincidence, in our opinion, that Quintino's plans for a nationalist clergy were begun in 1924, less than a year after Fr. Macedo was appointed as the new vicar of Joaseiro.

Indeed, even a cursory examination of Fr. Macedo's pastoral activities within Joaseiro reveals how much the young priest fitted Dom Quintino's nationalist mold.[7] Macedo was most enlightened towards the *romeiros*. Unlike Esmeraldo, and most every other member of the hierarchy since 1891, Macedinho did not reproach, condemn, and lament their "fanaticism." Nor, like his predecessor, did he heap disrespect upon the Patriarch of Joasciro. Instead, the new vicar sought to win the friendship and loyalty of the "New Jerusalem's" lower class *romeiro*-settlers. At the same time, he attempted to rechannel the questionable religious beliefs of the people into the orthodox liturgical celebrations of the church. Several examples amply illustrate these new policies, implemented by Fr. Macedo with the approval of both Dom Quintino and Padre Cícero. During Holy Week of 1923, Macedinho revived the ancient celebrations of the Nazarene's last days. That year, the entire city took part in the processions which dramatically reenacted the suffering, death, and resurrection of the Lord. But Macedinho did not limit himself to liturgical duties. When he attempted to reconstruct the east tower of the church, begun by Fr. Esmeraldo, the new vicar personally went with his parishioners to beg for the money needed to make the repairs. When the work itself was about to begin, Fr. Macedo personally led the volunteer workmen, mostly *romeiros*, to the Patriarch's doorstep to ask and receive his blessing on their undertaking. Unlike Esmeraldo, Macedinho understood and took advantage of the people's admiration for Padre Cícero. To convince the people that he himself was acting with the Patriarch's consent, Macedo, not perhaps undemagogically, appropriated the use of the Patriarch's cane. That symbol of authority the young vicar always carried with him whenever he marched at the head of a band of parishioners. Indeed, as Floro was reluctantly to observe: With Macedo's arrival in Joaseiro "the contentment of the people was indescribable."[8]

The "contentment" was not limited to *romeiros*. Above all, it extended to all but a few of Joaseiro's most prominent native sons (*filhos da terra*). They, of course, had been instrumental in persuading Dom Quintino to appoint Fr. Macedo in January 1923, after Joaseiro had been without a vicar for more than sixteen months. These same native sons became the new "pillars of the church." The long-abandoned parish associations for laymen (*irmandades*) were revived, new ones created and over both the *filhos da terra* presided as officers.[9] Two of these associations became especially prominent. One was the St. Vincent de Paul Society (*Conferências Vicentinas*) under the presidency of Sr. José Geraldo da Cruz, who since 1917 was the proprietor of the *Farmácia dos Pobres* (and discoverer of a pharmaceutical preparation, *Balsamo da Vida,* highly prized and widely purchased among the "pilgrim-tourists" of the Northeast). The other was the Association of the Ladies of Charity in which there participated the wives and daughters of Joaseiro's prominent families. With the moral and financial support of these two organizations, Fr. Macedo continued his efforts to extend the influence of orthodoxy over Joaseiro's lower classes. The contruction of chapels in "Brejo Sêcco" and "Padre Cícero," two outlying rural districts of the *município,* were symbolic of the new vicar's efforts to win back the pilgrim-settlers to orthodoxy.[10]

Macedinho's religious activities were not, however, devoid of political significance. It is only necessary to recall the traditional internal division of Joaseiro into "two cities": that of the newcomers and that of the native sons. In this light, Fr. Macedo had become the first *filho da terra* to bid effectively for the leadership of the resident *romeiros,* the largest segment of Joaseiro's newcomer population. As Padre Cícero increasingly accorded his religious prestige among the masses to the vicar, Floro's leadership became seriously challenged for the first time since 1913 when Col. João Bezerra de Menezes had assumed the prefecture with Rabelo's aid.

Fr. Macedo's revival of the parish organizations of the laity was thus of profound political significance. In the *município,* where Floro had effectively monopolized all political power in Cícero's name, the parish brotherhoods once again emerged (as during Lôbo's day) as the functional equivalent of an opposition political party.[11] In a word, Macedo, himself a native son, had not only attempted to revive Joaseiro's religious life, but also—by reinvigorating the traditional organizations of the laity—had provided the structure through which the patient but resentful native sons might at last challenge Floro's leadership. That Joaseiro's parish brotherhoods were tantamount to an opposition party is clearly confirmed by the presence in them of both Col. João Bezerra, one-time prefect deposed by the revolution of 1913–1914 and José Xavier de Oliveira, the manager of the Patriarch's estates, whose son, Antonio, was among the first to contest Floro's authority.[12]

The Native Sons' Quest for Power

Indeed, Floro's rapid ascent to power in 1908 and his dominant influence over the Patriarch had been resented by Joaseiro's native sons and, for that matter, by some of the established families of the Cariry. In 1913, it was a Cariryense, Fr. Joaquim de Alencar Peixoto, ex-editor of *O Rebate,* who launched the first public attack against the Patriarch and his "alter ego." Peixoto's libelous tract, *O Joaseiro do Cariry,* had been clearly provoked by Floro's successful maneuver which deprived Peixoto of his bid for prefect of Joaseiro. Then, in 1920, the Patriarch and Floro came under an equally bitter attack by one of Joaseiro's prominent native sons. That year, Dr. Antonio Xavier de Oliveira, a young physician trained in Rio de Janeiro, whose father José had become active in Macedinho's St. Vincent de Paul Society, published his celebrated work, *Beatos e Cangaceiros.*[13] While this work may be considered but another defense of the Northeast as "the very soul of Brazil,"[14] it was also a political platform on which Dr. Antonio made a veiled bid to defeat Floro in the congressional elections scheduled for 1921. Dr. Antonio's key argument suggested that Floro, among other Valley *chefes,* was directly responsible for the rise of *cangaceirismo* in the Cariry. This social cancer would disappear only when there arose in the region new leaders intent on bringing progress. The author considered himself just such a new leader and in the introduction of his work cryptically made his bid for electoral support: "Will the government of Ceará and the [prominent] men of the Cariry [agree with my proposals to better the Valley]? I can't be certain. But it's possible that they already have."[15]

Floro, however, neither agreed with his fellow physician nor was he oblivious to Dr. Antonio's veiled bid for electoral support. In 1921, Floro easily won election to the federal congress, while the outflanked Xavier de Oliveira was forced to bide his time until 1934, when he again ventured unsuccessfully to become the Valley's federal deputy.[16] In 1923, moreover, Floro took revenge on his challenger. In the deputy's celebrated defense of the Patriarch before the Federal Congress, Dr. Floro resoundingly denounced Xavier de Oliveira and branded *Beatos e Cangaceiros* a "colossal lie." With this attack, Floro had opened a new round in an old struggle.[17]

Incensed by Floro's 1923 speech, Joaseiro's native sons were provoked into rallying behind Fr. Macedo.[18] Moreover, their local campaign to depose Floro could now derive strength from two new sources. On the one hand, the Roman Catholic clergy tacitly supported Floro's defeat. His speech in the federal congress which also branded the clergy as "hypocrites and 'Nero-like persecutors' " of the Patriarch was more than sufficient cause for the churchmen's enmity. On the other hand, political fissures within Ceará's state party structure gave rise to a faction in Fortaleza sympathetic to the anti-Floro elements in Joaseiro. That faction was led by Manoel do Nascimento Fernandes Távora, a former *rabelista*. In 1920, Távora had broken from the *Partido Democrata* after its chief, state Governor Manuel Moreira da Rocha, formed a coalition government with remnants of José Accioly's conservatives. Távora soon after created his own party, the *Partido Republicano*, whose branch in Joaseiro was led by José Geraldo da Cruz, the renowned pharmacist and president of Joaseiro's St. Vincent de Paul Society.[19] Thus, the ensuing attempt to rally native sons against Floro was not merely a local affair, but intimately bound to both an increasingly politicized church and a state-wide opposition political party with counterparts elsewhere in Brazil.

Within Joaseiro, the political "mise-en-scène" was building towards a showdown. The parties to the dispute and their place in the broader political structure of Brazil were as follows. In the forestage there was Macedinho and the prominent *filho da terra* families, mobilized "politically" within Joaseiro's parish organizations. It was a curious mixture of politics, religion, and the traditional family! Yet, here was a foreshadowing of national politics in the decade of the not-too-distant thirties. That era witnessed not only Brazilian Catholicism's bid for power within a corporativist state (when the church nationally supported its own candidates in the LEC, the Catholic Electoral League). It also witnessed the subsequent rise of Brazilian fascism (when the slogan, *"Deus, Patria e Familia"* became the rallying cry of the *Partido Integralista,* a Brazilian variant of Italian Fascism).[20]

In the wings, but in opposition to Fr. Macedo, stood Floro. His trump card, of course, was his overwhelming control of an isolated and aging Patriarch; while his allies within Joaseiro were now few, they were powerful. There were fifteen prominent newcomer merchants and a handful of the most important state and federal civil servants whose appointment to Joaseiro was owed largely to Floro's munificence and political influence in Rio de Janeiro.[21] Floro and his supporters were also a curious mixture: antiquated "Old Republic" *bacharéis* and acquisitive bourgeois merchants. In the short run, both realized that power and wealth depended on main-

taining their ties to the sources of federal patronage as well as promoting
pilgrim-tourists to the Patriarch's "New Jerusalem." They too foreshadowed
a significant trend which emerged in Brazil after 1930 when, even though
civilian *bacharéis* momentarily took a back seat to middle-class military
interventores, power and upward mobility were to become increasingly dependent on the graces bestowed by a centralized, federal government.

The showdown between Macedinho's native sons and Floro's newcomers came in 1924. During that entire year, each camp rallied its supporters. Midyear brought two well-chosen tests of strength. For example,
Macedo's attempt to transfer Joaseiro's traditional market day (*feira*) from
Sunday to a weekday ended in a victory for Floro, who with the merchants
of Joaseiro, Crato, and Barbalha successfully argued for maintaining the
Sunday market.[22] Then in June 1924, Macedo won the day. He had led
eight thousand "pilgrims" from Joaseiro to Barbalha under the pretext
of paying a *promessa* to that city's patron saint for earlier granting the
Cariry a rain filled winter. The event was in fact a political rally in support
of Barbalha's prefect. Macedo's purpose was to ally Joaseiro's native sons
with Barbalha's landed interests in an effort to oppose the merchant forces
of Joaseiro and Crato led by Floro and tacitly supported by Col. Antonio
Luis.[23]

Although each camp had won a victory, by late 1924 "Macedinho"
was clearly in the lead. This was made possible by the successful launching
of an "independent" weekly newspaper in Joaseiro. Understandably, *O Ideal*
was as partisan as its chief editor, José Geraldo da Cruz, leader of Joaseiro's
"*tavorista*" party and the president of the St. Vincent de Paul Society.[24]
As a steady stream of pro-Macedo dispatches from *O Ideal* found their way
into Fortaleza's *O Nordeste,* the recently founded daily of Ceará's Roman
Catholic hierarchy, Fr. Macedo felt his hand strengthened by clerical supporters in the capital. Then, at Christmastide, 1924, Macedo publicly defied
Floro's authority.[25]

"Joaseiro em Fóco"

The issue in question was the *jogatina,* or games of chance.[26] In the backlands, it was customary for the towns to sponsor a kermess, dominated by
the *jogatina,* each Christmas when the rural population traditionally came
to the city to enjoy both the annual religious celebrations and the secular

social diversions. Usually, it was the city council which contracted a con-
cessionaire to provide the games of chance and other pastimes; the fee
paid represented an important annual revenue to the municipal treasury.
In Joaseiro in 1924, it was Floro, rather than the city council, who granted
the *jogatina* concession for the handsome sum of eight *contos*. When Floro
allegedly relegated a portion of this income to defray personal expenses
incurred earlier that year in the beautification of Joaseiro's Freedom Square
and the erection of the statue in honor of Padre Cícero, his political opponents seized upon the issue as but one more proof of Floro's political
tyranny.

Fr. Macedo, however, did not directly attack Floro for his alleged
peculation.[27] Rather, several days before Christmas, Macedinho mounted
the pulpit in Joaseiro and unleashed an unexpected and violent campaign
against the end-of-the-year *jogatina*. Gambling, Fr. Macedo charged, was
a gross "immorality" and its sponsors were, by implication, desecrators of
the religious feast of Christmas. Moreover, inherent in Macedinho's argument was both the equation of gambling with profanity and his own puri-
tanical stance about the sacred, moral supremacy of the church. As a consequence, Fr. Macedo had converted a purely local power dispute into a
much larger issue: a conflict between Ceará's church hierarchy and secular
political authority.[28]

In Joaseiro, Macedinho's sermon was unmistakenly understood to be
an attack against Floro. In fact, the priest issued an ultimatum: either the
jogatina was suppressed or he himself would refuse to celebrate mass on
Christmas day. When Floro quietly yielded ground by persuading the
gambling concessionaires to transfer their games from street booths into
private homes, Fr. Macedo was obliged to take the issue one step further:
he threatened to resign as vicar of Joaseiro unless the gambling concessionaires were immediately arrested and imprisoned.[29]

But this time Macedo had gone too far. Floro refused to yield again
and called the priest's bluff; without fanfare he defiantly waited for
Macedinho to leave Joaseiro as promised. Like Floro, Macedo believed
Padre Cícero was his trump card: He was convinced that the Patriarch,
intent on reentering the priesthood, would prefer a militant clergyman to an
irate congressman. However, at an urgent and secret meeting, in Padre
Cícero's residence held shortly after Macedinho threatened to resign his
post, the Patriarch finally cast his lot with Floro only after an attempt to

persuade the young vicar to drop his campaign ended in failure.[30] Indeed, Macedinho had miscalculated: Apparently the Patriarch put Joaseiro's continued survival and progress, guaranteed as it was by the *município's* link to the federal government via Floro, above his own passionate hope to return to the priesthood. That decision not only obliged Macedo to leave Joaseiro in defeat but also precipitated one of the most vicious political campaigns ever perpetrated against the Patriarch and Joaseiro.

That campaign, which Floro subsequently branded as "diabolic," was initiated in early 1925. Its author was the despondent Fr. Macedo, who left for Fortaleza in late 1924 in order to rally political supporters in the capital. When the Governor, Moreira da Rocha, proved reluctant to support the ex-vicar, Macedinho appealed to Dom Manuel Gomes, Archbishop of Fortaleza. The latter appears to have obliged insofar as he allowed the young priest to launch his campaign in the columns of *O Nordeste,* the Catholic archdiocesan daily. In May 1925, there appeared the first of Macedinho's partisan articles (later collected and published under the title, *Joazeiro em Fóco*), destined ostensibly to liberate his "Martyred Land" from Floro's yoke.[31] Macedo's crusade was not restricted to a mere vindication of Joaseiro's native sons. It was also the instrument with which the entire clergy of Ceará sought to settle an old score with Floro, who had publicly condemned the church hierarchy in his congressional speech of 1923. That speech, Macedo recalled, was "the Calvary of this clergy, . . . of this Cearense clergy, incontestably the primary civic element of the glorious Land of Light." In defending the church hierarchy, *Joazeiro em Fóco* marked the entry of Ceará's clergy into the political life of the state as an organized political entity.[32]

Precisely because Macedo had emerged as the advocate of both the Roman Catholic hierarchy and Joaseiro's native sons, the campaign against Floro was doubly bitter. Floro was not spared; Macedo denounced him as the "tyrant of Joaseiro" as well as the unprincipled slanderer of the "immaculate clergy of Ceará." Floro's contributions to Joaseiro were belittled, while charges of peculation, profiteering, and even the "murder" of common criminals were leveled against him.[33] Nor was Padre Cícero spared. Fr. Macedo, it is true, limited his portrayal of the Patriarch as the hapless victim of his "alter ego." But other men of the cloth who joined the crusade were far less cautious in their denunciation of their suspended colleague. One priest went so far as to revive the "religious question" of Joaseiro, again condemn the Patriarch as a disobedient priest, and even insinuate that Joaseiro's faithful were as heretical as Protestants, a horrendous charge at that time.[34]

Indeed, Joaseiro emerged as the center of a nationwide controversy which continued months after Fr. Macedo published his last article in *O Nordeste*. In July, Floro personally responded by launching a new newspaper in Joaseiro, *A Gazeta do Joazeiro,* the vehicle for his own series of biting articles against Macedo, entitled "Um Padre Ordinário."[35] At once the nation was treated to another spectacle when Floro proceeded to take Fr. Macedo to court. But soon after he dropped the charges of libel on the advice of prominent *acciolysta* politicians in Fortaleza.[36] Finally, in September 1925, the conflict was carried into the Legislative Assembly of Ceará where the conservative party deputy, Godefredo de Castro, passionately defended Floro, the Patriarch, the material progress, and the political *status quo* of Joaseiro.[37]

The debate in the Assembly was clearly inspired by the successful efforts of the *acciolystas* to come to Floro's defense. Days earlier, Floro's coreligionists had persuaded Ceará's Governor, Moreira da Rocha, to visit the Cariry.[38] His ostensible purpose was to inaugurate the arrival of the main railroad line at nearby Missão Velha. However, when the Governor reached Joaseiro, the real purpose of his visit to the Valley became manifest. The Patriarch, Floro, and a multitude of prominent citizens of Joaseiro turned out to welcome the Governor. Triumphal àrches decorated the principal thoroughfares, while a caravan of autos transported political and public officials on a tour of the city. After a round of banquets and rallies, the unity of the party in power in Fortaleza and the political *status quo* of Joaseiro proved invincible; Macedo's attempt to bring victory to the native sons had clearly failed.

The following October, Floro was hailed in Fortaleza's weekly news magazine, *Ceará Illustrado,* as "the politician of the greatest electoral prestige in the south of the state";[39] he was to retain power until his untimely death in March 1926. Only then, did the Cariry begin to lose its superior political position vis-à-vis Ceará's coalition politics and the patronage of the federal government. Thereafter, the Patriarch, too, lost the political prestige he once enjoyed. Not even his decision (if indeed it was his own) to support Julio Prestes, the conservative presidential candidate in 1929, proved of any avail in restoring either his own political power or the Valley's privileged "third force" position in Ceará's unideological politics.[40]

However, neither Floro's death, the Patriarch's decline, nor Macedo's crusade were wholly responsible for the subsequent political victory won at last by Joaseiro's native sons in late 1930. That victory came with the Vargas revolution of October. It saw Fernandes Távora, founder (in 1920) of Ceará's *Partido Republicano* (*tavoristas*) and brother of the famous *tenente,* Juarez Távora, appointed to the post of interventor of Ceará. As virtual governor of the state, Fernandes Távora then turned to his one-time political supporters in Joaseiro and appointed as prefect the former leader of Joaseiro's *tavorista* party, Sr. José Geraldo da Cruz. In the person of this pharmacist, publisher of *O Ideal,* and ex-president of Fr. Macedo's St. Vincent de Paul Society, Joaseiro's native sons had at last come to power, thanks mostly to political changes far beyond the "New Jerusalem."

A final comment is in order. Fr. Macedo's 1925 crusade was not only a political failure.[41] It was, from Joaseiro's point of view, an historical disaster. The national debate inspired by the Floro-Macedo feud and aided by the writings of the Catholic clergy helped distort the image of the Patriarch beyond further recognition. Joaseiro was now transformed not only into a "Mecca of fanatics," an "outpost of *cangaceiros,*" but also into a redoubt of criminality and political despotism. Even today this image of Joaseiro has altered little and to its own citizens' dismay much of its history has appeared to outsiders to be more legend than fact. Unfortunately, much of that legend must be attributed to Fr. Macedo's *Jouseiro em Fóco,* Xavier de Oliveira's *Beatos e Cangaceiros,* and Fr. Alencar Peixoto's *Joaseiro do Cariry.* Ironically then, the inescapable conclusion is that much of the historiographical basis of Joaseiro's distorted past is largely the work of two of its own native sons and that of a fellow Cariryense. All three, it must always be remembered, were aspirants to political power; in their hopes for victory or in the aftermath of defeat, they became the unintentional creators of a mythical Patriarch and a mythical city, both of which have survived into the present at the hands of uncritical writers: writers unwilling or unable to unmask the truth.

The Last Journey

One of the myths which has persisted into the present is that Padre Cícero went to his death unreconciled with his church. Two factors within the Patriarch's own lifetime clearly contributed to that view. The first was the attitude of his bishop. Dom Quintino, it will be remembered, had resuspended the cleric in 1921. The resignation of Joaseiro's first vicar, Fr. Esmeraldo, further convinced Dom Quintino that neither the Patriarch nor his city was worthy of further solicitude. The bishop apparently had no change of heart: In April 1924, one of the Patriarch's friends in Rio de Janeiro reported confidentially to him that Dom Quintino considered the octogenarian to be an incurable "reprobate." According to this source, Quintino had made it clear to influential churchmen in Rio de Janeiro that "Joaseiro merited nothing."[42]

The second factor was the startling 1925 affirmation of Fr. Macedo that "Floro had prevented Padre Cícero from reacquiring orders to celebrate mass."[43] Macedo's charge, leveled in *Joaseiro em Fóco,* was clearly a political one directed against Floro. But, once made and left unrectified, it helped confirm the myth that the Patriarch remained outside the "one, true fold." A recent article also by a priest from the Cariry, has unfortunately reaffirmed that myth.[44] Moreover, there is a widespread impression that the Patriarch's failure to return fully to the cloth was entirely his own responsibility (or, irresponsibility, as orthodox clergymen contended). For these reasons, it is best to review that last decade of Padre Cícero's life and his repeated efforts to regain orders.

The basis for Fr. Macedo's contention in *Joaseiro em Fóco* was an event which took place in November 1924. That month, the Benedictine Abbot, Dom Bento Lopez, arrived in the Cariry.[45] As Apostolic Visitor and personal emissary of the Holy Father, Dom Bento had come to examine the needs and progress of various dioceses throughout Brazil. When he reached Crato, he appears to have turned a sympathetic ear to the Patriarch's long standing case. With Dom Quintino's consent, both Dom Bento and Padre Cícero agreed to discuss the steps necessary for the Apostolic Visitor to present the Patriarch's appeal directly to the Holy See. A meeting of the two was scheduled for 7 December 1924, but it never took place as planned. Floro rather than Padre Cícero met with the papal emissary. The alleged results of that encounter became a burning political issue in the subsequent conflict between Macedinho and Floro. Dom Bento's account to Rome is still unavailable. As to the public record, it is obviously partisan. Fr. Macedo's account contends that Floro had physically prevented the Patriarch from meeting with Dom Bento.[46] When Floro appeared in Padre Cícero's stead, he betrayed the ancient Patriarch by assuring the papal emissary that both Padre Cícero's absence and his disobedience to his superiors were a sign of "bad conscience." Floro's account vehemently denied Macedo's charges.[47] He claimed he had neither interfered in the early discussions between the Patriarch and Dom Bento nor prevented Padre Cícero from meeting later with the Apostolic Visitor. The Patriarch's ill health, Floro insisted, was the sole reason for his decision to meet with Dom Bento in Padre Cícero's place. At that encounter, according to Floro, it was Dom Bento who reneged on his earlier promise to provide Padre Cícero with the necessary canonical assistance. Instead, Floro wrote, Dom Bento then suggested that the Patriarch appeal directly to the Holy Father; the Apostolic Visitor's earlier pledge to carry personally the case to Rome was hence null and void. Padre Cícero's unpublished correspondence barely clarifies the matter.[48] He confirmed Floro's claim that Dom Bento had suggested that the Patriarch appeal directly to the Pope; nowhere, however, did Padre Cícero imply that that suggestion represented the emissary's denial of an earlier promise to aid him more directly.

Rather than dwell fruitlessly on the "*affaire* Dom Bento," it is far more satisfactory and relevant to turn to the Patriarch's efforts—undertaken at this time—to establish ties with his eventual heirs, the Salesian Fathers. The Salesians are an Italian missionary congregation founded in the late nineteenth century. Its purpose has been to provide vocational training for underprivileged boys. The Salesians' founder was Don John Bosco, who was later canonized as a saint of the church and who during his lifetime enjoyed a close friendship with the popes of Rome. His order established a mission field in Brazil around the turn of the century; by the 1920s, there were vocational centers in Niterói, Recife, and other major cities of Brazil.[49]

Exactly when Padre Cícero first decided to contact the Salesians is uncertain.[50] But it is beyond doubt that the intimate ties which later bound him to the Italian missionaries represented the most significant fact of the last decade of his life. The first traces of the Patriarch's correspondence with the Salesians date from September 1924.[51] Letters at that time to Frs. Rota and Della Via indicate that Floro and Padre Cícero's friends in Rio de Janeiro had shortly before made contact with the order, probably in Niterói. In these same letters Padre Cícero expressed his profound pleasure over the Salesians' avowed willingness to found a vocational school in Joaseiro. That deed, the Patriarch exclaimed in a letter, would constitute "the greatest benefice that I could leave to this people whom I have educated in the most austere principles of our divine religion."[52] Padre Cícero then added in confidence that he had willed all of his possessions to the Salesians for the success of that "great work."

Ironically, the Patriarch had made the bequest to the Salesians as early as October 1923, almost a full year before the first written exchange of letters preserved in his archives. It will be recalled that prior to this October 1923 will, Padre Cícero had bequeathed most of his possessions to Fr. Macedo's seminary mentors of the Premonstratensian Order. Why the Patriarch altered his will is unknown. One hypothesis rests on Floro's congressional speech of September 1923, in which he vehemently branded the Brazilian churchmen as "hypocrites." Perhaps the Patriarch interpreted this attack as fatal to his own hope that his fellow Brazilian priests would assist him in regaining orders. As a result, it can be speculated that one month after Floro's speech, the cleric named as his heirs an Italian congregation whose intimate ties with the papacy may have appeared to him as the last and only means of returning to the cloth. Unfortunately, this plausible hypothesis still awaits confirmation in contrast to the Patriarch's professed rationale for providing the Salesians with his fortune, namely, to found a vocational agricultural school in Joaseiro.

Like the Franciscans whom the priest had invited in 1914 to erect a school and seminary in Joaseiro, the Salesians too were reluctant to undertake the enterprise "without the expressed authorization of the bishop."[53] Fr. Rota, the chief Salesian in Brazil, frankly advised the Patriarch to make his peace with Dom Quintino. Padre Cícero professed his willingness to do so, but in a confidential letter to Fr. Rota, he also expressed his fear that the bishop would respond unfavorably.[54] For that reason, the suspended Patriarch appealed directly to Fr. Rota to intervene in Rome on his behalf. So eager was the ailing octogenarian to regain his orders that he even informed his Salesian friend of his readiness to journey to Rome, if that should prove necessary![55] Despite the Patriarch's eagerness to return to the cloth and the Salesians' interest in establishing another school, Fr. Rota made it clear that all depended on the priest's act of submission to episcopal authority. The question remained unresolved. Neither Fr. Rota nor the Patriarch weakened. At best, their correspondence between 1924 and 1929 bears witness to the moving personal drama of an aging cleric, too proud to submit to his peers and too convinced of the efficacy of his own course.

In 1929, the intractable Dom Quintino died. Three years later, the consecration of Dom Francisco de Assis Pires as Crato's second bishop made it possible for the Patriarch to reopen his case.[56] Dom Francisco proved more amenable than his predecessor to the plight of the Patriarch who was now nearing his nintieth year. However, the ecclesiastical records of the Crato diocese reveal little of their transactions except that the disposition of the Patriarch's personal fortune had now become an impediment to his reinstatement. An important question arose: Were the Patriarch's possessions the rightful patrimony of the diocese to whose *obras pias* Rome had once demanded they be donated? Or, if in truth acquired under the pretext of false miracles, could they be bequeathed to the Salesians as the Patriarch had prescribed in his will? This problem was ultimately resolved not by Rome's canon lawyers whose earlier decisions had resulted in Padre Cícero's suspension but rather by the Brazilian civil law. It appears that the government's fiscal authorities refused to exempt the Patriarch's vast fortune from taxes. Church officials then apparently approved the cleric's bequest to the Salesians provided that the foreign missionaries accepted the duty to pay the taxes. In this expedient manner, the Salesians, rather than the diocese of Crato, became the Patriarch's legal heirs.[57]

This resolution did not bear on the priest's reinstatement. In fact, his hope to regain holy orders was never fulfilled. However, the Patriarch did not die outside the "one true fold," as some writers have implied. While he never again performed the duties of a priest, he appears to have reconciled himself to living out his last days as a faithful communicant of his church.[58] One of the younger priests of the diocese, Msgr. Joviniano Barreto, who had served in the 1930s as Joaseiro's pastor, later offered this view of the Patriarch's last days: "He never missed Sunday mass. He was always patient and never uttered a word of protest nor the slightest gesture [of revolt] in regard to events which he endured as a religious. This does not prove a disdain towards religion which he loved from the depths of his priestly soul but to the contrary [it demonstrates] a deep faith in Catholicism from which he never parted."[59]

During the Patriarch's last days, illness, blindness, and age conspired with the reluctance of his church to deter him from the last, longed-for journey to Rome about which he had written Fr. Rota and from which he believed his reinstatement would ensue. Instead, in the early hours of 20 July 1934, the nonagenarian embarked on that final journey from which neither patriarch nor politician is spared. Moments before his death he raised his arm and in defiiance of every past prohibition, he thrice traced the sign of the cross in the air, and then succumbed.[60]

There is a moving acount of the tumult which shortly thereafter fell upon Joaseiro on the morning of 20 July 1934. It was written by Lourival Marques, the son of one of the Patriarch's personal secretaries, and is recorded here:[61]

I was awakened by a stampede of people in the streets. For a moment, I didn't know what to make of those strange sounds. When I got to the window, it struck me that something monstrous was taking place in the city. What a frightening spectacle, those thousands of stupefied people racing through the streets, crying, shouting, pulling their hair out. . . . And then it became clear . . . Padre Cícero was dead. I, myself, was never a "fanatic" and yet I felt, like all the others, like crying, shouting and racing towards the home of that man who was equaled neither in goodness nor in the calumny heaped upon him. A torrent of more than forty thousand people crowded each other, and some fainted in the anxiety to reach the priest's home. The telegraph office overflowed with people who had come to dispatch telegrams to all the cities of Brazil. . . . As soon as the cables reached the nearest towns, an unbelievable pilgrimage—of dozens of overflowing trucks, of thousands upon thousands of persons on foot—began its march upon Joaseiro. Joaseiro experienced and still is experiencing a moment that neither London nor New York will ever equal. . . . The people, an enormous tidal wave of people, has invaded everything, hurling down anything in its path, breaking down doors, climbing over everything. The police were asked to keep order, but they refused to do so, claiming that Padre Cícero belonged to the people and that he would continue to belong to the people.

Meanwhile, [those who had attended the cleric at the hour of his death] managed to [tie] his corpse [to a plank] and placed it in the window frame exposed [to the crowd, but] at a height out of people's reach. . . . Throughout the entire day, certain persons were responsible for pressing rosaries, medals and other religious artifacts to the corpse so that [these objects] might be kept as relics. Thousands of persons continued to arrive from all four points of the compass, on foot, on horseback, in cars, trucks and every possible means of transport.

Four o'clock in the afternoon . . . above the first army plane crosses the heavens. Then another. Now they dive and loop, soaring six feet above the roof of the old Padre's residence. The flights last for a long time. It is a most heartfelt homage that the pilots are paying to the great Brazilian who has fallen. . . . Later, they landed at our airfield and personally presented a very expensive funeral wreath in the name of the nation's air force.

The city is an immense anthill; an anthill of sixty thousand people, now that some twenty thousand outsiders have arrived. Not a store is open; barber shops, cafes, bars, everything is closed. The mayor's office officially decreed three days of mourning. Crato, Barbalha and other cities followed suit. Every organization and society flew the flag, draped in black ribbon, at half mast. . . .

Throughout the night of 20 July and the morning of the following day, thousands filed past the corpse, held erect in the open window frame of the miracle worker's residence. At one point, the corpse's arm swung loose from its binds and a cry went up "Padre Cícero lives; he is risen from the dead." The town fathers swiftly moved to disabuse the credulous; fearful of panic, they reassured the mourners that the Patriarch was indeed dead. Earlier, the attending physicians had left the scene through backyards and alleyways as a precaution against the expected retaliation of the lower classes.[62]

Then, early on the morning of the twenty-first, the Patriarch's bier was made ready for the last journey to the Chapel of Our Lady of Perpetual Help, where his mother, a sister, and Maria de Araújo had already been put to rest. Sixty thousand people and almost a dozen priests from the Valley's cities accompanied the cortege; four hours elapsed before the chief mourners and priests reached their destination just a few blocks from the cleric's residence, today the "Padre Cícero Museum." By noon, the solemn mass had been intoned and the marble slab was fitted into place above the grave dug earlier within the sanctuary of the chapel in close proximity to the altar.[63]

The Patriarch was dead. In the minds of some of Joaseiro's prominent citizens and merchants, so too was Joasciro. Pessimists began to close their shops and take leave of the city whose green pastures they expected to wither. Certainly, the life-size bronze statue of the cleric, erected in Freedom Square in 1925, was a poor substitute for a Patriarch. But the pessimists notwithstanding, the *romeiros* continued to arrive. In their perennial misery, many believed, and still beileve, that Padre Cícero will soon return! Meanwhile, by their labors, the once insignificant hamlet continued to grow. Its population today is about eighty thousand souls. Its cotton gins boom, its schools expand, new industries have taken root, and even the church hierarchy has become reconciled to the impoverished "fanatics," upon whom justice has yet to shine.[64] Indeed, until the poor inherit the earth or better, until the poor lay claim to what is rightly theirs, Joaseiro—with its past and present promise of a miracle—seems destined to remain the most sought-after way station of the Brazilian Northeast.

Abbreviations

Archives

ABC: Arquivo do Bispado do Crato. Crato, Ceará.

ABS: Personal Archive of D. Beatriz Santanna. Juàzeiro do Norte Ceará.

ACS: Arquivo do Colégio Salesiano "Dom João Bosco." Juàzeiro do Norte, Ceará.

AXO: Personal Archive of D. Amália Xavier de Oliveira. Juàzeiro do Norte, Ceará.

CN: "Côpias dos telegrammas do Padre Cícero recibidos nesta Estação do Joaseiro de 29 de setembro de 1912 em diante," 3 vols. Now in the possession of Dr. F. S. Nascimento, Fortaleza, Ceará; referred to as the Coleção Nascimento.

GBM: Personal Archive of Dr. Geraldo Bezerra de Menezes. Niterói, Rio de Janeiro.

LTJ: Livro do Tombo da Freguezia de Nôssa Senhora das Dôres. Juàzeiro do Norte, Ceará.

PCC: Personal Archive of Padre Cícero Countinho. Juàzeiro do Norte, Ceará.

RGM: Personal Archive of Dr. Raimundo Gomes de Mattos. Fortaleza, Cearà.

Journals

Itaytera: *Itaytera, Orgão do Instituto Cultural do Cariri* (Crato, Ceará).
RIAHGP: *Revista do Instituto Arqueológico, Histórico e Geográfico de Pernambuco* (Recife).
RIC: *Revista do Instituto do Ceará* (Fortaleza).
RIHGB: *Revista do Instituto Histórico e Geográfico Brasileiro* (Rio de Janeiro).

Notes

Chapter 1
The Social Origins of the Miracle

1. The date of Padre Cícero's arrival in Joaseiro is cited in Irineu Pinheiro, *Efemérides do Cariri* (Fortaleza, 1963), p. 156. This is the posthumous work at one of Padre Cícero's personal physicians, who was also prominent in the political, intellectual, and financial circles of Crato. The volume contains many hitherto unpublished documents from Padre Cícero's personal archives to which Sr. Pinheiro had access.

2. Our account of Padre Cícero's arrival in Joaseiro and of the reasons that ultimately persuaded him to reside permanently in the hamlet is based on the detailed and unpublished memoir of his close personal friend, Pelusio Correia Macedo, whose father was one of the two prominent inhabitants of the hamlet who urged the priest to come there in April 1872. The document is entitled "A pedido do Am[ig]o José Bernadino lhe oferece o pequeno am[ig]o Pelusio C[orreia] Macedo, Juàzeiro, 19 de Março de 1955." It is found in the personal archives of the Cearense lawyer, Dr. Raimundo Gomes de Mattos of Fortaleza, Ceará (hereinafter cited as RGM).

3. The two citizens in question were Pedro Correia Macedo, then *professor regio* at Joaseiro, and his father-in-law, Capt. Domingos Conçalves Martins, the

largest resident landowner at that time in Joaseiro, who were, respectively, the father and maternal grandfather of Pelusio Correia Macedo. It is presumably their testimony which is contained in Macedo's "A pedido . . . 1955," RGM.

4. Our detailed account of this dream is a paraphrase of the one found in Macedo, "A pedido . . . 1955," RGM. An earlier published version appeared in one of the most curious and yet fundamental accounts ever written about Joaseiro, M[anuel] Dinis, *Mistérios do Joazeiro* (Joazeiro, Ceará, 1935), p. 10.

5. According to *The Catholic Encyclopedia* (New York, 1913), VII, 163-167, private devotions to the Sacred Heart of Jesus were in evidence among mystics and ascetics as early as the eleventh and twelfth centuries. Then in the seventeenth century, Margaret Mary Alacoque (1647–1690), a French Visitandine nun at Paray-le-Monial, France, had an apparition of Christ (1673) in which He commanded her to propogate a public devotion "of expiatory love" to Him "under the figure of His Heart of flesh. . . ." The doctrinal lines of this devotion were underscored in 1675, the year of the "great vision," when Christ again appeared to the nun and explained: "Behold the Heart that has so loved men . . . instead of gratitude I receive from the greater part of [mankind] only ingratitude. . . ."

Throughout the eighteenth century, the devotion spread rapidly within France and to other parts of Western Europe, even though Rome continually rejected innumerable appeals to endorse officially the widespread popular practices. Then, in 1856, "at the urgent entreaties of the French bishops," Pope Pius IX formally "extended the feast to the universal Church" (*Ibid.*, p. 166). In 1889, Pope Leo XIII decreed that the devotion be celebrated with the most solemn rituals of the Church.

The significance, to our study, of this devotion is made clearer by the following excerpts from the *Catholic Encyclopedia*: "The [public] acts of consecration and of reparation were everywhere introduced together with the devotion. Often times, especially since 1850, groups, congregations, and States have consecrated themselves to the Sacred Heart and in 1875 this consecration was made throughout the Catholic world." In 1899, by fiat of Pope Leo XIII, "all mankind was solemnly consecrated to the Sacred Heart" (*Ibid.*, p. 166).

Also of importance to this study is the fact that "the Catholics of France, especially, cling firmly to it [the devotion] as one of their strongest hopes of ennoblement and salvation" (p. 167). In 1864, priests of the Congregation of the Missions, better known as the Lazarist Fathers in South America and as the Vincentian Fathers in North America, came to Ceará to administer the seminary at Fortaleza where they propagated this devotion among the newly ordained native Brazilian priests.

On the widespread devotion to the Sacred Heart in the Northeastern backlands at the turn of the century, see Dinis (1935), p. 8, and Dom Joaquim G. de Luna, "Os monges beneditinos no Ceará," *Revista do Instituto do Ceará* (Fortaleza), LXV (1951), 192-228, esp. 210, hereinafter cited as *RIC*.

6. Macedo, "A pedido . . . 1955," RGM.

7. *Ibid.*; also in Dinis (1935), pp. 1-2.

8. An excellent study of the Cariry Valley is Joaquim Alves, "O Vale do Cariri," *RIC*, LIX (1945), 94-133.

9. *Ibid.*, 110.

10. For a brief sketch of Crato's role in securing Ceará's independence, see the historical survey by Raimundo Girão, *A Pequena História do Ceará* (2d ed.; Fortaleza, 1962), *passim*. The work contains bibliographical references to all the standard secondary sources relevant to Ceará's history.

11. Factors in the Cariry's decline after independence are traced in the pioneering study—the first to sketch Ceará's political history from independence to the present—of Abelardo Montenegro, *História dos Partidos Políticos Cearenses* (Fortaleza, 1965), pp. 6-18.

12. On the immoral state of the clergy at this time, see the special publication commemorating the fiftieth anniversary of the founding of the diocesan seminary at Fortaleza, *Album Histórico do Seminário Episcopal do Ceará* (Fortaleza, 1914), pp. 1-3, hereinafter cited as *Album Histórico*.

Observations about the Clergy in Crato are contained in George Gardner, *Viagens no Brasil, principalmente nas províncias do norte e nos distritos do ouro e do diamante durante os anos de 1836–1841* (São Paulo, 1942), pp. 153-154. The original English edition was published in London in 1846.

On the state of disrepair of church properties in Crato and elsewhere in the Cariry Valley, see one of the most invaluable sources for the study of the region, Ireneu Pinheiro, *O Cariri: Seu Descobrimento, Povoamento, Costumes* (Fortaleza, 1950), p. 225.

Notes on the use of churches as polling places and their frequent misuse as the loci of often violent political conflicts are found in João Brigido, *Apontamentos para a História do Cariri: Crônica do Sul do Ceará* (Fortaleza, 1888), pp. 102-103.

13. Friar Vitale da Frascarolo (1780–1820) is better known in the Northeast under the Brazilianized name of Frei Vidal. He was not a mythical figure; a semi-official history of the Capuchin missions in Brazil notes that Frei Vidal was known throughout the Northeast "for his impassioned popular preaching, laced with prophetic references, which still remains alive in the memory and traditions of the 'backlanders,'" cited in P. Metodio da Nembro, *I Cappucini nel Brasile, Missione e Custodia del Maranhão, 1892–1956* (Milano, 1957), p. 5.

For some firsthand recollections of the missions preached in the Cariry Valley—which often resembled American revival meetings—at the end of the nineteenth century and of the miracle-working powers attributed to the preachers, see Paulo Elpídio de Menezes, *O Crato do Meu Tempo* (Fortaleza, 1960), p. 56.

14. A pioneering attempt to study the folk religion of Ceará is the work of Abelardo Montenegro, *História do Fanatismo Religioso no Ceará* (Fortaleza, 1959). About half of this volume concerns Padre Cícero.

Our references to folk religion, its beliefs and practices, are based largely on two works of the noted Cearense folklorist, Eduardo Campos, *Folclore do Nordeste* (Rio de Janeiro, 1960a), especially the chapter entitled "O Sertanejo e as suas superstições," pp. 59-68, and *Estudos do Folclore Cearense* (Fortaleza, 1960b), especially the chapter entitled "Magia e Medecina Popular," pp. 99-106. On the customary recourse of the ailing backlanders to healers (*rezadores*), see Luis da Câmara Cascudo, *Dicionário do Folclore Brasileiro* (2d ed., 2 vols.; Rio de Janeiro, 1962), I, 259-261. On folk religion in the Cariry, see Pinheiro (1950), pp. 137-141.

15. Our account of the Valley's revitalization in the 1850s was suggested by Pinheiro's account (1950), pp. 81-84.

16. The Crato city council law (No. 640, art. 50) is cited in Pinheiro (1963), p. 138.

17. Our statistics are drawn from the most comprehensive short account of the history of sugarcane cultivation in the Cariry: José de Figueiredo Filho, *Engenhos de Rapadura do Cariri* (Rio de Janeiro, 1958), p. 69.

18. Most of these cottage industries were located in the *Casas de Caridade* which were equipped with looms. On the *Casas*, see pp. 18-20 of this text and relevant footnotes.

19. For a succinct discussion of the traditional social structure of rural Brazil, see Charles Wagley, *An Introduction to Brazil* (New York, 1963), pp. 99-114.

20. For a discussion of the *compadrio*, see Wagley (1963), pp. 190-191.

21. Pinheiro (1950), pp. 81-84. On the first *sobrado* built in 1857 in Crato, see Pinheiro (1963), pp. 143-144.

22. For details about *O Araripe* and other newspapers published in Crato, see F. S. Nascimento, "Subsídios para a história do Jornalismo cratense," *A Província* (Crato III 1955), 3-14; 99-112.

23. For details about the plan to create a new province with its seat in Crato, see Pinheiro (1950), pp. 31-34. It is also clear that one of the chief reasons for the establishment of the Cratense newspaper, *O Araripe*, was to promote the campaign and disseminate propaganda in favor of the new province; on this subject, see Décio Teles Cartaxo, "Pela Instalação de um Órgão de Cadéia Associada em Crato," *A Província*, III (1955), 61-64.

24. For a brief account of similar proposals and efforts in 1828, 1839, 1846, 1940, and 1957, see the special campaign publication, *Estado do Cariri*, Separata da Revista *Itaytera* (Crato, 1957).

25. Our account is based chiefly on Celso Mariz, *Ibiapina, Um Apostolo do Nordeste* (João Pessôa, Paraíba, 1942), *passim*. Also see Msgr. Silvano de Souza, "Padre Mestre Ibiapina," *Itaytera* (Crato, 1961), VI, 89-108.

26. The episcopal prohibitions against Ibiapina are recorded in the Livro do Tombo of the parish of Sobral and are cited verbatim in Mariz (1942), pp. 68-70.

27. The best account of the Charity Houses and of the sisterhoods which Ibiapina established is José de Figueiredo Filho, "Casa de Caridade de Crato, Fruto do Apostolado Multiforme do Pe. Ibiapina," *A Província*, III (1955), 14-25; also see Mariz (1942), pp. 202-203.

28. On the use of the Charity Houses, especially that of Crato, as a "cottage industry" for the production of cheap cotton cloth, see Figueirdo Filho (1955), *passim*.

29. Ibiapina's "rule" is appended in Mariz (1942).

30. Technically speaking, the Crato Charity House was not the first school for women in the Cariry. In 1861, one of Crato's three primary schools was for girls, according to Thomaz Pompêo de Souza Brasil, *Diccionário Topographico e Estatístico da Província do Ceará* (Rio de Janeiro, 1861), p. 34.

31. *Album Histórico* (1914), pp. 1-3. For additional biographical data on Dom Luis Antônio dos Santos, who was consecrated in 1880 as Archbishop of Bahia, see Apolônio Nóbrega, "Dioceses e Bispos do Brasil," *Revista do Insituto Histórico e Geográfico Brasileiro* (Rio de Janeiro), Vol. 222 (janeiro-março, 1954), pp. 3-328, esp. pp. 166-168 (hereinafter cited as *RIHGB*) and Arnold Wildberger, *Os Presidentes da Província da Bahia* (Salvador, Bahia, 1949), p. 684.

For the bishop's obituary in which he was hailed as one of the church's reformers, consult Guilherme Studart, *Datas e Factos para a História do Ceará* (3 vols. Fortaleza, 1896-1924), III, p. 26.

32. Data on the clergy are contained in Nertan Macêdo, *O Padre e a Beata* (Rio de Janeiro, 1961), p. 44; also see *Album Histórico* (1914), p. 83.

33. Our notion of the "romanization" of Brazilian Catholicism was suggested by the provocative analysis of religion in Brazil written by Roger Bastide, "Religion and the Church in Brazil," in T. Lynn Smith and Alexander Marchant (eds.), *Brazil, Portrait of Half a Continent* (New York, 1951), pp. 334-355.

For Bastide, the concept of "romanization" (although his own term is "romanized church") consists of: (1) the assertion of the authority of an institutional and hierarchical (episcopal) church over all popular variants of folk Catholicism; (2) the reformist upsurge of the episcopacy in the mid-nineteeth century to control the doctrine, faith, institutions and education of the clergy and laity; (3) the increased reliance of the Brazilian church upon foreign (European) priests, especially those of the missionary orders and congregations, to achieve "the transition from colonial Catholicism to universalist Catholicism, with complete doctrinal and moral rigidity" (341); and (4) the pursuit of these objectives apart from and even against the interests of local politics.

To these dimensions of the process of "romanization," it is necessary to add a fifth, viz., (5) the systematic integration of the Brazilian church, on both an ideological and institutional level, into the highly centralized structures of the Roman Catholic church directed from Rome. Signs of this last process are abundant, such as the establishment of the South American College or Colégio Pio Latino-Americano in 1858, where twenty-six Latin American archbishops and bishops had been trained by 1922 and from which Latin America's first cardinal, Brazil's Dom Joaquim Arcoverde (1906), had received his degree in sacred theology; the increased participation of the Brazilian clergy and laity in the Holy Year pilgrimages to Rome; the convocation in Rome in 1899 of the first synod of Latin American bishops under papal auspices.

This last process, in our minds, makes clearer Bastide's perceptive remark: "In becoming Romanized, the [Brazilian] church denationalized itself" (p. 343).

It is important to note, however, that the revitalization of the Brazilian church did not take place in a vacuum. In Europe, the reform of the church and the clergy and an increasing emphasis on personal saintliness and supernatural devotions (such as that to the Sacred Heart of Jesus) were in full force under the papacy of Pius IX; for the European background, see the excellent study of Paul Droulers, S. J., "Roman Catholicism" in Guy S. Métraux and François Crouzet (eds.), *The Nineteenth-Century World* (New York, 1963), pp. 282-315, esp. pp. 306-307.

34. *Album Histórico* (1914), esp. chapters II and III, pp. 19-44; for a eulogistic biography of Fr. Pierre Chevallier, see chapter VIII, pp. 106-115.

35. For an account of the miracles attributed to Ibiapina at Caldas, Barbalha, and also at the public dam which the missionary had ordered built near the Charity House in the *município* of Milagres, see Pinheiro (1950), pp. 161-163 and Mariz (1942), p. 96, n. 32.

The "miracles" at Caldas probably resulted from the high mineral content of the salubrious spring water; about a decade ago, the state government of Ceará authorized the erection of a hydro-mineral station at the Caldas spring, according to Antonio Marchêt Cullou, "Barbalha," *Itaytera*, V (1959), 127-133, esp. 128.

36. See *A Voz da Religião no Cariri* (Crato), 14 March 1869, as cited in Nascimento (1955), pp. 4 5.

37. Dom Luís' prohibition is cited in Pinheiro (1950), p. 168.

38. For an example of the Charity House hymns in which Ibiapina himself is the object of the *beatas'* religious devotion, see "Hino do Pe. Ibiapina reproduzido da tradiçao popular por Teresa Rosando Simões," *Itaytera*, IV (1959), p. 109.

39. For an astute critique of the *beatas'* inadequate religious training and for observations on their frequent deviation from orthodox Catholicism, see Figueiredo Filho (1955), *passim*.

40. "Declaração que faz o Padre Ibiapina aos Irmãos, Beatos e Irmãs das Santas Casas de Caridade do Cariri-Novo . . . Cravatá, Paraíba, 16 de setembro de 1872," cited in Pinheiro (1950), pp. 161-162, n. 30.

41. For an account of the Crato seminary's first fifty years, see *Album do Seminário do Crato* (Rio de Janeiro, 1925), hereinafter cited as *Album*.

42. *Ibid.*, p. 30. For Fr. Chevallier's views, see text of this chapter p. 29.

43. *Ibid.*, p. 32.

44. The Pastoral Letter is cited in Nóbrega (1954), p. 168.

45. The imperial religious question" is discussed in J. Lloyd Mecham, *Church and State in Latin America: A History of Politico-Ecclesiastical Relations* (Chapel Hill, 1934), pp. 316-321.

On the Vatican's opposition to Freemasonry, see Droulers (1963), pp. 302-306.

46. "If the Masonic lodges were anti-clerical elsewhere, they certainly were not in Brazil," Mecham (1934), p. 317.

47. One Brazilian scholar interprets the 1872 *affaire* as the critical turning

point in Brazilian church-state relations. Thereafter, Brazilian Catholicism was to affirm the ultramontanist principle of the "total independence of the church in matters within its own jurisdiction. The beginnings of differentiation that is outlined therein, is therefore one of a recapturing of attributions, substantially religious, by the episcopal hierarchy," cited in Cândido Mendes, *Memento dos Vivos: A Esquerda Católica no Brasil* (Rio de Janeiro, 1966), p. 35.

On the episcopacy's attack against Freemasonry, see note 50 below.

48. Excerpts of the Collective Pastoral Letter of the Brazilian Episcopacy in 1890 are cited in one of the most important works on Catholicism during the early decades of the Brazilian "Old Republic": Padre Júlio Maria [de Morais Carneiro], *O Catolicismo no Brasil, (Memória Histórica),* (Rio de Janeiro, 1950), pp. 213-218. It was originally published in 1900.

While the Pastoral recognized the Republic, it expressed the hope that the new constitution (proclaimed in 1891) would contain not " 'a word that might offend the freedom of the religious conscience of the country, which is, in the great majority, Catholic, apostolic, roman' " (p. 216).

That the Republic was accepted by the church in order to acquire the liberty by which it could proceed to defend itself against the very doctrines which erected the Republic is made amply clear by the following statement of Padre Júlio Maria: "The Republican period cannot yet be for religion one of splendor as was the colonial [period]. Nor is it one of decadence as was that of the Empire. It is, it cannot be otherwise—the period of combat" (p. 242).

Undoubtedly the Brazilian church's dilemma, posed by the new Republic, might have been unresolvable had it not been for the sharp modification of the papacy's attitude towards the modern world as expressed in the many encyclicals of Pope Leo XIII. It was he who contributed "most to domestic peace in all countries by encouraging Catholics to be loyal to the existing political system," according to Droulers (1963), p. 312.

49. For a more systematic discussion of the doctrines discussed here, see Mecham (1934), pp. 321-330 and João Cruz Costa, *A History of Ideas in Brazil* (Berkeley, 1964), *passim*.

50. On Dom Luis' actions in favor of his confreres and against the emperor, see the chapter "O Ceará e a Questão Religiosa" in Geraldo Bezerra de Menezes, *Homens e Idéias à Luz da Fé* (2d ed., Rio de Janeiro, 1959), pp. 194-209; and Nóbrega (1954), p. 168.

Despite the customary historiographical interpretation of the religious question which asserts that most bishops "observed a discreet silence" (Mecham, [1934] p. 319) in regard to the arrest of their two confreres, it is important to note that many bishops soon thereafter openly condemned Masonry. A perusal of Nóbrega, cited above, indicates eight of the fifteen reigning bishops between 1872 and 1875 issued pastoral letters attacking Masonry or in support of their confreres; four bishops apparently remained silent despite pressure from their colleagues to act, while information about the stand of the remaining three bishops is not specified in this source. That more than half of the members of the Brazilian episcopacy did speak out against Masonry may require historians to revise the literature on this question.

51. Some notes on the spread of Protestantism in the Brazilian Northeast during the last quarter of the nineteenth century are contained in Luis da Câmara Cascudo, *História do Rio Grande do Norte* (Rio de Janeiro, 1955), pp. 252-255. In the years 1890–1891, Fortaleza's daily newspaper, *A República,* published a number of proselytizing articles by the minister, Rev. De Lacy Wardlow.

52. See Msgr. José Quinderé, *Dom Joaquim José Vieira* (Fortaleza, 1958), for relevant biographical data and his achievements as bishop of Ceará.

53. Dom Joaquim José Vieira, *Carta Pastoral . . . exhortando os seus Diocesanos a orarem pela Egreja e pela Pátria e premunindo-os contra os vícios oppostos à Santa Religião . . . 25 de março de 1893* (Fortaleza, 1894). An edited version is found in Macêdo (1961), pp. 139-156.

54. Manoel Monteiro, "Carta Aberta . . . a Gomes de Mattos," *Unitário* (Fortaleza), 27 April 1952.

55. Dom Luis' vow and the solemn consecration of Ceará are cited in *Album Histórico* (1914), p. 5. About similar public acts throughout the Catholic world in 1875 and of their origin in a papal decree, see n. 5 of this chapter.

56. Montenegro (1959), p. 32.

57. Fr. Antonio Gomes de Araújo, "Padre Pedro Ribeiro da Silva, O Fundador e Primeiro Capelão de Juàzeiro do Norte," *Itaytera,* IV (1958), 3-7.

58. Our account of Joaseiro around 1875 is based on Lívio Sobral (pseud. of Fr. Azarias Sobreira), "Padre Cícero Romão," *RIC,* LVII (1943), 285-296; this was the last of a series of four consecutive articles bearing the same title, the first of which was published in *RIC,* LIV (1940). A more critical study is that of Joaquim Alves, "Juàzeiro, Cidade Mistica," *RIC,* LXXI (1948), 73-101, esp. 84-91. Among the most recent accounts is that of Otacílio Anselmo e Silva, "A História do Padre Cícero," *Itaytera,* V (1959)—VII (1961), *passim.*

Since the completion of the present manuscript in early 1968, a very thorough biography has appeared: Otacílio Anselmo e Silva, *Padre Cícero: Mito e Realidade* (Rio de Janeiro: Editôra Civilização Brasileira, 1968). It is one of the first Brazilian studies to use extensively selected documents from the ecclesiastical archive of the Diocese of Crato (see Chapt. II, n. 1); it omits material from the cleric's personal archive (see Chapt. II, n. 4) to which Anselmo had no access.

Time has not permitted me to evaluate Anselmo's work in detail in this study. His interpretation, however, subscribes to the historiographical school critical of Padre Cícero—exemplified in the writings of Fr. Antonio Gomes de Araújo and other authors whose contributions are discussed in Chapt. VI, n. 1 and elsewhere in the footnotes.

59. See Sobral (1943), *passim* and Alves (1948), p. 87.

60. This viewpoint that Ibiapina and Padre Cícero bear a striking resemblance in their devotion to the church and in their pastoral methods has been hotly

contested by orthodox Catholic writers of the Cariry. An example of this view-point is "Carta de Otacílio Anselmo e Silva ao Padre Antonio Gomes de Araújo, 22 de janeiro de 1957," in *Ecos de "Apostolado do Embuste,"* Separata da Revista *Itaytera* (Crato, [1957 ?]), pp. 13-19.

61. On the educational work of Isabel da Luz which Padre Cícero encouraged, see Amália Xavier de Oliveira, "Minha Mestre," in the commemorative volume of Joaseiro's fiftieth anniversary as a *município, Revista do Cinqüentenário do Juàzeiro de Norte* (Fortaleza, 1961), pp. 25-30 (hereinafter cited as *Rev. do Cinqüentário*).

62. On Padre Cícero's poverty and disinterest in worldly matters, see Menezes (1960), p. 62; and Manuel do Nascimento Fernandes Távora, "O Padre Cícero," *RIC* LVII (1943), 35-69, *passim*.

63. Alves (1948), pp. 89-90; Pinheiro (1950), pp. 220-221.

64. Alves (1948), pp. 85-86.

65. On Fr. Felix and his penitent society in Crato, see *Album* (1925), pp. 85-86; Pinheiro (1950), p. 230; José Alves de Figueiredo, *Ana Mulata* (Crato, 1958), p. 181; Menezes (1960), p. 40-41, pp. 54-56. On the origins and contemporary survival of these societies, see Fernando Altenfelder Silva, "As Lamentações e os Grupos de Flagelados de São Francisco," *Sociologia* (São Paulo), XXIV (março, 1962), 1, 15-28.

66. A biographical note on Msgr. Francisco Rodrigues Monteiro is contained in *Album* (1925), pp. 92-94. On his pastoral activities in Iguatú, see Alcântara Nogueira, *Iguatú, Memória Sócio-Histórico-Econômico* (Fortaleza, 1962), p. 104. On his role in the events of Joaseiro, see Menezes (1966), pp. 63-64.

67. Typical of the innumerable popular accounts of Padre Cícero which circulate widely throughout the Northeast even today is Tristão Romero, *Vida Completa do Padre Cícero Romão Batista (Anchieta do Século XX),* (Juàzeiro do Norte, 1950).

68. On Padre Cícero's role in encouraging the cultivation of manioc in the Cariry after 1877, see Celso Gomes de Mattos, "Em Defesa da Serra do Araripe," *A Provincia,* III (1955), 31-34.

69. A reference to this vow is contained in J. Machado, *Duas Palavras, Excertos da Vida do Padre Cícero* (Juàzeiro do Norte, 1948), p. 14. This is one of several published versions of Padre Cícero's last will and testament of 1923. An incomplete text of the will is cited in Macedo (1961), pp. 113-120. On Padre Cícero's personal devotion to the Sacred Heart, see Dinis (1935), p. 8.

70. Biographical data about Maria de Araújo (1862–1914) are in Pinheiro (1963), p. 148.

71. This account of the miracle is based on a letter from Padre Cícero to Dom Joaquim Jose Vieira [7 January 1890]; it is one of several important documents found in the personal archive of Sr. Hugo Catunda which were published under the title, "Documentos Sôbre a Questão Religiosa do Juàzeiro," in RIC, LXXV (1961), 266-297, esp. 266-269 (hereinafter cited as "Documentos").

72. *Ibid.,* 268.

Chapter 2
The Ecclesiastical Conflict

1. Dom Joaquim José Vieira to Padre Cícero Romão Batista, 4 November 1889, Arquivo do Bispado do Crato, Crato, Ceará (cited hereinafter as ABC).

2. *Ibid.,* Dom Joaquim clearly states that "Msgr. Monteiro publicized the facts . . . without consulting me. . . . As Bishop of this Diocese, I cannot be kept in the dark about this. . . . How does one intend to establish a new state of affairs in religious matters without a hearing of the Bishop!"

3. Between March 1889, and April 1891, only four articles about the miracle appeared in the Brazilian press: *Diário do Comércio* (Rio de Janeiro), 19 August 1889; *Diário de Pernambucco* (Recife), 29 August 1889. These are referred to by José Joaquim Teles Marrocos in his letter to Fr. Clycério da Costa Lôbo, 12 October 1891, cited in "Documentos" (1961), pp. 285-288.

The third article, also favorable to the miracle appeared in *Estrêla da Aparecida* (São Paulo), 29 December 1889 and was allegedly written by Msgr. Francisco Monteiro, on 11 November 1889, cited in Pinheiro (1963), pp. 477-480. Previously, Monteiro categorically denied that he had ever written anyone about the event; see Monteiro to Joaquim, 27 October 1889, ABC. The fourth and only unfavorable article was published in *O Estado do Ceará* (Fortaleza), 19 August 1890.

4. The reconstruction of events between 1889 and 1891 are based on many unpublished letters found in ABC and in the Arquivo do Colégio Salesiano "Dom João Bosco," Juàzeiro do Norte, Ceará (cited hereinafter as ACS). The latter is essentially the extant personal archive of Padre Cícero Romão Batista, inherited upon his death by the Salesian Fathers.

5. Joaquim to Cícero, 4 November 1889, ABC.

6. Joaquim to Cícero, 3 November 1888, ABC; published in Pinheiro (1963), pp. 448-450.

7. Joaquim to Cícero, 19 January 1890, ABC.

8. Cícero to Joaquim [7 January 1890], ABC; published in "Documentos" (1961), pp. 266-269.

9. The Joaseiro branch of the Apostleship of Prayer was solemnly founded on 19 October 1888; see Acta da fundação solene da Associação do Apostolado da Oração do Sagrado Coração de Jesus, na povoação do Juàzeiro, da paróquia do Crato, Diocese do Ceará, ACS.

10. Padre Cícero's admission that the *beata* since childhood had suffered nervous seizures is contained in the Auto de Perguntas feitas ao Revdmo. Padre Cícero Romão Batista, perante o Exmo. e Revdmo. Dom Joaquim José Vieira, . . . Fortaleza, 17 July 1891, in "Documentos" (1961), pp. 269-272 (hereinafter cited as Auto de Perguntas. . .).

11. Cícero to Joaquim [7 January 1890], ABC; published in "Documentos" (1961), p. 268.

12. Joaquim to Cícero, 5 November 1889, ABC.

13. Joaquim to Cícero, 19 January 1890, ABC.

14. *Ibid.*

15. Joaquim to Cícero, 27 January 1890, and 7 March 1890, ABC.

16. Joaquim to Cícero, 4 June 1890, ABC.

17. Cícero to Joaquim [7 January 1890], ABC; published in "Documentos" (1961), p. 268.

18. *Ibid.*

19. These are the same priests who had attended the solemn foundation of the Apostleship of Prayer in Joaseiro in 1888, Acta da fundação, . . . ACS.

20. Fr. Manuel Fêlix de Moura to the Vice-Rector of the Seminary, 25 January 1898; published in "Documentos" (1961), pp. 291-292. The relevant text is: "In the beginning, when things remained under secrecy, I was inclined to believe. . . ."

21. "Communicado: Milagres na provoação do Joazeiro do Crato," *Cearense* (Fortaleza), 24 April 1891.

22. *Ibid.*

23. This was Dom Joaquim's interpretation as expressed in his letter to Dr. Madeira, 15 November 1892, ACS.

24. *Cearense* (Fortaleza), 10 May 1891.

25. These included Fr. Laurindo Duettes, *vigário* of Triúnfo, Pernambuco who was ordained with Msgr. Monteiro. Duettes had founded the Catholic Party of Triúnfo in 1890 and finally resorted to arming several thousand peasants whom he led against republican forces; cited in *Album Histórico* (1914), 100. The other two were Frs. Manoel Antônio Martins de Jesus, *vigário* in Salgueiro, Pernambuco, and Cícero Torres of Paraíba.

26. Manoel Antônio Martins de Jesus, "Letter to the Editors," *Era Nova* (Recife), 18 May 1891, cited in the pamphlet by Fr. J. Soares Pimental (ed.), *Os Milagres do Joazeiro ou Grande Collecçã de documentos que attestam a veracidade da transformação da Sagrada Hóstia em sangue, sangue precióso de N. S. Jesus Christo, na povoação do Joazeiro. . . .* (Caicó, Rio Grande do Norte, 1892), pp. 5-8.

27. Cited in Dinis (1935), pp. 19-22. Dr. Ildefonso's "attestado" is dated 30 May 1891.

28. *Ibid.,* pp. 22-28. The original "attestado" is dated 29 April 1891.

29. *Os Milagres do Joaseiro ou Nosso Senhor Jesus Christo Manifestando Sua Presença Real no Divino e Adoravel Sacramento da Eucharistia,* Donaciano de Norões Maia and José Manoel de A. Façanha (eds.) (Crato, 1891), hereinafter cited as *Os Milagres.*

30. Padre Cícero dispatched copies of this pamphlet to D. Joaquim but flatly denied that he had taken any part in publishing it; Cícero to Joaquim, 18 June 1891, ACS.

31. *Os Milagres* (1891), pp. 24-29.

32. Pe Cícero's arrival in Fortaleza on 16 July 1891 was noted in *Libertador* (Fortaleza), 16 July 1891.

33. Auto de Perguntas . . ., in "Documentos" (1961), pp. 269-272.

34. Portaria de . . . 19 July 1891, published in "Documentos" (1961), pp. 275-276.

35. Joaquim to Cícero, 22 July 1891, Confidential, ABC; published in Pinheiro (1963), pp. 466-467 and "Documentos" (1961), pp. 277-278.

36. Petição de Apelação, 28 July 1891, in "Documentos" (1961), pp. 278-279.

37. Cícero to Joaquim, 14 August 1891, ABC; also in "Documentos" (1961), pp. 279-281 and partially paraphrased in Pinheiro (1963), pp. 456-457.

38. *Ibid.*

39. Details of the commission's activities in Joaseiro and Crato are contained in one of the two notebooks kept by one of the miracle's leading proponents, José Joaquim Telles Marrocos. The notebook or copybook in question was the second to be found by the author in the Personal Archives of Fr. Cícero Coutinho, a native and resident of Juàzeiro do Norte, Ceará (hereinafter cited as PCC). For the purpose of clarity, the notebook referred to above will hereinafter be cited as the Marrocos Copybook II, PCC.

40. Biographical data on Frs. Clycério and Antero are contained in *Album Histórico* (1914), *passim;* Msgr. José Quinderé, "História Eclesiastica do Ceará," Raimundo Girao and Martins Filho (eds.), *O Ceará* (Fortaleza, 1939), pp. 351-366, esp. p. 364; and Victor Hugo Guimarães, *Deputados Provinciais e Estaduais do Ceará—Assembléias Legislativas, 1835-1947* (Fortaleza, 1952), p. 260.

41. Quinderé (1939), p. 364.

42. Antero was also renowned for his devotion to the Sacred Heart of Jesus. He erected "a beautiful Chapel to the Divine Heart, the first constructed under this invocation in our *sertões,*" *Album Histórico* (1914), 96.

43. Marrocos Copybook II, PCC.

44. Fr. Clycério da Costa Lôbo to Pe. Cícero, 24 November 1891, cited in Pinheiro (1963), pp. 469-470.

45. "Côpia Authéntica do Processo do Inquêrito Instruido pelo Excmo. e Revdmo. Dr. Dom Joaquim José Vieira sôbre os factos extraordinários occuridos em Joazeiro, 1891," (hereinafter cited as "Côpia Authéntica") ABC.

46. *Ibid.,* ff. 25v—30r.

47. *Ibid.,* ff. 28v—29r.

48. *Ibid.,* f. 22v.

49. The following description of the popular enthusiasm which the commission's investigation generated in Crato sheds some light on the possible pressures that may have been imposed on the two priests: "In order to learn what was happening, a multitude of young and old thunderously besieged the grounds of the Charity House of Crato.

"Those who were unable to enter through the main gate of the cloister jumped the fences, scaled the walls and thronged into the church building, the anterooms and the hallways in an effort to see at least the poor Maria de Araújo."

The above description was found in the first notebook of José Marrocos, now preserved in the ACS and hereinafter cited as the Marrocos Copybook I, ACS.

50. See the articles of the Protestant missionary, Rev. De Lacey Wardlow in *A República* (Fortaleza) during 1890 and 1891.

Clerical concern over the spread of Protestantism dated at least from the 1880s in Ceará. In 1883, for example, an unidentified Fortaleza priest wrote Padre Cícero: "My friend: unfortunately, the *evangelical* minister (whose name is Lacy Badalo [?]) is still protestantizing our capital; but it seems to me that he doesn't dare set foot from here to the *sertão* after what happened to Albina in Bat[urit]é." Fr. [?] to Cícero, 13 September 1883, ACS.

51. Rdo. Dor. Fran.co Ferreira Antero to Msgr. Saluci, Commissioner of the Holy Office, Rome, 5 August 1892, ACS, Pasta Marrocos.

52. Clycério to Cícero 21 November 1891, cited in Pinheiro (1963), pp. 467-469.

53. *Album Histórico* (1914), *passim*.

54. Quinderé (1958), pp. 56-59.

55. *Ibid.,* p. 57.

56. Pinheiro (1963), p. 504.

57. Clycério to Cícero, 24 November 1891, ACS.

58. Antero to Dom Jerônymo, 5 October 1893, Marrocos Copybook I, ACS.

59. Antero to Saluci, Rome, 5 August 1892, ACS, Pasta Marrocos.

60. For a popular analysis of the significance of foreign priests in Latin America, see Ralph della Cava, "Ecclesiastical Neo-Colonialism in Latin America," *Slant* (London, October-November 1967, n. s. 3), 5, pp. 17-20.

61. See Despacho do Revdmo. Bispo Diocesano in "Documentos" (1961), p. 279.

62. "Côpia Authéntica," ff. 82v.-83, ABC; also cited in "Documentos" (1961), pp. 278-279.

63. Antero to Dom Jerônymo, 5 October 1893, Marrocos Copybook I, ACS.

64. Our biography of Marrocos is based on Fr. Antonio Gomes de Araújo, "Apostolado do Embuste," *Itaytera,* II, 3-63, and Fr. Azarias Sobreira, *Em Defesa de um Abolicionista (Resposta ao "Apostolado do Embuste"),* (Fortaleza, 1956).

65. Fr. A. E. Frota to José Marrocos, 5 September 1890, PCC.

66. F. S. Nascimento, "Esboço da Evolução Literária do Crato," *Itaytera,* IV (1958), 56-70.

67. Marrocos to Cícero, June 1889 [?], PCC. In this letter, Marrocos urged Padre Cícero to hold a solemn celebration in honor of the coming Feast of the Precious Blood to which Monteiro ought to be invited. Marrocos further encouraged the cleric to set up palm arches along the main street and organize the people for a mass procession. Everything in the letter indicates that it was written one month before Monteiro led 3,000 citizens of Crato in procession to Joaseiro.

68. See note 3.

69. See Depoimento e Considerações do Professor José Joaquim Teles Marrocos in "Documentos" (1961), 285-288.

70. Copies of Marrocos' *consultas* sent to the bishops of Maranhão, Pará Bahia,

and Rio Grande do Sul (in Brazil), Funchal and Guarda (in Portugal) are found in ACS, Pasta da Questão Religiosa.

Chapter 3
A Movement in the Making

1. A most valuable source illuminating the growing concern of the Brazilian hierarchy over events in Joaseiro is the hitherto unpublished correspondence between Fortaleza's bishop and Dom Joaquim Arcoverde, who in 1906 became Brazil's first cardinal. Between 18 October 1891 and 20 May 1893, the two bishops exchanged almost two dozen letters. However, only 12 of Arcoverde's and a copy of only one of Dom Joaquim's were found in ABC, Pasta Arcoverde.

It is ironic that Arcoverde was a classmate of Pe. Cícero's and Msgr. Monteiro's at the Colégio of Frei Rolim in Cajazeiras, Paraíba. Even more ironic, José Marrocos was his professor there. On 7 September 1891, Marrocos sent his former pupil one of the original *consultas*. But Arcoverde refused to offer any advice whatsoever and admonished Marrocos to prove his fidelity to the church by acting in harmony with his bishop's views.

It was Marrocos' letter that prompted Arcoverde to write Dom Joaquim on 18 October 1891. The future cardinal included both a copy of the *consultas* and his own reply to Marrocos.

In later correspondence (27 November 1891 and 12 December 1891, ABC, Pasta Arcoverde) Arcoverde frankly and harshly criticized Dom Joaquim for failing "to cut at the roots (of Joaseiro) with an act of energy." Arcoverde was convinced that the Crato pamphlet, *Milagres do Joaseiro*, "proved beyond a shadow of a doubt that there (in Joaseiro) ridicule is the predominant characteristic. As a consequence there is nothing there of the divine." Arcoverde to Dom Joaquim, 27 November 1891, ABC, Pasta Arcoverde.

In Arcoverde's letter of 12 December 1891, he articulated the course of action Dom Joaquim ought to follow.

In his reply of 28 December 1891, Dom Joaquim honorably pleaded for understanding. "Could I prohibit or suspend," he asked, "more than twenty priests who believe in the miracle, even if they are deluded?"

2. This promise to allow the dissidents to appeal to Rome was repeated in a letter from Dom Joaquim to Fr. Francisco Ferreira Antero (Secretary of the Commission of Inquiry) on 10 November 1892, Marrocos Copybook I, ASC.

3. On the equality of the miracle of Josseiro with identical ones in Europe, see the letter from Antero to Saluci, Rome, 5 August 1892, ASC, Pasta Marrocos.

4. An illustrious inhabitant of Crato who was an eyewitness to the events in Joaseiro recalls the impact of the events: "[They] were received in Crato as being a boon, conceded by God to the people of the Cariri. Fr. Monteiro, deeply loved by the people, proclaimed the good news. He sincerely believed in the holy revelations." Cited in Menezes (1960), p. 64.

5. Among the more notorious *beatas,* often referred to as the "false" *beatas,* were: Anna Leopoldina d'Aguiar Melo, Maria de Soledade, Maria Caminha, and Maria das Dôres.

6. The following account based on: Aderson Ferro, "Milagres em Joaseiro" in *Combate* (Fortaleza), 31 August; 2, 6, 14 September; 25, 28 October 1892; Côpia Authéntica, ABC; and correspondence of Msgr. Alexandrino to Dom Joaquim, ABC.

7. Testimony of the 19 year old *beata,* Anna Leopoldina d'Aguiar Melo, a native of Crato, 19 September 1891, in Côpia Authéntica, f. 67 v., ABC.

8. Testimony of Maria de Araújo, 11 September 1891, Côpia Authéntica, f. 22 v., ABC.

9. Testimonies of the 31 year old *beata,* Joaquina Timotheo de Jesus, a native of Crato, 18 September 1891, Côpia Authéntica, f. 45 v.; and of the 45 year old curate of Milagres, Fr. Manoel Rodrigues Lima, 17 September 1891, Côpia Authéntica, f. 38., ABC.

10. Testimony of the 33 year old native of Joaseiro, Joel Wanderlei Cabral, 5 October 1891, Côpia Authéntica, f. 74, ABC.

11. A list of the twenty-seven is indicated in "Termo de Declaração d'algumas graças obtidas mediante votos feitos ao Preciôso Sangue," 3 October 1891, in Côpia Authéntica, ff. 78-79 v., ABC.

12. The account that follows is based on Ferro (1892). The religious effervescence which reigned in Joaseiro between June and September 1892 is described in the letters of Msgr. Alexandrino to D. Joaquim, ABC: that of 28 June notes an increase in pilgrimages; that of 14 July speaks of *beatas* who are imitating Maria de Araújo; those of 9 August and 16 September report "new miracles" of bleeding crucifixes presented by Maria das Dôres, Maria Caminha, and Maria da Soledade.

13. The bishop granted Cícero the faculty, usually reserved to the bishop, to absolve Masons and Protestants from their sins· provided they signed a public declaration of obedience to the Catholic Church and its credo; Joaquim to Cícero, 25 June 1891, ABC.

According to District Judge of Barbalha, João Firmino de Hollanda who visited Joaseiro on 15 May 1891, Pe. Cícero had given a sermon that consisted in: "the history of the persecution of the Christian religion from the time of the Roman Emperors up to the present day; in the conversion of Constantine; in the end of the world, which was imminent according to the promise of Jesus Christ; and finally in the duty of those sent by God to Joaseiro to confess their sins." At this point in the sermon Pe. Cícero energetically counseled confession and repeated the following: "in this matter . . . I am not crazy, I'm not an idiot, I have no calling for magic. What I tell you, that which you see, I heard, it was predicted to me—Jesus Christ sheds His blood to save you, those who believe, He said, He will save. He chose this place, and I'll have you know that it is He who sends you here for your salvation; therefore, confess yourselves here or whereever you can." Copy of notes of visit made by João Firmino to Joaseiro on 15 May 1891, in Côpia Authéntica, ff. 109-114 v, dated 30 June 1892, ABC.

14. An important factor that led D. Joaquim to suspect the *beata,* was the confidential report submitted to him by Fr. Quintino Rodrigues de Oliveira e Silva, vice-rector of the Crato Seminary. Secretly solicited by the bishop, Quintino's confidential report substantially rectified his earlier and less critical testimony given to the Commission of Inquiry on 25 September 1891 (in Côpia Authéntica, ff. 55v-58, ABC). In his secret reply to the eight questions raised by D. Joaquim, Quintino stated that he never saw the host transform itself into blood. This occurred only after the *beata* had reopened her mouth *several minutes after* she originally received communion. He also intimated that the *beata* had lied to him about her apparent visions. Both remarks led D. Joaquim to the conclusion that the *beata* may have substituted the original consecrated host with another that emitted something that appeared to be blood. Furthermore, dishonesty was not a characteristic of sanctity.

An edited version of Quintino's confidential report and of his change of heart about the alleged miracles is in Gomes de Araújo (1956), pp. 3-64, esp. pp. 14-15.

Unfortunately, it is difficult to date Quintino's confidential report. It appears in the Côpia Authéntica, ff. 93v-96, ABC, as "Relatorio do Pe. Quintino." There, it is cited as being written in Fortaleza on 31 October 1891. However, Dom Joaquim's letter to Fr. Quintino (in which the eight questions are raised) is dated 26 December 1891, ABC. It seems plausible that Quintino did not submit his reply until 31 December 1891 (not 31 October). It seems unlikely that Dom Joaquim could have sent the eight questions to Fr. Quintino in October because the bishop did not see the "Proceedings" in which Quintino's original testimony is transcribed until November 1891.

As late as 1894, Dom Joaquim still blamed himself for not acting more vigorously against Joaseiro. In a confidential letter to Msgr. Monteiro, who first announced the miracle from the pulpit in Crato, the bishop wrote: "I am partially to blame for this business, because in 1889 I acted weakly. [When you abusively proclaimed it a miracle and Pe. Cícero began to venerate the urn] it was my duty to suspend you both immediately; I didn't in the hope that you'd act upon my fraternal warnings; now I am paying for that weakness." Joaquim to Monteiro, 5 March 1894, Marrocos Copybook I, ACS.

15. According to Fr. Antonio Gomes de Araújo (1956), p. 5, his grandfather, Basílio Gomes da Silva, the political chief of Brejo dos Santos from 1893–1927, had visited Joaseiro during the heyday of the miracle, presumably in 1891. After three days there, he told his wife: "Let's go home. There's nothing of the other world here. Padre Cícero is mistaken." Despite the *coronel's* lucid insight, neither he nor any other prominent layman of the Cariry Valley owned up to their disbelief, until July 1892, three months after Dom Joaquim's plan to expose the hoax had been initiated.

16. In addition to the twenty "activist" priests, there were others for whom the miracles were a source of inspiration. For example, Fr. A. Xisto Albano,

son of the Baron of Aracatanha and future bishop of Maranhão, heard of the events in Joaseiro and wrote Pe. Cícero: "More than ever do I desire to come and witness these extraordinary facts." Meanwhile he asked Pe. Cícero to pray for him "in order that I obtain from the Sacred Heart the true priestly sanctity, today more than ever indispensable." A. X. Albano to Cícero, 12 December 1891, ASC, Pasta da Questão Religiosa.

From União, the curate, Fr. Agostinho José de Santiago Lima, requested Pe. Cícero to remember him in his prayers. Fr. A. J. de Santiago Lima to Cícero, 15 November 1891, ACS, Pasta da Questão Religiosa.

17. The two priests in question are Frs. Quintino Rodrigues de Oliveira e Silva, vice-rector of the Crato seminary and Manoel Cândido dos Santos, curate of Barbalha. The former had given testimony in favor of the miracles before the Commission of Inquiry on 25 September 1891. The latter did not.

18. Sketchy data on Alexandrino's career is found in Pinheiro (1963), p. 172. Why Dom Joaquim chose this native son of Assaré (sometimes considered the westernmost city within the Cariry Valley), is as unknown as the reasons for the removal of his predecessor, Fr. Antonio Fernandes Távora. The latter was a close friend of Pe. Cícero, but was presumably critical of the "miracles." Nonetheless, Távora's dismissal was highly praised by Dom Joaquim Arcoverde (Arcoverde to D. Joaquim, 23 February 1892, ABC) and may indicate D. Joaquim' dissatisfaction with Fr. Távora.

Alexandrino departed from Quixadá for Crato on 2 February 1892 according to *Estado do Ceará* (Fortaleza), 10 February 1892.

19. Correspondence between Alexandrino and Dom Joaquim reveals that the bishop had frequently accused his appointee of being overly sympathetic to the dissidents. On occasion, Alexandrino admitted to being tolerant of them but retorted that this was indeed effective since, in consequence, Pe. Cícero had never preached against the teachings of the church. While Alexandrino admitted that he never "was in the camp opposed to the facts of Joaseiro" he nonetheless assured the bishop that he "never believed in them." Such was his disbelief, Alexandrino alleged, that there were very few pilgrims to Joaseiro from his former parish of Quixadá, Alexandrino to Joaquim, 31 August 1892, ABC. On later occasions Dom Joaquim's doubts were so strong that Alexandrino felt obliged to reassure the bishop of his loyalty, Alexandrino to Joaquim, 4 July 1893 and 26 September 1894, ABC.

The dissidents came to believe that Alexandrino had been chiefly responsible for many of the key episcopal orders against them. In fact, prior to Alexandrino's transfer to a parish in Piauí state in 1900, he allegedly went to Joaseiro. There, "from the altar of the church, with tears in his eyes, in a loud voice, he begged the people's pardon for the injustices he perpetrated in the [second] inquiry against the priest [Pe. Cícero] and other accused persons . . . by claiming that he was under obligation to follow the bishop's orders." This account was offered by Pe. Cícero's political aide, Floro Bartholomeu, in his celebrated defense of the cleric before the Federal Congress in 1923. It was offered as proof that the priests of the Valley had given sufficient reason for the people to continue to believe in the veracity of the miracles. See Floro Bartholomeu da Côsta, *Joazeiro e o Padre Cícero (Depoimento para a História)*, (Rio de Janeiro, 1923), pp. 48-49.

20. The second inquiry was conducted on three successive mornings in the chapel of the Charity House of Crato, 20-22 April 1892. Four priests, three physicians, and several other lay witnesses took part. Among them were Dr. Marcos Rodrigues Madeira and Col. Joaquim Secundo Chaves. The former's testimony that there was no natural explanation of the miracles of 1891 had precipitated the ecclesiastical conflict. The latter, a lifelong friend of Pe. Cícero, was one of the three "procurators."

It appears that the hosts used in the second inquiry were brought from Fortaleza. Apparently Dom Joaquim had suspected the *beatas* of Crato—among whose tasks was that of preparing the hosts from flour and water—of substituting adulterated hosts for natural ones. Gomes de Araújo (1956), 7, 8, and 26 n. 2 also gives a chemical formula which, if used in the preparation of the host, would cause them to turn red upon contact with saliva.

The original account of the second inquiry is contained in the Cópia Authéntica, ff. 115-116v, ABC. An allusion to it is contained in Gomes de Araújo (1956), pp. 15-16.

21. The theft of the urn was discovered on 22 April 1892 according to Msgr. Alexandrino's letter to D. Joaquim, 22 April 1892, ABC. This same letter noted that Padre Cícero and Fr. Joaquim Soter had personally submitted the urn to Msgr. Alexandrino in March 1892.

At the time of the theft, Mons. Alexandrino reported that suspicion in Crato fell upon José Marrocos, Alexandrino to Dom Joaquim 22 April 1892, ABC. Dom Joaquim had also corroborated the report about Marrocos' culpability with Fr. Francisco Ferreira Antero: "Fr. Antero, it was you who told me here [in Fortaleza] that Sr. Marrocos had written you saying that he had arranged the theft of [the urn] . . . in such a way so as not to compromise Padre Cícero!", Dom Joaquim to Fr. Antero, 10 November 1892, Marrocos Copybook I, ACS. In the same letter, the bishop declared: "I was almost certain that the theft of the cloths was done by Sr. Marrocos . . . after Y. Revd. confirmed this thought to me. . . ."

The discovery of the urn among José Marrocos' personal effects shortly after his death on 14 August 1910 was made by Dr. Raul de Souza Carvalho, the substitute District Judge of Crato. That discovery was not made public, however, until late 1953 when Dr. Carvalho published his article "Um Capítulo Inédito sôbre o Padre Cícero," in *Unitário* (Fortaleza) 27 December 1953, 3 and 10 January 1954. (It was republished in *O Povo*, Fortaleza, 22 July 1961.)

The account of the theft in Gomes de Araújo (1956), pp. 13-14, which places its occurrence in *July 1891*, is clearly in error. Apparently Fr. Gomes de Araújo had confused the events of the first Commission of Inquiry in 1891 with those of the second inquiry in April 1892. A more careful reading of the Cópia Authéntica (the source used extensively by the priest-author) reveals that the first Commission of Inquiry examined the urn's contents in Joaseiro on 12 September 1891 (See Côpia Authéntica, "Termo da abertura de caiza . . . ." f. 24v., ABC) but never removed it to Crato as Gomes de Araújo alleges (1956), p. 14. That occurred only in April 1892, as Alexandrino's letter indicates.

Gomes de Araújo's study (1956), intent on accusing José Marrocos not only of preparing the hoax but also of "feigning to believe in its divine origin" (p. 29, n. 9), also errs seriously in its major line of interpretation: by casting Marrocos into the culprit's role, Fr. Gomes de Araújo unjustly exonerates his fellow-priest-predecessors from the lion's share of the guilt in inculcating and sustaining the popular belief in the miracle. Father Gomes' desire to protect the Cariry's priests is understandable, but it does not justify some of his omissions which tend to distort the active role of the priests in propagating the belief in the alleged miracles. The following are two examples of such omissions.

First, in spite of ample documentary evidence in the Côpia Authéntica regarding the involvement of Crato's Msgr. Francisco Monteiro, nowhere in Fr. Gomes' study does he allude to this cleric's preeminent role. It was Msgr. Monteiro, after all, who first announced the miracles from the pulpit, who led the first pilgrimage to Joaseiro in 1889, who guided the principal *beatas* involved in the "miracles" and who encouraged Padre Cícero to reject Dom Joaquim's order to desist from propagating the miracles. On the contrary, Fr. Gomes pleads that Msgr. Monteiro and other priests whom he admits believed at first, were innocent victims of the ruse perpetrated by Marrocos. This view, however, greatly underestimates the actions and reasons of the Cariry clergy in defending Joaseiro.

In a second instance, Fr. Gomes only partially transcribes a letter from Fr. Manuel Felix de Moura to Dom Joaquim on 25 January 1893 (1956), pp. 39-40, n. 25. He cites the following sentence: "In the beginning, when the things [of Joaseiro] were kept secret, I was inclined to believe, but after . . . the facts becoming every moment more *deceitful . . . I withdrew my belief*" [*itali*cs his]. The complete sentence cited in "Documentos" (1961), pp. 291-292, is as follows: "In the beginning when the things [of Joaseiro] were kept secret, I was inclined to believe, but after Msgr. Francisco Rodrigues invited the people [from the pulpit in Crato] to go to Joaseiro to adore the blood of Jesus Christ, the facts becoming every moment more deceitful, I withdrew my belief." The excluded passage incidentally confirms again the important role played by Msgr. Monteiro.

The above comments in no way seek to deny Fr. Gomes' ample and accurate documentation, (1956), pp. 3-4 and *passim,* that José Marrocos was widely believed to have engineered the hoax. His claim that the priests were nothing more than innocent victims is, on the other hand, a serious distortion of historical reality.

22. The effect of the subsequent testimony of laymen upon the public was extremely limited since their letters were confidential and not published. They were, however, sent to Rome in 1893.

The three prominent laymen who gave confidential testimony to Dom

Joaquim were: (1) João Firmino de Hollanda, District Judge of Barbalha, (2) João Batista de Siqueira Cavalcanti, District Judge of Crato, and (3) Col. Juvenal de Alcântara Pedrosa, a merchant-landowner of Crato. Their letters are respectively identified: (1) 30 June 1892—allegedly transcribing notes made by the author immediately after visiting Joaseiro on 15 May 1891 is contained in the Côpia Authéntica, ff. 109-114v, ABC; (2) 28 July 1892, fully transcribed in "Documentos" (1961), 289-290; and (3) 10 August 1892, contained in Côpia Authéntica, ff. 118-120v, ABC.

According to Msgr. Alexandrino's letter to Dom Joaquim of 9 August 1892, both Col. Juvenal and Dr. Siqueira Cavalcanti had been requested by Dom Joaquim to submit their written testimony after the second inquiry was concluded in April. Both claimed that Dr. Marcos Rodrigues de Madeira, the physician who first swore publicly to the "miraculous nature" of the "miracles," had personally confessed that he had arrived at an erroneous conclusion. According to Col. Juvenal's letter, Dr. Madeira was prepared to make a public retraction. However, despite two requests to do so from Dom Joaquim, Dr. Madeira consistently refused to alter in writing his original declaration of 1891. His offer to go personally to Fortaleza, at the bishop's expense, was summarily rejected by Dom Joaquim who insisted that the physician put his views in *writing* for the benefit of Rome. The physician's views were expressed in two unpublished letters to Dom Joaquim on 13 December 1892 and 25 January 1893; both are contained in the Côpia Authéntica, ff. 126-128v, ABC, and in Marrocos Copybook I, ACS. The recantation of another prominent physician who witnessed the 1891 events in Joaseiro is found in the letter of Dr. Inácio de Sousa Dias to Dom Joaquim, 16 October 1892, in "Documentos" (1961), pp. 290-291.

23. The record of the simultaneous "miraculous events" in Icó, Aracaty, União, are documented in the articles of Aderson Ferro (1892). Perhaps, because of clerical involvement in those events, they are disproportionately underestimated in Gomes de Araújo (1956), p. 42, n. 30.

In October 1892, just three months after the above-mentioned episode, one of the Joaseiro *beatas,* Maria de Soledade, appeared in Barbalha. She presented a "miraculous" and bleeding host to the assistant curate, Fr. Joaquim Soter de Alencar, who placed it on the altar of a family chapel before which he and members of the family prayed in a vigil. The incident received publicity in *A Provincia* (Recife), 20 January 1893 and prompted Dom Joaquim to interrogate Fr. Soter and his priest-brother, Fr. Vincente Soter de Alencar; Fr. Vincente to Dom Joaquim, 23 April and 12 July 1893, Marrocos Copybook I, ACS.

On 28 December 1892, Maria de Soledade appeared in the city of Jardim, where Fr. Vincente Soter was curate. A host she could not consume was placed on the altar. Later that evening, many prominent citizens came to worship. On 21 January 1893 these citizens, including a member of the state legislature and other local officials signed an official document attesting to the "miracle." It was notarized on 7 February 1893 in Jardim. A copy is in ACS, Pasta da Questão Religiosa.

24. In a letter to Padre Cícero several months after the events, Fr. Clycério recollected that the *beata* Maria Caminha had disclosed to him several "revelations . . . relative to the punishment of several places and especially of Aracaty"; Fr. Clycério to Padre Cícero, 5 October 1892, Marrocos Copybook I, ACS.

The same letter reveals that Fr. Clycério may have owned up to his own gullibility: "On top of all my misfortunes, the Devil inspired more than one pious woman to present several hosts as miraculous . . . ." Nonetheless, Clycério alone was responsible for communicating, as true, the "revelations" concerning the divine destruction of the cities of Limoeiro and Cascavel; Fr. Clycério to the respective curates, 28 and 29 July 1892, ABC. He also wrote to Dom Joaquim's secretary that, according to the prophecy, Fortaleza would suffer "a great chastisement" unless the city's inhabitants repented within fifteen days; Fr. Clycério to Msgr. Vicar-General of the Diocese of Fortaleza, 29 July 1892, ABC.

The call for police intervention appeared in *A República,* (Fortaleza), 9 August 1892.

In late 1893, Dom Joaquim ordered an inquiry into the events of Aracaty and União. It took place in the city of União on 9 November under the direction of Fr. Agostinho José de Santiago Lima. Of the three *beatas* interrogated, one was Maria de Soledade, who after the July 1892 events in União appeared later in Joaseiro, according to Ferro (1892). The record of the unpublished inquiry is listed as "Autoamento" in Côpia Authéntica, ff. 146-155, ABC.

25. Padre Cícero was suspended by the Portaria of 5 August 1892 according to the letter from Msgr. Alexandrino to Dom Joaquim, 15 August 1892, ABC.

A copy of this Portaria is located in Marrocos Copybook I, ACS. It lists six reasons for suspension: (1) for proclaiming the events of 1889 miraculous and initiating their cult; (2) Cícero's refusal to desist from proclaiming the miracles in public despite the bishop's order to desist; (3) for sustaining and inculcating audacious doctrines, presumedly that of the second Redemption; (4) for lacking intellectual and emotional balance to direct the faithful; (5) for encouraging people to make vows on the basis of false principles; (6) for causing anxiety among Christian families; (7) for concurring indirectly in the theft of the urn. In conclusion, Cícero was not only suspended but also prohibited from keeping consecrated hosts in the tabernacle of Our Lady of Sorrows chapel.

Fr. Clycério was suspended two days earlier, on 3 August 1892, Fr. Clycério to Dom Joaquim, 5 August 1892, ABC. By October 1892, he made arrangements to move to Mossoró, Rio Grande do Norte, then under the ecclesiastical jurisdiction of the Diocese of Olinda and Recife (Pernambuco), Fr. Clycério to Padre Cícero, 5 October 1892, Marrocos Copybook I, ACS.

Undoubtedly the events of União and Aracaty were decisive in compelling Dom Joaquim to suspend Pe. Cícero.

26. Dom Joaquim José Vieira, "Carta Pastoral de 25 de março de 1893," published in Macêdo (1961), pp. 139-156.

27. Dom Joaquim sent the case to Rome in May 1893, two months after is-

suing his Pastoral Letter. In addition to the report of the first Commission of Inquiry of 1891 (which he originally hesitated to dispatch), he added the report of the second inquiry of April 1892, the Pastoral of 1893 and several other documents, including the confidential letters of the three laymen, cited in n. 22 above. This accretion of documents was later contested by the dissidents.

However, Rome had already been advised of the case by Dom Joaquim Arcoverde. The future first cardinal of Brazil took it upon himself to do so prior to September 1892. Later, he wrote to Dom Joaquim: "I tell you in the strictest confidence [that] I have had alerted certain persons in Rome, members of the Congregation of the Holy Office [of the Inquisition], and I sent them that pamphlet [*Milagres do Joaseiro* (Crato, 1891)], and also excerpts from Y. Exc.'s letters, duly translated into Italian and commented upon," Arcoverde to Dom Joaquim, 22 September 1892, ABC, Pasta Arcoverde. It is possible that Arcoverde may have also requested Rome to act energetically so as to destroy Joaseiro, as he had advised Dom Joaquim to do in December 1891; see n. 1.

When Arcoverde wrote Rome is unknown. However, Cardinal Monaco, chief of the Holy Office wrote Dom Joaquim on 17 July 1892, ABC, requesting complete details of the "facts of Joaseiro."

28. Fr. Antero traveled to Rome without Dom Joaquim's expressed permission and during the latter's absence from Fortaleza. He also "pilfered" a copy of the report of the first Commission of Inquiry. Dom Joaquim publicly alluded to this unsavory affront to his authority in his second Pastoral Letter of 25 July 1894, in Macedo (1961), 162.

Fr. Antero later retorted that Dom Joaquim had given him *carte blanche* to undertake the trip. According to Antero, the bishop even offered to pay for the trip. Dom Joaquim encouraged Fr. Antero to make the trip as further proof of the dissidents' complete liberty. Dom Joaquim's intent to send Fr. Antero to Rome with the 1891 report is clearly stated in the bishop's letter to Dom Jm Arcoverde, 28 December 1891, ABC, Pasta Arcoverde.

Antero's illicit trip to Rome, under the pretext of visiting a sick nephew who was a seminarian there, may have prompted Arcoverde to alert secretly the members of the Inquisition about Joaseiro (see n. 27); at least, Arcoverde assured Dom Joaquim: "Y. Exc. can rest assured [now that Rome is alerted] that Fr. Antero will come back on the double and ashamed of the sad role he played . . . ," Arcoverde to Dom Joaquim, 22 September 1892, ABC, Pasta Arcoverde.

In Rome, Antero nonetheless presented the report (apologizing for its weaknesses) and made a strong appeal on Joaseiro's behalf. He argued (or perhaps threatened) that if Rome did not legitimate the "miracles of Joaseiro," it would have a difficult task to explain to the faithful why they should continue to believe in other "similar" miracles. He also stressed that the large number of conversions that already took place in Joaseiro was a sign of the veracity of the events; Antero to Msgr. Salucci, Rome, 5 August 1892, Marrocos Copybook I, ACS.

29. Msgr. Monteiro's trip to Rio took place after 29 September 1893; he re-

turned around mid-November; Msgr. Alexandrino to Dom Joaquim, 27 September 1893 and 20 November 1893, ABC. Dom Joaquim alluded to Monteiro's trip in his Pastoral Letter of 1894, cited in Macêdo (1961), pp. 162-163.

Among the "fresh documents" that Monteiro took to Rio de Janeiro was a lengthy letter from Dr. Marcos Rodrigues Madeira. In this letter, the physician attempted to destroy in detail two points raised in Dom Joaquim's Pastoral of 1893, which was aimed at invalidating the physician's earlier declarations; Dr. Madeira to Msgr. Monteiro, 28 September 1893, Marrocos Copybook I, ACS. Certainly Dr. Madeira's refusal to deny the supernatural quality of the "miracles" encouraged the dissidents to persist in their appeals. On Madeira's refusal to recant see note 22.

30. José Marrocos to Fr. Felippe Sottovia, 30 November 1893 and 28 December 1893, Marrocos Copybook I, ACS.

31. Alexandrino to Joaquim, 28 June 1892, ABC and Ferro (1892).

32. Alexandrino to Joaquim, 16 September 1892, ABC.

33. Alexandrino to Joaquim, 28 June 1892, ABC.

34. Fr. Antonio Gomes de Araújo, "Um Civilizador do Carirí," in *A Província*, III (1955), 127-146, esp., 136.

35. Alexandrino to Joaquim, 31 August 1892, ABC. Later, Alexandrino wrote that even though the inhabitants of Crato were "increasingly changing their opinion about Joaseiro, they are, however, revolted by Padre Cícero's suspension . . . ," Alexandrino to Joaquim, 16 September 1892, ABC.

36. Alexandrino to Joaquim, 18 October 1892, ABC.

37. Copy of the Petition, December 1892, ACS, Pasta da Questão Religiosa. The petition referred to two proofs of Padre Cícero's respect for the civil authorities: (1) that he had broken up several family fueds, and (2) that he had performed the first civil marriage in the *sertão*. A description of the former event, which occurred in 1888, is contained in Bartholomeu (1923), pp. 112-113, n. 30.

38. Alexandrino to Joaquim, 15 May 1892; 4 July 1893; 20 November 1893, ABC. References to the wide-spread view among the common people that Dom Joaquim was "a Mason and a Republican" are contained in *A República* (Fortaleza), 20 June 1893.

39. Alexandrino to Joaquim, 20 November 1893, ABC.

40. This prohibition was reconfirmed by Dom Joaquim in his Portaria of 23 January 1894: "In order to avoid any misinterpretation of our [previous] . . . prohibition against celebrating any religious service in the chapel of Joaseiro, We declare that . . . it applies to all priests of this diocese, including Your Reverend as vicar of the parish, and regardless of the [degree of] solemnity . . .," cited in Pinheiro (1963), 168.

41. José Marrocos to Fr. Felippe Sottovia, 30 November 1893, Marrocos Copybook I, ACS.

42. One example was the mass rally which took place in Joaseiro on 3 July 1893 to commemorate the return of Fr. Antero from Rome. More than 1,000 persons met him beyond the hamlet's walls, among them Padre Cícero and Msgr.

Monteiro. Two hundred arches decorated the streets, illuminated by admirers carrying candles. Young girls welcomed him with speeches.

At 8 p.m. fireworks and pyrotechnic displays took place. Banners declared "Viva Padre Antero; Viva Padre Cícero." The next day a mass was celebrated; there were eight priests in attendance, a most impressive display; Alexandrino to Joaquim, 4 July 1893, ABC.

43. Dom Joaquim José Vieira, Pastoral Letter of 1894, cited in Macêdo (1961), p. 161. In July 1893 Dom Joaquim had expressly prohibited any priest from blessing medals and any layman from venerating them. His prohibition was published in *A Verdade* (Fortaleza), 23 July 1893.

44. Alexandrino to Dom Joaquim, 8 January 1894, ABC. This letter reports that priests and laymen continued to believe in the miracles.

45. "Decisão e Decretos da S. Congregação do Santo ofício," 4 April 1894, cited in Macêdo (1961), pp. 164-165.

46. *Ibid.*

47. Ofício, Dom Joaquim to Padre Cícero, 9 August 1894, ABC: this ordered the priest to come to Fortaleza within thirty days under pain of suspension *ipso facto*. The other priests similarly summoned to Fortaleza were: Fr. Antero, Msgr. F. Rodrigues Monteiro, Fr. Manoel Rodrigues Lima and Fr. João Carlos Augusto. According to Marrocos Copybook II, PCC, Padre Cícero left Joaseiro on 28 August 1894 and arrived in Fortaleza on 2 September 1894.

Dom Joaquim's "master plan" is contained in his "Instrucções que devem ser fielmente observados pelo [Rvdmo. Pe. Alexandrino] . . . no tocante as pessoãs envolvidas nos factos de Joaseiro," Joaquim to Alexandrino 20 August 1894, ABC.

48. According to Marrocos Copybook II, PCC, forty state troops had arrived in Crato several days before Padre Cícero's departure on 23 August. They were under the command of Captain Fialho. On 22 August, a sergeant (Alferes) Porfírio was already stationed in Joaseiro with several men.

In 1906, José Marrocos referred to this incident as one of the occasions in Padre Cícero's life when he had "escaped from under the sword of the government before whom [*sic*] he was denounced as a conspirator," see "Draft of the Historical Account to the Members of Congress," 10 August 1906, ACS, Pasta Marrocos. It is unknown whether this "Draft" was ever sent to the Federal Congress.

49. The indented transcript is a faithful paraphrase of the report from Alexandrino to Joaquim, 20 September 1894, ABC.

50. A possible allusion to the trial of Maria de Araújo's relatives is found in Gorgônio Brigido dos Santos' article "O milagre do Joazeiro do Crato no Estado do Ceará," *Diário de Pernambuco* (Recife), 6 September 1893. Gorgônio Brigido was apparently the public prosecutor in Crato. In the above article, he accused Padre Cícero (1) of demanding that he not prosecute "the mother, uncle and cousin of Maria de Araújo for the murder perpetrated in the sugar mill of José Dias and [(2)] of succeeding in sidetracking the testimonies of three witnesses so that at the trial the accused went scot-free while an innocent youth went to

jail but was finally absolved by the jury and the case was never appealed."

Alexandrino's account of course was written a year after the above article. Perhaps he was referring to another crime committed or to a retrial.

51. Alexandrino to Joaquim [23-26 September 1894?], ABC.

52. Alexandrino to Joaquim, 26 September 1894, ABC.

53. The subsequent information is based on Dom Joaquim's Portaria of 13 September 1894, published in *A República* (Fortaleza), 22 October 1894, and Alexandrino to Joaquim, 26 September 1894, ABC.

54. See "Instrucções . . ." in n. 47.

Several *beatas* recanted under Mons. Alexandrino's pressure and threats of loss of residence and habit. Here is a list of those who declared their earlier claims were false:

1) 22 September 1894, *Beata* Antonia Maria de Conceição
2) 14 October 1894, Rachel Sisnando Lima
3) 25 October 1894, Maria Joanna de Jesus.

These are contained in the Côpia Authéntica, ABC.

55. Here is a partial list of the priests who formally recanted and whose statements were published in the secular and religious press. (Those marked with an asterisk were summoned to Fortaleza with Padre Cícero):

Name	Date of Recantation	Place and Date of Publication
1. Fr. Laurino Duettes, curate in Triumfo, Pbco.	24 September 1894	*Era Nova* (Recife), 27 September 1894 *A República* (Fortaleza), 5 October, 1894
2. Fr. Cícero Joaquim de Siqueira Torres, diocese of Pernambuco	8 October 1894	*A Verdade* (Fortaleza), 28 October 1894
*3. Fr. Manuel Antonio Martins de Jesus, curate of Salgueiro and Belmonte, Pbco.	21 October 1894	*A Verdade* (Fortaleza), 11 November 1894
*4. Fr. João Carlos Agosto	26 November 1894, (letter to D. Joaquim, ACS)	*A Verdade* (Fortaleza), 2 February 1895 *A República* (Fortaleza), 4 February 1895
5. Fr. Jacintho Ramos, diocese of Pbco.	13 December 1894	*Era Nova* (Recife), 15 December 1894 *A Verdade* (Fortaleza), 13 January 1895
*6. Msgr. Francisco Rodrigues Monteiro	February [1895]	*A Verdade* (Fortaleza), 2 February 1895 *A República* (Fortaleza), 4 February 1895

7. Fr. Manuel Rodrigues Lima,   February   *A Verdade* (Fortaleza),
    curate of Missão Velha   [1895]   2 February 1895
                                                      A República (Fortaleza),
                                                      4 February 1895
8. Fr. Clycério da Côsta   February 1895   *A Verdade* (Fortaleza),
    Lôbo   2 February 1895
                                                      A República (Fortaleza),
                                                      4 February 1895
*9. Fr. Francisco Antero   12 June   *Ceará* (Fortaleza),
    (NB Fr. Antero's refusal   1897   30 June 1897
    to recant in December
    1894 led to his complete
    suspension from orders,
    communicated in the Portaria
    of 22 February 1895, Marrocos
    Copybook I, ACS.)

The Pernambucan press, both secular and religious consistently opposed the dissidents. In 1894, articles against the "schismatic fanatics" appeared in the *Diário de Pernambuco* (Recife), 1 May 1894 and in August 1894. The latter was transcribed in *A República* (Fortaleza), 14 September 1894, and concluded with an urgent appeal to the bishop of Olinda and Recife that he not tolerate that his priests in the interior continue to give publicity to "those detestable facts."

56. Alexandrino to Joaquim, 20 October 1894, ABC.
57. Alexandrino to Joaquim [18 January 1895?], ABC.
58. Alexandrino to Joaquim, 26 September 1894 and 20 October 1894, ABC.

Chapter 4
The Movement Organizes

1. Biographical data on José Lôbo is taken from the unpublished manuscript entitled "O Joaseiro e Seu Legítimo Fundador, Padre Cícero Romão Batista" (unpublished manuscript, 1963, Juàzeiro do Norte), by Joaseiro's recently deceased popular historian Octávio Aires de Menezes. Sr. Octávio was the grandson of José Lôbo. He was a self-educated man who vehemently opposed the fanaticism of Joaseiro's lower classes and that of some of Joaseiro's elites. He was also critical of the church's exploitation of fanaticism but at the same time had a passionate distaste for the critics of Padre Cícero, the man whom he defended as the true founder of Joaseiro, and without whom there would be no city. His brief accounts of Joaseiro's history and personages were read daily over Joaseiro's radio station. His manuscript merits publication.

2. In an undated (probably c. 1895 or 1896) appeal to Pope Leo XIII, ACS, Pasta Legião da Cruz, the following parish organizations are listed with their respective chief officers: Antonio Landim da Chaves, President of the Conference of Our Lady of Sorrows; Pedro Feitosa e Silva, President of the Conference of the

Most Blessed Sacrament; Antonio Claudio Alves da Côsta, President of the Conference of the Precious Blood; José Julio Carneiro Côsta, Second Secretary of the
Legion of the Cross. José Lôbo is listed as Second Vice-President and Propagator
of the Óbulo de S. Pedro (which is known in the English-speaking world as the
Peter's Pence annual collection).

In later documents it is clear that the Óbulo was the same organization as
the Legion of the Cross. Why the same organization is listed here as two distinct
entities is unclear, except perhaps to convey the impression that there was one
more organization than really existed. This, however, is an unsatisfactory answer
because the St. Vincent de Paul Society which was founded in Joaseiro in 1888—
see Studart (1896–1924), II, 356—existed at the time of this listing. Indeed, after
Lôbo arrived in 1894 he played an important role in its Joaseiro affiliate.

3. "Livro do Registro do Apostolado da Oração do Santíssimo Coração de
Jesus" (Joaseiro), 13 January 1898, ACS, Pasta Legião da Cruz. Also, see Chapter
Five, n. 11.

4. In the senatorial elections of May 1889, the Sixth Electoral District of
Ceará, consisting of Crato, Barbalha, Joaseiro, São Pedro, Porteiras, and Brejo
dos Santos collectively cast a total of 1,942 votes. Crato's electorate of 652 votes
was the largest of the Valley, cited in *Cearense* (Fortaleza), 9 June 1889. Figures
on the national electorate since the Republic are cited in Gueirreiro Ramos, *A
Crise do Poder no Brazil: Problemas da Revolução Nacional Brasileira* (Rio de
Janeiro, 1961), p. 32.

5. The account is of a meeting of the Legion of the Cross, Actas da Legião
da Cruz, Sessão Ordinária, 4 April 1897, ACS, Pasta Legião da Cruz.

6. Aires de Menezes (1963, ms.), 37-38.

7. A petition, in the form of a letter, was dispatched on 27 December 1894,
Padre Cícero to Pope Leo XIII, Marrocos Copybook I, ACS. A telegram requesting a reply was sent on 5 January 1895, *Ibid.*

8. Padre Cícero to Pope Leo XIII, 27 December 1894, *Ibid.*

9. Marrocos Copybook I, ACS.

10. Letter of the Joaseiro branch recommending José Joaquim de Maria
Lôbo to the Superior Council of the Conferences of St. Vincent de Paul, Joaseiro,
March 1895, Marrocos Copybook I, ACS.

11. Details of Lôbo's travels and discussions in Rio and Petropolis are contained in Marrocos Copybook II, PCC; see note 25.

12. There are no records of the actual discussions between Lôbo and Dom
Jerônymo de Maria Gotti. Our assumption about Lôbo's arguments are based
on his letter to Dom Jerônymo, 20 July 1895, ACS. These arguments, written
after Lôbo returned from Rio, are so similar to Padre Cícero's appeal of December 1894, that it is unlikely that Lôbo would have presented any startlingly different proposal. Only one point of difference merits recording. While Cícero had
asked Rome to authorize an "Apostolic Commission" to review the details of the
miracles, Lôbo, in his letter of 20 July 1895 asked for an "investigating commission" (*commissão fiscalizadora*) which might be made up of confreres of the

St. Vincent de Paul Society and whose two qualifications were to be: (1) "active Catholics of exemplary life and service to religion" and (2) "uninvolved in the business here [at Joaseiro]" ("alhéios ás cousas daqui . . .").

On 26 January 1896, José Marrocos and José Lôbo in the name of the religious organization of Joaseiro cabled the nuncio in Petropolis: "The people of Joaseiro are still awaiting confirmation of the promises of Petropolis . . ."; telegram in ACS, Pasta Legião da Cruz.

13. The Legion was founded in Niterói, Rio de Janeiro province, in 1885. See Dom Joaquim's Fourth Pastoral, 1898, in Macêdo (1961), 179.

14. According to the *New Catholic Encyclopedia* (New York, 1967), XI, 235, the "modern Peter's Pence collection originated in the 1860s as a subsidy to compensate for the loss of revenue from the States of the Church. Through the encyclical *Saepe venerabiles fratres* (1871), it was given official approval. Today, even after the Lateran Pacts, it remains a free offering of Catholic dioceses to the Pope."

15. According to Lôbo, the meeting with Dom João Esberard took place on 2 April 1895, Lôbo to Dom Joaquim, 10 August 1898, ACS, Legião da Cruz. On Dom João's authorization, Lôbo subsequently met with Dr. Carneiro Leão, a prominent Catholic lay leader.

16. Dom Joaquim, Fourth Pastoral, 1898, in Macêdo (1961), pp. 179-180. In this Pastoral Dom Joaquim declared that Canon Law reserves the right to each bishop to authorize the establishment of a religious institution in his diocese. He indicated further that even if the Pope, instead of Dom João Esberard, had "authorized" the Legion in Joaseiro, it could not be allowed to function in the Diocese of Ceará "without the expressed *placet* of its Prelate."

17. Actas da Legião da Cruz, Sessão Ordinária, 4 April 1897, in ACS, Legião da Cruz. This document indicates there were 5,467 members present at the meeting. It is likely, that these 5,467 members also participated in Joaseiro's five other religious brotherhoods.

18. Lôbo to the Cardinals of the Holy Congregation of Bishops, Rome, 1 August 1899, in ACS, Legiao da Cruz.

From various Legion documents it has been possible to identify tentatively the location of the ten chapters: (1) Joaseiro; (2) Santa Quitéria and (3) Riacho de Guimarães, both situated near the city of Sobral, Ceará; (4) Varjota or Varajota near the city of Ipú; (5) Capeztre (?); (6) Sussuana; (7) São Francisco and (8) Junco, identified in the cited documents merely as *povoados* or *povoações* with no other reference to either the *município* or state in which they are located; (9) *sítio* Loreto in Santa Luzia de Saboia, State of Paraíba; and finally (10), Cajazeira in the parish of Tamboril, Ceará.

In Dom Joaquim's Fourth, Pastoral, 1898, reference is made to chapters in the parishes of Ipú, São Benedito, and Meruoca, see Macêdo (1961), p. 181.

The dates of the establishment of three branches are known: that of Joaseiro, as we have seen, was founded in 7 July 1895; see note 2. The Varjota chapter was established on 12 September 1897 according to Eusébio de Souza "A Vida da

'Legião da Cruz,' " *RIC* (1915), pp. 315-322, esp. p. 316. That of the *povoado* of Junco was founded in mid-1898 by forty-eight males and eight females "under the honorary chairmanship of the vicar" of the parish of Our Lady of the [Immaculate] Conception who urged the establishment of the Legion, according to the letter from its founder, Adolpho Pácio de Oliveira Pedrosa to Lôbo, 16 August 1898, ACS, Legião da Cruz. No data have been found to determine either the date of establishment of the other seven chapters or the membership size of each chapter.

19. Information about the monthly dues of Legion members is based on the letter from Lôbo to the Cardinals of the Holy Congregation of Bishops, Rome, 1 August 1899, ACS, Legião da Cruz.

All rates of exchange (U. S. dollars and Brazilian milreis) used in this study are based on the table found in Julian Smith Duncan, *Public and Private Operations of Railroads in Brazil* (New York, 1932), p. 183.

20. *A República* (Fortaleza), 28 May 1895 published the following account of taxes received in 1894 from selected *municípios* of the Cariry Valley:

Jardim	7:033$186
Brejo dos Santos	2:570$111
Milagres	1:702$773
Missão Velha	5:412$373
Porteiras	2:621$123
Vareza-Alegre	2:614$974

21. *Table of Donations Contributed to the Legion of the Cross*

Date	Totals Collected from 10 Chapters	Totals Collected in Joaseiro Alone	Destination and Amount
7 July 1895- 26 April 1896	3:000$000(est.)	?	2:359$000 (a)
27 April 1896- 7 May 1897	6:137$000	?	4:685$000 (b)
June-July 1897	?	?	?
July 1897- August 1898	8:504$860	5:054$260	6:790$400 (c)
September 1898	3:129$700 (d)	?	?

SOURCE: Actas da Legião da Cruz, Joaseiro Branch, 7 June 1896 to 2 October 1898, ACS, Legião da Cruz.

(a) sent to National office of Óbulo de São Pedro, Rio de Janeiro.
(b) destination unknown, but most likely same as (a).
(c) given to Holy Father in Rome on 18 April 1898; Actas, 7 August 1898.
(d) of this figure, 2:524$000 was contributed by a chapter near Sobral; Actas, Sess. Extra., 20 September 1898.

22. Dom Joaquim's report is contained in the Fourth Pastoral Letter, 1898, in Macêdo (1961), p. 183.

The donation of 6:790$000 from the Legion was personally submitted to Leo XIII by Lôbo on 18 April 1898 in Rome. His transatlantic trip may have cost as much as two contos, thus raising the Legion's fund for 1898 to nine contos, in comparison to the Diocese's total of over eleven!; see Actas da Legião da Cruz, Sessão Ordinária, 7 August 1898 and Sessão da 3.ª Assembléia Geral, 15 August 1898, ACS, Legião da Cruz.

23. Dom Joaquim José Vieira, Portaria of 13 April 1896 suspending Padre Cícero from celebrating mass. This text was published in full in *A Verdade* (Fortaleza), 19 April 1896 and in *Diário de Pernambuco* (Recife), 30 July 1896.

24. Cited in full in note 23. Also see Third Pastoral Letter, 1897, in Macêdo (1961), p. 172. The reason stated here for the suspension was "the follies committed upon follies."

25. Lôbo traveled to Rome in late 1896, mid-1897 and early 1898 on behalf of the Legion. On his first trip he appealed the decree of 1894. The purpose of his second trip was to counter the decree of 1897 which threatened Padre Cícero with excommunication. His third trip coincided with that of Padre Cícero's to Rome. A fourth visit was made in 1899 in order to appeal the Fourth Pastoral Letter of Dom Joaquim in which the bishop denounced the Legion of the Cross and its founder, José Lôbo.

	Left Joaseiro	*Returned to Joaseiro*
1st trip	2 September 1896	27 February 1897
2d trip	28 May 1897	21 September 1897
3d trip	30 January 1898	6 August 1898
4th trip	29 April 1899	2 September 1899

Source: Marrocos Copybook II, PCC.

26. The entire account of the religious boycott of Crato and the attempted assassination of Padre Cícero is based on the lengthy report submitted by Msgr. Alexandrino to Dom Joaquim, 6 November 1896, ABC.

27. This Holy Office decree was issued in Rome on 10 February 1897 and was published verbatim in Dom Joaquim's Third Pastoral Letter, dated 30 July 1897. The Pastoral is cited in Macêdo (1961), pp. 168-178, esp. pp. 177-178.

Dom Joaquim received the decree on 25 March 1897, *Ibid.*, p. 174. In April, the bishop addressed a sealed communiqué to Padre Cícero. It did not contain the Roman decree. Nonetheless, rumors immediately began to circulate in Joaseiro. One version contended that Cícero had been defrocked; another, that he had been fully reinstated. Not even Msgr. Alexandrino was aware of its contents; Alexandrino to Dom Joaquim, 25 April 1897, ABC. On orders of Dom Joaquim, Msgr. Alexandrino attempted to arrange a confidential meeting with Padre Cícero in Crato on 13 June. The cleric refused, and insisted that all exchanges be conducted in writing since ". . . verba volant et scripta manent;" Alexandrino to Joaquim, 13 June 1897 and 24 June 1897, ABC. Padre Cícero's reply to Msgr. Alexandrino of 19 June 1897 is contained in Irineu Pinheiro (1963), p. 169, where it is incorrectly dated as 21 June 1897. In this letter, Padre Cícero once again expresses the

view that "calumny and ill-will persecute me and make me their victim. . . ."
He disavowed any of the crimes and acts of disobedience attributed to him and
which "through God's mercy I never thought of."

28. Msgr. Alexandrino personally delivered the 1897 excommunication threat
to Padre Cícero at *Sítio* Paul outside of Crato on 21 June 1897. There were two
official witnesses, Antônio Arino Gomes Coimbra and Antônio Coimbra Vila
Nova. The meeting lasted for more than an hour. According to Msgr. Alexandrino, Padre Cícero denied ever disobeying the church but accused Dom Joaquim
"of wanting to destroy everything and of having imposed upon him [Padre
Cícero] canonical penalties [even though Padre Cícero was] innocent." Furthermore, the cleric insisted that he would never assert that the miracles of Joaseiro
were a hoax because "he [Padre Cícero] was certain that everything was true."

As the public encounter continued, a huge crowd assembled. Padre Cícero
then took the decree and proceeded to talk at length "in defense of the facts of
Joaseiro." Alexandrino concluded: "Never have I heard such nonsense from the
mouth of a priest which seems to indicate total mental imbalance." Alexandrino
was ordered to read the decree on Sunday, 4 July 1897, in the event that Padre
Cícero failed to reply to it by 30 June 1897. (The above account is taken from
the Memorandum sent by Alexandrino to Dom Joaquim on 28 June 1897, ABC).

Padre Cícero made no reply whatsoever. Instead, he left for Salgueiro on the
evening of 29 June 1897 without communicating his destination to Alexandrino.
His departure created in Joaseiro deeper hostility towards church officials. All
blamed Msgr. Alexandrino for the incident, Alexandrino to Joaquim, 30 June
1897, ABC.

29. Lôbo left for Rome, via Portugal, in May 1897. During his absence, José
Marrocos remained in Crato from where he proceeded to direct Cícero's new
campaign.

It was Marrocos' idea to prepare Italian translations of all major documents
concerning the "religious question" of Joaseiro. This he did without Cícero's
prior consent in order "to prevent the Bishop from remitting a false translation
[to Rome]." Marrocos also insisted in publishing various documents and an
account of the miracles of Joaseiro in the Roman newspaper, *Giornale di Roma.*
Despite Padre Cícero's disapproval, Marrocos had it done "at my own risk and
expense." In his Pastoral Letter of 1898, Dom Joaquim attacked Cícero for publishing articles in Rome.

Among the dissidents' contacts in Rome were two Brazilian priests: Fr.
Fernandes da Silva Távora, former vicar of Crato and Friar Bessa, otherwise
unidentifiable. Petitioned by telegrams on 9 July 1897 to intercede on Padre
Cícero's behalf, both refused. Fr. Fernandes Távora, however, counseled Cícero
that "without your presence the appeal is impossible." This was apparently
decisive in persuading Padre Cícero of the necessity to go personally to Rome.
The telegram to Fr. Távora is published in Pinheiro (1963), p. 169.

All other information above is a summary of the unpublished correspondence
between José Marrocos and Padre Cícero during the latter's exile in Salgueiro;

Marrocos to Cícero, 24 July 1897, 4 August 1897, 5 October 1897 and 26 November 1897; Cícero to Marrocos, 31 July 1897, ACS, Pasta Salgueiro.

30. Padre Cícero to D. Quinôu and D. Angêlica (his mother and sister) 20 October 1897, ACS. In this letter the cleric declared: "I find so very disagreeable this persecution that forces me to wander as a vagabond, exile, orphan and good-for-nothing [even though] thanks be to God, I never committed any crimes— [all this] only because of the iniquity and despotism of men without consciences that [sic] I don't know to what lengths this overwhelming oppression will go."

31. The classical account of Antonio Conselheiro is found in the celebrated literary work of Euclydes da Cunha, *Os Sertões*. It is beautifully rendered into English by Samuel Putnam, tr., *Rebellion in the Backlands* (Chicago, 1944). When the work appeared in 1902, it repeated the accusation that Pe. Cícero intended to overthrow the Republic: "In Joazeiro, in the state of Ceará, a sinister heresiarch, Padre Cícero, was gathering fresh multitudes of schismatics for the Counselor" (p. 284). One of the many critical views of da Cunha's opinion is Lauro Nogueira, "A Segunda Conferência do Dr. Gomes de Mattos sôbre o Padre Cícero," *Unitário* (Fortaleza), 14 May 1952.

Two studies that probe beyond the religious aspects and into the political are: Abelardo Montenegro, *Antônio Conselheiro* (Fortaleza, 1954), and Ralph della Cava, "Brazilian Messianism and National Institutions: a reappraisal of Canudos and Joaseiro," *Hispanic American Historical Review*, XLVIII, 3 (August, 1968), 402-420. Also see Rui Facó, *Cangaceiros e Fanáticos* (Rio de Janciro, 1963) and Maria Isaura Pereira de Queiroz, *O Mêssianismo—no Brasil e no Mundo* (São Paulo, 1965).

32. Dom Joaquim, Third Pastoral Letter, 1897, in Macêdo (1961), p. 170.

33. The preceding details are based on: Luiz Torres, "O Governador da Bahia e Canudos. Calumnia" in *A Bahia* (Salvador), 14 September 1897 and *A República* (Fortaleza), 10 August 1897.

34. "Desordens do Joazeiro," *Diário de Pernambuco* (Recife), 30 December 1896.

35. Telegrams. Gov. Joaquim Corrêa Lima to Juiz de Direito and Delegado de Polícia of Salgueiro, 14 August 1897, and Bishop of Olinda to vicar of Salgueiro, 14 August 1897, cited in Bartholomeu (1923), pp. 108-112 and also in one of the most important accounts about a later period in Joaseiro's history, Irincu Pinheiro, *O Joaseiro do Padre Cícero e a Revolução de 1914* (Rio de Janeiro, 1938), pp. 159-161, n. 28.

36. In addition to the telegrams sent on 14 August 1897 to the Governor and bishop of Pernambuco by Salgueiro's Juiz de Direito, Manuel Lima Borges, and vicar, Fr. João Carlos Augusto, the local officials of the neighboring *municípios* —Leopoldina, Granito, Ouricury, and Cabrobó—also dispatched telegrams of support to the Governor. The above documents are cited in Bartholomeu (1923), pp. 110-112 and originally appeared as appendices to the article "Veritas Super Omnia," *Diário de Pernambuco* (Recife), 7 October 1897.

The above article in defense of Padre Cícero, signed by "many Catholics" but presumedly written by José Marrocos, illuminates two important questions. First, in regard to Padre Cícero's political stance, the article denounces the "inhuman persecution" designed to cast the cleric in the role of a conspirator. It noted that a state-wide protest in Pernambuco was raised in order to prove that the cleric was a peaceful and law-abiding citizen who respected the civil authorities. Second, in regard to the "religious question" of Joaseiro, the article stressed the national significance of the miracles of Joaseiro. It contrasted the church's approval of similar events in Italy and Portugal with its denunciation of those of Joaseiro (and the subsequent persecution of Padre Cícero). It attributed Rome's negation of the miracles of Joaseiro to a substitute account that was "Machiavellianly and clandestinely prepared," presumedly by Dom Joaquim, in order to undermine the original "Proceedings" that contained "exuberant proofs and testimony of the highest value."

Additional telegrams to ecclesiastical authorities, including one to the Archbishop of Bahia requesting his aid in furthering the cause of the miracles—"this great good that God deigned to manifest *in our fatherland*"—are found in Pinheiro (1963), pp. 492-494 (italics mine).

37. The Canudos episode prompted Marrocos and Padre Cícero to turn also to the political leaders of the Cariry Valley for support. Between September and November 1897, documents attesting to Padre Cícero's good standing as an obedient priest and citizen were issued by the civil authorities of Crato and Barbalha. Letters attesting to the cleric's "civil, moral and religious comportment" were sought from eight priests in the Cariry Valley. The above documents are found in ACS, Pasta da Questão Religiosa.

During Padre Cícero's later journey from the interior to Recife, enroute to Rome, he was hailed everywhere by the political chiefs of Pernambuco as well as by the people. In Alagôa de Baixo (Pbco.), he resided in the home of Col. Chico Bernardo and was befriended by other powerful local political chiefs, according to Ulysses Lins de Albuquerque, *Um Sertanejo e o Sertão* (Rio de Janeiro, 1957), pp. 74-75.

38. In October 1897, Salgueiro's Juiz de Direito, M. Lima Borges, solicited Governor Joaquim Corrêa Lima for Padre Cícero's passage to Rome, Cícero to D. Quinou and D. Angélica, 20 October 1897, ACS. In late December, the Governor agreed to arrange 500$000 reis for the trip as well as meetings with friends in Recife who might provide additional sums. The Governor requested that Padre Cícero leave by early January 1898; M. Lima Borges to Cícero, 28 December 1897, ACS, Pasta Roma.

Padre Cícero, however, arrived in Recife, at the home of the M. Lima Borges family only on 3 February 1898 after a brief return to Joaseiro in order to take leave of his family. On 8 February he met with the Bishop of Olinda and on the following day with Governor of Pernambuco from whom he received the promised 500$000 reis, cited in a letter from the wealthy Joaseiro merchant who accompanied the priest to Rome, João David de Silva to D. Angélica, 10 February

1898, ACS. Before embarking for Rome on 11 February 1898, Padre Cícero borrowed an additional 250$000 from the Governor's friend, Sebastião Sampaio, from whom he later requested an additional loan of 750$000; Cícero to Snr. Mendo Sampaio, Rome, 4 July 1898, ACS, Pasta Roma.

39. Padre Cícero arrived in Rome on 25 February 1898. Until 4 July, he resided at the Albergho dell'Orso, Via Monte Brionzo, 94; João David da Silva to D. Angélica, Rome, 26 February 1898, ACS, Pasta Roma. Later, he resided at the Church of S. Carlo al Corso, apparently befriended by an Italian priest, Fr. Vincenzo Bucceri.

In July, he had requested a loan from his Recife benefactor, Sebastião Sampaio (see n. 37). But apparently this was not granted. Instead, the Salgueiro Judge, M. Lima Borges, and a Recife woman identified only as D. Engracinha took up a subscription and sent the priest 930 Liras, almost one and a half contos; Cícero to Fr. João Carlos Augusto, Rome, 13 September 1898, ACS, Pasta Roma.

The reason for requesting additional financial assistance was the unexpected request of the Holy Office to remain in Rome longer than he had expected to, Cícero to M. Lima Borges, Rome, 4 July 1898, ACS. However, it is inexplicable why Padre Cícero had not advised the Holy Office of his presence in Rome before April, two months after his arrival; Cícero to Cardinal Parocchi, 23 April 1898, ACS, Pasta Roma.

40. The following table is based primarily on a document in Padre Cícero's hand entitled "Missas Distribuídas pelo Padre Cícero Romão Baptista, Joaseiro, Ceará para serem celebradas em Roma" as well as on additional receipts found in ACS, Pasta Missas.

Date	Person	Number of Masses	Value in Italian Lira
7 June 1898	Fr. Alberto Pequeno	400	500.00
		10	12.50
8 June 1898	Fr. Albano Maciel	50	62.50
10 June 1898	M. Cardinal Ledchowski, Prefect of the Propaganda Fidei	2,591	3,250.00
?	Dr. Fr. Ant.º Fernandes da Silva Távora	50	93.50
		129	162.35
?	Dr. Conego Antonio Murta	50	93.50
8 June 1898	Fr. Vincenzo Bucceri of the Church of S. Carlo in Rome	50	62.50
13 June 1898	Fr. Giusseppe M. Albani, General of the Servite Order	400	500.00
14 June 1898	Fr. Andreas Frühwirth, General of the Order of Preachers (Dominicans)	1,000	1,250.00

Date	Person	Number of Masses	Value in Italian Lira
?	Fr. Aloysius Lauer, General of the Order of Friars Minor (Franciscans)	874	1,093.50
?	Fr. Alberto Antero	400	500.00
?	Cardinal Goite [?]	2,600	3,250.00
?	Cardinal Parocchi, Prefect of the Holy Office	2,600	3,250.00
8 June 1898	Fr. Antonio Vessiani di [?]	50	62.50
3 October 1898	Fr. Pio Valeri	100	125.00
		11,354	14,367.85

The total value of the masses in Brazilian currency was 22.708$000 reis or more than 22 contos. At the exchange rate of 1898 this equaled $3,406.20 U.S.

This amount represented more than a third of the lifetime income of an average Brazilian priest in the interior of the Northeast. Apart from gifts, inheritance, etc., a curate derived his income entirely from stipends offered for (a) the celebration of the mass and (b) administration of baptism, marriages, and burials. In a single year he would receive about 830$000 reis for (a) and perhaps a maximum of 700$000 reis for (b). His annual income was therefore about 1:500$000. In forty years in the ministry he might expect to earn sixty contos. Many people probably earned less. This barest of living wages may explain the noted tendency of the Brazilian clergy's active participation in local politics.

It should be noted here that Padre Cícero had distributed mass-stipends in Rome long before his visit in 1898. Below is an account of the sums, considerably vast for the period, that were dispatched to Rome prior to 1898. It is based on the memoranda and receipts kept by the priest and conserved in ACS. These figures do not include mass-stipends distributed among the Brazilian clergy during the period.

Year	Number of Masses	Total in Milreis	Exchange Rate of Milreis (1$000) in U.S. Cents	Total Value in Dollars
1891	420	840$000	30	$ 252.00
1892	2,797	5:594$000	24	1,320.00
1893	2,933	5:866$000	24	1,392.00
1894	7,342	14:684$000	20	2,800.00
1895 (incomplete)	150	300$000	19	570.00
1896	5,500	11:000$000	18	1,980.00
1897	5,000	10:000$000	16	1,600.00
7 Year Total	24,142	48:284$000	—	$9,914.00

41. See notes 21 and 22.

42. Indicative of the cleric's mood is this excerpt from a letter to one of his closest friends: "If it weren't that so many ties bind me, I would never again return to Brazil, not because I do not love her very much, but because disappointments have filled my life with so many difficulties and problems that all I want [to do] is to remain quietly in some forgotten corner of the world, caring only for my soul's salvation," Padre Cícero to Secundo Chaves, Rome, 25 May 1898, cited in Pinheiro (1938), pp. 162-164, n. 29.

For additional letters of Padre Cícero to family and friends, see Pinheiro (1963), pp. 494-503.

43. Padre Cícero appeared before the Holy Office on four occasions prior to 17 August 1898. On that day, the Inquisition issued the new decree. It is published Macêdo (1961), pp. 188-190. Padre Cícero met with the Holy Office for a fifth and last time on 1 September 1898; see letter from Lucido Maria Cardinal Parocchi, Rome, 7 September 1898, also cited in Macêdo (1961), p. 190. The analysis of the 17 August 1898 decree in the text is based on the document.

44. Padre Cícero to Fr. João Carlos Augusto, Rome, 13 September 1898, ACS. According to an entry in the margin of his Roman Breviary, now in the personal archive of D. Amália Xavier de Oliveira of Juàzeiro do Norte, Ceará (hereinafter cited as AXO), Padre Cícero celebrated mass on 5 September 1898 in the church of S. Carlo al Corso, in Rome. Permission to celebrate mass in Brazil, subject to Dom Joaquim's approval, was not formally granted him until 4 October 1898; see letter from Cardinal L. M. Parocchi to Padre Cícero, Doc. Number 7849, Rome, 4 October 1898, ACS, Pasta Roma.

45. Padre Cícero departed from Rome for Naples at midnight, 7 October 1898. At noon the previous day, Msgr. Cagiano de Azevedo presented the cleric to Pope Leo XIII: "I spoke alone with the Holy Father and he offered me a gold rosary of the Most Blessed Virgin and he blessed two crucifixes that I planned to give to my bishop, Dom Joaquim, and to Sm. D. Manoel, Bishop of Olinda." He left Italy via Genoa on 10 October and arrived in Recife on 26 October. He arrived in Fortaleza on 12 November, departing on the twentieth for Joaseiro where he arrived on 4 December 1898; this account based on Padre Cícero's marginalia Roman Breviary, AXO.

46. Dom Joaquim, Fourth Pastoral Letter, 1898, cited in Macêdo (1961), pp. 178-190.

Dom Joaquim attacked the Legion of the Cross for utilizing the money it collected from the poor to feign "zealous fervor for the welfare of the Chair of St. Peter, with the intention of gaining the attention of the Holy Office in favor of the pretended miracles" (p. 180).

He further attacked the Legion for using funds for the costly journeys of José Lobo to Rome and for the expense account of the Legion's representative (perhaps Msgr. Bessa) before the Holy See (p. 180). The bishop then implied that the Legion's financial resources enabled Cícero to rely on unidentified persons "who advocated his cause, employing all measures necessary for success" (p. 186).

47. Four days after Padre Cícero's arrival in Joaseiro, on 4 December 1898, he withdrew to Crato as he had promised Dom Joaquim, Cícero to Joaquim, Fortaleza, 15 November 1898, in Pinheiro (1963), pp. 503-504. There he would wait until the bishop received authorization from Rome that would permit the priest to celebrate mass in Joaseiro.

In the interim, however, Cícero's followers spread the rumor that the cleric had been fully reinstated by Rome but that the bishop had withdrawn all his privileges. There was renewed "indignation against Dom Joaquim," Msgr. Alexandrino to Dom Joaquim, 14 December 1898, ABC. This popular reaction may have persuaded Dom Joaquim to restrict Cícero's privilege to celebrate mass only beyond the walls of Joaseiro; this privilege was made public in Dom Joaquim's Fourth Pastoral Letter, 1898, cited in Macêdo. (1961), p. 187. There is every reason to believe that Dom Joaquim's severity in this matter—in contrast to Rome's generosity—once again embittered the relations between the two men.

On 1 March 1899 Padre Cícero returned to Joaseiro once and for all, Padre Cícero, notes in Roman Breviary, AXO.

Chapter 5
From Religion into Politics

1. Alexandrino Rocha, "Juàzeiro, A Mêca do Padim Ciço," in the weekly magazine *Manchete* (Rio de Janeiro), 4 December 1965, pp. 118-121. Data on the two annual pilgrimages to Joaseiro are found in Expedito Cornélio, "Festa da Gratidão," *Rev. do Cinqüentenário* (1961), pp. 7-8. For a highly impressionistic account of a recent pilgrimage by a French traveler, see François Vilespy, "Juàzeiro do Norte et le Padre Cícero," *Caravelle* (Toulouse, France), 5 (1965), pp. 61-70.

2. The condemnation of the Legion appeared in Dom Joaquim's Fourth Pastoral Letter, 1898, cited in Macêdo (1961), pp. 178-190, esp. pp. 180-181.

On 19 June 1898, the weekly *A Ordem* (Sobral, Ceará) ran an editorial, entitled "Os Jagunços da Legião da Cruz," in which it accused José Lóbo of exploiting the good faith and generosity of ignorant believers. It also asked whether the "police did not have the imperious duty to intervene in order to put an end to these disorders."

The Catholic weekly, *A Verdade* (Fortaleza), 10 July 1898, published a communique from Ipú in which it accused local Legion leaders of creating a "terrible . . . sect" that "was a kind of *Canudos* not lacking its *Conselheiro* and its *conselheiristas*. . . ."

The details about the alleged threat of assassination against the Ipú *coronel* and other general information about the Legion are contained in de Souza (1915), pp. 315-322.

3. Fr. Quintino Rodrigues de Oliveira e Silva was named to the post of vicar of Crato on 23 May 1900. He took office on 10 June according to Pinheiro (1963), p. 170.

The twenty-two page, unpublished confidential report written by one Fausto Sobrinho, otherwise unidentifiable, was based on his visit to Joaseiro and Crato between October 1902 and January 1903. It is entitled "Apontamentos sobre o fanatismo no Juazeiro," a copy of which is preserved in ABC. It is the only eye-witness account of Joaseiro during the decade 1899 and 1909, a period for which very little historical data exist or have been found; it is hereinafter cited as "Apontamentos . . .," 1903, ABC.

The description of the "New Jerusalem" in 1903 in our text accurately follows the "Apontamentos . . .," unless otherwise noted.

4. The account of the "*beato* da Cruz" is based on [Antonio] Xavier de Oliveira, *Beatos e Cangaceiros* (Rio de Janeiro, 1920), pp. 37-46. The accuracy of this account is disputed by Bartholomeu (1923), pp. 113-122.

5. An *oração forte* is a supplication addressed to God or the saints according to a formula that must be used only in extraordinary circumstances.

These *orações* probably originated in the sixteenth and seventeenth centuries on the Iberian peninsula as prayers and formulas used against witches. They "are most common throughout all Brazil . . . , where they are transmitted either orally or in written form. In the latter case, the paper on which they are written is usually carried in a small cloth bag worn around the neck or in billfolds or in other hidden places on one's person. In moments of extreme stress, affliction etc., the prayer may be said." For other details, see "Oração Forte," in Câmara Cascudo (1962), II, 534-537.

6. Padre Cícero refers to the vow made by him and Frs. Manoel Felix de Moura, Francisco Rodrigues Monteiro, and Antonio Fernandes Távora, vicar of Crato in 1890 in his last will and testament, *Cópia do Testamento com que faleceu nesta cidade o Revmo. Padre Cícero Romão Batista* (Joaseiro, n.d.), pp. 6-7 (hereinafter cited as *Cópia do Testamento*). Excerpts of the will are found in Macêdo (1961), pp. 113-120; a lengthy discussion of the controversy regarding the building of the chapel, as well as photographs are contained in Bartholomeu (1923), pp. 57-59.

According to Bartholomeu (1923), p. 58, Dom Joaquim had granted Padre Cícero authorization to build the chapel in 1890. The bishop's first prohibition is dated 13 April 1896 and is contained in the letter from Msgr. Alexandrino to Padre Cícero, 28 April 1896, ACS, Legião da Cruz. Dom Joaquim's second prohibition is found in his letter to Fr. Quintino, 17 September 1903, ABC: "the continuation of these works would in some way sanction the false principle on which it was begun. . . ."

The shell of the cathedral remained intact until about 1939, five years after Padre Cícero's death. Then, the Salesian priests to whom he had willed his estate destroyed it in order to put the building materials to other uses; see Alves (1948), p. 62, pp. 72-101, esp. p. 94.

Despite the church's earlier ban, the Hôrto's cathedral ruins remained for decades the principal convergence point of the annual Holy Week processions of the people of Joaseiro. In 1955, however, the church hierarchy at last succeeded in banning the practice; see Durival Aires, "A Morte de Uma Tradição," in *O Estado* (Fortaleza), 17 April 1955.

7. This important viewpoint is cited in Bartholomeu (1923), p. 59, n. 9.

8. The expectation of Christ is cited in "Apontamentos . . . ," 1903, ABC. It is also alluded to in Alves (1948), p. 84. Alves also notes that "the Serra do Hôrto is an obligatory stop-off for the visiting pilgrim who finds there in the terrain some resemblance to the Holy Land," (p. 95). The pilgrims' mental transformation of Joaseiro's topography into that of the Holy Land is amply discussed in Dinis (1935), pp. 100-101.

9. "Apontamentos . . . ," 1903, ABC.

10. These words were attributed to the Chief Commissioner of the first Commission of Inquiry, Fr. Clycério da Costa Lôbo, by the priest, Msgr. José Teixeira da Graça in the latter's letter to Dom Joaquim, 9 November 1892; the letter is cited in Montenegro (1959), pp. 27-28.

For a vivid description of Joaseiro and the Hôrto cathedral ca. 1904, see Joaquim Pimenta, *Retalhos do Passado* (Rio de Janeiro, 1949), pp. 40-42.

11 Joaseiro's Population:

1890	2,245 (a)
1898	more than 5,000 (b)
1905	12,000 (c)
1909	15,050 (d)

SOURCES:

(a) "Descripção da Cidade do Crato em 1882 pelo Dr. Gustavo Horácio," in *Itaytera,* V (1959), 165-171, esp. 169.

(b) estimated on "Livro do Registro do Apostolado da Oração do Santíssimo Coração de Jesus" (Joaseiro), 13 January 1898, ACS, Pasta Legião da Cruz.

(c) Draft of Letter, José Marrocos to the Fedral Congress, 10 August 1906, ACS, Pasta Marrocos.

(d) "1° de Janeiro de 1909—A Povoação do Joaseiro . . . tem na presente data 18 ruas, 4 travessas, etc., com a população de 15,050 habitantes," document submitted to the Legislative Assembly of Ceará in support of Joaseiro's bid for municipal autonomy, in ACS (hereinafter cited as "A Povoação do Joaseiro," 1 January 1905).

12. The role of the merchants in encouraging the pilgrimages is alluded to in Dom Joaquim's Third Pastoral Letter of 1897, cited in Macêdo (1961), pp. 172-173. However, no specific details are given in the Pastoral or found elsewhere for this period.

The role of the Legion in stimulating pilgrimages was cited in the Fourth Pastoral Letter, 1898, in Macêdo (1961), pp. 178-182

13. Fourth Pastoral Letter, 1898, Macêdo (1961), pp. 181-182.

14. Allusions to the early influx of Alagôans into Joaseiro are cited in Joaquim Alves, *Nas Fronteiras do Nordeste* (Fortaleza, 1932[?]), p. 240. The continuing influence of Padre Cícero in Alagôas is cited in Alves (1948), pp. 93-94.

Reference to Alagôans and their descendants among Joaseiro's population in

1963 is found in Frei Antonio Rolim, O.P., "Levantamento Sócio-Re...
Diocese de Crato" (Rio de Janeiro, 1964, mimeographed), as cited in Ann M...
"Religion in Juàzeiro (Ceará, Brazil) Since the Death of Padre Cícero—A Ca...
Study in the Nature of Messianic Religious Activity in the Interior of Brazil"
(unpublished Master's Essay, Columbia University, 1966).

Regretfully, the author has been unable to find specific data that would
illustrate the historical conditions accounting for the large-scale immigration of
Alagôans into Jouzeiro in this century.

15. Alves (1932 and 1948), passim, unduly emphasizes the "religious" motivation of the pilgrims.

16. These letters were found in ACS. In citing them in the notes only the city
or town of origin (and state, where identified) and the date of the letter will be
noted, in that order.

17. "Apontamentos . .," 1903, ABC.

18. Sertãozinho, 11 March 1910, ACS.

19. Baixanalzinho, 30 March 1910, ACS.

20. Rozaduilio, Alagôas, 12 July 1910, ACS.

21. Lourenço, January 1913, ACS.

22. Tôrres, 21 July 1911, ACS.

23. Cited in Pe Pereira Nóbrega, Vingança Não (Depoimento sóbre Chico
Pereira e Cangaceiros do Nordeste), (Rio de Janeiro, 1961), pp. 84-93, esp. p. 86.

24. Caprichó, 2 May 1910, ACS.

25. Belo Horizonte, Minas Gerais, 3. April 1910, ACS.

26. Pilões de Gorabeira, Pernambuco, 10 July 1910, ACS.

27. Se Facó (1963), pp. 53-58.

28. Padre Cícero to Fr. L——, 18 July 1918, ACS, Pasta da Correspondência
com o clero.

29. Joaquim Alves, História das Sêcas (Séculos XVII a XIX), (Fortaleza,
1953), p. 240; and Th. Pompeu Sobrinho, História das Sêcas (Seculo XX), Fortaleza, 1953), p. 191.

30. Celso Furtado, The Economic Growth of Brazil (Berkeley and Los
Angeles, 1965), p. 145.

31. Djacir Menezes, O Outro Nordeste (Rio de Janeiro, 1937), pp. 158-160.

32. Facó (1963), pp. 29-37, esp. p. 30; and Thomaz Pompeu de Souza Brasil,
O Ceará no Centenário da Independência do Brasil (2 vols.; Fortaleza, 1922 and
1926), I, 231.

33. Facó (1963), pp. 30-31; and Rodolpho Theophilo, A Secca de 1915 (Rio
de Janeiro, 1922b), pp. 138-140. The subsequent insight into the Northeast labor
shortage is based primarily on Facó (1963), pp. 29-37, and Furtado (1965), pp.
141-148.

34. Rodolpho Theophilo, Seccas do Ceará (Segunda Metade do Século XIV),
(Fortaleza, 1901), pp. 65-66, p. 141 and p. 156; also Furtado (1965), p. 147.

35. See the annual governors' reports to the State Legislature during this
period, esp. the Mensagem apresentada á Assembléa Legislativa do Ceará pelo

*Presidente do Estado, Dr. Antonio Pinto N gueiro Accioly em 1° de Julho de
1897:* (Fortaleza, 1897), pp. 26-27. Various schemes to contract Asiatic and
European laborers for Ceará were discussed in the Fortaleza daily, *A República,*
6 June 1894 and 17 August 1896.

36. Labor remained relatively fixed in the Northeast after 1919 when the
federal government began to subsidize a vast program of public works, including
the construction of dams, roads, and wells. See Pompeu Sobrinho (1953), pp.
330-47 and Albert O. Hirschman, *Journeys Toward Progress* (New York, 1963),
pp. 13-91, p. 30.

37. During the droughts of the late 1850s, one observer noted, the Cariry
Valley became a center of convergence not only of those in search of supplies
but also in search of a haven from the droughts which struck from Bahia to Piauí:
"The Valley of the Cariry is, without exaggeration, like unto those oases of Libya
to which the Arabs of the desert flee;" Souza Brasil (1861), p. 34.

Shortly after the official proclamation of the drought of 1888, Fortaleza newspapers vividly described the usual pattern of migration that had begun into the
Valley: "The absence of rain is also a fact in the central *municípios* of Rio Grande
do Norte and Paraíba *whose inhabitants customarily descend upon the Cariry*
as the first stopoff of their exodus; resulting from this are the great waves of
emigrants who come from there [the Cariry] to deluge the capital [Fortaleza]
when local resources dry up; in the present crisis they have begun to move early,"
in *Pedro II* (Fortaleza), 21 June 1888 (italics mine). Also see Pinheiro (1950), 20.

38. Bartholomeu (1923), pp. 44-45; p. 90, n. 23.

39. See Pimenta (1949), p. 43, regarding the rivalry between Barbalha and
Crato; see also Guilherme Studart, "Descripção do município de Barbalha,"
RIC, II (1888), 9-13. For a more recent account of Barbalha, see Marchêt Callou
(1959), pp. 127-133.

40. José de Figueiredo Brito, "A Contribuição dos Romeiros na Construção
Econômica do Carirí," *Itaytera,* II (1956), 227-229, esp. 228. The author notes that
the cultivation of the serras by the pilgrims was so successful that the large landowners subsequently "invaded" the newly cultivated areas and dispossessed the
pilgrims of their land (228).

41. Pinheiro (1938), p. 173. Also see note 45, Chapt. VI of this study.

42. Unless otherwise stated, all data for the year 1909 is based on the document "A povoação do Joaseiro . . .," 1 January 1909, ACS.

Data for 1917 is based on Lt. José Pinheiro Bezerra de Menezes, "Joazeiro
do Cariry," *Correio do Ceará* (Fortaleza), 18 October 1917. According to the
article the author was an engineering officer who compiled statistics on Joaseiro
on behalf of the General Staff of the Brazilian army.

43. Pinheiro (1950), p. 21. As early as 1896–1897, *maniçoba* rubber was
recognized as an important export of Ceará, see the articles in *A República*
(Fortaleza), 26 November 1896 and 2 August 1897. Peak production years were
from 1897–1917 according to Pompeu de Souza Brasil (1926), II, 244. According
to Bartholomeu (1923), p. 45, n. 4, "the cultivation of *maniçba* [rubber] in the

Serra do Araripe within an area of about ten leagues is due solely and exclusively to Padre Cícero."

44. Pinheiro (1950), p. 64.

45. "A povoação do Joaseiro . . .," 1 January 1909, ACS.

46. A letter from the merchant to Pe. Cícero's sister is cited in Chapter IV, note 38.

47. Facó (1963), 179.

48. "A povoação do Joaseiro . . .," 1 January 1909, ACS.

49. Facó (1963), p. 180.

50. Bartholomeu (1923), pp. 170-171; also partially cited in Facó (1963), p. 181.

51. Pinheiro (1963), pp. 209, 213.

52. José Maria Bello, *A History of Modern Brazil, 1889–1964,* trans. James L. Taylor with a new concluding chapter by Rollie E. Poppino (Stanford, 1966), pp. 162-171, esp. pp. 164-166.

53. *Ibid.,* p. 169; the denomination of Campos Sales' political policies as "the politics of the governors" is found in José Maria dos Santos, *A Política Geral do Brasil* (São Paulo, 1930), 352-353.

54. Unfortunately neither a biography of Accioly nor a monographic account of his twenty-year influence on Ceará's politics exists. A contemporary series of vitriolic articles attacking his administration was written by [J. G. da] Frota Pessôa and published in book form as *O Olygarcha do Ceará (A Chrônica de um despota),* (Rio de Janeiro, 1910). Also see Martin Soares (pseudonym of Antonio Salles), *O Babaquara,* (Rio de Janeiro, 1912). An equally partisan denunciation of the Accioly administration and perhaps the single most valuable printed source for any future monograph is Rodolpho Theophilo, *Libertação do Ceará (Queda da Oligarchia Accioly),* (Lisboa, 1914).

A revisionist's eulogy is contained in the pamphlet by José Waldo Ribeiro Ramos, *Centenário do Comendador Nogueira Acioli* (Fortaleza, 1940). A cursory examination of the Accioly "oligarchy" is contained in the previously cited work of Abelardo Montenegro on Ceará's political parties (1965), pp. 38-42; and Glauco Carneiro, *História das Revoluções Brasileiras* (Rio de Janeiro, 1965), I, 196-203, esp. 186-190.

Scattered references to the period are contained in the memoirs of Pimenta (1949), *passim,* and in Msgr. José Quinderé, *Reminiscências* (Fortaleza, 1947), *passim.*

Biographical data on Gov. Accioly are contained in Guimarães (1953), pp. 192-195.

55. For example, the transition from Empire to Republic in Crato did not in itself result in the deposition of Col. José Antonio de Figueiredo who retained de facto political control until 1892; see José de Figueiredo Brito, "Maxixes & Malabares (Episódio Inédito da História Política do Crato)," in *Itaytera,* V (1959), 37-57, esp. 38-40.

On *coronelismo,* the classic study is Victor Nunes Leal, *Coronelismo: Enxada e Voto* (Rio de Janeiro, 1948). A recent study of four contemporary *coronéis* of the Northeast is Marcos Vinicius Vilaça and Roberto C. de Albuquerque, *Coronel e Coronéis* (Rio de Janeiro, 1965).

56. Bartholomeu (1923), pp. 170-171 clearly indicates that taxes paid by Joaseiro to the state government were considerably higher than those paid to the federal government:

Year	State Taxes	Federal Taxes
1916	19:500$000	2:440$000
1917	24:600$000	5:717$000
1918	31:500$000	19:942$000
1919	43:000$000	19:140$000
1920	32:100$000	18:831$000
1921	47:900$000	24:831$000
1922	52:100$000	31:800$000

From this data it is clear that the combined annual state and federal taxes paid by Joaseiro had increased almost 400 per cent in seven years.

57. Orlando Carvalho, *Política do Município* (Rio de Janeiro, 1946), p. 165, indicates that from 1868 to 1910, the percentage of all governmental revenue collected by the *municípios* increased more than seven times. The implication is that municipal government was made "more real" and that the possibilities increased both for corruption and legitimate rewards doled out by the local political chiefs, thus assuring them of even greater power than under the Empire.

58. Pinheiro (1938), pp. 180-184 and pp. 189-191. The depositions took place in Missão Velha in 1901; Crato, 1940; Barbalha, 1906; Lavras, 1907 and 1910; Santana do Cariri and Campos Sales in 1908; in Aurora and Araripe, 1908. In 1909, Crato's "little oligarchy" was threatened, but survived; also see Pinheiro (1950), p. 187.

Only the 1904 Crato struggle is amply documented in both Pinheiro (1938 & 1950) and Figueiredo Brito (1959). Additional light is shed in the recent memoirs of [Sen. Manuel do Nascimento] Fernandes Távora, *Algo de Minha Vida* (2d ed., Fortaleza, 1963), pp. 30-32.

59. As early as 1912, Gustavo Barroso noted in his celebrated maiden-work, *Terra de Sol* (6th ed., Fortaleza, 1962) that the "geography of banditry" was not limited to the Cariry Valley alone but extended its borders into Paraíba and Pernambuco, pp. 102-103. Also see Figueiredo Brito (1959), pp. 50-51, and Pinheiro (1938), p. 191, in regard to the *cangaceiros* hired in Pernambuco for the conflict in Crato in 1903–1904.

60. A pioneer study of *cangaceirismo* is Abelardo Montenegro, *História do Cangaceirismo no Ceará* (Fortaleza, 1955).

61. Frota Pessôa (1910), pp. 231-232.

62. Notarized copies of petitions dated 2 February 1900, to the Holy Father; 4 September 1902 to the nuncio in Petropolis and 29 September 1903 to Pope Pius X, are located in ACS, Pasta da Questão Religiosa.

On 25 November 1905, the *Jornal do Cariry* (Barbalha) in a special one-page edition erroneously announced that Rome had reinstated Padre Cícero in response to a telegraphed request sent by the people of Joaseiro earlier in the year. Also see note 63, below.

On 30 March 1906, a commission of Fortaleza merchants received from Dom Joaquim a formal refusal to transmit a request to Rome on Padre Cícero's behalf; cited in Pinheiro (1963), pp. 174-175.

Finally in 1908 the papal nuncio in Petropolis wrote one of the members of the above commission that only Rome could restore Padre Cícero's orders; Dom Alessandro to Adolpho Barroso, 26 August 1908, ACS, Pasta da Questão Religiosa.

63. The copies of the notarized petitions sent to Dom Joaquim were found in ACS, Pasta da Questão Religiosa. That of Santana do Cariri is dated 10 December 1905; Barbalha's, 10 January 1906; Brejo dos Santos', 8 February 1906; Crato's, 19 February 1906.

64. The cleric's neutrality in local disputes was further attested to by his financial support of the Empreza Typographica Cariryense of Barbalha. Organized by José Marrocos in 1904 and 1905, the "empreza" launched an apolitical, nonpartisan weekly newspaper. Interestingly enough, the purpose of the *Jornal do Cariry* was to promote the development of the entire region. It strongly condemned rivalries between *coronéis* and *municípios* as the cause of the "lamentable impediments whenever great undertakings of common interest are involved . . .," based on documents and the "Estatutos da Empreza Typographica Cariryense" found in ACS, Pasta Marrocos.

65. The requests to Padre Cícero to prevent local hostilities are contained in the following letters: Fr. Pedro Esmeraldo to Padre Cícero, 24 February 1903, PCC, re: Missão Velha; Julio A. Pequeno to Padre Cícero, 17 August 1907, PCC, re: Lavras; Col. Domingos Leite Furtado to Padre Cícero, 1 January 1909, ACS, re: Aurora; and Dr. Ant°. P.N. Accioly to Padre Cícero, 29 April 1911, PCC, re: Barbalha's political chief, Col. Jôca de Macedo.

66. Testament of José Lôbo: "Attesto que sendo Cariryense d'origem . . .," 25 December 1910, in ACS, Pasta da Questão Religiosa.

Floro Bartholomeu also notes this more than a decade later: "during this period, in spite of being a simple hamlet, Joaseiro was the refuge of the defeated and Padre Cícero, the unofficial intermediary between the government and the litigants [who] . . . pacified ruffled spirits and prevented personal conflicts.

"Because [Padre Cícero] was not a politician at the time, his intervention was always solicited," cited in Bartholomeu (1923), p. 177, n. 22.

Chapter 6
Padre Cícero Enters Politics

1. The first and perhaps most violent denigration of Padre Cícero was published by a fellow priest, Fr. Joaquim de Alencar Peixoto, *Joazeiro do Cariry* (Fortaleza, 1913). In a chapter, entitled "Aman-Ra," Alencar Peixoto compared

Cícero to an ancient ruler of Egypt and declared that "as a priest, citizen and politician, he is the kiss of death. . . ." (pp. 80-81). Ironically, the priest-author was both the founder of Joaseiro's first newspaper, O Rebate, and one of the principal proponents of Joaseiro's autonomy.

Rodolpho Theophilo (1914) claimed that it was the splendor of the papal court which convinced Padre Cícero that "to be rich would not prevent him from going to heaven since even the head of the church was" (p. 79). Once rich, "he decided to run the political show in the Cariry . . ." (p. 80).

Scholars have also contributed, perhaps unintentionally to this line of analysis. In 1926 the now world-renowned Brazilian educator, Manuel Bergström Lourenço Filho, published the widely-read, and prize-winning account of Joaseiro, Joaseiro do Padre Cícero (Scênas e quadros do fanatismo no Nordeste), (2d ed., São Paulo, 1926). Unfortunately this work, more than any other, was responsible for portraying Padre Cícero, then 82 years of age and ailing, as a megalomaniac and paranoiac (pp. 64-75). This portrayal, despite the many merits of Lourenço Filho's study, may have done much to deter a more dispassionate inquiry into Joaseiro and the priest for more than two decades. Alves (1948) was the first student to take up that task. In 1943 the distinguished Senator from Ceará and physician, Manuel do Nascimento Fernandes Távora, classified Padre Cícero as a "paranoiac" (1943), pp. 35-69. The most recent attack against Padre Cícero is Fr. Antonio Gomes de Araújo's "Apostolado do Embuste" (1956), cited earlier; it has been recently amplified in the author's latest article, "A Margem de 'A Margem da História do Ceará'," Itaytera, VIII (1962), 5-19.

Two apologetic works, now almost forgotten, were written in the cleric's lifetime, well after he had become politically notorious. L. Côsta Andrade, Sertão a Dentro (Alguns dias com o Padre Cícero), (Rio de Janeiro, 1922), argues that "the beloved priest, far from being a fanatizer, a demoniac, a demolisher . . . is a priest of suggestive and cultured ideas . . . always up to date with the forward advances of humanity . . ." (pp. 94-95). Equally praiseful is Antonio Carlos Simõens da Silva's O Padre Cícero e a População do Nordeste (Elementos de defesa, história, "folklore" e propaganda), (Rio de Janeiro, 1927). This work was written as a "defense of Padre Cícero" (p. 19) and may have been commissioned by the cleric or his advisors.

After Padre Cícero's death, Irineu Pinheiro's (1938) study was the first to rehabilitate the priest's reputation without flattery. In recent decades, the task of defending Padre Cícero has been taken up by a native of Joaseiro, also a priest, Fr. Azarias Sobreira. His writings under the pseudonym, Lívio Sobral. (1940–1943), are cited in full in Chapter I, n. 58 of this work. His most recent work, a series of articles, appeared under his proper name, Fr. Azarias Sobreira, "Padre Cícero, Enigma de Hontem e de Hoje," O Povo (Fortaleza), October 1965 through February 1966. Only after the completion of this study were the above articles published in book form under the title, O Patriarca de Juàzeiro (Juàzeiro, 1969).

2. Cópia do Testamento (n.d.), p. 3. The other reason given by the Patriarch

was his desire "to heed the repeated requests of the then Governor of the State, my erstwhile friend, Comendador Antonio Pinto Nogueira Acioli . . ." (p. 3). However, the evidence cited further in the text and in the next footnote clearly shows that the initiative to prevent the "other citizen's" designation as prefect of Joaseiro lay with Padre Cícero and not Accioly. At this time, prefects were not elected, but appointed by the Governor.

3. Padre Cícero to Accioly, 18 June 1911, ACS. The letter was clearly prompted by "rumors current in Joaseiro" that the "other citizen," therein identified as Major Joaquim Bezerra de Menezes, was "pressing for an official post once Joaseiro was raised to a *município*." From the text of Padre Cícero's will, it is clear that the Major sought nothing less than the post of prefect.

4. The identification of Major Joaquim Bezerra de Menezes is explained above in note 3. He is mentioned in Pinheiro (1950), p. 64, as one of two prominent cotton planters in the Cariry Valley. He held the honorific rank of Major in the National Guard. Among his descendants are the prominent cotton planters and politicians of Joaseiro, Major Humberto Bezerra de Menezes, a Brazilian Army officer, former prefect of Joaseiro and at present Federal Deputy from the Cariry Valley to the National Congress, and his brother Adauto, now serving his second term as a member of the Legislative Assembly of Ceará. Both provided the author with information in Joaseiro during September 1964.

5. In interviews conducted in August and September 1964, with Joaseiro historians, the late Octávio Aires de Menezes and the octogenarian, José Ferreira de Bezerra de Menezes, neither could shed light on the 1907 rally sponsored by Major Joaquim.

The cleric's "boycott" of the meeting is adduced indirectly from his own subsequent failure, as well as the failure of these two famous local historians, to assign the 1907 meeting any place in their history.

6. The text of this rare handbill, entitled "Ao Povo do Joazeiro" is contained in Dra. Amália Xavier de Oliveira (ed.), "Inquêrito do Juàzeiro," (unpublished MS, 1943), pp. 4-5.

Dra. Amália is one of Joaseiro's most prominent educators and at present is the director of the state-supported Escôla Normal Rural, established in Joaseiro in 1934.

7. On Col. Antonio Luis' petition to the bishop in 1906, se Chapter V, n. 63.

8. On José Marrocos' political views see Chapter V, n. 64. José Lôbo's political views are discussed by his grandson, Aires de Menezes (unpublished MS, 1963): "Zé Lôbo with his monarchist views hated the Republic . . ." (p. 67).

9. The discussion of Joaseiro's social structure is partly drawn from José Fabio Barbosa da Silva, "Organização Social de Juàzeiro e Tensões entre Litoral e Interior," *Sociologia,* XXIV (1962), 3, 181-194, esp. 181-187; and Amália Xavier de Oliveira (unpublished MS, 1943), pp. 43-47. Our discussion seeks to illuminate the historical roots of the "two Joaseiros."

10. Information about the Silva Brothers and João Batista de Oliveira was given the author by D. Maria Gonçalves da Rocha Leal in Fortaleza on 4 July

1964. D. Maria Gonçalves was Joaseiro's first professionally trained school teacher. She returned to Joaseiro in 1924; three years later she directed the city's first *"grupo escolar."* See Tarcila Cruz Alencar "A Evolução das Letras em Juàzeiro do Norte," *Rev. do Cinqüentenário* (1961), pp. 22-24.

11. Aires de Menezes (unpublished MS, 1963), pp. 66-67), lists the following native sons "who, while not turning into enemies of Padre Cícero, did keep their distance. . . . Aristides Ferreira de Menezes, old João da Rocha, Col. Joaquim da Rocha, Pedro Jacintho da Rocha, Col. Coimbra, Joaquim Inácio de Figueiredo, the old-timer, Benjamin Callô. . . ." The division over the religious issue is confirmed in Pinheiro (1938), p. 172.

12. For a biographical sketch of Pelusio Macedo, see Raimundo Gomes de Mattos, "Perece Um Gênio do Sertão," *Unitário* (Fortaleza), 12 May 1955. Also see *Album* (1925), p. 107.

13. Letter, Pelusio Correia de Macedo to José Marrocos, 24 January 1905, PCC.

14. Pinheiro (1938), p. 172.

15. Barbosa da Silva (1962), p. 183; Amália Xavier de Oliveira (unpublished MS, 1943), pp. 44-45, and information given to the author by Dra. Amália Xavier de Oliveira in Joaseiro, 13 September 1964.

16. Amália Xavier de Oliveira (unpublished MS, 1943), p. 45.

17. This is the viewpoint of such critics as Lourenço Filho (1922), pp. 79-84; Fernandes Távora (1943), p. 45; and Alves (1948), p. 95. It is shared by Fr. Azarias Sobreira, "O Revolucionário," in *Rev. do Cinqüentenário* (1961), pp. 14-16. Fr. Sobreira writes: "It was the arrival of Floro Bartholomeu in 1908, it was his gradual ascendancy over Padre Cícero that imprinted a new direction upon everything. It was Floro who . . . innoculated the aging priest with the idea of accelerating the forward march of his beloved homeland towards full and definitive self-determination . . ." (p. 14).

18. The date of arrival is in Bartholomeu (1923), p. 106 n. 29, p. 137.

Published biographical data on Floro Bartholomeu (1876-1926) are contained in: Azarias Sobreira, "Floro Bartholomeu—O Caudilho Bahiano," *RIC,* LXIV (1950), 193-202; Guimarães (1952), pp. 244-245; Pinheiro (1963), pp. 160-161, 213; newspaper obituaries published in *Jornal do Commêrcio* (Fortaleza), 9 March 1926, *Correio do Ceará* (Fortaleza), 10 March 1926, *Diario do Ceará* (Fortaleza), 10 and 11 March 1926; and of course the autobiographical allusions contained in Bartholomeu (1923), *passim.*

19. Floro's encounter with Conde Adolpho is cited in Bartholomeu (1923), pp. 136-137.

Published biographical data on Conde Adolpho Van den Brule is contained in: Bartholomeu (1923), pp. 132-137; and Sílvio Froes de Abreu, "Schisto Bituminoso da Chapada do Araripe, Ceará," *RIC,* XXXVIII (1924), 363-377, esp., 363-364.

20. Details of Conde Adolpho's early activities are few. Some are contained in Bartholomeu (1923), pp. 135-137 and Abreu (1914), pp. 363.

In 1904, Conde Adolpho first visited the Cariry and found copper in Coxá, mistakenly thought to lie within the *município* of Aurora. Shortly after, thanks to his brother who still lived in Paris, the Conde had incorporated in Paris a firm known as the "Societé Anonyme d'Exploitation des Mines de Cuivre d'Aurora (Brésil)." According to another document also found in ACS, Pasta do Conde Adolpho, the Frenchman's chief partner was Fr. Augusto Barbosa de Menezes, the Vicar of São Pedro do Carirí (today Caririaçú) who was an intimate friend of Padre Cícero. In 1907, news that landowners intended to seize Coxá and develop the copper fields without Conde Adolpho's participation sent the Frenchman back to the Cariry, according to Bartholomeu (1923), p. 136.

21. There is no record of either the Patriarch's purchase or date of purchase of Coxá. Pinheiro (1938), p. 164, insists that it was bought "in the first decade of the present century" and clearly implies that this occurred before the arrival of Dr. Floro and Conde Adolpho (p. 165). It is most likely the Padre Cícero's friend and the Conde's partner, Fr. Barbosa, was instrumental in the Patriarch's decision to do so.

22. An almost complete account of the Coxá land dispute was written by Dr. Floro Bartholomeu, "Minas do Coxá: Ligeiras Considerações para refutar os argumentos adduzidos pelo Illmo. Snr. Cel. José Francisco Alves Teixeira no 'Correio do Cariry' de 5 do Corrente," a forgotten series of twelve articles which appeared in Joaseiro's first newspaper, *O Rebate,* between 22 August 1909 and 25 July 1910.

It is interesting to note that, upon advice provided by Ceará's eminent historian, Dr. Guilherme Studart, to Fr. Barbosa, Padre Cícero corresponded with the Benedictine missionaries in Quixadá, Ceará, who held title to some of the lands at Coxá. According to this correspondence dated 14 September, 28 October 1908, and 1 January 1909 and found in ACS, Correspondência com as Ordens Religiosas, the Patriarch prevailed upon Abbot Bonifácio Jansen not to sell their Coxá holdings to other interested landowners in the Cariry.

Information on the Benedictines is found in D. Joaquim G. de Luna, "Os monges beneditinos no Ceará," *RIC,* LXVI (1952), 220-240 as well as in Luna (1951).

23. Details about the armed conflict at Coxá are contained in an undated letter from Dr. Floro to Padre Cícero, cited in Pinheiro (1938), pp. 164-167, esp. p. 165, n. 30. Interestingly, no reference whatsoever to this event is contained in Bartholomeu (1909-1910).

24. The familial relationship between Col. Antonio Luis and Col. J. F. Alves Teixeira is cited in Pinheiro (1938), pp. 183-184.

Bartholomeu (1909–1910; 26 September 1909), noted that Col. Antonio Luis owned land near Coxá and implied that he, rather than his relative, Col. J. F. Alves Teixeira, had instigated the attack against Dr. Floro's party. In an unspecified issue of the neighboring Barbalha newspaper, *A União,* an unsigned article openly accused Col. Antonio Luis of sending henchmen to stop the Coxá demarcation. The article was later reprinted under the title "Inedictoriaes—Os Últimos Acontecimentos," in *O Rebate* (Joaseiro), 25 July 1909.

The incident at Coxá was later used by Alencar Peixoto (1913), to portray Padre Cícero as a "captain of the infamous, of bandits, of criminals. . . ." (pp. 208-211).

25. Evidence that Padre Cícero began to work for the erection of the new diocese as early as 1907 is contained in the article by Manuel Benício, "Dr. Leandro Bezerra," which appeared in the newspaper *O Fluminense* (Niterói), 11 June 1907: "Recently, Leandro Bezerra de Menezes, *backing up* the enormous efforts of the virtuous priest, Padre Cícero Romão Batista, his close personal friend, has been engaged in the creation of a bishopric that *may* have Crato as its seat" (italics mine).

Leandro Bezerra de Menezes was a native son of Crato, an imperial senator from Alagôas and an arch-conservative Catholic. Because of his close contacts with the Brazilian hierarchy in Niterói and Rio as well as with the papal nuncio in Petropolis he became, despite his advanced age, the chief promoter in the South of the new diocese in the Cariry. Information on him is contained in "Leandro Bezerra" *RIC*, XXVI (1912), 206-214 and in Pinheiro (1963), p. 89.

In a letter from Padre Cícero to Dr. Leandro Bezerra, 25 September 1908, ACS, Pasta do Bispado do Cariri, the cleric wrote: "There's no longer any doubt about the creation of the Diocese of the Cariry. You are the agent charged by Providence for the task. . . . When I was in Rome in '98, I made such a request, writing through someone else, to His Holiness, Leo XIII; and here, later, I had published in newspapers the necessity [*sic*] of establishing that Diocese in the very center of the different states that border on the Cariry . . . Joaseiro is the key point . . . , the point desired and loved by all, appropriate for a great Chair of learning in civilization and Faith among populations that are becoming more barbarous than they ever were . . . . '[It was you] who saw in the humble birthplace of your ancestors the Seat of a Bishopric [here] at the chapel of Our Lady of Sorrows. . . '."

26. Padre Cícero was made aware that the creation of a bishopric in Crato would be detrimental to him. Evidence of this is contained in Bartholomeu (1923), p. 72, where Dr. Floro cites an undated letter that was written to the Patriarch at a time, probably in 1907, when it was widely believed that Padre Cícero had favored Crato as the site of the new diocese (see n. 24): "Another monsignor was so sure of the possibility that a bishopric in Crato, two and a half leagues from Joaseiro, would add to the martyrdom of his friend, Padre Cícero, that upon learning of the latter's efforts of getting it [in Crato], he told him in a letter something like the following—'I'm amazed by your insistence in wanting the bishopric there; *si vôce com um bispo distante, vae amargando o pão que o demônio amassou, quanto mais com um trepado na sua garupa'*."

27. *Ibid.*

28. Pinheiro (1963), p. 175; pp. 504-505.

29. Telegram, Padre Cícero to Dr. Leandro Bezerra, 10 December 1908. The original is in the Personal Archive of Dr. Leandro Bezerra's grandson, Dr. Geraldo Bezerra de Menezes (hereinafter cited as GBM) who is a resident of Niterói, Rio de Janeiro State.

30. In a letter to Padre Cícero from Dom Ruperto Rudolph, the Benedictine Abbot at Quixadá, and successor of Dom Bonifácio (see n. 22), the monk offered to sell the Patriarch the monastery's holdings in Coxá. He said that, from the Patriarch's previous correspondence with the order, he knew of his intention "to make them a part of the patrimony of the future diocese of the Cariry," Dom Ruperto to Padre Cícero, 16 August 1913, ACS, Pasta da Correspondência com as Ordens Religiosas.

31. Padre Cícero to Dr. Leandro Bezerra, 21 April 1909, GBM.

32. Padre Cícero to José Marrocos, 21 April 1909, ACS, Bispado do Cariri. According to this letter, the cleric intended to leave on 23 April. His first stop was Fortaleza where Dom Joaquim required him to make the annual retreat of the clergy. From there, he went by ship to Rio de Janeiro where he was expected to arrive on 31 May 1909 according to the *Hebdomidário Cathólico* (Rio de Janeiro), 27 May 1909. That newspaper noted: "One of the purposes of the voyage of the virtuous priest from Ceará is to promote the creation of a bishopric in the *sertão* of Crato or Joaseiro. . . ."

That Padre Cícero expected to erect the Diocese in Joaseiro is certain from his request to José Marrocos, 19 January 1909, ACS, Bispado do Cariri, to prepare a fund-raising circular. In a copy of the circular, it was proposed that Joaseiro be the seat of a diocese which would embrace all of the Cariry Valley as far north as Icó, Ceará; west to Picos, Piauí; east to Cajazeiras, Paraíba, and south to Petrolina, Pernambuco.

33. *Unitário* (Fortaleza), 29 June 1909. This paper was founded in 1903 by Ceará's brilliant journalist João Brígido dos Santos (1829–1921). Its appearance marked Brígido's inexplicable break with the government of Gov. Accioly, whom he had served as editor of *A Républica*, the official organ of the PRC-C. Oddly, after Brígido had helped overthrow Accioly in 1912, he later worked to restore the oligarch's power. Unfortunately, there is no biography of this man who recorded so much of, and actively played a significant part in, Ceará's political history from the 1860s until 1921.

In 1948, *Unitário* republished many of João Brígido's articles as well as assessments of him. This tribute ran from 13 July to 18 July 1948 and constitutes an important source for any future study of the journalist.

34. Our account is based on Pinheiro (1938), pp. 183-184. Pinheiro claims that "one of the causes of the aggression against Crato was the demarcation of the Coxá fields. . . ." (p. 183).

35. The preceding account of the Furtado-Antonio Luis feud is factually documented in the excellent and detailed study of Figueiredo Brito (1959), pp. 39-40, 51-53, and alluded to with reservations in Pinheiro (1938), p. 191. The interpretation is my own.

The family and political ties between Col. Antonio Luis and Dr. Accioly are cited in Figueiredo Brito (1959), pp. 47, 54-55, and Souza Carvalho (1953–1954).

Biographical data on Col. Antonio Luis Alves Pequeno (1864–1942) can be found in Guimarães (1952), pp. 184-186. He should not be confused with his father and grandfather whose names are exactly the same, an error that seriously distorts the account of Pereira de Queiroz (1965) in regard to the Crato-Joaseiro rivalry.

36. The important theme of conflict between landowners and merchants in the interior as a consequence of the changing economic structure of the Northeast is suggested, but in a very different context, by Facó (1963), pp. 149-168. Unfortunately, unavailable statistical data prevent a more systematic pursuit of this theme, other than that presented throughout this chapter.

In the case at hand, there is abundant evidence that Furtado's opposition was due to his dislike of the common practice of Valley merchants to invest a good share of their profits in agricultural enterprises. Thus the merchant-*fazendeiros* were far more secure in times of drought than were the traditional solitary *fazendeiros*.

37. See Pinheiro (1938), pp. 183-184. According to the article "Inedictoriaes— As Ultimos Acontecimentos," *O Rebate* (Joaseiro), 25 July 1909, the three merchants from Barbalha had prevented the armed conflict by having all the parties agree to attend a conference that never took place. According to this account, the possibility of violence ended by May 1909. A leading role in the conciliatory initiative was played by Raimundo Gomes de Mattos, Governor Accioly's son-in-law.

38. *O Rebate* (Joaseiro), 18 July 1909. Its last issue, the one hundred and fourth, appeared on 3 September 1911. An incomplete collection is located at the Biblioteca Nacional, Rio de Janeiro. A more complete collection is in the hands of Fr. Cícero Coutinho of Joaseiro, to whom I am deeply grateful for his generous permission to microfilm this invaluable source.

Dr. Floro referred to Cícero's return in Bartholomeu (1923), pp. 106-107, n. 29. He erroneously dated the journey as 1910 instead of 1909.

Dr. Floro did note the exceptional reception which Padre Cícero received during his overland trip to Joaseiro in Alagôas, where the governor officially greeted him, and in Bahia and Pernambuco. This visit, still remembered by the old-timers of the region, may partially explain the extraordinary influence of the priest among the inhabitants of the São Francisco River region. See Chapter V, n. 14, of this work.

Several references to the influx of Alagôans into Joaseiro between 1903 and 1911 are contained in Alencar Peixoto (1913), pp. 117, 165, 171.

39. An incomplete biographical sketch of Fr. Joaquim de Alencar Peixoto (1871–1957) appeared in *O Rebate* (Joaseiro), 26 April 1911. Fr. Peixoto stoutly refused to accept any pastoral duties, an attitude that led the vicar of Crato, Fr. Quintino, to raise indirectly the issue of the former's suspension: "I never spoke of his suspension; clearly that is not my prerogative even though I believe him to merit that punishment," Fr. Quintino to D. Joaquim, 28 October 1907, ABC.

In 1904, Fr. Peixoto, a part-time journalist, actively supported Col. Antonio Luis in the deposition of Col. Belém. In 1907, however, the maverick priest broke with Antonio Luis and, without permission of his bishop, went to Joaseiro where he resided after 15 August 1907. Although Fr. Peixoto attended the spiritual needs of Joaseiro without authorization, he most likely went there with the intent of inciting the hamlet to seek its autonomy from Crato, in his mind, a decisive act of political revenge against his enemy, Col. Antonio Luis.

40. The exchange of telegrams between Padre Cícero, Governor Accioly and Col. Antonio Luis were published, undated, in *O Rebate* (Joaseiro) 25 July, 15 August, and 22 August 1909. Proof that these telegrams were exchanged in July 1909 is contained in the *O Rebate* editorial (*artigo de fundo*) published the following year on 25 September 1910, "Quem não gostar que se morda": "In July of last year [1909] upon returning from Rio and learning of what had come to pass in the Cariry, Padre Cícero resolved to telegraph H. Exc., the President of the State and Snr. Antonio Luiz to the same effect [i.e., in regard to Joaseiro's elevation to municipal status]."

41. In a bitter mood, Dom Joaquim wrote Fr. Quintino of Crato shortly after Padre Cícero left Joaseiro: "Let me tell you once and for all: even if Padre Cícero manages to put together a patrimony of a thousand contos, I shall never agree to the erection of the diocese in Joaseiro which is inhabited by exploiters and the exploited." He went on to encourage Fr. Quintino to accept the challenge and, in return, promised to take the lead himself. He gave Quintino two years to raise the money, Dom Joaquim to Fr. Quintino, 19 April 1909, ABC.

According to two letters from Msgr. Antonio de Macedo Costa, an influential priest in Petropolis, to Padre Cícero, 8 and 15 June 1909 ACS Dom Joaquim's charges against the Patriarch proved so detrimental that neither the Archbishop of Rio, Dom Joaquim Cardinal Arcoverde nor the papal nuncio could act contrary to the wishes of the Ceará bishop.

Apparently Dom Joaquim and Padre Cícero had met at the Mosteiro de São Bento in Rio. Msgr. Macedo then added: "After seeing the cordial manner in which Dom Joaquim received you at the Monastery and hearing the terrible accusations that he made against you [later] to the nuncio, *mystério . . . mystério . . . mystério. . . .*" Cited in Bartholomeu (1923), pp. 177-178, n. 43.

42. Crato's inability to raise funds for the patrimony of the new diocese was so evident that when the Holy See finally granted the privilege to Crato, in 1914, the patrimony had still not been raised; Pinheiro (1963), p. 505.

After the Patriarch's return to Joaseiro in July 1909, he continued to work for Joaseiro's selection as the diocesan seat. On 11 April 1910, he wrote to the widow of the Baron of Ibiapaba asking her to contribute 150 contos to the patrimony. Correspondence between the Patriarch and the Baroneza began on 25 September 1908 and continued through 1914. These letters are in ACS, Bispado do Cariri.

The view that Padre Cícero entered politics because of his problems with the church hierarchy is expressed by two authors. Abelardo Montenegro (1955) imprecisely argues: "Fearing that his prestige before the backland masses might be destroyed by the church, he entered into partisan politics" (p. 89).

A more authoritative view which takes into account the violent antecedents at Coxá, but at the same time inexplicably ignores the question of the bishopric, is Irineu Pinheiro's (1938): "one comes to the conclusion that Padre Cícero finally judged that through political influence he could be better able to resolve the question [assumedly that of his clerical reinstatement] which interested him so much. Henceforward, his gradual entry, perhaps without perceiving it, into the always charged field of politics" (p. 166).

43. Information about Dom Manuel Antonio de Oliveira Lopes, and the pastoral visit to the Cariry—Joaseiro was purposely excluded from the itinerary—are contained in Pinheiro (1963), pp. 178-180 and in the memoirs of Dom Joaquim's then secretary, Msgr. José Quinderé (1957), pp. 45-51.

44. Bartholomeu (1923), p. 57. The priest in question was Fr. Antonio Tabosa Braga.

45. Bartholomeu (1923), p. 57. Dr. Floro's original articles are: Manuel Ferreira de Figueiredo [pseudonym of Floro Bartholomeu], "Justa Defeza," "Olho por Olho, Dente por Dente" and "Os Effeitos da Imprudencia," *O Rebate* (Joaseiro), 29 August, 12 and 19 September 1909.

46. The term "alter ego" was used for the first time by Fr. Manuel Macedo, a native son of Joaseiro, in a series of articles originally published in the Catholic weekly, *O Nordeste* (Fortaleza), June 1925 and subsequently collected and re-published as a book, entitled *Joazeiro em Fóco* (Fortaleza 1925), p. 10. The term "alter ego" became (and still is) the most celebrated characterization of Dr. Floro after it was popularized as a chapter title in Lourenço Filho's work (1926), Chapter VI: "O 'Alter-Ago' . . . ," pp. 77-84.

Fr. Azarias Sobreira's characterization of Floro as the "Bahian Caudilho" (1950) has never caught on.

47. For information about D. Hermínia see the unflattering portrait by Alencar Peixoto (1913), pp. 147-152 and Floro's own account in Bartholomeu (1923), pp. 60-63.

48. Bartholomeu (1923), pp. 60-61.

49. Padre Cícero to José Marrocos, 5 October 1906, ACS: "I was passing the cemetery that is almost finished except for some plastering and I began the foundations [*sic*] of the chapel of O. L. of Perpetual Help.

"The vicar [of Crato] ordered me to request the bishop for the license and I have taken it upon myself to build [the chapel]." The "license" may refer either to canonical permission required to open the cemetery or build the church. It is unclear from the text of the letter but it presumably referred to the latter.

50. Bartholomeu (1923), p. 61.

51. Hermínia died on 15 November 1908. On the first anniversary of her death a requiem mass was celebrated for her in Joaseiro, according to *O Rebate* (Joaseiro), 21 November 1909.

52. Bartholomeu (1923), p. 62.

53. *Ibid.* This episode over D. Hermínia led the cleric to include in his will both a defense of the woman's virtue and, hence, a justification for his decision to bury her in the Chapel of Our Lady of Sorrows; see *Cópia do Testamento* (n.d.), 8. Although the chapel was not consecrated until after the Patriarch's

death, he had both his mother and sister buried there, as well as Maria de Araújo. In his will, he asked that he himself be laid to rest there, a request that was fulfilled upon his death on 20 July 1934.

54. In 1913, two years after *O Rebate's* editor, Fr. Joaquim de Alencar Pexioto, broke with the Patriarch over political matters, the priest-journalist published his own account of *"l'affaire* D. Hermínia." In it, he implied that the Patriarch had seduced the virtuous woman; Alencar Peixoto (1913), pp. 147-152, esp. pp. 150-151.

It was this accusation, the first and last ever made against Padre Cícero's celibacy, that prompted the Patriarch to declare proudly in his will: "I must also declare, because it is for me a great honor and one of the many effects of Divine grace upon me, that by virtue of a vow made by me at the age of twelve after reading about the Immaculate life of St. Francis de Sales, I have remained chaste and pure until this day," *Cópia do Testamento* (n.d.), p. 3.

55. Aires de Menezes (unpublished ms., 1963): in the early 1900s "it was José Lôbo who kept abreast of all of Padre Cícero's affairs including his correspondence with pilgrims from all the Northeastern states. . . . Zé Lôbo had the responsibility of answering all these letters giving replies to the many requests on behalf of Padre Cícero," (p. 43). By 1908 and 1909, the correspondence was greatly reduced, partly because the pilgrims preferred "to come personally to Joaseiro" (p. 68).

56. Aires de Menezes (unpublished MS, 1963), pp. 68-72.

57. José Marrocos to Padre Cícero, 19 July 1909, PCC.

58. José Marrocos to Padre Cícero, 22 July 1909, PCC.

59. [José Marrocos], *Joaseiro: A Carta do Snr. Nicodemos Resposta de José de Arimatea* (1909 [?], no publisher), an original copy of this pamphlet was kindly presented to the author in 1964 by the late Sr. Odílio Figueiredo, a native of Joaseiro and resident in Fortaleza.

60. Alencar Peixoto (1913), pp. 81 and 215-216, is the author of this accusation.

61. On 21 August 1910, *O Rebate* (Joaseiro) devoted its entire issue to the memory of José Marrocos. In it, Dr. Floro's funeral oration was published under the title "Oração Funebre."

62. This viewpoint, perhaps, based on oral history, was presented only recently by Gomes de Araújo (1962), p. 15, n. 25:

"The version is that Floro Bartolomeu da Costa was the author of the poisoning because Padre Cícero, long since entreated by Comendador Nogueira Accioly to join the *Partido Repúblicano do Ceará,* always refused [sic], on the counsel of . . . Professor José Joaquim Teles Marrocos. The victim [Marrocos] had hardly shut his eyes, [when]the executioner [Floro] took off for his *fazenda,* "Barreiros' [in Missão Velha]. *Inasmuch as no suspicion arose against him,* he returned to Joaseiro and even delivered the funeral oration beside the tomb of his victim . . ." (italics mine).

In our opinion, Fr. Gomes de Araújo has no evidence whatsoever to prove that Floro poisoned Marrocos. His chief source, Alencar Peixoto, was noted for his exaggeration as well as a deep streak of political vengeance which he vented on Padre Cícero and Floro alike. Also, Fr. Gomes de Araújo *himself* notes that, at the time of Marrocos' death, Floro was in no way held suspect!

63. Alencar Peixoto (1913), pp. 79-83, accused Padre Cícero of being a "fatal influence" over his friends. In the author's fashion, he relates the "fate" of the Patriarch's former defenders: José Marrocos; Msgr. Monteiro; Fr. Joaquim Sother; Fr. João Carlos; Fr. Vincente Sother de Alencar; Fr. Clycério da Costa Lôbo; Fr. Francisco Ferreira Antero; Dr. Marcos Rodrigues Madeira; Dr. Ildefonso Lima; Col. Secundo Chaves; Lt. Col. José Joaquim de Maria Lôbo; Maj. João Cyriaco; Capt. Belmiro Maia and Lt. José Duda. Despite Alencar Peixoto's exaggeration, all these persons who ranked among Padre Cícero's intimates were either dead or aged or too distant geographically to exert any influence over the Patriarch in 1908, except for Marrocos. In a sense, Padre Cícero had outlived his "era" and, as a result, needed Floro more than ever before.

64. See Raimundo Girão, *História Econômica do Ceará* (Fortaleza, 1947), pp. 380-382, 401-460.

65. A critical view of *bacharelismo* is found in Sergio Buarque de Holanda, *Raizes do Brasil* (Rio de Janeiro, 1936), pp. 114-118. Under the Republic, the *bacharel* degree increasingly became a "mere entrée to a niche in a bureaucratic urban order," according to Richard Morse, *From Community to Metropolis* (Gainseville, Florida, 1958), p. 154. Although this assessment primarily refers to São Paulo, it is in our opinion, applicable also to the smaller "urban centers" of the *sertão*.

66. The celebrated Cearense novelist and sociologist Jader de Carvalho has documented the rise of the *bacherel* and the decline of the *coronel* in the *sertão* of Ceará in his satirical novel, *Sua Majestade, O Juiz* (São Paulo, n.d.). For a fictional commentary on the changes produced in Ceará after 1930, see Carvalho's *Aldeota* (São Paulo, 1963), the account of Fortaleza's most fashionable suburban area whose rise was closely linked to the profitable contraband activities of some of its residents.

67. Relevant data can be found in Souza Carvalho (1953–1954) and Pinheiro (1963), p. 209.

68. Based on [Guilherme] Barão de Studart, *Para a História do Jornalismo Cearense, 1824–1924* (Fortaleza, 1924), pp. 151-174.

69. Floro's favorable reception in Joaseiro by villagers and the Patriarch alike—an admission few writers have been willing to concede—is found in the work of Joaseiro's erstwhile chief historian, Aires de Menezes (unpublished MS, 1963), pp. 73-74: "Upon his arrival here he installed an *ambulatório* (clinic) on Rua S. Pedro where he began his practice. Given the lack of doctors at that time in Joaseiro, Dr. Floro quickly built up a vast clientele and became the private physician of Padre Cícero. . . . Floro realized that the sure road to win the sympathy and support of the people would be [through] his profession as a doctor; he could give himself entirely to his work in favor of the people and with

no need for personal profit. With this in mind, he set himself to the task. Dr. Floro was a dynamo, he attended whomever sought him with the solicitude of a true apostle of medicine. Soon, there was not a home that had not received Dr. Floro when sickness arrived. The people saw in Dr. Floro a friend and a charitable doctor who attended the rich and poor with the same solicitude and without regard to their social position. The seed was planted, the people were on his side, it was only necessary to wait for an opportunity." Floro's favorable reception was also confirmed by D. Maria Gonçalves Rocha Leal in an interview in Fortaleza on 4 July 1964.

Another probable boost to Floro's success as a physician was the discovery, just about this time, that Sr. Ernesto Rabello, Joaseiro's chief pharmacist and self-styled doctor, had adulterated his pharmaceutical preparations with homegrown substitutes. Several deaths were attributed to this malpractice and the charlatan was quickly run out of town, according to Alencar Peixoto (1913), pp. 133-136.

70. For a modern political scientist's discussion of the doctor as an alternative type of "political chief," see Jean Blondel, *As Condições da Vida Politica no Estado da Paraíba* (Rio de Janeiro, 1957), pp. 57-72, esp. pp. 70-72, "o médico."

Chapter 7
Joaseiro Bids for Autonomy

1. Pinheiro (1963), p. 505.
2. See Chapter V of the text.
3. Bartholomeu (1923), p. 57, n. 8 gives details on the strike. According to Manuel Ferreira de Figueiredo [pseudonym of Floro Bartholomeu], "Os Effeitos da prudência," *O Rebate* (Joaseiro), 26 September 1909, the "strike" was apparently called by Padre Cícero to protect his pilgrims from "any cranks who might . . . mistreat them . . . [and thus] precipitate conflicts [between Joaseiro and Crato]."

In this article, Dr. Floro also defended the pilgrims whom Fr. Tabosa had condemned as "followers of Satan." Dr. Floro's arguments further illustrate the important contribution of the pilgrims to the economy of the Cariry (see Chapter V): While everywhere in the Northeast there is a massive emigration to the rubber forests of the Far North, "the *sertão* progresses and especially the Cariry because of the influx of pilgrims to Joaseiro. . . ."

Floro contrasted the pilgrim (*romeiro*) to the bandit (*cangaceiro*): "if it weren't for the *romeiro,* the productive element of these regions, concentrating his energies in favor of material development, we would consequently have the predominancy of the *cangaceiro,*—the destructive element.

"Do you think these pilgrims would come, making up [by their presence] for the scarcity of the local population, making us happy by their efforts, were it not for the providential influence of Rev. Padre Cícero?

". . . Immigration [is] a force for progress; therefore the *romeiros* of Joaseiro, because they are hard-working, are truly useful immigrants."

4. Montenegro (1959), p. 32, correctly observes: "The struggle between Joaseiro and Crato had an undisguiseable economic cause."

5. See "Abaixo a Intriga!" in *O Rebate* (Joaseiro), 5 December 1909. This article alludes to the statement in Crato's *Correio do Cariry*.

6. Flávio Gouvêia [pseudonym for Floro Bartholomeu], "Joaseiro," in *O Rebate* (Joaseiro), 29 May 1910.

7. *Correio's* attack is cited in "A Mentira," *O Rebate* (Joaseiro), 19 June 1910.

8. Attitudes toward Peixoto are cited in the only published, but sometimes inaccurate, secondary account of Joaseiro's campaign for autonomy written by a native of Joaseiro, Fr. Cícero Coutinho, "A Política em Juàzeiro, logo após sua Independência," *O Jornal do Cariry* (Juàzeiro do Norte), 30 July 1950b.

In a letter from Crato's Vicar, Fr. Quintino to Dom Joaquim, n.d. (but ca. 25 December 1910–1 January 1911), ABC, Fr. Peixoto was reportedly confessing the young women of Joaseiro in the home of a private citizen whose own daughter, it was rumored, became the object of Fr. Peixoto's affections.

9. The Fortaleza import-export agent, Adolpho Barroso, chief buyer of Joaseiro's *maniçoba* rubber, was an ardent advocate of Joaseiro's cause before Governor Accioly. In a letter from Barroso to Padre Cícero, 30 August 1910, PCC, the merchant claimed that Accioly said: "Tell Padre Cícero that he merits my full attention, however, insofar as he favors Fr. Peixoto, I [Accioly] cannot take a single step on his behalf. . . ."

Souza Carvalho (1953–1954: 3 January 1954) also asserts that Accioly would not grant Joaseiro autonomy "without the 'placet' of his friend and relative, Col. Antonio Luis Alves Pequeno."

10. "A Mentira," *O Rebate* (Joaseiro), 19 June 1910.

11. See an earlier article by Fr. Cícero Coutinho, "A Independência do Joaseiro," in *Jornal do Cariry* (Juàzeiro do Norte), 23 July 1950a. This article was republished in *O Pioneiro* (Juàzeiro do Norte), 22 July 1953.

12. Padre Cícero to Governor Accioly, 26 July 1910, ACS.

In an earlier letter from Padre Cícero to Accioly, 16 June 1910, ACS, the cleric had attempted to keep the police battalion out of Crato for fear that Col. Antonio Luis might use them against Joaseiro.

This fear was not unfounded since despite Accioly's claim that the battalion was sent to put down *cangaceiros*, Adolpho Barroso advised Padre Cícero that the troops were really dispatched "because of the injurious articles of *O Rebate*. Here [in Fortaleza] everyone expected a revolution," Barroso to Padre Cícero, 30 August 1910, PCC.

13. On Accioly's neutrality or reticence, see Pinheiro (1938), p. 30.

14. According to the octogenarian José Ferreira Bezerra da Menezes, a native son of Joaseiro and Dr. Floro's intimate friend and right-hand man, the first meeting of Joaseiro's politicians had taken place on 10 July 1910 in the dry-goods store of the merchant, Manoel Victorino da Silva. There, it was resolved to hold a rally on 15 August. This information is contained in the author's unpublished manuscript, which he kindly put at our disposal, "A Minha Historia sôbre as cousas antigas e modernas do Juaseiro" unpublished MS, 1936).

15. Based on Sousa Carvalho (1953–1954). In the article of 3 January 1954, the author denies that Col. Antonio Luis Alves Pequeno intended to blackmail Padre Cícero with the cloths, an assertion that fails to hold up under careful scrutiny.

16. Telegram, Accioly to Padre Cícero, 20 August 1910, ACS; also the letter from Accioly to Padre Cícero, 20 August 1910, PCC, in which Accioly wrote: "With satisfaction, I note that Y. Rev. approved the creation of a mobile force [*companhia volante*] that is there for the purpose of giving chase to *cangaceiros* who have caused so much evil in those zones of the state." Thus, Antonio Luis' pride was preserved.

17. Antonio Luis' refusal was noted in "A Questão do Joaseiro—como o Snr. Antonio Luiz Abusou da Prudência do Povo do Joaseiro," in *O Rebate* (Joaseiro), 4 September 1910.

18. Souza Carvalho (1953–1954), *passim*.

In addition to the box, there were supposedly two manuscripts of Marrocos' which dealt with the religious question of Joaseiro, as well as a chemistry book in French that contained the chemical formula allegedly used by the deceased to transform hosts into blood; on this point, also consult Gomes de Araújo (1956), *passim,* and (1962), pp. 14-16.

The Patriarch's fear that Dom Joaquim might have obtained the box is implied in Alencar Peixoto (1913), pp. 216-218.

19. The telegram is quoted, unsigned, in Alencar Peixoto (1913), p. 218. The author claims that shortly after Governor Accioly had gotten the box, he dispatched the telegram in order to force Padre Cícero to join the PRC-C. This seems unlikely, since the Patriarch had already acceded to Accioly's various demands which, in turn, had proven satisfactory enough for the oligarch to promise on 20 August 1910 to elevate Joaseiro (see n. 85).

Who had the box has been open to debate. In light of subsequent events we agree with Souza Carvalho (1953–1954) who says that it always remained in Antonio Luis' possession. Alencar Peixoto (1913), pp. 218-219 and Gomes de Araújo (1962), pp. 14-16 claim that Accioly had received it.

Furthermore, Father Quintino's hitherto unpublished letter to Dom Joaquim, n.d. (but ca. 25 December 1910–1 January 1911), ABC, has this to say: "In regard to the cloths of the Joaseiro question, it's not worth trying to get them because they are not in the possession of any official *but rather in the hands of Col. Antonio Luis* who ordered them to be stored safely there [in Fortaleza]. . . . With the cloths, all dated and signed by Padre Cícero, [Antonio Luis] is counting [on using them] *to put pressure on the very same priest*. The fact that Padre Cícero has been unable to get back his 'sacred' package . . . has been the chief reason for the truculent combat—of unknowable consequences—in which the two paladins of our press, *O Rebate* and *O Correio do Cariry* are now engaged . . ." (italics mine).

20. The undated meeting which probably took place after Col. Antonio Luis had returned to Crato on 31 August 1910, is recalled in Souza Carvalho (1953–1954: 10 January 1954). The author, who was not present, claims that Padre

Cícero confessed to Antonio Luis both his disbelief in the miracles and his fear of revealing this to his followers. Details and a supposedly verbatim transcript of the alleged conversation are contained in Montenegro (1959), pp. 5-7.

In our opinion the charge of duplicity made against the Patriarch does not seem adequately documented. Moreover, Irineu Pinheiro (1963) insists that Padre Cícero died in the conviction that the miracles of 1889–1891 were of divine origin (p. 533).

21. Based entirely on the published contemporary account "Independência do Joaseiro-Passeiatas e Discursos," *O Rebate* (Joaseiro), 4 September 1910.

22. Pinheiro (1963), 505.

23. Maj. Joaquim Bezerra's attempt is alluded to in "A Questão do Joaseiro," *O Rebate* (Joaseiro), 18 September 1910, and in "Quem não Gostar, que se morda . . . ," *O Rebate* (Joaseiro), 25 September 1910.

24. "A Questão do Joaseiro," *O Rebate* (Joaseiro), 11 and 18 September 1910.

25. *Ibid.,* 18 September 1910.

26. Adolpho Barroso to Padre Cícero, 2 January 1911, ACS, noted that telegrams had reached Fortaleza officials alleging that Joaseiro's position was a defensive one. He then saw to it that this viewpoint was presented to high level federal officials in order "to call this to the attention of the federal government inasmuch as the State Government refuses to budge."

27. See Coutinho (1950a and b), *passim.*

28. "Independência do Joaseiro-Passeiatas e Discursos," in *O Rebate* (Joaseiro), 4 September 1910.

29. The *cámara municipal* of Missão Velha submitted its full agreement to the new boundaries with Joaseiro in an official communiqué addressed to Ceará's Legislative Assembly on 23 August 1910, ACS.

A similar declaration from Barbalha was not found.

30. This explains why it was the Barbalha merchants, Srs. S. Sampaio, A. S. Filgueiras, J. C. de Sá Barretto, and A. Grangeiro who rushed to mediate (with partial success) the feud of May 1909; Chapter VI, see n. 37.

Talks between the merchants of Barbalha and Missão Velha regarding their "common political interests" date from 1909; see "Inedictoriaes—Os Ultimos Acontecimentos," in *O Rebate* (Joaseiro), 25 July 1909.

31. See *O Rebate* (Joaseiro), 18 and 25 September 1910. On the Aurora question, see the partial account in Pinheiro (1938), p. 182.

32. Floro Bartholomeu da Costa, "De Água Abaixo, Não Irá o Joaseiro," in *O Rebate* (Joaseiro) 8, 15, 22, 29 January, 5 February 1911a.

33. On Col. Nelson Franca de Alencar's last minute alliance with Antonio Luis in the revolt of 1904, see Figueiredo Brito (1959), pp. 46-47. The chief reason for his change of heart appears to have been his brother-in-law's audacious shooting of Belém's despised police chief. It is unknown whether Col. Nelson's brother-in-law, Horácio Jacome, intentionally sparked the revolt or not. If affirmative, it must be asked why the powerful Col. Nelson did not become the new prefect of Crato, but rather, the merchant Antonio Luis? Much of the

answer may rest with the fact that Antonio Luis was the first cousin of both Jacome and Ceará's Governor Accioly.

Information on Col. Nelson is found in the eulogy of Alves de Figueiredo (1958), pp. 67-69.

34. Details are found in Dr. Floro Bartholomeu de Côsta "Última Palavra," *O Rebate* (Joaseiro), 26 February 1911b.

35. An account of the agreement is contained in a letter from Padre Cícero to Governor Accioly, 22 February 1911, ACS.

36. Padre Cícero to Cols. Abdon Franca de Alencar, et al., 3 March 1911, ACS. This letter, written in Floro's hand, still insisted that Joaseiro be made a police district, a concession that was confirmed by the Legislative Assembly and thus gave the new *município* the right to quarter troops there.

37. Accioly to Padre Cícero, 7 October 1910, PCC.

38. See Montenegro (1965), *passim,* esp. p. 42.

39. Under the pseudonym of Martin Soares, the celebrated Cearense writer Antonio Salles published a book, entitled *O Rabaquara* (Rio de Janeiro, 1912).

40. The most detailed account of the growth of opposition to Accioly is contained in Theophilo (1914), 5-88.

41. Bello (1966), p. 213.

42. See note 34.

43. In the letter from Padre Cícero to Accioly, 22 February 1911, ACS, the Patriarch noted that on 15 February—three days before the official Crato peace delegation arrived in Joaseiro—Fr. João Carlos Augusto came to Joaseiro. It was he who, on "the request of Crato's merchants and other prominent persons of Crato such as . . . Irineu Pinheiro," initially proposed peace talks.

Evidence that Accioly most probably had inspired the peace talks is alluded to in the above letter. The Patriarch acknowledged Accioly's communiqué of 6 February 1910. The gist of Padre Cícero's reply is that Accioly had advised him of the plan for peace talks.

The role of Fr. João Carlos Augusto is also cited in Bartholomeu (1911b).

44. *O Rebate's* (Joaseiro) entire issue of 26 April 1911 was devoted to Fr. Peixoto's birthday. Four days later the issue was dedicated to Dr. Floro's *formatura*. The fact that the latter edition appeared three days before schedule clearly indicates the intensity of the competition between Dr. Floro and Fr. Peixoto.

45. The PRC-C platform was published in two installments in *O Rebate* (Joaseiro), 14 and 28 May 1911.

46. [Fr. Joaquim de Alencar Peixoto], "Ao Público," *O Rebate* (Joaseiro), 27 August 1911.

47. Padre Cícero to Accioly, 18 June 1911, ACS.

48. José André's demotion to *intendente,* soon after which he disappeared from Joaseiro's political scene is noted in Coutinho (1950b). However, the author offers no explanation for this move other than Dr. Floro's ambition to get "the plate of lentils."

49. Theophilo (1914), *passim*; for the role of the Commercial Association of

Ceará in the demonstrations against Accioly in December, 1911, see pp. 91-92.

50. Padre Cícero to José Accioly, 18 October 1911, ACS.

51. Padre Cícero to Government Accioly, 18 June 1911, ACS. In this letter the Patriarch reminded the Governor, with some exaggeration, that Joaseiro would be the "largest [bailiwick] in the *sertão* of the State." This was clearly a case of political pressure on the Governor.

52. In a most important letter from Padre Cícero to Col. Antonio Luis Alves Pequeno, 1 October 1911 [?], ACS, the Patriarch wrote that the pact was the "wish of Dr. Accioly . . . *compadre* Sant'Anna was appointed by Dr. Accioly to propose this accord. . . ."

Fr. Gomes de Araújo's (1962) claim that the pact was conceived and executed by Barbalha's judge, Arnulpho Lins da Silva, seems invalidated (p. 11). His account of the pact's significance is also inaccurate, since it makes no reference to Accioly's role or broader political concerns.

53. Padre Cícero to Col. Antonio Luis, 1 October 1911 [?], ACS.

54. The pact is found in Pinheiro (1938), pp. 174-180 and in Macêdo (1961), pp. 120-123.

55. Padre Cícero to Adolpho Barroso, 18 October 1911, ACS.

56. Theophilo (1914), p. 72.

57. *Ibid.*, p. 77.

Chapter 8
The Cariry Bids for Statewide Power

1. Theophilo (1914).

2. Two recent studies which clearly place Accioly's downfall within a national political perspective are: Afonso Arinos de Melo Franco, *Um Estad ista da República* (Rio de Janeiro, 1955), II, 701-703, 722-741; and, Nelson Werneck Sodré, *Históri ta Militar do Brasil* (Rio de Janeiro, 1965), pp. 190-198.

3. Bello (1966), p. 213. It must also be remembered that Rui Barbosa was supported by the influential coffee interests of São Paulo without which all his middle class support elsewhere would have been of little avail.

4. In 1908, Accioly succeeded himself in the governorship after first rigging a 1907 amendment to the state constitution that until then prohibited consecutive reelection. These two events did much to rally opposition forces prior to the 1910 "civilianist" campaign. Both events are discussed in Frota Pessôa (1910), pp. 135-170 and Theophilo (1914), pp. 21-35.

The fraudulent elections of 1910 in Ceará are cited in Theophilo (1914), p. 170.

5. Melo Franco (1955), II, 702.

6. Melo Franco (1955) asserts that this shift was due to "ambitions unchained within the new dominant political party that was the army," II, 702. Sodré (1965) perceptively notes that "Rui's campaign was conducted in the name of *civilismo* which gave rise to a contradiction between civilians and the military that in reality did not exist" (p. 190).

For an excellent bibliographical summary of the middle-class origins of the officer corps prior to 1910, and also for the pitfalls of this hypothesis, see June E. Hahner, "Brazilian Civilian-Military Relations, 1889-1898" (Ithaca, Latin American Studies Program, Dissertation Series, Cornell University, 1967), pp. 117-119, n. 29. (Mimeographed.)

7. Besides Melo Franco (1955), *passim*, Sodré (1965), *passim*, Bello (1966), pp. 217-225, additional descriptive information and bibliography about the *salvações* can be found in Pedro Calmon, *Historia do Brasil* (Rio de Janeiro, 1959), VI, 2124-2140.

The historical interpretations about why the military intervened are unclear. Some writers contend that the military were seeking revenge against the urban middle classes, which, during the "civilianist" campaign, were staunchly anti-military. Our preference is for the hypothesis that, (a) the military were themselves of middle-class origins and sympathy and, (b) local opposition forces welcomed the military as the only instrument then capable of helping the former to seize power.

8. See Costa Porto, *Pinheiro Machado e Seu Tempo: Tentativa de Interpretação* (Rio de Janeiro, 1951), pp. 151-158. A less satisfactory biography is Cyro Silva, *Pinheiro Machado* (Rio de Janeiro, n.d.).

The earliest split between Minas Gerais and São Paulo, the two states which dominated the federal government of the Republic, was caused by the latter's refusal to allow a *mineiro* or *carioca* presidential successor who might prove detrimental to São Paulo's coffee interests. The issue is discussed in Santos (1930), pp. 432-433.

9. A description of Pinheiro Machado as the "Black Pope" is found in Santos (1930), p. 436; Calmon (1959), however, refers to him as the "homem forte," or strong-man (VI, 2136), apparently a more common term of the era.

It is important to note that Pinheiro Machado's quest for power and the presidency was symptomatic of his home-state's ambition to break the almost invincible control which Minas Gerais and São Paulo exercised over the federal government. The temporary split in this axis in 1910 saw Rio Grande do Sul, Brazil's third most populated and wealthy state, support Pinheiro Machado's efforts. This bid was successful only in 1930, when another native son, Getulio Vargas, came to power on the heels of the October revolution. Unsuccessful as Rio Grande was until 1930, its "third-force" position within a national political system otherwise dominated by the "politics of coffee and cream" (the phrase characterizing the coffee and dairy economies of the São Paulo-Minas political tandem) was largely responsible for generating a dynamism in the politics of Brazil after 1910. Without Rio Grande's offers of alliance, it seems unlikely that the Brazilian Northeast, whose relative economic stagnation had long since reduced its political importance within the Union, would have been able to demand greater regional benefits from the nation as was the case after 1915.

10. Theophilo (1914), pp. 74-76.

11. Theophilo (1914), pp. 82-85. Biographical data on Franco Rabelo (1861–

1920) can be found in Eusébio de Souza, *História Militar do Ceará* (Fortaleza, 1950), p. 306, n. 160.

12. Theophilo (1914), pp. 85-88; Melo Franco (1955), II, 724-725.

13. Theophilo (1914), pp. 38-48, 60-70. The importance of the Amazon rubber boom to Ceará is cited on p. 42. It is regrettable that no monographic study on Ceará's links to the Far North yet exists. Veritable panegyrics to the role of the Commercial Association are cited on p. 164 and 267-268.

14. Facó (1963), *passim*, and Sodré (1965), *passim*; Melo Franco (1955), II, 702-703.

15. These events are discussed in detail in Theophilo (1914), pp. 89-92, 103-106, 108-117.

16. Theophilo (1914), pp. 112, 122.

17. Theophilo (1914), pp. 118-157; esp., pp. 120-126, 138-140, 143.

18. Theophilo (1914), pp. 141, 160 for example, reluctantly recognized that proletarian action, quite independently of the middle-class anti-Accioly leadership, had greatly accounted for the oligarch's defeat. But he easily criticized their terrorism and branded the proletariat "as a child who easily deludes himself."

19. Theophilo (1914), pp. 140, 145, 148, 151. It is important to note that Accioly's 800-man mounted cavalry, called the *Força Pública*, deserted the battle (pp. 122, 147).

Msgr. José Quinderé, in his revisionist assessment of these events, *Comendador Antonio Pinto Nogueira Accioly* (Fortaleza, 1950), denies that Accioly resigned because of the inability of the federal military inspector, Col. José Faustino, to defend the oligarch. On the contrary, Mons. Quinderé says, it was Ceará's bishop, Dom José Joaquim Vieira, who persuaded the federal troops to desist from defending Accioly because the church leader believed the situation to be "irremediably lost" (pp.4-5).

Quinderé's study also praised Accioly for contributing to Ceará's progress and claims that the oligarch's downfall was detrimental to the very public advances which the middle class was clamoring for (pp. 5-6).

20. Theophilo (1914), pp. 141, 157-162.

21. Unfortunately, no study of Ceará's proletarian political history exists. Our revisionist interpretation of their role in the events of 1911–1912 is adduced from Theophilo's (1914) continuous repudiation of their acts of violence. Two workers parties that formed in Fortaleza on the heels of the proclamation of the Republic were subsequently betrayed by the elites; see Montenegro (1965, 36-38). A personal allusion to radical and marxist trade-unionism in Fortaleza around 1930 is found in a recent sensationalist, journalistic account of Joaseiro by Edmar Morel, *Padre Cícero, O Santo de Juazeiro* (Rio de Janeiro, 1946), pp. 215-222. Also see Pimenta (1947), *passim*.

22. The congressional elections are discussed in Theophilo (1914), pp. 102; 168-170.

23. For biographical details about Dr. Francisco de Paula Rodrigues, a descendant of the Paula Pessôa family which had opposed the Acciolys since the

Empire and to whom Franco Rabelo entrusted the leadership of the *"rabelista"* party in 1912, see the article by Plácido Aderaldo Castelo, "Deputado Paula Rodrigues," *RIC*, LXXVIII (1963), 307-312. The article also traces the disputes between the two families from the closing days of the empire until the 1930 revolution. Also see the viewpoint of a former political opponent, Manuel do Nascimento Fernandes Távora, "Dr. Francisco de Paula Rodrigues," *RIC*, LXXVIII (1963b), 299-306.

24. The components of *"rabelismo"* are noted in Theophilo (1914), pp. 141, 160. Another source and one of the best *rabelista* analyses of the events of 1912 was written by a member of *rabelismo's* "inner circle", Hermenegildo Firmeza, "A Revolução de 1912 no Ceará" (ed. by his son-in-law, Dr. José Bonifácio de Sousa), *RIC*, LXXVII (1963), 25-59. It is one of the most illustrative documents of Brazilian "clientele" politics during the old Republic.

25. Theophilo (1914), pp. 168-170.

26. Theophilo (1914), pp. 209-219.

27. Theophilo (1914), pp. 175-202; 222-252.

28. For the *rabelista* version of the pact with José Accioly, see Firmeza (1963), pp. 40-52; also, Theophilo (1914), 252-255. Our account excludes the finer points of the political wheeling and dealing, the various attempts to impose conciliatory candidates and a number of violent episodes, all of which played an important role in the final three-way division. For such details, consult the above works as well as Carneiro (1965), I, 188-189. The conclusions of our account however, are faithful.

29. Rabelo's electoral victory in Fortaleza was a resounding one; he received 1,491 votes to 210 votes given to Gen. José Bezerril Fontenele, who ran as the candidate of Pinheiro Machado, after the gaúcho strong-man and Cavalcante failed in their attempt to have Bezerril accepted as a "conciliatory" candidate by the *rabelistas* and *acciolystas*. Rabelismo's refusal is understandable, while Accioly refused because he feared that Bezerril, once elected, would resign the governorship and turn it over to Cavalcante, whose alliance with Pinheiro Machado had made him an enemy of the Acciolys. See Theophilo (1914), pp. 175-176; 179; 186-189; 192; 253.

The small size of Fortaleza's electorate, a total of 1,701 votes, gives some idea of the political scale and the basis of clientele politics.

30. For details on Rabelo's lack of a majority in the Assembly, see Theophilo (1914), pp. 255-265; Firmeza (1963), pp. 52-59.

31. Pereira de Queiroz (1965), pp. 321-327, speaks of a dichotomy between coast and backland. Unlike da Cunha (1944), *passim*, Pereira de Queiroz admits of interpenetration between backland and coastal cultures that need not be violent. However, contrary to our opinion, the author cites Joaseiro as an example of limited interpenetration (p. 320). For a critique of this theory of dualism, see Rodolpho Stavenhagen, "Seven Erroneous Theses about Latin America," *New University Thought*, IV (1966–1967), 4, 25-37, esp. 25-29.

32. According to Coutinho (1950b), Col. José André had assumed the post of

president of the city council in late 1911 but "did not remain very long in the slot which had been carved out for him." In fact, minutes of the city council's meetings in mid-year 1912 (cited below in n. 35) would seem to confirm that fact since his name does not appear among those participating in the meetings.

A rare copy of the handbill, entitled "Ao Povo", directed against José André was kindly made available by Sr. Odílio Figueiredo, a Joaseirense now residing in Fortaleza. A facsimile and a translation appear elsewhere in the text.

Floro Bartholomeu subsequently acknowledged his role in preventing José André's candidacy in one of a series of seven articles entitled "Formal Desmentido," *Unitário* (Fortaleza), 14 July 1915.

The charge that José André's family was held hostage appears in Peixoto Alencar (1913), pp. 224-225.

The view that José André remained the candidate of the native sons is expressed in the unpublished article of Octávio Aires de Menezes (1964), cited in full in n. 33, below.

33. The only secondary source that in any way illuminates Joaseiro's political history in 1912 is the unpublished article by the late Aires de Menezes, "Col. Franco Rabelo e a Revolução do Joaseiro" (unpublished MS, 1964). This was written to combat what Menezes considered to be a hostile article authored by Glauco Carneiro, "A Revolta dos Jagunços," *O Cruzeiro* (Rio de Janeiro), 4 August 1964, but it unfortunately never reached the press. He was kind enough to allow me to photograph his only copy shortly before his death.

Carneiro's article was later included in Volume I of his two-volume work on Brazilian revolutions (1965) I.

In a letter from Col. Joaquim Alves da Rocha to Padre Cícero, 25 February 1912, PCC, there are indications of the deep concern of the pro-Accioly *chefes* of Crato, Barbalha, and Jardim over retaining their political power.

34. Theophilo (1914), p. 229.

35. "Actas da pôsse dos veradores [do Joaseiro], José da Cruz Neves, secretário da câmara, reunião do 10 de junho de 1912," ACS. This document was notarized by the secretary and given to Padre Cícero. Unfortunately, the book in which the 1911-1912 *actas* (minutes) of the city council were recorded has been missing for decades from the archives of Joaseiro's *câmara municipal*.

36. Adolpho Barroso to Padre Cícero, 12 July 1912, PCC.

In one of the letters from the Fortaleza importer-exporter, Adolpho Barroso, to Padre Cícero, 24 May 1912, ACS, in which Rabelo's failure to secure a majority of votes in the Legislative Assembly was discussed, Barroso told the Patriarch: "In politics, you are more informed than I."

This view, in our opinion, is but another indirect indicator that the backlands kept abreast of coastal politics and was generally well-informed. It must be remembered that telegraphic communications between Crato and Fortaleza had existed since 1899. The telegraph station in Joaseiro was established about 1908 or 1909. Technological advance was of considerable importance in integrating a three-tiered political system in which region, state, and nation were bound up.

37. Adolpho Barroso to Padre Cícero, 30 August 1912, ACS.

38. "Circular No. 1 do Comité Executivo do Partido Marreta," 30 July 1912, addressed to Padre Cícero and found in PCC.

This circular announced that the party convention would be held in Fortaleza on 25 August 1912. Its principal goal was to nominate Marreta candidates for state deputies in view of the November 1912 elections. The circular openly condemned the "illfated accord celebrated in Rio . . ." between *rabelistas* and *acciolystas*.

39. Aires de Menezes (unpublished MS, 1964), p. 2.

40. *Ibid.,* pp. 2-3. Unfortunately, we have found no conclusive evidence about when and if a municipal election was held in Joaseiro. Aires de Menezes' account clearly speaks of local elections, although he gives no exact date. In contrast, the octogenarian, Col. João Bezerra de Menezes, in an interview he gave us on 1 August 1964 in Joaseiro, claimed that he was "selected" for the post by Padre Cícero. At that time, we were not aware of how significant Col. Bezerra's interview was to our work and, out of ignorance, did not press him for details.

41. Coutinho (1950b).

42. Aires de Menezes (unpublished MS., 1964) notes that by virtue of the alliance between Floro and Col. João Bezerra, "the candidacy of Snr. José André was liquidated without any possibility of victory. As it could not have been otherwise, João Bezerra was elected by an overwhelming majority of votes" (p. 3).

43. Rabelo's campaign pledge to have municipal prefects elected rather than appointed was contained in the only public speech he ever made during the entire campaign. It was given at a banquet offered in his honor by, (not surprisingly), the Commercial Association of Ceará on 21 March 1912. See Lt. Col. Marcos Franco Rabelo, "Plataforma, lido por occasião do banquete politico realizado no dia 21 de Março de 1912 no theatro José de Alencar pelo Tenente Coronel Dr. Marcos Franco Rabello, candidato á presidência do Ceará no quatrénio de 1912 à 1916," in Theophilo (1914), pp. 273-282.

The other seven planks in his platform reveal his strong appeal to middle-class demands: (1) end luxury spending and consumption by state authorities, impose austerity; (2) a balanced budget; (3) return budgetary control of *municípios* to local prefects; (4) expand educational facilities, especially in Fortaleza; choose professors according to individual merit; (5) reduce both the costs and size of the state's police force; institute a citizen-police force made up of members of the voluntary Rifle and Shooting Associations (then in vogue in Brazil); (6) judicial reform; (7) improve public sanitation, sewerage, and potable water supply and beautify the capital.

Item 3 was clearly a bid to gain support of interior chiefs who had been the traditional supporters of Accioly.

44. Figuereido Brito (1959), p. 55. The candidate of the successful coalition was Col. Francisco José de Britto, a merchant and rabid *rabelista,* unlike his purely pragmatic and conservative coalition partners, led by Col. Nelson da Franca Alencar. The account of Antonio Luis's removal from office is found in Pinheiro (1938), pp. 43-44.

45. Reported in the *rabelista* organ *Folha do Povo* (Fortaleza) 28 October

1912 and cited in Montenegro (1955), p. 73. The interpretation of this *rabelista* convention in Barbalha as comparable to the "Little Hague" (*Haya-mirim*) held in Joaseiro in October 1911 is our own. Regrettably, only the latter, because of Padre Cícero's presence, has been subject to study. The lack of adequate documentation at this writing prevents a more detailed analysis of the 1912 Barbalha meeting on behalf of Col. Franco Rabelo. The Cariry towns represented by *rabelistas* at the meeting were: Barbalha, Crato, Joaseiro, Milagres, Missão-Velha, Jardim, Brejo dos Santos, Santanna do Carirí, Aurora, Araripe, Campos Sales, Porteiras, São Pedro (Caririaçu), Assaré, Saboeiro; the peripheral towns of Iguatú, Quixadá, and São Mateus also sent representatives; Lavras did not.

46. Praise of Franco Rabelo's campaign against *cangaceirismo* is found in a series of articles by his nephew-in-law, Boanerges Facó, "Homens e Cousas— Ceará: Govêrno Franco Rabelo," *Unitário* (Fortaleza), 2, 9 and 15 August 1959a, esp. 9 August 1959.

47. Rodolpho Theophilo, *A Sedição do Joazeiro* (São Paulo, 1922), p. 28: the troops were commanded by Capt. Júlio Ladislau Lourenço de Sousa.

The above work is a sequel to Theophilo's *Libertação do Ceará* (1914) and is a detailed account of the fall of Franco Rabelo.

48. See Montenegro (1955), pp. 32-61, on the history of banditry in Ceará; Theophilo (1883), *passim,* on the rise of bandit groups (*cangaços*) during the drought of 1877–1879; and Facó (1963), *passim,* for a modern and marxian interpretation of *cangaceirismo*. The last contains important bibliographical references on the subject.

Unfortunately, there are few studies on *cangaceirismo* in the border states of Ceará, viz., Pernambuco, Paraíba, and Rio Grande do Norte, which were, in addition to the Cariry Valley the traditional "protected" zones of the *cangaceiros*. Until such studies are done and until a Northeastern region-wide perspective obtains in them, there can be no satisfactory evaluation of this problem in regard to the Cariry Valley.

49. One of the few bandit groups, if not the only one, that was able to retain its relative independence from local political chiefs was that led by the celebrated, Pernambucan-born, folk-hero, Antônio Silvino. Silvino, whose real name was Manoel Batista de Moraes (b. 1875), was willing to hire out his services to *coronéis* in several states, not unlike the Japanese *samurai*. For a long time, he was the one-man opponent of the extension of the Great Northwestern RR into the backlands of Pernambuco. A partial biography of Silvino is found in Gustavo Barroso's *Heróes e Bandidos (Os Cangaceiros do Nordeste),* (Rio de Janeiro, 1917), pp. 225-278, and in his *Almas de Lama e Aço* (São Paulo, 1930), pp. 75-89.

The most celebrated popular poetic account of Antônio Silvino is by one of the Northeast's most famous *cantadores* (a popular troubadour), F[rancisco] das Chagas Baptista, *História Completa de Antônio Silvino, Su Vida de Crime e seu Julgamento* (Rio de Janeiro, 1960).

50. The key piece of legislation which altered the police structure of Ceará was Law No. 146, adopted by the Legislative Assembly on 1 September 1894; cited in Montenegro (1955), p. 63.

51. The broader causes of Belém's downfall, viz., the emerging conflict between modern commercial and traditional agrarian interests have been alluded to elsewhere in this study.

52. Figueiredo Brito (1959) pp. 50; 53. Unfortunately, two generations of Crato historians (several of whom were related to Col. Antonio Luis) have consistently refused to lay any blame for the rise of *cangaceirismo* in the Cariry on the political chief's doorstep, where in our opinion a portion of it rightly belongs.

53. See Gomes de Araújo (1962), *passim.*

54. Details based on an interview with Col. João Bezerra de Menezes in Joaseiro on 1 August 1964.

55. Pinheiro (1950), p. 21.

56. Padre Cícero to Governor Accioly, 20 June 1911, ACS.

57. *Ibid.*

58. Pinheiro (1950), p. 21.

59. Padre Cícero to Santa Cruz, 10 November 1911, ACS.

60. Santa Cruz and his ally Col. Franklin Dantas had, incidentally, employed the services of the celebrated *cangaceiro,* Antônio Silvino, in their attack against the government of Paraíba; see Barroso (1917), p. 254.

This fact clearly illustrates that the lines between social protest, criminal banditry, and purely paid-for and partisan political brutality were never clearly drawn among the Northeastern *cangaceiros* during this period. Such confusion also existed among Italian bandits during the 19th century as shown in the study of E. J. Hobsbawm, *Primitive Rebels: Studies in Archaic Forms of Social Movement in the 19th and 20th Centuries* (New York, 1965), pp. 23-29. This lack of clarity in goals seriously puts into question Rui Facó's (1963) interpretation of Northeastern *cangaceirismo* as a significantly conscious form of social protest.

61. This was reported in the letter from Padre Cícero to Gen. Bizerril Fontenele, 19 May 1912, ACS. In this missive, the Patriarch assured his correspondent that he had never aided Santa Cruz and, to the contrary, had done everything possible to persuade the vengeful *chefe* to withdraw permanently to a life of work and peace.

For a listing of Paraíban governors, see Luis Pinto, *Síntese Histórica e Cronológica da Paraíba* (Rio de Janeiro, 1953), esp. p. 107.

62. Most interpretations of Rabelo's campaign against banditry refuse to recognize its obviously political objectives. For various reasons, historians of Ceará today also refuse to acknowledge the charges of João Brigido, Rabelo's political opposition leader, that the campaign was both ineffective and of partisan political inspiration. References to Brigido's position, which merit a more objective reevaluation, are cited in Montenegro (1955), p. 75.

63. Commenting on the state police's campaign against Cariry bandits, Rodolpho Theophilo (1922a) observed that "wealthy local *chefes* of political prestige were tried and made to answer to the jury" (p. 29).

64. Aires de Menezes' (unpublished MS., 1964) expressive account of the showdown is as follows: "Dr. Floro presumed that João Bezerra, once elected to [the prefecture], would remain obsequious to [Floro's] pretensions and orienta-

tion inasmuch as Floro had been the advocate and organizer of the victory won by João Bezerra. However, on Floro's part, this turned out to be pure deception; João Bezerra, once sworn in and shielded by Franco Rabelo's government, refused to accept the [political] demands and direction of Dr. Floro" (p. 3).

In an interview in Joaseiro on 1 August 1964, the octogenarian João Bezerra de Menezes explained that he had requested the archives because Gov. Franco Rabelo had demanded from him a full account of the *município's* financial standing. Bezerra added: "Franco Rabelo sent me two notices. . . . But, I couldn't [give him the account he requested] since I didn't have the books. It was Floro . . . who had everything. Padre Cícero had lots of good will but no power [to force Floro to give me the archives]. If I didn't reply [to Rabelo] by the 2nd [of September, 1912], Rabelo threatened to sequester my personal property.

"I then dispatched Cincinato Silva to Fortaleza to talk with the Secretary of the Interior [Frota Pessôa]. He did so and [later] met with Rabelo. They [then] sent [Capt.] José do Valle [to Joaseiro, on my behalf]."

João Bezerra's claim that Franco Rabelo had threatened him if a financial account were not made, seems in retrospect to have been either a prearranged pretext or a post-facto rationalization to justify Bezerra's public break with Floro.

65. A letter recommending Capt. José do Valle to Padre Cícero was sent by Col. Vicente Motta, interim Governor of Ceará (between Accioly's fall and Rabelo's inauguration). Motta noted that even though Valle was "our political adversary, he tells me that he desires to act [in Joaseiro] in perfect harmony with Y. Rev.," letter from Col. Vicente Motta to Padre Cícero, 14 September 1912, in the Personal Archive of D. Beatriz de Santanna, Joaseiro (hereinafter cited as ABS).

An undated official communiqué from Franco Rabelo to Padre Cícero, PCC, introduced "Captain of the State Military Batallion, José Ferreira do Valle, who today departs for [Joaseiro] where he will exercise his duties as Police Chief, to which post he was appointed today."

66. Coutinho (1950b) asserts that Rabelo had sent Capt. Valle to Joaseiro to force Floro to give the municipal archives to Bezerra.

Telegram from Padre Cícero to José Accioly, 11 October 1912, cited in Pinheiro (1938), p. 36, n. 15: "I inform you that the actual police-chief here, Capt. José do Valle, is proceeding incorrectly to the point of threatening city councilmen [*vereadores*], who support me, with imprisonment and beatings and even threatening attacks on my home in order to abuse Dr. Floro. I see an imminent danger, especially since I was advised last night that on the arrival today of Moreira Souza I would be attacked. Demand energetic safeguards through your father's intercession before the central [federal] government."

Telegram, Franco Rabelo to Padre Cícero, 11 October 1912.: "Urgent. In view of your telegram I have decided to transfer from Barbalha to Joaseiro as police chief, Lt. Júlio Ladislau, an officer of moderation and sound judgement, trusting you will afford him your valuable support [and] assistance on behalf of peace and order of [your] *município*."

The preceding telegram is contained in the first of three volumes of telegrams received and dispatched from the telegraph office of Joaseiro, "Côpias dos telegrammas do Padre Cícero recibidos nesta Estação do Joaseiro de Padre Cícero de 29 de setembro de 1912 em diante." These three volumes, which contain telegrams sent and received in Joaseiro from 1912 until early 1916, are now in the possession of Dr. F. S. do Nascimento of Fortaleza (hereinafter cited as CN, i.e., Coleção Nascimento) and to whom I happily express my gratitude for the opportunity to transcribe and cite them here.

This collection was most likely used by the Cratense historian, Irineu Pinheiro, whose two valuable works on Joaseiro and the Cariry (1938 and 1963) were the first to publish some of the telegrams contained in CN.

67. Padre Cícero to José Accioly, 11 January 1913, ACS. In this letter, the Patriarch noted that "persecution against me continues" and cited as an example the removal of Pelusia Macedo. It is in this letter that Padre Cícero established a secret code to be used in his future telegraphic correspondence with the Acciolys who were now in Rio.

Clear evidence of the code is contained in the telegraphic correspondence found in CN between the Patriarch and Dr Floro after the latter went to Rio in mid-1913.

It is most probable that at least two of the three volumes of telegrams (for late 1913 through 1916) were drawn up by Pelusia Macedo after he was reappointed to the telegraph office in Joaseiro later in 1913.

68. Information on the interstate pact is contained in Barroso (1917), pp. 254-255; Theophilo (1922a), p. 30; and Montenegro (1955), p. 73. The interpretation of its significance to Rabelo's policy in the Cariry is our own.

69. In a telegram from Franco Rabelo to Padre Cícero, 1 December 1912, CN, I, the Governor dismissed as out of hand the widespread rumors of an imminent inter-governmental invasion of the Cariry. These rumors had apparently led the Patriarch to withdraw his support from Franco Rabelo. In an attempt to dissuade the Patriarch from that course of action, Rabelo cabled: "My government, I repeat, is proud to recognize in the personage of its Vice-president [Padre Cícero] one of the greatest forces for order, lamenting [his] respectable motives [that] oblige [him] to deny it [the government] his invaluable political participation. At this very moment the states of Pernambuco, Parahyba, Rio Grande do Norte, Ceará in solemn meeting in Recife are laying foundations for complete extinction of banditry in bordering regions for peace of families.

"Therefore it is inconceivable that governments which sacrifice themselves for a common peace may consent to disturbance [for] unconfessable ends."

Unfortunately, Padre Cícero's telegram in which he withdrew his support from Rabelo was not found in any archive.

70. Theophilo (1922a), pp. 13-22; Melo Franco (1955), II, 726.

71. Theophilo (1922a), p. 21.

72. After the November 1912 outbreak, Rabelo's party consisted of the Paulo Pessôa clan, middle-class professionals and merchants. It was opposed by a united

front comprising: (1) Acciolystas; (2) the historic Accioly dissidents of 1903 led by João Brigido; (3) those loyal to Sen. Cavalcante; and (4) a faction of former enemies of Accioly who had been exiled in the Far North and refused any voice in Rabelo's government; they were led by Solon Pinheiro.

The best discussion of the political alignments in November 1912 is found in Theophilo (1922a), pp. 9-14. Theophilo clearly blames Rabelo for having failed to create a government and party which would have "all the political groups" who had opposed Accioly. In his opinion, Dr. Francisco de Paula Rodrigues, the heir to the Paula Pessôa faction, was not up to the task (pp. 11, 24-25). However, Joaquim Pimenta, in *Retalhos do Passado* (1949), squarely blames Rabelo; just after Rabelo's candidacy was declared, Pimenta met Rabelo and recalled thus: "One thing that surprised and displeased me was his complete estrangement and ignorance of Ceará's political situation. He could recall or vaguely knew of only one political faction, that of the Paula Rodrigueses, one-time correligionists of his father-in-law, General José Clarindo deposed as Governor of the State . . . in 1893. He [Rabelo] referred to that group exclusively as if it were the only partisan force in Ceará or [the one] worthy of greater esteem, although he himself had long ago withdrawn into a comfortable inactive ostracism, [and] without any hope of seeing his own ephemeral prestige one day restored. . . . Unfortunately . . . I never succeeded in disabusing him of [those political] ideas. . . ." (pp. 145-146).

For biographical data on Dr. Paula Rodrigues, see n. 23.

73. Theophilo (1922a), pp. 23-24; 31.

74. Among other causes for the rupture, Irineu Pinheiro (1938), p. 36, places great importance on Capt. José do Valle's threat to arrest Joaseiro's councilmen loyal to Padre Cícero (see n. 66). In respect to that incident Pinheiro states: "In the Cariry, the [Rabelo] 'ins' (*situacionistas*) committed the unforgivable error of creating hostility in Padre Cícero and his large, massive following. And this [was done] for the love of local elements [*rabelistas*] of [notable] mediocrity or almost no political significance."

75. Padre Cícero to José Accioly, 11 January 1913, ACS: referring to *rabelismo's* political victory and the burnings in Fortaleza, the Patriarch wrote, "if it weren't for that ill-starred accord of June, nothing like this would have happened." He then reminded José Accioly of the certainty of the Portuguese proverb, "Quem se fia em inimigos, nas mãos delles cae."

76. In November, Antonio Luis, as an incumbent state deputy, left for Fortaleza to attend the November session at which anti-*rabelista* forces intended to declare Rabelo's tenure unconstitutional. From the capital he telegraphed Padre Cícero thus: "Friends in Rio insist we present a slate for State Deputies. All is well. Floro [is a] candidate. Advise neighboring *municípios;*" Antonio Luis to Padre Cícero, 15 November 1912, CN, I.

77. Irineu Pinheiro (1938), the Crato historian and close relative of Antonio Luis long ago pointed out that after Joaseiro won its autonomy relations between

Floro and Col. Antonio Luis turned cordial and "with time they became intimate" enough for Floro to visit the ex-*chefe* "from time to time in Crato, lodging in [the latter's] home" (pp. 30-32).

Because Pinheiro was probably privy to these events his observations of the growing amity between Floro and Antonio Luis are cited here in full: "After Col. Franco Rabelo came to power in 1912, there continued the same cordial relations between the two Carirense political chiefs and in the face of the *govêrno de prepotências* of that president, the obligatory subject of their conversations was the necessity of a reaction [revolution] against [an] arbitrary and violent adversary.

"Victim of the reigning demagogery of the day, the ousted political chiefs throughout the state waited for the opportune moment to react, convincing themselves of the idea of a revolution.

"I am convinced [says Pinheiro] that those conversations between Col. Antonio Luis and Dr. Floro Bartholomeu contributed significantly towards the [decision to] undertake the revolutionary movement [of 1913–1914]. Thanks to those [conversations] the conviction became firmer each day that their party was at a crossroads: either [the party] must triumph shortly via armed reaction (and the large contingents of men from Joaseiro were a factor of victory) or else everyone would be fatally doomed bit by bit to ostracism [with the result that], their intimate alliance [would be] undone, the number of their [political] supporters reduced and their prestige as leaders fallen," cited in Pinheiro (1938), pp. 31 32.

78. The accounts among others, which blame Padre Cícero for the revolution of 1913-1914 are Theophilo (1922a), Gomes de Araújo (1962), and Bello (1966).

Naturally, Pinheiro (1938) could not fully inculpate his relative, Col. Antonio Luis, to whom recent historians continue to attribute all the advances made in the Cariry. It is unfortunate that much of the Cariry's past remains in the realm of either "hagiography" or "demonology," rather than history.

In 1923, Floro impassionately inquired before the congress: "Is it possible that even today it is not known that I was the leader of the revolution of Joaseiro and the only one responsible for it?" Bartholomeu (1923), p. 89; also, p. 88, n. 22.

In his public will and last testament, the Patriarch affirmed unequivocally that he was neither a revolutionary nor was he a contributor to the revolution; see *Cópia do Testamento* (n.d.), p. 4.

79. That Col. Antonio Luis must be viewed as a key author of the revolution can be deduced from the following passage contained in Pinheiro (1938), p. 32:

"Without a doubt, those exchanges between the two chiefs [Floro and Antonio Luis], the balancing of the probabilities of victory by revolt, the mutual encouragements, etc., sparked Floro into action and determined that he, who until then [was] a neophyte in state politics, put himself at the head of an armed revolt against the government.

"When it was decided to overthrow the government by revolution, Dr. Floro personally knew none of Ceará's party chiefs. He had never even been to Fortaleza!"

80. During Floro's absence from Joaseiro, his personal secretary and *compadre,* José Ferreira de Menezes, received and transmitted news to Padre Cícero exactly as Floro prescribed. This fact is confirmed by the letters from Floro to the octogenarian José Ferreira, who kindly gave us several taped interviews in September 1964 and who also allowed us to microfilm his correspondence with Floro.

On the role of rumors and tension in the Cariry in 1913, see Pinheiro (1938), pp. 33-41 and Aires de Menezes (unpublished MS, 1964) *passim.*

81. *Cópia do Testamento* (n.d.), p. 10.

82. Theophilo (1922a), pp. 37-39. The victim was Dr. Gentil Falcão, a *rebelista* who early switched his support to João Brigido and the *marretas.*

83. In a letter from Accioly to Padre Cícero, 9 March 1913, ACS, the ex-oligarch noted that Rabelo's pledge of loyalty to Pinheiro Machado, professed at the same time as he led Ceará into the *Bloco do Norte,* had "demoralized [Rabelo] before the public because of his lack of coherence and sincerity."

In a later letter from José Accioly to Padre Cícero, 20 June 1913, ACS, the oligarch's son, who was now in command of the PRC-C, observed this about Rabelo: "The Salvador has fallen into the greatest discredit in political circles, thanks to his duplicity with which he declared himself in solidarity now with Pinheiro Machado, now with Gen. Dantas Barreto." As a result, Machado could no longer tolerate Rabelo. Accioly then urged that "our local *chefes* stay at their posts, exerting every effort to hold the party together in their respective *municípios,* arranging among themselves a unified plan of action against the tyranny that oppresses the State. Inasmuch as [Rabelo] no longer enjoys the Federal Government's support, it [the government] will find it difficult to resist the effects of whatever effort we put our shoulders to."

84. Theophilo (1922a), p. 33. On Pinheiro Machados role in Cearás politics, see F. S. Nascimento, "Caudilho Gaúcho Ganha Capítulo na História Política do Ceará," *O Povo* (Fortaleza), 24 and 25 August 1963.

85. Theophilo (1922a), pp. 35-47.

86. Telegram, Floro to Padre Cícero, 4 August 1913, CN, I. This was sent from Petrolina, Pernambuco, a few days horseback journey from Joaseiro. Pinheiro (1938), p. 33, simply states that Floro left in "mid-1913."

87. Telegram, Fortaleza Police Chief to Padre Cícero, 3 July 1913, CN, I. Telegram, Padre Cícero to Franco Rabelo, 4 July 1913, cited in Pinheiro (1938), pp. 36-37, n. 15.

Franco Rabelo replied to Padre Cícero (Telegram, 5 July 1913, CN, I) that his Fortaleza police chief had in no way intended to be disrespectful to the Patriarch. Despite this attempt to pacify the priest, Rabelo concluded threateningly: "there will be no anarchy [in the Cariry] because the constituted authorities would never permit themselves to be disobeyed and disrespected with impunity."

88. It is clear that the St. John's episode provoked Padre Cícero, undoubtedly under Floro's influence, to create a National Guard unit in Joaseiro. The first communiqué of this subject is a Rio telegram from ex-Governor Accioly to Padre Cícero, 1 July 1913, CN, I. Willingly, Accioly agreed to transmit the appeal to the government. His efforts were only partially successful, according to his subsequent telegrams to the cleric on 12, 13, 19 July 1913, CN, I.

Only after Floro's arrival in Rio was the Joaseiro guard unit finally approved, Telegram, Floro to Padre Cícero, 19 August 1913; 3 September 1913, CN, I. Undoubtedly, Pinheiro Machado had played an important role in securing this for Joaseiro.

89. The benefactor was the Baroness of Ibiapaba. Two telegrams from Floro to Padre Cícero (12 and 20 September 1913, CN, I) dealt with this question. In the end, the Baroness refused to help.

90. The attention paid to Floro shortly after his arrival in Rio de Janeiro on 11 August 1913 by some of Brazil's most prominent politicians is recorded in telegrams from Floro to Padre Cícero, 13, 16, and 19 August 1913, CN, I. Here was the rare occasion when he seemed to have been overwhelmed by his own importance; Floro, the prospector-physician, had indeed arrived at the top.

91. Padre Cícero was made privy to the Rio conspiracy by a letter from one of Brazil's celebrated public officials of the "old Republic," Francisco Sá. One-time Minister of Transport and then senator from Ceará, this *mineiro* official was ex Governor Accioly's son-in-law. His letter was delivered to the Patriarch by Floro upon his return to Joaseiro in November 1913. The transcript which follows is found in Pinheiro (1963), p. 182:

"Rio, 29 October 1913. Ex. Rev. Padre Cícero: In a letter dated today which we, members of the commission elected by the [congressional] representatives of Ceará to direct [in Rio] the political interests of the state, address to Y. Rev., a letter borne by our illustrious friend, Dr. Floro Bartholomeu da Costa, we advise Y. Rev. that all the measures necessary to regain peace and tranquility [for Ceará] have been taken. We shall not go into details now, leaving it up to our friend [Floro] to do so. There is one [detail], however, that I think ought to be gotten straight from the beginning. It concerns the election of the president of the legal [rump] Assembly [which is to be] convened in Joaseiro. For that post, there must be elected the one person who has most worked for the measures that are being taken in favor of our policies and who [in Joaseiro] will be assured of the guarantees of prestige and power which the [new] legal order requires. That person is the very same Dr. Floro whose name will meet with the most decided support of federal politics. Advising Y. Rev. of my opinion with which our most prominent *chefes* are in total agreement, I take the liberty of asking you to communicate this to the members of the Assembly, when it is convened, in order that they will understand the necessity of selfless and joint action [together with] the elements here [in Rio de Janeiro] who are favorable to our cause. . . . Francisco Sá."

92. Telegram, Rabelo to Padre Cícero, 11 September 1913, CN, I. In this, Rabelo insisted that the mission of Lt. Col. Torres Melo to Crato was merely

disciplinary and for the purpose of transferring existing units. This was Rabelo's reply to a telegram from Padre Cícero, sent on 10 September 1913 and cited in Pinheiro (1938), pp. 33-34, n. 13.

93. Padre Cícero's conviction that Rabelo intended to invade Joaseiro seems to have been based on information gathered by Col. Antonio Luis and other Valley *chefes*. See the telegram from Padre Cícero, Antonio Luis, *et al.,* to Floro, 10 September 1913, cited in Pinheiro (1938), p. 33, n. 13.

94. A veiled allusion to the *rabelista* plan is contained in Pinheiro (1938), pp. 33-34.

The details upon which our account is based, however, appear in the recently published work of Otacílio Anselmo e Silva, *Padre Cícero: Mito e Realidade* (Rio de Janeiro: Editôra Civilização Brasileira, 1968), p. 385.

95. *Ibid.*

96. Telegram, Rabelo to Padre Cícero, 13 September 1913, CN, I. The allegedly "seditious" handbills were circulated in connection with the arrival of troops in Crato.

97. This important unpublished letter from Padre Cícero to Accioly, 21 October 1913 is in ACS; italics mine.

98. *Cópia do Testamento* (n.d.), p. 4.

99. "Rumors' that Padre Cícero tried to conciliate with Rabelo in order to avoid armed conflict against Joaseiro prompted Floro to insist on the Patriarch's denial; Telegrams, Floro to Padre Cícero, 15 and 16 September 1913, CN, I; also cited in Pinheiro (1938), p. 34.

In our opinion, Cícero's efforts to conciliate with Rabelo may have been more than rumor. On 30 October 1913, Adolpho Barroso, the Patriarch's trusted merchant-friend in Fortaleza, telegraphed Padre Cícero thus: "Conde Adolpho [Van de Brule] will leave Saturday. [He is] bearer of my letter that gives guarantees for Joaseiro's peace from Franco Rabelo's government. He is a great admirer of your celebrated virtues. Trust his judgment about cooperation [for the] progress of that region. You can confide frankly," A. Barroso to Padre Cícero, 30 October 1913, CN, I.

100. Padre Cícero's letter was dated 21 October. Floro left Rio de Janeiro on 30 October 1913, according to the telegram, Floro to Cícero, 30 October 1913, CN, I.

101. Telegram, João Brigido to Padre Cícero, 10 November 1913, CN, I, notes that Floro departed from Salvador, Bahia on 2 November by land to Joaseiro.

Although troops were stationed along the Ceará-Pernambucan border, Floro successfully reached Joaseiro because Gen. Torres Homen in Fortaleza refused to arrest him, according to Theophilo (1922a), p. 48.

102. Theophilo (1922a), p. 48, discusses the purloined letter.

Brigido telegraphed Padre Cícero, 9 December 1913, CN, I, inquiring whether his letter dated 5 December had been received. That very night the revolution had commenced (p. 49).

103. A useful chronology of the military events is found in Souza (1950), pp. 306-311; in Theophilo (1922a), *passim,* and Pinheiro (1938), *passim.*

Important telegraphic communications on the revolution are published in Pinheiro (1938), pp. 194-240, and (1963), pp. 182-200.

A little-known contemporary account is A. Gusmão, *O Ceará Conflagrado— O Movimento Revolucionário do Juazeiro—Subsídio para a História do Ceará* (Fortaleza, 1915).

104. Telegram, Pinheiro Machado to Padre Cícero, 16 December 1913, cited in Pinheiro (1963), p. 187. From this it was clear that Cattete planned only to sit and wait.

105. According to Montenegro (1955), *"rabelistas* and anti-*rabelistas* recruited into their forces a great number of criminals and *cangaceiros"* (p. 76). This view is confirmed by a Crato eyewitness to the events of December through January: C. Livinio de Carvalho, *A Couvada*, Recife, 1959, pp. 57-81 (entitled, "A Tomada do Crato"); earlier published as "A Tomada do Crato" in *RIC*, LXVI (1952), 119 136. This was originally written in 1915 at the request of Floro Bartholomeu.

106. Cited in Pinheiro (1963), p. 186.

107. The best description of Joaseiro in December, 1913 is in Pinheiro (1938), 46-55. On the role of the refugee from Canudos who helped build the trenches, see Nertan Macêdo, *Memorial de Vilanova* (Rio de Janeiro, 1964), pp. 139-140. Also about the *vallados,* see Lourenço Filho (1926), pp. 124-126.

108. Telegram, Col. Alípio Lopes to Padre Cícero 19 December 1913, cited in Pinheiro (1963), p. 188.

109. *Cópia do Testamento* (n.d.), p. 1.

Although Fr. Antonio Gomes de Araújo (1962), pp. 11, 14, has recently accused Padre Cícero of leading the revolution of 1913-1914, another Cearense clergyman has vindicated the Patriarch's name. The opinion of Fr. José Quinderé (1957) merits considerable credibility since as a state deputy and secretary to Dom Joaquim during the "Old Republic," his views have a firsthand quality. Quinderé contended that only when Cícero was threatened with arrest and Joaseiro with destruction, did the Patriarch sanction "armed defense" (pp. 92-93).

110. Pinheiro (1963), p. 189; Pinheiro (1938), pp. 41, 51.

111. For a number of popular verses about Joaseiro written by backland poets, see Lourenço Filho (1926), pp. 165-194, "O Joaseiro no folc-lore," and Luis da Câmara Cascudo, *Vaqueiros e Cantadores* (Pôrto Alegre, 1939), pp. 97-107.

112. Pinheiro (1963), p. 191; Pinheiro (1938), p. 104.

113. Comment written on telegram, Jm. Lima to Padre Cícero, 30 January 1914, CN, I. Quinderé (1957) exonerates the Patriarch from any responsibility for those barbarous acts: "I am convinced that no blame for these excesses rests with the old priest, himself incapable in any way whatsoever of vengeance and evil-doing" (p. 93).

114. For a partisan account of the death of Capt. J. da Penha, see J. H. de Holanda Cavalcante, *Um Crime Político* (Fortaleza, 1934). Another account, by Francisco Souta, is found in Pinheiro (1963), pp. 516-521.

For remarks on the attitude of Fortaleza's middle classes, also see Raimundo de Menezes, "No tempo do Padre Cícero . . . O Canhão de Emilio Sá . . . ,"

O Povo (Fortaleza), 30 and 31 March 1963.

115. The "state of siege" decree was issued on 9 March 1914. The decree calling for federal intervention was issued on 14 March 1914. Texts of both documents are cited in Studart (1896–1924), III, 224-227.

116. The officer assumed the governship of Ceará on 15 March 1914. His own account of these events is recorded in Marechal Setembrino de Carvalho, *Memórias (Dados para a História do Brasil)* (Rio de Janeiro, 1950), pp. 104-125.

An important secondary account of early 1914 is Boanerges Facó, "Homens e Cousas—Ceará: Intervenção Federal" in *Unitário* (Fortaleza), 6 September, 11, 18, and 25 October 1959b.

Chapter 9
Joaseiro in National Perspective

1. Theophilo (1922a), p. 212: "The candidate for the presidency . . . *Coronel* Benjamin Liberato Barroso . . . was imposed by Rio. . . ."

2. Quinderé (1957), p. 106, notes that the choice of Barroso was the "initiative of Marshal Hermes in order to undo the bad impression which was created within the army by the violence to which a comrade-in-arms [Rabelo] had fallen victim. . . ."

3. En route to Fortaleza, Barroso gave an interview to a Recife newspaper in which he recalled his political feuds which dated from the 1890s; see "O 'Jornal do Recife' entrevista o Coronel Liberato Barroso, novo Governador do Ceará," *Jornal do Recife* (Recife), 21 June 1914.

4. Theophilo (1922a), p. 232: "Dr. Benjamin Barroso was surrounded by *marretas* who informed him about the situation in Ceará according to their own hatreds and interests."

Clearly the cause of the rupture between the *marretas* and the *acciolystas,* now led by Floro, was Cavalcante's refusal to disband the local units of the *marreta* party in Ceará; Cavalcante's adamant refusal to do so is contained in his telegram to Padre Cícero, 4 August 1914, CN, III.

5. On the split in the 1914 Assembly, see Theophilo (1922a), pp. 264-265.

6. On Floro's attempt to obtain indemnization from the state government, see Theophilo (1922a), pp. 260-263. His own account of this episode is: Floro Bartholomeu, "Formal Desmentido," *Unitário* (Fortaleza), 9, 10, 11, 13, 14, 15, 17 July 1915.

7. For some of the telegrams from Pinheiro Machado to Padre Cícero, see Pinheiro (1938), pp. 233-237.

8. Telegram, Floro to Cícero, 20 September 1914, CN, III; also published in Pinheiro (1938), pp. 237-239.

9. References to Barroso's campaign against banditry in the Cariry are contained in Montenegro (1955), p. 79.

10. Telegram, Floro to Cícero, Rio, 11 November 1914, CN, III: "I recommend you not reply to any telegram about politics or other matters [concerning

Joaseiro] without consulting me in order to stop the perfidy [of] certain Cearense politicians."

Although Padre Cícero sent no formal reply, it is clear from his subsequent telegrams that thereafter he acquiesced to Floro's demand to leave all political questions to him.

11. The attempt to produce a new *rabelista-acciolysta* axis and the proposal to the Supreme Court are discussed in Theophilo (1922a), pp. 273-274; the worsening economic crisis of 1914-1916 is cited in pp. 269-270.

On 18 August 1914, Padre Cícero received an anonymous telegram, CN, III, giving him a detailed account of the European war and the death of Pope Pius X. An annotation in the margin of CN, III, notes that Cícero was shocked and ordered churchbells to toll from 3 p.m. on 18 August until the same time on 21 August. As a result, Joaseiro's population was perhaps among the few in the interior to become conscious of world events.

12. A one-time state deputy loyal to Accioly, Msgr. José Quinderé, observed that the period from 1812 to 1930 was, unlike the days of Accyoline unanimity, one of political division and coalition governments; see Quinderé (1957), p. 59. For biographical data on Quinderé, see Guimarães (1952), pp. 384-385.

13. For the exact dates of these administrative changes, see Girão and Martins Filho (1939), p. 255.

14. Antonio Luis was returned as prefect of Crato in 1914 and retained that post until 1928. He held the post of deputy during the Barroso administration (1915-1916); see Guimarães (1952), p. 42.

15. On the advancements made in Fortaleza, see Raimundo Girão, *Geografia Estética de Fortaleza* (Fortaleza, 1959), *passim*, esp. pp. 221-227.

16. Two recent documents which attest to the Cariry's demands on Fortaleza for a greater share in the spoils of the state are: Joaquim Alves, "O Vale do Cariri," *Almanaque do Cariri* (Crato, 1949), pp. 13-14 (this is not to be confused with Alves' 1950 article of the same title); and the previously cited *Estado do Cariri* (1957).

17. *Ibid.*

18. Based on various telegrams from candidates to Padre Cícero, CN, III.

19. On the visit of Governor João Thomé de Saboia to the Patriarch in 1917, see Bartholomeu (1923), 24, n. 1. The visit of Governor Moreira da Rocha in September 1925 is the subject of the entire issue of the discontinued Fortaleza illustrated weekly, *Ceará Illustrado* (Fortaleza), II (25 October 1925), 68. For the visit of Governor Matos Pexioto, see Morel (1946), *passim*, esp. 81-82.

On the visit of politicians to Joaseiro after Cícero's death in 1934, see Montenegro (1965), *passim*.

20. Floro's career as a state deputy is recorded briefly in Guimarães (1952), pp. 244-245. Floro was elected for two terms as federal deputy, 1921-1923 and 1924-1927; information received from Dr. Hugo Catunda of Fortaleza in a letter from Sr. José Oswaldo de Araújo of Fortaleza to the author, 12 January 1968.

21. Morel (1946), p. 137. On efforts of both parties to recruit Padre Cícero as their candidate, see *Jornal do Commercio* (Fortaleza), 23-29 March 1926.

22. Morel (1946), pp. 241-242.

23. Hirschman (1963), *passim*.

24. Bartholomeu (1923), pp. 12-13.

25. On *Tenentismo,* see Virgínio Santa Rosa, *O Sentido do Tenentismo* (Rio de Janeiro, 1933).

26. On the Prestes Column in Ceará, see Morel (1946), pp. 124-133; and Eusébio de Souza, *História Militar do Ceará* (Fortaleza, 1950), pp. 315-326.

27. See *Diario do Ceará* (Fortaleza), 10 March 1926.

28. Raimundo Girão, *História Economica do Ceará* (Fortaleza, 1947).

29. During the drought of 1915, the chief source of alleviation was money and foodstuffs donated, not by the government, but by private citizens and voluntary organizations, including the church, Quinderé (1957), p. 119. In Joaseiro, the situation was desperate. Padre Cícero had received 300$000 reis to distribute among the *município's* 30,000 inhabitants, letter from Pe. Cícero to Dom Bonifácio Jansens, 24 December 1915, ACS. Less than two decades later, Floro praised the priest for his heroic efforts to keep the city from starvation; see Bartholomeu (1923), p. 127, n. 33.

On efforts to exploit local iron and coal deposits, see Bezerra de Menezes (1917) and Abreu (1924), *passim.*

Information on the prolonged legal struggle over the Coxá copper deposits, which was settled only in the 1960s, was given to the author in September 1964, by Fr. Gino Moratelli, Director of the Colégio Salesiano "Dom João Bosco," Juàzeiro do Norte, and one of the judges of the case, Dr. Boanerges Facó of Fortaleza.

30. The revival of cotton in the twenties and the statistics cited in the text are found in Girão (1947), pp. 225-231, 425-437.

31. See the delegation's report: Arno Pearse, *Cotton in North Brazil* (Manchester, 1923).

32. On Campina Grande, see the work by Elpídio de Almeida, *História de Campina Grande* (Campina Grande, Paraíba, n.d.), esp. pp. 357-392; reference to the growing textile industry in Pernambuco is in Othen L. Bezerra de Mello, "A Evolução da Indústria de tecidos de Algodão em Pernambuco," *Revista do Instituto Arqueológico, Histórico e Geográfico de Pernambuco,* XXX (1915–1916), 51-60.

33. Bartholomeu (1923), p. 90, n. 23. For photographs of the foreign civil engineers and prominent Brazilian visitors to Joaseiro, see Reis Vidal, *Padre Cícero: Joazeiro Visto de Perto; O Padre Cícero, Sua Vida e Sua Obra* (2d. ed., Rio de Janeiro, 1936), *passim.*

34. Cited in Dinis (1935), p. 32. On the *consagrações,* see, among others, Bartholomeu (1923), p. 50.

35. Lampeão's visit to Joaseiro was widely reported in the Cearense press: *Correio do Ceará* (Fortaleza), 17 March 1926; *O Nordeste* (Fortaleza), 17 and 20 March 1926.

Lampeão's visit in 1926 is recorded in Dinis (1935), p. 113, while the controversy engendered by the visit is noted in Reis Vidal (1936), p. 61-70.

Lampeão came to Joaseiro in order to obtain a commission in the Brazilian army in exchange for his and his band's services to defeat the Prestes Column; see Leonardo Motta, *No Tempo de Lampeão* (Rio de Janeiro, 1930), esp. the chapter entitled "Quem Escreveu a Patente de Lampeão?" (pp. 27-34).

The bibliography on the celebrated bandit is vast and extends across many disciplines, literature being considerably more cultivated than history. Three standard works on Lampeão are: Optato Gueiros, *Lampeão* (4th ed., Salvador, Bahia, 1956); Luiz Luna, *Lampião e seus cabras* (Rio de Janeiro, 1963); and Rachel de Queiroz, *Lampião* (Rio de Janeiro, 1953).

Vast quantities of folk literature about Lampeão, as well as Padre Cícero, exist; an important attempt to catologue these is Casa de Rui Barbosa, *Literatura Popular em Verso,* Catálogo (Rio de Janeiro, 1962), v. I.

The only successful attempt to analyze the significance of Northeastern banditry is Facó (1963), esp. pp. 38-46, 169-176. However, Facó's analysis is but a start in the still uncultivated field of popular social history.

36. Bartholomeu (1923), p. 176.

37. *Ibid.,* pp. 89; 94, n. 25.

38. *Ibid.,* p. 11.

39. Alves (1945), pp. 123-127.

40. Amália Xavier de Oliveira (unpublished ms, 1943), pp. 57-60.

41. Pinheiro (1963), p. 209.

42. Cícero to Accioly, 16 June 1910. ACS.

43. Bartholomeu (1923), p. 97.

44. *Ibid.,* p. 99, and Dinis (1935), pp. 102-103. Also see the article by Crato's bishop, Dom Quintino, "A Côrte Celeste," which appeared ca. 1918 in Crato's diocesan newspaper, *A Região,* and which is transcribed in full in Azarias Sobreira, *O Primeiro Bispo do Crato (Dom Quintino),* (Rio de Janeiro, 1938), pp. 69, 72-78.

45. On the *beato* José Lourenço, see Bartholomeu (1923), p. 97, and the exaggerated account of Lourenço Filho (1926), pp. 97-105.

In 1936, the Brazilian military destroyed the agricultural community initiated in Caldeirão by the *beato*. The destruction was justified by the officer in charge, José Góes de Campos Barros, *A Ordem dos Penitentes* (Fortaleza, 1937), a copy of which was made available to me by our beloved friend, D. Alba Frota, whose sudden death in 1967 has deprived Fortaleza of one of Ceará's most extraordinary talents.

Recently, the *beato* and Caldeirão have become symbols for progressive thinkers about Brazil's agrarian structure; see "Apontamentos para a reforma agrária do Nordeste," *Boletim da Federação das Associações Rurais do Estado do Ceará,* (Fortaleza, março de 1955), pp. 9, 1-9, esp. pp. 5-7; and Facó (1963), "Um Saldo Positivo: Caldeirão" (pp. 97-105).

46. Interview with D. Maria Gonçalves da Rocha Leal in Fortaleza, 4 July 1964.

47. See Cruz Alencar (1961), p. 23; and Dinis (1935), pp. 84-92.

48. The chief critic of Joaseiro's educational system was Lourenço Filho, who in 1922 was appointed as Ceará's Director of Public Education. His criticism is contained in Lourenço Filho (1926), pp. 195-204, 212-213. Two shortcomings of Lourenço Filho's criticisms are: (1) his neglect to analyze Joaseiro's educational plant in relation to Crato's monopoly over education; (2) the possibility that political judgments may have influenced his professional ones inasmuch as Padre Cícero had not originally supported the then Governor of the state, Justiniano da Serpa. Also see Bartholomeu (1923), pp. 94-95, and n. 47.

49. Amália Xavier de Oliveira (unpublished MS, 1943), pp. 82-83.

50. Telegram, Cícero to Federal Interventor, 23 September 1932, ABS this contains the cleric's offer of the Sítio Stọ Antonio as the site of the school.

For a brief account of the school, see Plácido Alderado Castelo, "Histórico da Escola Normal Rural do Juàzeiro, Estado do Ceará," in *Anais da Semana Ruralista de Juàzeiro* (Fortaleza, 1938), pp. 129-139.

51. Pinheiro (1963), p. 209 Amália Xavier de Oliveira (unpublished MS, 1943), p. 88.

52. On the erection of the statue of Padre Cícero, see Eusébio de Sousa, "Os Monumentos do Estado do Ceará," *RIC*, XLVII (1932), pp. 51-103, esp. pp. 89-90; and Raimundo Gomes de Mattos, *Discurso proferido . . . na solemnidade da Inauguração da Estatua do venerando Padre Cícero Ramão Baptista, em Joazeiro, no dia 11 de Janeiro de 1925* (Fortaleza, 1925).

53. On the airfield in Joaseiro, see *Gazeta do Cariry* (Crato), 4 February 1928.

54. *Cópia do Testamento* (n.d.): in the cleric's 1923 will, both Floro and Antonio Luis were named as his executors.

55. Hirschman (1963), *passim*. on the drought polygon.

56. Barroso (1962), *passim*. Ironically, Barroso who seemed devoid of racist views in 1912 became in 1932 one of the leading *Integralista* exponents of racism. Barroso's elevation of the Northeastern *sertanejo* into a national and nationalist symbol may have been inspired by the similar viewpoints expressed for the first time by Brazil's most important modern historian, João Capistrano de Abreu, in many works published between 1899 and 1922.

57. Leonardo Motta, *Cantadores* (3d. ed., Fortaleza, n.d.); first published in 1921.

58. Cited in Hernan Lima, "Era êle mesmo o sertão," in Leonardo Motta, *Violeiros do Norte* (3rd. ed., Fortaleza, 1962); first published in 1925.

59. José Américo de Almeida, *A Parahyba e Seus Problemas* (João Pessôa, Parahyba, 1923).

60. Bartholomeu (1923), 158-170, esp. 170.

61. Costa Andrade (1922); Simõens da Silva (1927); Reis Vidal (1936).

62. On the qualities of the *sertanejo* in comparison to European immigrants, see Simõens da Silva (1927), 23, 33-34, 108-111; on Cícero's nationalism, see Reis Vidal (1936), 79-94; on Cícero's opposition to the concessions granted to Henry Ford in Amazônas, see Morel (1946), 143.

Chapter 10
The Patriarch and the Church

1. According to Amália Xavier de Oliveira (unpublished MS, 1943), pp. 50-53, Joaseiro's prefects were:

1) 1911–1912: Padre Cícero Romão Batista
2) 1912–1913: Col. João Bezerra de Menezes
3) 1914–1927: Padre Cícero
4) 1927–1929: José Eleutério de Figueiredo
5) 1929–1930: Alfeu Farias de Aboim
6) 1930–1933: José Geraldo da Cruz
7) 28 July 1933–7 October 1934: Lt. João Pinto Pereira and Sr. Zacarias de Albuquerque
8) 8 October 1934–31 May 1935: José Geraldo da Cruz

2. The cleric's declining health is discussed in Dinis (1935), p. 96.

3. Our discussion is based partly on Dinis (1935), pp. 91, 94-95, 123.

4. Padre Cícero's mother, D. Joaquina Vicência Romana, better known as D. Quinôu, died on 4 or 5 August 1914 in Joaseiro, according to telegrams of condolence found in CN, III.

Maria de Araújo (1862-1914) died on 17 January 1914, at the very height of the revolution of Joaseiro; see Pinheiro (1963), pp. 148, 191.

José Marrocos died in 1910; José Lôbo in 1918.

5. See Reis Vidal (1936), *passim*.

6. Biographical data on D. Joanna Tertuliana de Jesus, better known, as "*Beata* Mocinha", are contained in Morel (1946), pp. 168-169; Menezes (1960), pp. 120-121; and Sobreira (1965-1966), article 50.

7. Data on D. Angélica Romana are contained in Sobreira (1965-1966), 29 October 1965; she was born in 1849 in Crato and died in Joaseiro on 6 October 1923. His older sister, also a spinster, D. Maria Angélica Romana, also known as D. Mariquinha (b. 1842), had died in Crato in 1878, during the great drought.

8. Documents found in ACS, Pasta Mocinha, fully testify to the *beata's* wide range of activities. Her role in erecting Joaseiro's *matadouro modelo* (slaughterhouse) is cited in *O Ceará* (Fortaleza), 27 November and 12 December 1928.

9. Based on letters in ACS, Pasta da Correspondência Geral. One of the commercial uses to which Padre Cícero's prestige was put—without his knowledge—occurred ca. 1914. The Studart Pharmacy in Fortaleza coined an aluminum medal: the face contained a portrait of Padre Cícero; the obverse, an ad for a pharmaceutical elixir. One of these medals was graciously presented to the author by the noted Cariry historian, Fr. Antonio Gomes de Araújo, in Crato in 1964.

10. On the role of *santeiros*, see Dinis (1935), pp. 24-32, esp. p. 26.

11. See *ibid.,* pp. 26, 97, for a criticism of those members of the household whom Dinis accused of stealing contributions from pilgrims. Also see Sobreira (1965-1966), article 49, for a scathing critique of one Benjamin Abrahão, a Lebanese immigrant, who allegedly dominated the Patriarch's household; for another view of Abrahão, see Morel (1946), pp. 207-208.

12. On the fear that Joaseiro's inhabitants would depart from the city after Padre Cícero's death, see Bartholomeu (1923), p. 153.

The same thought was expressed in a public lecture in Fortaleza in 1952 by Raimundo Gomes de Mattos; excerpts from his lecture found in RCM. Also see Lauro Nogueira "A Segunda Conferência do Dr. Gomes de Matos Sobre O Padre Cícero," *Unitário* (Fortaleza), 14 May 1952.

The idea for the statue was Floro's two years before its erection; there was considerable opposition to the idea from the Catholic Church, according to Bartholomeu (1923), pp. 73-74.

The most thorough account of the erection of the statue in January 1925 is "A Erecção da Estatua do Padre Cícero," *O Sitiá* (Quixadá, Ceará), I, 22 February and 8 March 1925. Also see Gomes de Mattos (1925) and Sousa (1932).

13. On the dismemberment of the Diocese of Ceará and creation of the Diocese of Crato, see Pinheiro (1963), p. 204.

14. Telegram, Cícero to Accioly and Floro, 21 December 1914, CN, III; also published in Pinheiro (1963), pp. 204-205.

15. Padre Cícero's offer to the Franciscans to establish a school in Joaseiro was first made on 10 September 1914, according to the reply of Frei Cyriaco Hielscher to Padre Cícero, Rio, 22 October 1914, ACS, Pasta da Correspondência com as Ordens Religiosas.

16. Padre Cícero to Frei Cyriaco, 19 November 1914, ACS.

17. A semi-official view of Padre Cícero was contained in the Fortaleza seminary's fiftieth anniversary publication, *Album Histórico* (1914), pp. 74-75: Padre Cícero "got involved and entangled in the sad question of Joaseiro [and has become] today the Patriarch of the fanatics of that region."

18. The privilege to celebrate mass was acknowledged by Cícero in a letter to Dom Quintino, 28 December 1916, ACS; in it Cícero reaffirmed his friendship and the homage paid to the bishop during his pastoral visit. Also see Montenegro (1959), p. 35.

19. Provisão de creação da Freguezia de N[ôssa] S[enhora] das Dôres do Joazeiro, cited in Livro do Tômbo da Freguezia de N. S. das Dôres do Joazeiro, ff. i-iv (hereinafter cited as LTJ).

20. The archives of the Diocese of Crato contain few records of the transactions between Cícero and Dom Quintino by comparison to the voluminous records kept by Dom Joaquim. A major reason for this difference is simply geography; far distant from Joaseiro, Dom Joaquim required regular communications from his agents in Crato. Once Crato was made the episcopal see, the "religious question" of Joaseiro, just 18 kilometers away, could be more frequently dealt with in person. The resulting lack of documentation accounts for our strong reliance on a few basic documents as well as the more speculative nature of several of our hypotheses about this later period.

21. For biographical data on Dom Quintino, see Sobreira (1938). Also see two recent accounts: Fr. Azarias Sobreira, "Dom Quintino—Centenário," *RIC*, LXXIX (1965), 75-88; and Andrade Furtado, "O Centenário de Dom Quintino," *RIC*, LXXVII (1963), 60-62; also *Album* (1925), pp. 114-120.

22. Sobreira (1965–1966), 22 November 1965.

23. Sobreira (1961), p. 16; Pinheiro (1938), *passim*.

24. Montenegro (1959), p. 32, for example, contends: "Padre Cícero had already reflected enough about his situation as a suspended priest. Fearing that his prestige among the masses would be destroyed by the church, he entered into party politics."

25. At the time of the revolution, Fortaleza's bishop decided to dispatch the Italian Capuchin, Friar Marcellino da Cusano, to the interior to pacify the *jagunços* (a maneuver reminiscent of Canudos). It was Friar Marcellino who observed that "among revolutions this was one of the least bloody and that the secret of the *jagunços'* victory consisted in the immense fear that preceded them everywhere, affording them easy access to a victorious advance." The archival report is cited in da Nembro (1957), p. 302, n. 92.

26. Telegram, Irmão em Christo to Cícero, 10 February 1914, CN, I.

27. Bartholomeu (1963), p. 63.

28. One other source of bitterness was Padre Cícero's participation in the *"solidarísticas,"* the pseudo-banking institutions which promised depositors a 1,000 per cent return on their investment. The cleric had allowed an otherwise respectable insurance agent to establish a *solidarística* in October 1914 in Joaseiro; it was given the name, *Banco da Mãe de Deus* (Bank of the Mother of God). When the agent skipped town with the revenues, resentment against Padre Cícero arose. It is important to note that the *solidarísticas* mushroomed throughout Ceará, Fortaleza not excluded.

This literature on the *solidarísticas* is scattered in: Theophilo (1922a), *passim.*; Bartholomeu (1923), pp. 124-127; Dinis (1935), pp. 135-136; Duarte Junior, "Solidarísticas," *Itaytera,* IV (1958), 185-187; Menezes (1960), p. 97; and Sobreira (1965–1966), article 51.

29. The relevant documents are: D. Maria Martins de Macedo (D. Maroca) to D. Lucas [Heuzer], O.S.B., 10 October 1915, ACS, Correspondência com as Ordens Religiosas; D. Lucas to Cícero, 10 November 1915, ACS.

30. Bartholomeu (1923), p. 88, n. 22.

31. *Ibid.*

32. Gomes de Araújo (1962), p. 8. The decree was issued in Rome on 21 June 1916, according to a letter from Dom Quintino to Cícero, 29 April 1920, ABC.

33. No copy of Rome's excommunication order was found in ABC. The account of Dom Quintino's justification for not executing the decree is found in drafts of a memorandum he wrote in Rio de Janeiro to the Holy Father, 9 November 1920, ABC.

34. Interestingly enough, the November 1915 exchange between Quintino and Dom Giusseppe, Archbishop of Sardi and apostolic nuncio in Petropolis, originated in the nuncio's inquiry about a certain Pelusio Macedo of Joaseiro who had earlier written directly to the Pope asking for the reinstatement of Cícero, 2 November 1915, ABC.

35. Gomes de Araújo (1962), pp. 8-9, claims that Dom Quintino did not

execute Rome's order because "of the threats Floro Bartholomeu da Costa made to the bishop through the intermediary of the late Msgr. Pedro Esmeraldo da Silva."

36. According to the census of the Crato Diocese for 1925 contained in the semi-official ecclesiastical document, *Album* (1925), there were ca. 350,000 Catholic inhabitants in twenty-six parishes of the Cariry Valley; there were a total of thirty-four priests. The following data are found on pp. 221-225:

Município	*Population*	*No. of Priests*
Joaseiro	32,060	1 (excluding Padre Cícero)
Crato	29,774	10
Milagres	23,360	1
Barbalha	19,900	1
Icó	15,005	4
Total of 26 *município*:	c.350,000	34

37. On Joaseiro's parish wealth, see Bartholomeu (1923), p. 175.

38. Portaria de transferência de Vigário do Crato para o Joaseiro em favor do Padre Pedro Esmeraldo da Silva, 20 January 1917, LTJ.

For a biography of Joaseiro's first curate, see *Album* (1925), pp. 99-100; and Sobreira (1965–1966), article 38.

39. Bartholomeu (1923), p. 56.

40. Sobreira (1965–1966), 22 November 1965.

41. Pinheiro (1963), p. 209; and Sobreira (1938), pp. 104-105.

42. Bartholomeu (1923), p. 82; and Sobreira (1938), p. 53.

43. The following remarks are based on records in ACS, Pasta das Missas.

44. Presently, recourse to "reduction" is generally at the bishop's discretion, especially if his diocese lacks sufficient patrimony. Prior to the 1960s, the right was usually conferred directly by Rome in the "quinquenials" issued a bishop. None of those documents were found in ABC, which explains the purely hypothetical nature of the remarks in the text.

45. Rocha (1965).

46. Quintino to Cícero, 31 December 1916, ABC.

47. Quintino to Rvdo. Sr. Vigário do Joaseiro [Fr. Pedro Esmeraldo], 6 February 1917, ABC.

48. Esmeraldo to Quintino, 6 February 1917, ABC.

49. *Ibid.*

50. Apostolic nuncio to Quintino, Document No. 61, 14 April 1917, ABC.

51. Quintino to Cícero, 25 June 1917; 23 December 1917; 16 January 1918, ABC. Padre Cícero's replies are dated: 28 June 1917, published in Pinheiro (1963), pp. 528-533; 30 December 1917, ABC; [?] January 1918, ABC.

52. Bartholomeu (1923), p. 65, n. 13.

53. *Ibid.*, p. 66.

54. See n. 33.

55. Bartholomeu (1923), p. 69.

56. Suprema Sacra Congregatio Sancti Officii to Quintino, Protocol No. 319/14, 3 March 1921, ABC.

57. Quintino to Cícero, 3 June 1921, ABC. Floro's views are in Bartholomeu (1923), p. 67.

58. An interesting account of Esmeraldo's ineptness was written by a successor, Fr. Manoel Macedo: História da Successão, ff. 3-7, LTJ.

59. Another account of this incident is in Sobreira (1965–1966), 22 November 1965.

Chapter 11
The Last Days

1. A biographical note on Fr. Manuel Macedo is in *Album* (1925), pp. 186-187. The data found in Amalia Xavier de Oliveira (unpublished MS, 1943), p. 12, are useful except for the claim that Fr. Macedo had assumed the vicariate of Joaseiro in 1924, rather than 1923. The latter date is confirmed in Provisão de Vigário encomendado da Freguezia de N. S ª das Dores do Joazeiro em favor de Pe. Manual Macedo, por 1 anno, 26 de janeiro de 1923, LTJ, (f. 2v)

2. A copy of the rescinded 1922 will is in ABS. It is dated 7 March 1922 and was notarized and legally stamped.

3. In addition to the Premonstratensian Order of St. Norbert, Cícero bequeathed remaining properties to the Sisters of Charity of Saint Vincent de Paul. Were both orders not to erect schools within two years, they would be disinherited in favor of the Holy Father. Neither religious group was included in the legally binding will of 1923, cf. *Cópia do Testamento* (n.d.).

4. See the letter from Quintino to Fr. Azarias Sobreira, 5 December 1919, in Sobreira (1938), pp. 148-149.

5. Sobreira (1938), pp. 105-107.

6. *Ibid.*

7. The following account is based on Floro Bartholomeu da Costa, "Um Padre Ordinário," *Gazeta do Joazeiro* (Joaseiro), 6, 13, 21 June, 18 July, 1 August 1925, esp. 6 June 1925.

8. *Ibid.*

9. Based on Msgr. Joviniano Barreto, "Organização Religiosa," in Amália Xavier de Oliveira (unpublished MS, 1943), pp. 55-65, esp. p. 60.

10. *Ibid.*

11. Floro denounced the members of the two brotherhoods as political "Tartuffes" who after receiving communion went about plotting; see Bartholomeu (1925), 21 June.

12. Membership is noted in Bartholomeu (1925), 13 June.

13. Xavier de Oliveira (1920).

14. *Ibid.*, pp. 246-248.

15. *Ibid.*

16. In October 1934, Xavier de Oliveira ran for congress on the Catholic Electoral League slate; see the issues of *O Nordeste* (Fortaleza), 13 October 1934 and *Correio do Ceará* (Fortaleza), 6 November 1934; also Dinis (1935), p. 142.

17. Bartholomeu (1923), pp. 113-122; and (1925), 21 June.

18. In the work of Xavier de Oliveira's sister, Amália Xavier de Oliveira (unpublished MS, 1943), the decision to oppose Floro is called "the revolt of the native sons"; here is her account of the reason for that revolt: "With the year 1925, a new phase in the history of Joaseiro began. Until then, the 'native sons' had had almost no direct control over the movements in favor of the city's advancement" (pp. 11-12).

19. On the establishment of the *Partido Republicano* by Fernandes Távora, see Montenegro (1965), p. 47. Reference to José Geraldo da Cruz as leader of the party branch in Joaseiro is noted in Bartholomeu (1925), 1 August; and in Dinis (1935), pp. 70, 161.

20. For data on the Catholic Electoral League and the Integralista Party in Ceará, see Montenegro (1965), pp. 66-69, 72-73.

21. Floro's supporters advertised in the *Gazeta do Joazeiro*; they were comprised of: six dry-goods merchants, one *santeiro,* a dentist, a pharmacist, one lawyer, two hardware merchants, one baker, and one goldsmith. In addition, there were the local, state, and federal appointees: the district court judge of Joaseiro, Dr. Juvéncio Sant'anna; the state tax collector, Alpheu Aboim; the federal tax collector, Dr. Pedro Uchôa de Albuquerque. For the most part, Floro's supporters were newcomers (*adventícios*); based on various issues of the *Gazeta do Joazeiro* (Joaseiro), 1925.

22. Bartholomeu (1925), 13 June.

23. *Ibid.*

24. *O Ideal* (Joaseiro) was a weekly; it was probably founded in July or August 1924. The first issue of this rare collection, which was made available to us by Sr. Odílio Figueiredo of Fortaleza, is number 48, dated 8 July 1925.

25. Consult *O Nordeste* (Fortaleza) for 1924. In early 1925, *O Nordeste* published Fr. Macedo's bitter attack against Floro; see n. 31.

26. Our account is based on Bartholomeu (1925), 13 June; and M. Macedo (1925a), pp. 13, 33.

27. The charge of peculation is made in M. Macedo (1925a), pp. 12-13, 61-71, and is also noted in Dinis (1935), p. 68.

28. M. Macedo (1925a), pp. 6-7.

29. This account is based on Bartholomeu (1925), 13 June.

30. The secret meeting is discussed in a letter from Juvéncio Sant'anna to Floro, 9 June 1925, which was published in *Gazeta do Joazeiro* (Joaseiro), 13 June 1925. Padre Cícero's own account of his decision was published in *O Ceará* (Fortaleza), 20 September 1925.

31. The articles appeared in *O Nordeste* in April and May 1925; they were subsequently published as *Joazeiro em Fóco* (1925a).

32. M. Macedo (1925a), pp. 6-7, 11, 23-24, 82.

33. *Ibid.*; see "Mortes," p. 44 and *passim*.

34. Padre Dubois, "Um Pseudo-Martyr," *Correio do Ceará* (Fortaleza), 29 August 1925.

35. Full citation in n. 7.

36. Bartholomeu (1925), 21 June.

37. Godofredo de Castro, *Joazeiro na Assembléa Legislativa do Ceará* (Fortaleza, 1925).

38. The visit was the subject of two issues of the *Gazeta do Joazeiro* (Joaseiro), 13 and 20 September 1925.

39. *Ceará Illustrado* (Fortaleza), 25 October 1925, II, 68.

40. See Dinis (1935), pp. 158-163; he suggests that the decision to support Julio Prestes and not Getúlio Vargas was not really Cícero's. Also see Morel (1946), pp. 181-183.

41. Fr. Macedo admitted to that failure in a series of articles written after his return to Crato in July 1925; see Pe. Manuel Macedo, "O Joaseiro Ideal," in *O Ideal* (Joaseiro, 1925b), 8, 11, 18, 25 July and 1, 8, 15 August.

42. Letter, José Geraldo Bezerra de Menezes to Cícero, 17 April 1924, ACS. On continued hostilities between Dom Quintino and Cícero in 1929, see Morel (1946), pp. 163-164.

43. M. Macedo (1925a), p. 17.

44. Gomes de Araújo (1962), *passim*.

45. M. Macedo (1925a), pp. 16-18.

46. *Ibid.*

47. Bartholomeu (1925), 15 August.

48. Cícero to Padre Pedro Rota, 20 December 1924, and 21 June 1925, ACS, Pasta dos Salesianos. This file contains Cícero's correspondence with the Salesians, the congregation to which he willed almost his entire estate in 1923.

49. Interview in September 1964 with Frs. Gino Moratelli, Director of the Colégio Salesiano "Dom João Bosco" in Juàzeiro do Norte and Mario Balbi, professor of English.

50. Morel (1946), p. 53, claims this occurred in Recife in 1898 prior to Cícero's departure for Rome; no evidence, however, is given.

It is more likely that this contact was made for the Patriarch in 1923 by Dr. José Geraldo Bezerra de Menezes, the son of Leandro Bezerra who had aided Cícero to establish the Diocese of the Cariry, and whose own son, João, was a student at the Salesian school in Niteroí, Rio de Janeiro state. This is alluded to in a letter from J. G. Bezerra de Menezes to Cícero, 15 April 1925, ACS.

51. Cícero to Frs. Rota and Della Via, 22 September 1924, ACS, Pasta Salesianos.

52. Cícero to Rota, 22 September 1924, ACS.

53. Rota to Cícero, 23 September 1924, ACS.

54. Cícero to Rota, 11 July 1925, ACS: Cícero was convinced that Dom Quintino would "impose such vexatious conditions upon me that I would perhaps

be forced not to accept them." The Patriarch also noted that the chief bone of contention was Quintino's adamant stand against the pilgrimages. Any agreement, Cícero thought, would oblige him to stop seeing the *romeiros*. To this Cícero countered:

"Now, these poor *sertanejos,* in the great majority, my *compadres* and *afilhados* . . . come to seek my counsel whenever they have difficulties . . . my advice can only result in religious, social and domestic benefits which, as a rule, has been the case. How many homes have I not reconstituted, how many crimes have I not prevented, how many erring souls have I not [returned to] the sentiments of Christian faith as a result of my counsels!

"Therefore, it would be an unpardonable lack of charity to deny me [the opportunity to continue] to come to their aid."

55. Cícero to Rota, 11 July 1925, ACS: "Believe me that so great is my desire to be reinstated that if you, my dear friend, are disposed to assisting, I shall spare no sacrifice to go personally to Rome deal with the issue even despite my 82 years."

56. Dom Francisco de Assis Pires arrived in Crato on 10 January 1932; Pinheiro (1963), p. 215.

57. The previous discussion is based on: Cícero to Dom Manuel, Archbishop of Fortaleza, 1 January 1932, ACS; Cícero to Dom Francisco de Assis Pires, 1 July 1932, ACS; Dom Bento [Lopez ?], Nuncio Apostolico, to Dom Francisco, 5 June 1933, ACS.

58. Sobreira (1965–1966), article 42.

59. Barreto in Amália Xavier de Oliveira (unpublished MS, 1943), p. 58.

60. Dinis (1935), pp. 167-169; Reis Vidal (1936), pp. 119-126; Morel (1946), pp. 235-247.

61. Reis Vidal (1936), pp. 119-126; Morel (1946), pp. 245-246.

62. Interview with Dr. Pio Sampaio, one of the attending physicians, in Fortaleza, August 1964.

63. Accounts of the funeral are contained in *O Nordeste* (Fortaleza), 23 July 1934 and *O Povo* (Fortaleza), 18 August 1934.

64. The reconciliation of the church with the "fanatics" was reported in *O Povo* (Fortaleza), 30 March 1964: "Local Proibido em Juazeiro Foi Visitado Por Bispo e Padres Durante Semana Santa." The articles note that the Bishop of Crato, Dom Vicente de Araújo Matos, in the company of various priests, led the Holy Week pilgrimage to the Hôrto, the site on which Padre Cícero had planned to build his cathedral and which for decades had been the source of bitter enmities between the priest and the church. Also see Chapter V, n. 6.

Bibliography

Archives

Arquivo do Bispado do Crato. Crato, Ceará.

Arquivo do Colégio Salesiano "Dom João Bosco." Juàzeiro do Norte, Ceará.

"Copias dos telegrammas do Padre Cícero recibidos nesta Estação do Joaseiro de 29 de setembro de 1912 em diante," 3 vols. Now in the possession of Dr. F. S. Nascimento, Fortaleza, Ceará; referred to as the Coleção Nascimento.

Livro do Tombo da Freguezia de Nôssa Senhora das Dôres. Juàzeiro do Norte, Ceará.

Personal Archive of D. Amália Xavier de Oliveira. Juàzeiro do Norte, Ceará.

Personal Archive of D. Beatriz Santanna. Juàzeiro do Norte, Ceará.

Personal Archive of Dr. Geraldo Bezerra de Menezes. Niterói, Rio de Janeiro.

Personal Archive of Dr. Raimundo Gomes de Mattos. Fortaleza, Ceará.

Personal Archive of Pe. Cícero Coutinho. Juàzeiro do Norte, Ceará.

Published Documents

Côpia do Testamento com que faleceu nesta cidade o Revmo. Padre Cícero Romão Batista. Joazeiro, Ceará (n.d.).

"Declaração que faz o Padre Ibiapina aos Irmãos, Beatos e Irmãs das Santas Casas

de Caridade do Carirí-Novo . . . Cravatá, Paraíba, 16 de setembro de 1872," Irineu Pinheiro, *O Carirí: Seu Descobrimento, Povoamento, Costumes.* Fortaleza, 1950.
"Documentos Sôbre a Questão Religiosa do Juàzeiro," *Revista do Instituto do Ceará,* LXXV (1961), 266-297.
Mensagen apresentada á Assembléa Legislativa do Ceará pelo Presidente do Estado, Dr. Antonio Pinto Nogueira Accioly. Fortaleza, 1897.

Published Works

"Abaixo a Intriga!" in *O Rebate.* 5 December.
Abreu, Sílvio Froes de (1924). "Schisto Bituminoso da Chapada do Araripe, Ceará." *Revista do Instituto do Ceará,* XXXVIII, 363-377.
"A Erecção da Estatua do Padre Cícero," (1925). In *O Sitiá.* 22 February and 8 March.
Aires, Durival (1955). "A Morte de Uma Tradição." *O Estado.* 17 April.
Album do Seminário do Crato. (1925). Rio de Janeiro.
Album Histórico do Seminário Episcopal do Ceará. (1914). Fortaleza.
Alcântara Nogueira (1962). *Iguatú, Memória Sócio-Histórico-Económico.* Fortaleza: Imprensa Universitária do Ceará.
Alencar Peixoto, Pe. Joaquim de (1911). "Ao Público." *O Rebate.* 27 August.
—— (1913). *Joazeiro do Cariry.* Fortaleza.
Almeida, Elpídio de (n.d.). *História de Campina Grande.* Campina Grande, Paraíba: Edições da Livraria Pedrosa.
Altenfelder Silva, Fernando (1962). "As Lamentacões e os Grupos de Flagelados de São Francisco." *Sociologia,* XXIV, 1, 15-28.
Alves, Joaquim (1932?). *Nas Fronteiras do Nordeste.* Fortaleza.
—— (1945). "O Vale do Carirí." *Revista do Instituto do Ceará,* LIX, 94-133.
—— (1948). "Juàzeiro, Cidade Mística." *Revista do Instituto do Ceará,* LXII, 72-101.
—— (1949). "O Vale do Carirí." *Almanaque do Carirí,* Crato, pp. 13-14.
—— (1953). *História das Sécas (Séculos XVII a XIX).* Fortaleza: Edições "Instituto do Ceará."
Alves de Figueiredo, José (1958). *Ana Mulata.* Crato.
"A Mentira." (1910). In *O Rebate.* 19 June.
Américo de Almeida, José (1923). *A Parahyba e Seus Problemas.* João Pessôa, Parahyba.
Andrade Furtado (1963). "O Centenário de Dom Quintino." *Revista do Instituto do Ceará,* LXXVII, 60-62.
Anselmo e Silva, Otacílio (1959–1961). "A História do Padre Cícero." *Itaytera,* vv. V-VII.
—— (1968). *Padre Cícero: Mito e Realidade.* Rio de Janeiro: Editôra Civilização Brasileira.
"A Questão do Joaseiro—Como o Snr. Antonio Luiz Abusou da Prudência do Povo do Joaseiro." (1910). In *O Rebate.* 4 September.

Baptista, F[rancisco] das Chagas (1960). *História Completa de Antônio Silvino, Sua Vida de Crime e seu Julgamento*. Rio de Janeiro.

Barbosa da Silva, José Fabio (1962). "Organização Social de Juàzeiro e Tensões entre Litoràl e Interior." *Sociologia*, XXIV, 3, 181-187.

Barroso, Gustavo (1917). *Heróes e Bandidos (Os Cangaceiros do Nordeste)*. Rio de Janeiro.

—— (1930). *Almas de Lama e Aço*. São Paulo.

—— (1962). *Terra de Sol*. 6th ed. Fortaleza: Imprensa Universitária do Ceará.

Bartholomeu da Côsta, Floro (1900–10). "Minas do Coxá: Ligeiras Considerações para refutar os argumentos adduzidos pelo Illmo. Snr. Cel. José Francisco Alves Teixeira no 'Correio do Cariry' de 5 do Corrente." *O Rebate*. 22 August 1909–25 July 1910.

—— (1911a). "De Agua Abaixo, Não Irá o Joaseiro." *O Rebate*. 8, 15, 22, 29 January and 5 February.

—— (1911b). "Última Palavra." *O Rebate*. 26 February.

—— (1915). "Formal Desmentido." *Unitário* (Fortaleza). 9, 10, 11, 13, 14, 15, 17 July.

—— (1923). *Joazeiro e o Padre Cícero (Depoimento para a História)*. Rio de Janeiro.

—— (1925). "Um Padre Ordinário." *Gazeta do Joazeiro*. 6, 13, 21 June, 18 July, 1 August.

Bastide, Roger (1951). "Religion and the Church in Brazil." In *Brazil, Portrait of Half a Continent*, T. Lynn Smith and Alexander Marchant, eds. New York, pp. 334-355.

Bello, José Maria (1966). *A History of Modern Brazil, 1889–1964*, trans. James L. Taylor with a new concluding chapter by Rollie E. Poppino. Stanford: Stanford University Press.

Benício, Manuel (1907). "Dr. Leandro Bezerra." *O Fluminense*. 11 June.

Bezerra de Mello, Othen L. (1915–16). "A Evolução da Indústria de tecidos de Algodão em Pernambuco." *Revista do Instituto Arqueológico Histórico e Geográfico de Pernambuco*, XXX, 51 60.

Bezerra de Menezes, Geraldo (1959). *Homens e Idéias à Luz da Fé*. 2d ed. Rio de Janeiro.

Bezerra de Menezes, José Pinheiro de (1917). "Joazeiro do Cariry." *Correio do Ceará*. 18 October.

Blondel, Jean (1957). *As Condições da Vida Política no Estado da Paraíba*. Rio de Janeiro: Fundação Getúlio Vargas.

Boanerges Facó (1959a). "Homens e Cousas—Ceará: Govêrno Franco Rabelo." *Unitário*. 2, 9, 15 August.

—— (1959b). "Homens e Cousas—Ceará: Intervenção Federal." *Unitário*. 6 September, 11, 18, 25 October.

Brigido, João (1888). *Apontamentos para a História do Cariri: Crônica do Sul do Ceará*. Fortaleza.

Brigido dos Santos, Gorgônio (1893). "O milagre do Joazeiro do Crato no Estado do Ceará." *Diário de Pernambuco*. 6 September.

Buarque de Holanda, Sérgio (1936). *Raizes do Brasil*. Rio de Janeiro: Livraria José Olympio Editôra.

Calmon, Pedro (1959). *História do Brasil*. 7 vols. Rio de Janeiro: Livraria José Olympio Editôra.

Câmara Cascudo, Luis da (1939). *Vaqueiros e Cantadores*. Pôrto Alegre: Glôbo.

―――― (1955). *História do Rio Grande do Norte*. Rio de Janeiro.

―――― (1962). *Dicionário do Folclore Brasileiro*. 2 vols. 2d. ed. Rio de Janeiro: Instituto Nacional do Livro

Campos, Eduardo (1960a). *Folclore do Nordeste*. Rio de Janeiro: Edições "O Cruzeiro."

―――― (1960b). *Estudos de Folclore Cearense*. Fortaleza: Imprensa Universitária do Ceará.

Campos Barros, José Góes de (1937). *A Ordem dos Penitentes*. Fortaleza.

Carneiro, Glauco (1964). "A Revolta dos Jagunços." *O Cruzeiro*. 4 August.

―――― (1965). *História das Revoluções Brasileiras*. 2 vols. Rio de Janeiro: Edições "O Cruzeiro."

"Carta de Otacílio Anselmo e Silva ao Padre Antonio Gomes de Araújo, 22 de janeiro de 1957." (1957?). In *Ecos do "Apostolado do Embuste,"* Separata da Revista *Itaytera*, Crato.

Cartaxo, Décio Teles (1955). "Pela Instalação de um Órgão da Cadéia Associada em Crato." *A Província*, III, 61-64.

Carvalho, Jader de (n.d.). *Sua Majestade, O Juiz*. São Paulo.

―――― (1963). *Aldeota*. São Paulo.

―――― (1966). "Padre Cícero: Mito e Realidade—Prefácio ao livro do Otacílio Anselmo, no prelo." *O Povo*. 19, 20 February.

Carvalho, Orlando (1946). *Política do Município*. Rio de Janeiro.

Carvalho, Setembrino de, Marechal (1950). *Memórias (Dados para a História do Brasil)*. Rio de Janeiro.

Casa de Rui Barbosa (1962). *Literatura Popular em Verso*, Catalogo. Vol. I. Rio de Janeiro.

Castelo, Plácido Alderado (1938). "Histórico da Escola Normal Rural do Juàzeiro." *Anais da Semana Ruralista de Juàzeiro*. Fortaleza, pp. 129-139.

―――― (1963). "Deputado Paula Rodrigues." *Revista do Instituto do Ceará*, LXXVIII, 307-312.

Castro, Godofredo de (1925). *Joazeiro na Assembléa Legislativa do Ceará*. Fortaleza.

"Communicado: Milagres na povoação do Joazeiro do Crato." (1891). In *Cearense*. 24 April.

Cornélio, Expedito (1961). "Festa da Gratidão." *Revista do Cinqüentenário de Juàzeiro do Norte*. Fortaleza, pp. 7-8.

Costa Andrade, L. (1922). *Sertão a Dentro (Alguns dias com o Padre Cícero)*. Rio de Janeiro.

Costa Porto (1951). *Pinheiro Machado e Seu Tempo: Tentativa de Interpretação*. Rio de Janeiro.

Coutinho, Pe. Cícero (1950a). "A Independência do Joaseiro." *O Jornal do Cariry.* 23 July.

—— (1950b). "A Política em Juàzeiro, logo após sua Independência." *O Jornal do Cariry.* 30 July.

Cruz Alencar, Tarcila (1961). "A Evolução das Letras em Juàzeiro do Norte." *Revista do Cinqüentenário do Juàzeiro do Norte.* Fortaleza, 22-24.

Cruz Costa, João (1964). *A History of Ideas in Brazil.* Berkeley: University of California Press.

da Cunha, Euclydes (1944). *Rebellion in the Backlands,* trans. Samuel Putnam (from the original entitled *Os Sertões*). Chicago: Phoenix, University of Chicago Press.

da Nembro, P. Metodio (1957). *I Cappuccini nel Brasile, Missione e Custodia del Maranhão (1892–1956).* Milano.

della Cava, Ralph (1967). "Ecclesiastical Neo-Colonialism in Latin America." *Slant,* n. s. No. 3. October-November, 5, 17-20.

—— (1968). "Brazilian Messianism and National Institutions: A Reappraisal of Canudos and Joaseiro". In *Hispanic American Historical Review,* XLVIII, 3, 402-420.

[de Morais Carneiro], Pe. Júlio Maria (1950). *O Catolicismo no Brasil (Memória Histórica).* Rio de Janeiro: Livraria Agir.

"Descripção da Cidade do Crato em 1882 pelo Dr. Gustavo Horácio." (1959). In *Itaytera,* V, 165-171.

"Desordens do Joazeiro." (1896). In *Diário de Pernambuco.* 30 December.

Dinis, M.[anoel] (1935). *Mistérios do Joazeiro.* Joazeiro, Ceará.

Droulers, S. J., Paul (1963). "Roman Catholicism." In *The Nineteenth Century World,* Guy S. Métraux and François Crouzet, eds. New York: Mentor Books.

Duarte Junior (1958). "Solidarísticas." *Itaytera,* IV, 185-187.

Dubois, Padre (1925). "Um Pseudo-Martyr." *Correio do Ceará.* 29 August.

Duncan, Julian Smith (1932). *Public and Private Operations of Railroads in Brazil.* New York: Columbia University Press.

Estado do Cariri, Separata da Revista *Itaytera* (1957). Crato.

Facó, Rui (1963). *Cangaceiros e Fanáticos.* Rio de Janeiro. Editôra Civilização Brasileira.

Fernandes Távora, Manuel do Nascimento (1943). "O Padre Cícero." *Revista do Instituto do Ceará,* LVII, 35-69.

—— (1963a). *Algo de Minha Vida.* 2nd ed. Fortaleza.

—— (1963b). "Dr. Francisco de Paula Rodrigues." *Revista do Instituto do Ceará,* LXXVIII, 299-306.

Ferreira de Figueiredo, Manuel [pseud. Floro Bartholomeu da Côsta] (1909). "Justa Defesa." "Olho por Olho, Dente por Dente." "Os Effeitos da Imprudência." *O Rebate.* 29 August, 12 and 19 September, respectively.

Ferro, Aderson (1892). "Milagres em Joaseiro." *Combate.* 31 August, 2, 6, 14 September, 25, 28 October.

Figueiredo Brito, José de (1956). "A contribuição dos Romeiros na construção Econômica do Cariri." *Itaytera,* II, 227-229.

────── (1959). " 'Maxixes e Malabares' (Episódio Inédito da História Política do Crato)." *Itaytera*, V, 37-57.

Figueiredo Filho, José (1955). "Casa de Caridade do Crato, Fruto do Apostolado Multíforme do Pe. Ibiapina." *A Província*, III, 14-25.

────── (1958). *Engenhos de Rapadura do Cariri.* (Ministério da Agricultura, "Documentário da Vida Rural, no. 13"). Rio de Janeiro.

Firmeza, Hermenegildo (1963). "A Revolução de 1912 no Ceará." *Revista do Instituto do Ceará*, José Bonifácio de Sousa, ed., LXXVII, 25-59.

Frota Pessôa, [J. G. da] (1910). *O Olygarcha do Ceará (A Chrônica de um despota).* Rio de Janeiro.

Furtado, Celso (1965). *The Economic Growth of Brazil.* Berkeley and Los Angeles: University of California Press.

Gardner, George (1942). *Viagens no Brasil principalmente nas províncias do norte e nos distritos do ouro e do diamente durante os anos de 1836–1841.* São Paulo. Originally published in London: 1846.

Girão, Raimundo and Martins Filho, eds. (1939). *O Ceará.* Fortaleza.

Girão, Raimundo (1947). *História Econômica do Ceará.* Fortaleza: Editôra "Instituto do Ceará."

────── (1959). *Geografia Estética de Fortaleza.* Fortaleza.

────── (1962). *A Pequena História do Ceará.* 2nd ed. Fortaleza: Editôra "Instituto do Ceará."

Gomes de Araújo, Pe. Antônio (1955). "Um Civilizador do Cariri." *A Província*, III, 127-146.

────── (1956). "Apostolado do Embuste." *Itaytera*, II, 3-63.

────── (1958). "Padre Pedro Ribeiro da Silva, O Fundador e Primeiro Capelão de Juàzeiro do Norte." *Itaytera*, IV, 3-37.

────── (1962). "À Margem de 'À Margem da História do Ceará.' " *Itaytera*, VIII, 5-19.

Gomes de Matos, Celso (1955). "Em Defesa da Serra do Araripe." *A Província*, III, 31-34.

Gomes de Mattos, Raimundo (1925). *Discurso proferido . . . na solemnidade da Inauguração da Estatua do Venerando Padre Cícero Romão Baptista, em Joazeiro, no dia 11 de Janeiro de 1925.* Fortaleza.

────── (1955). "Perece Um Gênio do Sertão." *Unitário.* 12 May.

Gouvéia, Flávio [pseudonym of Floro Bartholomeu da Côsta] (1910)."Joaseiro." *O Rebate.* 29 May.

Gueiros, Optato (1956). *Lampeão.* 4 d. Salvador, Bahia: Livraria Progresso.

Guimarães, Hugo Victor (1952). *Deputados Provinciais e Estaduais do Ceará.* Fortaleza.

Gusmão, A. (1915). *O Ceará Conflagrado—O Movimento Revolucionário do Juàzeiro—Subsídio para a História do Ceará.* Fortaleza.

"Hino do Pe. Ibiapina, reproduzido da tradição popular por Teresa Rosando Simões." (1958). In *Itaytera*, IV, 109.

Hirschman, Albert O. (1963). *Journeys Toward Progress.* New York: The Twentieth Century Fund.

Hobsbawm, E. J. (1965). *Primitive Revels: Studies in Archaic Forms of Social Movement in the 19th and 20th Centuries.* New York: W. W. Norton and Co., Inc.

Holanda Cavalcante, J. H. de (1934). *Um Crime Político.* Fortaleza.

"Independência do Joaseiro—Passeiatas e Discursos." (1910). In *O Rebate.* 4 September.

"Inedictoriaes—Os Últimos Acontecimentos." (1909). In *O Rebate.* 25 July.

Lima, Hernan (1962). "Era êle mesmo o sertão." In *Violeiros do Norte,* Leonardo Motta. 3d ed. Fortaleza, pp. 9-17.

"Leandro Bezerra." (1912). In *Revista do Instituto do Ceará,* XXVI, 206-214.

Lins de Albuquerque, Ulysses (1957). *Um sertanejo e o Sertão.* Rio de Janeiro: José Olympio.

Livinio de Carvalho, C. (1952). "A Tomada do Crato.' *Revista do Instituto do Ceará,* LXVI, 119-136.

——— (1959). *A Couvada.* Recife.

"Local Proibido em Juàzeiro Foi Visitado Por Bispo e Padres Durante Semana Santa." (1967). In *O Povo.* 30 March.

Lourenço Filho, Manuel Bergström (1926). *Joaseiro do Padre Cícero (Scênas o quadros do fanatismo do Nordeste.* 2d ed. São Paulo: Edições Melhoramentos.

Luna, D. Joaquim G. de (1951). "Os monges beneditinos no Ceará" *Revista do Instituto do Ceará,* LXV, 192-228.

——— (1952). "Os monges beneditinos no Ceará." *Revista do Instituto do Ceará,* LXVI, 220-240.

Luna, Luiz (1963). *Lampião e seus cabras.* Rio de Janeiro: Editôra Leitura.

Macedo, Pe. Manuel (1925a). *Jouzeiro em Fóco.* Fortaleza.

——— (1925b). "O Joasciro Ideal." *O Ideal.* 8, 11, 18, 25 July and 1, 8, 15 August.

Macêdo, Nertan (1961). *O Padre e A Beata* Rio de Janeiro: Editôra Leitura, S. A.

——— (1964). *Memorial de Vilanova.* Rio de Janeiro: Edições O Cruzeiro.

Machado, J. (1948). *Duas Palavras (Excertos da vida do Pe. Cícero)* Juàzeiro do Norte.

Marchêt Callou, Antonio (1959). "Barbalha." *Itaytera,* V, 127-133.

Mariz, Celso (1942). *Ibiapina, Um Apóstolo do Nordeste.* João Pessoa, Paraíba.

[Marrocos, José] (1909?). *Joaseiro: A Carta Aberta do Snr. Nicodemus—Reposta de José de Arimatea.*

Mecham, J. Lloyd (1934). *Church and State in Latin America: A History of Politico-Ecclesiastical Relations.* Chapel Hill: University of North Carolina.

Melo Franco, Afonso Arinos de (1955). *Um Estadista da República.* 3 vols. Rio de Janeiro: Livraria José Olympio Editôra.

Mendes, Cândido (1966). *Memento dos Vivos: A Esquerda Católica no Brasil.* Rio de Janeiro: Tempo Brasileiro.

Menezes, Djacir (1937). *O Outro Nordeste.* Rio de Janeiro: Livraria José Olympio Editôra.

Menezes, Paulo Elpídio de (1960). *O Crato do Meu Tempo.* Fortaleza.

Menezes, Raimundo de (1963). "No Tempo do Padre Cícero . . . O Canhão de Emilio Sá. . . ." *O Povo.* 30, 31 March.

Monteiro, Manoel (1952). "Carta Aberta . . . a Gomes de Mattos." *Unitário.* 25 March.

Montenegro, Abelardo (1954). *Antônio Conselheiro.* Fortaleza.

—— (1955). *História do Cangaceirismo no Ceará.* Fortaleza: Editôra A. Batista Fontenele.

—— (1939). *História do Fanatismo Religioso no Ceará.* Fortaleza: Editôra A. Batista Fontenele.

—— (1965). *História dos Partidos Políticos Cearenses.* Fortaleza: [A. Batista Fontenele?]

Morel, Edmar (1946). *Padre Cícero, O Santo do Juàzeiro.* Rio de Janeiro: Empreza Gráfica "O Cruzeiro."

Morse, Richard (1958). *From Community to Metropolis.* Gainesville, Florida: University of Florida Press.

Motta, Leonardo (n.d.). *Cantadores.* 3d ed. Fortaleza: Imprensa Universitária do Ceará.

—— (1930). *No Tempo de Lampeão.* Rio de Janeiro.

—— (1962). *Violeiros do Norte.* 3d ed. Fortaleza: Imprensa Universitária do Ceará.

Nascimento, F. S. (1955). "Subsídios para a história do jornalismo cratense." *A Provincia,* III, 3-14, 99-112.

—— (1958). "Esboço da Evolução Literária do Crato." *Itaytera,* IV, 56-70.

—— (1963). "Caudilho Gaúcho Ganha Capítulo na História Política do Ceará." *O Povo.* 24 and 25 August.

Nóbrega, Apolônio (1954). "Dioceses e Bispos do Brasil." *Revista do Instituto Histórico e Geográfico Brasileiro,* vol. 222 (janeiro-março), 3-328.

Nogueira, Lauro (1952). "A Segunda Conferência do Dr. Gomes de Matos Sobre O Padre Cícero." *Unitário.* 14 May.

Nunes Leal, Victor (1948). *Coronelismo: Enxada e Voto.* Rio de Janeiro.

"O 'Jornal do Recife' entrevista o Coronel Liberato Barroso, novo Governador do Ceará." (1914). In *Jornal do Recife.* 21 June.

"Os Jagunços da Legião da Cruz." (1898). In *A Ordem.* 19 June.

Os Milagres do Joaseiro ou Nosso Senhor Jesus Christo Manifestando Sua Presença Real no Divino e Adoravel Sacramento da Eucharistia. (1891). Donaciano de Norões Maia & Jose Manuel da A. Façanha, eds. Crato.

Pearse, Arno (1923). *Cotton in North Brazil.* Manchester.

Peirera de Queiroz, Maria Isaura (1965). *O Méssianismo—no Brasil e no Mundo.* São Paulo: Editôra Dominus.

Pereira Nóbrega, Pe. (1961). *Vingança Não (Depoimento sôbre Chico Pereira e Cangaceiros do Nordeste).* Rio de Janeiro.

Pimenta, Joaquim (1949). *Retalhos do Passado.* Rio de Janeiro.

Pinheiro, Irineu (1938). *O Joaseiro do Padre Cícero e a Revolução de 1914.* Rio de Janeiro: Irmãos Pongetti Editores.

——— (1950). *O Cariri: Seu Descobrimento, Povoamento, Costumes.* Fortaleza.

——— (1963). *Efemérides do Cariri.* Fortaleza: Imprensa Universitária do Ceará.

Pinto, Luis (1953). *Síntese Histórica e Cronológica da Paraíba.* Rio de Janeiro.

Pompeu de Souza Brasil, Thomaz (1922 and 1926). *O Ceará no Centenário da Independência do Brasil.* 2 vols. Fortaleza.

Pompeu Sobrinho, Th. (1953). *História das Sêcas (Século XX).* Fortaleza: Editôra A. Batista Fontenele.

Queiroz, Rachel de (1953). *Lampião.* Rio de Janeiro: Livraria José Olympio Editôra.

"Quem não gostar, que se morda." (1910). In *O Rebate.* 25 September.

Quinderé, Mons. José (1939). "História Eclesiástica do Ceará." In *O Ceará,* Raimundo Girão and Martins Filho, eds., 351-366.

——— (1948). *Dom Joaquim José Vieira.* Fortaleza: Editôra "Instituto do Ceará."

——— (1950). *Comendador Antonio Pinto Nogueira Accioly.* Fortaleza.

——— (1957). *Reminiscências.* Fortaleza: Editôra A. Batista Fontenele.

Rabelo, Lt. Col. Marcos Franco (1914). "Platforma, lido por occasião do banquete político realizado no dia 21 de Março de 1912 no theatro José de Alencar pelo Tenente—Coronel Dr. Marcos Franco Rabello candidato á presidência do Ceará no quatrênio de 1912 à 1916." In *Libertação do Ceará (Queda da Oligarchia Accioly),* Rodolpho Theophilo. Lisbôa.

Ramos, Gueirreiro (1961). *A Crise do Poder no Brasil: Problemas da Revolução Nacional Brasileira.* Rio de Janeiro.

Reis Vidal (1936). *Padre Cícero: Joazeiro Visto de Perto; O Padre Cícero Romão Baptista, Sua Vida e Sua Obra.* Rio de Janeiro.

Ribeiro Ramos, José Waldo (1940). *Centenário do Comendador Nogueira Acioli.* Fortaleza.

Rocha, Alexandrino (1965). "Juàzeiro, A Mêca do Padim Ciço." *Manchete.* 4 December, 118-121.

Romero, Tristão (1950). *Vida Completa do Padre Cícero Romão Batista (Anchieta do Século XX).* Juàzeiro do Norte.

Santa Rosa, Virgínio (1933). *O Sentido do Tenentismo.* Rio de Janeiro.

Santos, José Maria dos (1930). *A Política Geral do Brasil.* São Paulo.

Silva, Cyro (n.d.). *Pinheiro Machado.* Rio de Janeiro.

Simõens da Silva, Antonio Carlos (1927). *O Padre Cícero e a População do Nordeste (Elementos de defesa, história, "folklore" e propaganda).* Rio de Janeiro: Imprensa Nacional.

Soares, Martin [pseud. of Antonio Salles] (1912). *O Babaquara.* Rio de Janeiro.

Soares Pimentel, ed., Pe. J. (1892). *Os Milagres do Joazeiro ou Grande Collecção de documentos que attestam a veracidade da transformação da Sagrada Hóstia em sangue, sangue preciôso de N. S. Jesus Christo, na povoação do Joazeiro. . . .* Caicó, Rio Grande do Norte.

Sobral, Livio [pseud. of Pe. Azarias Sobreira] (1943). Padre Cícero Romão. *Revista do Instituto do Ceará,* LVII, 285-296.

Sobreira, Pe. Azarias (1938). *O Primeiro Bispo do Crato (Dom Quintino)*. Rio de Janeiro: Editôra ABC.

—— (1950). "Floro Bartholomeu." *Revista do Instituto do Ceará*, LXIV, 193-202.

—— (1956). *Em Defesa de um Abolicionista (Reposta ao "Apostolado do Embuste."* Fortaleza: Editôra A. Batista Fontenele.

—— (1961). "O Revolucionário." *Revista do Cinqüentenário do Juàzeiro do Norte*, pp. 14-16.

—— (1965). "Dom Quintino—Centenário." *Revista do Instituto do Ceará*, LXXIX, 75-88.

—— 1965-66). "Padre Cícero, Enigma de Hontem e de Hoje." *O Povo*. October 1965–February 1966.

—— (1969). *O Patriarca do Juàzeiro*. Juàzeiro.

Sodré, Nelson Werneck (1965). *História Militar do Brasil*. Rio de Janeiro: Civilização Brasileira.

Souza, Eusébio de (1915). "A Vida da 'Legião da Cruz.'" *Revista do Instituto do Ceará*, XXIX, 315-322.

—— (1932). "Os Monumentos do Estado do Ceará." *Revista do Instituto do Ceará*, XLVII, 51-103.

—— (1950). *História Militar do Ceará*. Fortaleza: Editôra "Instituto do Ceará."

Souza, (Msgr.) Silvano de (1961). "Padre Mestre Ibiapina." *Itaytera*, VI, 89-108.

Souza Brasil, Thomaz Pompêo de (1861). *Diccionário Topographico e Estatístico da Província do Ceará*. Rio de Janeiro.

Souza Carvalho, Raúl de (1953–1954). "Um Capítulo Inédito sobre o Padre Cícero." *Unitário*. 27 December 1953, 3, 10 January 1954. Republished in *O Povo*. 22 July 1961.

Stavenhagen, Rodolpho (1966–1967). "Seven Erroneous Theses about Latin America." *New University Thought*, IV, 4, 25-37.

Studart, Guilherme [Barão de] (1888). "Descripção do município de Barbalha." *Revista do Instituto do Ceará*, II, 9-13.

—— (1896–1924). *Datas e Factos para a História do Ceará*. 3 vols. Fortaleza.

—— (1924). *Para a História do Jornalismo Cearense, 1824–1924*. Fortaleza.

Theophilo, Rodolpho (1901). *Seccas do Ceará (Segunda Metade do Século XIX)*. Fortaleza.

—— (1914). *Libertação do Ceará (Queda da Oligarchia Accioly)*. Lisboa.

—— (1922a). *A Sedição do Joazeiro*. São Paulo.

—— (1922b). *A Secca de 1915*. Rio de Janeiro.

Torres, Luiz (1897). "O Governador da Bahia e Canudos. Calumnia." *A Bahia*. 14 September. *A Republica*. 10 August.

"Veritas Super Omnia." (1897). In *Diário de Pernambuco*. 7 October.

Vieira, Dom José Joaquim (1894). *Carta Pastoral . . . exhortando os seus Diocensanos a orarem pela Egreja e pela Patria e premunindo-os contra vicios oppostos á Santa Religião . . . 25 de março de 1893*. Fortaleza.

Vilaça, Marcos Vinicius and Roberto C. de Albuquerque (1965). *Coronel e Coronéis*. Rio de Janeiro: Tempo Brasileiro.

Vilespy, François (1965). "Juàzeiro do Norte et le Padre Cícero." *Caravelle*, v.5, pp. 61-70.

Wagley, Charles (1963). *An Introduction to Brazil.* New York: Columbia University Press.

Wildberger, Arnold (1949). *Os Presidentes da Província da Bahia.* Salvador, Bahia.

Xavier de Oliveira, Amália (1961). "Minha Mestre." *Revista do Cinqüentenário do Juàzeiro do Norte,* pp. 25-30.

Xavier de Oliveira, [Antonio] (1920). *Beatos e Cangaceiros.* Rio de Janeiro.

Unpublished Manuscripts

Aires de Menezes, Octávio (1963). "O Joaseiro e Seu Legítimo Fundador Padre Cícero Rumão Batista." Juàzeiro do Norte.

—— (1964). "Col. Franco Rabelo e a Revolução do Joaseiro." Juàzeiro do Norte.

Barreto, Mons. Joviniano (1943). "Organização Religiosa." In "Inquérito do Juàzeiro," Amália Xavier de Oliveira, unpublished MS. Juàzeiro do Norte, 55-65.

Feirreira Bezerra de Menezes, José (1936). "A Minha História sôbre as Cousas antigas e modernas do Juazeiro." Juàzeiro do Norte.

Hahner, June E. (1967). "Brazilian Civilian-Military Relations, 1889-1898." Ithaca: Latin American Studies Program, Dissertation Series, Cornell University, Mimeographed.

Morton, Ann (1966). "Religion in Juàzeiro (Ceará, Brazil) Since the Death of Padre Cícero—A Case Study in the Nature of Messianic Religious Activity in the Interior of Brazil." New York: Columbia University, unpublished Master's Essay.

Rólim, Frei Anônio, O. P. (1964). "Levantamento Sócio-Religioso de Diocese de Crato." Rio de Janeiro: Mimeographed.

Xavier de Oliveira, Dr. Amália, ed. (1943). "Inquérito do Juàzeiro." Juàzeiro do Norte.

Newspapers

A Bahia. Salvador, Bahia.

A Ordem. Sobral, Ceará.

A Província. Recife, Pernambuco.

A República. Fortaleza, Ceará.

A Verdade. Fortaleza, Ceará.

Ceará. Fortaleza, Ceará.

Cearense. Fortaleza, Ceará.

Combate. Fortaleza, Ceará.

Correio do Ceará. Fortaleza, Ceará.

Diário de Pernambuco. Recife, Pernambuco.

Diário do Comércio. Rio de Janeiro, Guanabara.

Era Nova. Recife, Pernambuco.
Estado do Ceará. Fortaleza, Ceará.
Hebdomidário Cathólico. Rio de Janeiro, Guanabara.
Gazeta do Joazeiro. Juàzeiro do Norte, Ceará.
Gazeta do Cariry. Crato, Ceará.
Jornal do Cariry. Barbalha, Ceará.
Jornal do Recife. Recife, Pernambuco.
Libertador. Fortaleza, Ceará.
O Ceará. Fortaleza, Ceará.
O Estado do Ceará. Fortaleza, Ceará.
O Fluminense. Niterói, Rio de Janeiro.
O Ideal. Juàzeiro do Norte, Ceará.
O Jornal do Cariry. Juàzeiro do Norte, Ceará.
O Nordeste. Fortaleza, Ceará.
O Pioneiro. Juàzeiro do Norte, Ceará.
O Povo. Fortaleza, Cearà.
O Rebate. Juàzeiro do Norte, Ceará.
Pedro II. Fortaleza, Ceará.
Unitário. Fortaleza, Ceará.

Index